Understanding Dissidence and Controversy in the History of Psychoanalysis

Understanding Dissidence and Controversy in the History of Psychoanalysis

Edited by

Martin S. Bergmann

OTHER
Other Press
New York

Production Editor: Robert D. Hack

This book was set in 11 pt. Apollo by Alpha Graphics of Pittsfield, NH.

10 9 8 7 6 5 4 3 2 1

Library of Congress Cataloging-in-Publication Data

Understanding dissidence and controversy in the history of psychoanalysis /
edited by Martin S. Bergmann.
    p. cm.
Includes bibliographical references and index.
    ISBN 1-59051-117-4 (pbk. : alk. paper)
1. Psychoanalysis–History–Congresses.   2. Freud, Sigmund, 1856–1939–
Friends and associates–Congresses.   I. Bergmann, Martin S., 1913–
    BF173.U52 2004
    150.19'5'09–dc22

                                                    2004001442

Sponsored by the Psychoanalytic Research and
Development Fund, Inc.

The Fund dedicates this symposium to the mourned memory
of our first professional director, Sidney Selig Furst, M.D.
(September 21, 1921–May 26, 2000).

Conference Proceedings
February 14–15, 2003
New York, NY

Representatives of the Fund:
    Mortimer Ostow, M.D., *President*
    Peter Neubauer, M.D., *Vice President*
    Henry Nunberg, M.D., *Professional Director*

Initial Presenter, Chairman of the Conference,
and Editor of the Proceedings:
    Professor Martin S. Bergmann

Invited Participants:
    Harold P. Blum, M.D.
    Dr. André Green
    William I. Grossman, M.D.
    Otto F. Kernberg, M.D.
    Anton O. Kris, M.D.
    Jill Savege Scharff, M.D.
    Robert S. Wallerstein, M.D.
    Elisabeth Young-Bruehl, Ph.D.

Contributors

Professor Martin S. Bergmann is clinical professor of psychology in the post-doctoral program of psychoanalysis and psychotherapy at New York University. He is an honorary member of the American Psychoanalytic Association and a member of the International Psychoanalytic Association. He is coauthor of *The Evolution of Psychoanalytic Technique* (1976) and *Generations of the Holocaust* (1982) and author of *The Anatomy of Loving: Man's Quest to Know What Love Is* (1987) and *In the Shadow of Moloch: the Sacrifice of Children and Its Impact on Western Religions* (1992). A previous symposium, *The Hartmann Era*, also edited by him, was published by Other Press in 2000.

Harold P. Blum, M.D., is a former editor of the *Journal of the American Psychoanalytic Association*. He is the current executive director of the Sigmund Freud Archives and in this capacity the organizer of the Library of Congress exhibition on Freud. The last book he coauthored, *Psychoanalysis and Art* (2003), was the result of his creation of an interdisciplinary symposium that took place in Florence, Italy, in 1991. He is clinical professor of psychiatry at New York University's school of medicine.

Docteur André Green is considered by many to be the most original psychoanalyst active at the present time. His books appear in French but many have been translated into English. They include *On Private Madness* (1986), *The Work of the Negative* (1999), *The Fabric of Affect* (1999), *The Chains of Eros* (2000), and *Life Narcissism Death Narcissism* (2001).

William I. Grossman, M.D., is training and supervising analyst at the New York Psychoanalytic Institute and was formerly clinical professor of psychiatry at the Albert Einstein College of Medicine in New York City.

Otto F. Kernberg, M.D., F.A.P.A., has recently completed his term as president of the International Psychoanalytic Association. He is director of the Personality Disorders Institute at the New York Presbyterian Hospital, Westchester Division and professor of psychiatry at the Weill Medical College of Cornell University. He is training and supervising analyst of the Columbia University Center for Psychoanalytic Training and Research. He was the director of the Psychotherapy Research Project of the Menninger Foundation and book editor of the *Journal of the American Psychoanalytic Association* from 1977–1993. He was elected Doctor Honoris Causa by the University of Buenos Aires, Argentina, in 1998, and received the Austrian Cross of Honor for Science and Art in 1999. He is the author of 10 books and coauthor of nine others. His most recent books are *Aggressivity, Narcissism and Self-destructiveness in the Psychotherapeutic Relationship: New Developments in the Psychopathology and Psychotherapy of Severe Personality Disorders* (2004) and *Contemporary Developments and Controversies in Psychoanalytic Theory, Technique and their Applications* (in press).

Anton O. Kris, M.D., is a training and supervising analyst at the Boston Psychoanalytic Society and Institute and clinical professor of psychiatry at Harvard Medical School. He is also the author of *Free Association* (1982).

Peter Neubauer, M.D., is clinical professor of psychiatry and training analyst at New York University, as well as professor emeritus at Columbia University. He is editor of the *Psychoanalytic Study of the Child*.

Henry Nunberg, M.D., is the medical director of the Fund for Psychoanalytic Research and Development. He is a member of the New York Psychoanalytic Society.

Mortimer Ostow, M.D., Med. Sc.D., is president of the Psychoanalytic Research and Development Fund, attending psychiatrist at Montefiore Medical Center, visiting professor emeritus of pastoral psychiatry at the

Jewish Theological Seminary, and a faculty member at the New York University Psychoanalytic Institute. He is the editor of *Judaism and Psychoanalysis* and author of *The Psychodynamic Approach to Drug Theory* and *Sexual Deviation: Psychoanalytic Insight*.

Jill Savege Scharff, M.D., is codirector of the International Psychotherapy Institute and director of the International Institute for Psychoanalytic Training in Chevy Chase, Maryland, as well as clinical professor of psychiatry at Georgetown University and a teaching analyst at Washington Psychoanalytic Institute.

Robert S. Wallerstein, M.D., is past president of the International Psychoanalytic Association (1985–1989) and past president of the American Psychoanalytic Association (1971–1972). He was chair of the department of psychology at the University of California and a training and supervising analyst at the San Francisco Psychoanalytic Institute. He is the author of *Forty-two Lives in Treatment* (1986), *The Talking Cure* (1995), and *Lay Analysis: Life Inside a Controversy* (1998). His 1988 paper, "One Psychoanalysis or Many," was particularly relevant to this symposium, as was his paper "The Common Ground of Psychoanalysis" (1992).

Elisabeth Young-Bruehl, Ph.D., is on the faculty of the Columbia Center for Psychoanalytic Training and Research. She is the author of biographies of Hannah Arendt and Anna Freud, and three essay collections, the latest of which is *Where Do We Fall When We Fall In Love?* (2003).

Contents

An Editor's Personal Note of Thanks

The symposium upon which this book is based was conducted on my 90th birthday, a double privilege granted only to very few. I therefore wish to thank the participants and the Fund for Psychoanalytic Research and Development for so unusual a birthday present. I also wish to thank Stacy Hague, Judith Feher-Gurewich, and Ellen Vanook of Other Press for their enthusiastic acceptance of the manuscript. Thanks also go to Bob Hack, production editor, and the diligent copy editor, Dave Kaplan.

The section on Lacan was written while my wife and I had the privilege of staying in Joyce McDougall's house in Paris; her library on Lacan was of particular help. Catherine Alicot, secretary of the *Revue Française de Psychoanalyse*, was most helpful. Karen Duda, my secretary, shared the burden of writing this book with me with particular devotion.

Introduction

We, at the Psychoanalytic Research and Development Fund, feel proud and privileged to have sponsored this study.

It was not quite half a century ago that the Fund was organized by Dr. Herman Nunberg for the purpose of promoting research in psychoanalysis and dissemination of our findings. During the past fifty years we have tried to fulfill this mandate by conducting study groups, and by sponsoring public lectures and intensive symposia. Many of our projects have resulted in the publication of books; others were summarized in published essays. Over the years several hundred colleagues have participated in these endeavors.

Our contribution has included both the development of observations, theories, and technical advances, and the dissemination of this knowledge not only by our publications but also through the agency of the participants who, upon returning to their own institutes, have taught what they have learned.

This volume is the second in the series created by Professor Martin Bergmann. Both volumes are studies of particular issues in the history of psychoanalysis. The first was entitled *The Hartmann Era*, and this volume deals with a longitudinal view of the history of psychoanalysis rather than a description of a single era. We learn of the reaction to both psychoanalytic theory and practice on the part of those who have practiced it.

Professor Bergmann is a remarkable scholar who has an impressive ability to analyze complex situations and a prodigious memory. This is in a sense a history of the development of psychoanalysis and of the obstacles and challenges it has encountered.

This account of psychoanalytic history is especially important at present when psychoanalysis is encountering new challenges and new opportunities that, to be sure, were imagined and anticipated by Freud but not by many of his followers. I refer to the opportunity to coordinate psychoanalysis with pharmacotherapy, and to broaden its theory by incorporating new and relevant concepts elaborated currently in neuroscience. The challenge is to exploit and incorporate these innovations in such a way as to strengthen classical psychoanalysis and extend its reach. Professor Bergmann's summary of the past prepares us to confront the future with greater wisdom and confidence.

Mortimer Ostow, President

I

Rethinking Dissidence and Change in the History of Psychoanalysis

Martin S. Bergmann

I will argue in this presentation that in order to be true to itself and acknowledge its own history, psychoanalysis has to rethink anew the role that dissidents play in its history. Not so much the facts, but the interpretation of the facts is under dispute. It is my hope that because we are latecomers, distant from the events, we can return to the scene, neither to blame nor exonerate Freud or the dissidents, but rather to ask the phenomenon of the dissident to help us understand better what psychoanalysis is and what role it played in intellectual currents of the last century. I would like to use our "belatedness" as a way of reaching a deeper understanding of a historical process. My plea is for a psychoanalytic attitude toward the history of psychoanalysis and its dissidents. I am aware of the heavy demands I am making on the reader, for I am asking for an objective view of a historical process in which we are all involved, a process in which we all have been passionate partisans. However, should this effort succeed as a whole or in part, new vistas may open and the history of psychoanalysis will become richer and more interesting, and we will see psychoanalysis within a larger frame of ideas outside of psychoanalysis affecting its development.

In this presentation I will treat dissidence primarily as a battle of ideas, leaving aside the social aspects of these controversies. These social aspects and their heavy costs have been described in many books, including Hale (1995), Wallerstein (1998) and Fenichel (1998). As time goes on, this sociology will be of interest only to historians, whereas controversy and dissidence as a history of ideas is in my view of more enduring interest.

Freud (1912) and his early followers firmly believed that psychoanalysis would apply the techniques of natural science to the interiority of men, or as Fenichel (1945) put it, "The subject matter and not the method of psychoanalysis is the irrational; its methods are rational" (p. 4). What was painful was that dissidence showed that this hope was not achieved. Disagreements between psychoanalytic schools were not those encountered in the natural sciences, which further experiments eventually resolve, but more closely resembled religious and philosophical disputes, which cannot be resolved by rational means.

I will cite a passage by Anna Freud from the controversial discussions (King and Steiner 1991) because it articulates the very opposite of what I am trying to do. In the memorandum that Anna Freud submitted on September 29, 1943, she said:

> Though the idea of an open forum for psychoanalytic teaching may seem tempting at a first glance, I personally doubt whether it could be carried out effectively and whether the result would not fall far short of the intentions. It would not in effect turn out to be similar to institutes like the Tavistock Clinic with all their well-known shortcomings. If such a teaching procedure had been adopted from the beginning of psychoanalytic development, psychoanalysis of the present day would include the theoretical and technical teachings of, for instance, Stekel, Adler, Jung, Rank, etc. [p. 633]

These pregnant words were not uttered within a calm symposium on how best the history of psychoanalysis could be taught. Rather, they were a battle cry in a historical moment. When the British Psychoanalytic Society refused to give to the daughter the privileges of her father, because the Kleinians were not expelled, the history of psychoanalysis was radically changed.

The case of psychoanalytic orthodoxy has probably never been stated as forcibly or as well as Anna Freud put it. And yet some doubts linger: What was so deplorable about the Tavistock clinic? Going further, do we have only two alternatives—to teach the theoretical and technical innovations of each dissident or to pretend they never existed? Perhaps there is a third alternative to understand the dissident within his or her historical context—to ask whether there is a kernel of truth in what they are suggesting. Can we learn something about the nature of psychoanalysis itself from the dissidents? In this essay, I will argue that the dissidents can be so summarily dismissed only if psychoanalysis wants to continue to remain a narrow sectarian group and blind itself to the richness implicit in its own history. I am aware of the revolutionary implication of my position for psychoanalytic education, and I see its dangers, but in my view the potential benefits significantly outweigh the dangers. If, contrary to Anna Freud's position, the psychoanalytic student learns the full history of psychoanalysis with its controversies, I believe that a more realistic view of the place of psychoanalysis in the history of thought in the twentieth century will become possible. It is hoped this will also prepare the students to better deal with the fact that psychoanalysis is no longer a monolithic movement.

It was probably not an accident that the first analyst to understand that there were deeper psychological reasons for dissidence than the opposition to the painful truth discovered by Freud was Winnicott (1964) in his review of Jung's autobiography. I will discuss this review later; here I wish only to emphasize that he approached Jung with the empathy that any disturbed patient should expect from a psychoanalyst, without a trace of anger. A passage from André Green (1975b) can be cited as illustrating the dilemma that made this monograph necessary.

> Psychoanalysis could on the one hand attach itself to an embalmed and stiffened corpse, failing to pursue a critical evaluation of its theories as challenged by present practice. In this case it would be pledged to the mere safeguarding of its acquisitions, without ever calling into question the theory sustaining them. The alternative is a psychoanalysis which, periodically renewing itself, strives to extend its range, to subject its concepts to radical rethinking, to commit itself to self-criticism. In which case it must run the risks entailed by such self-examination, from which the best as well as the worst may emerge. [p. 287]

By 1910, when the first International was founded, Freud had developed a coherent set of ideas that heralded a new technique of therapy for the psychoneuroses. It was based on a radically different view of man from the one that prevailed during the Enlightenment. The thinkers of the Enlightenment considered what happens in the first years of life as unimportant because what happens is later forgotten. By introducing the distinction between forgotten and repressed, Freud reversed this verdict, making the first years of life particularly important. Freud's ideas will undergo refinement, further development, and even major revisions, but in essence they were in place by 1910 for anyone to learn. Only a year later the first dissident, Alfred Adler, appeared, followed by a long line of other dissidents—Stekel and Jung, and later Otto Rank, Ferenczi and Karen Horney. There were to be other dissidents after Freud's death, but if my interpretation is correct, dissidents during Freud's lifetime have a different character from that of the dissidents after his death.

In 1914, and again in 1925, Freud dealt with the problem of dissidence. In 1914, he had only Adler and Jung to address. But by 1925, Otto Rank had joined them. It turned out that at least the dissident during Freud's lifetime had a typical prehistory: Usually he was personally close to Freud and for a time made significant contributions to psychoanalysis. But for reasons that never quite lost their mystery, at some point the dissident turns vehemently against Freud and starts his or her own school. Freud's attempt to understand the dissident rested primarily on the concept of resistance. Psychoanalysis had discovered a truth many people find difficult to accept, namely that sexuality does not begin in adolescence, but during infancy, and that infantile sexuality culminates in the Oedipus complex, the wish to possess sexually one of the parents and eliminate the other. Infantile sexuality undergoes repression during the latency years. If conditions are favorable, in adolescence there is a turning away from the parental couple and the search for love and sexual relationships within one's own generation. Freud knew that when he attempted to reveal these facts to his patients, they often showed resistance, including denial of sexual intercourse among the parents themselves. Therefore, it was only a further step for him to think that it is possible for someone to be a psychoanalyst for a number of years and later on develop a similar kind of resistance to psychoanalytic ideas, in essence not different from resistance encountered in psychoanalytic work. But when, in subsequent events, psychoanalysis became divided into different schools, to continue to maintain that the other school is the resisting one became untenable.

However, to my knowledge no other explanations to account for psychoanalytic diversity were formulated and it is my hope that I can do so in this presentation.

I am not claiming that Freud was mistaken. The history of dissidents will show that resistance to Freud's ideas plays a role, but it was too narrow an interpretation that did not do justice to a more complex process. I also wish to stress that dissidence is not a blemish on the history of psychoanalysis. It forced Freud to clarify much that was left obscure; for example, Freud rejected Adler's view of aggression, but some of his views reentered psychoanalysis in 1920 with the formulation of the dual instinct theory.

The idea that the dissident school is the resisting one had a major impact on the history of psychoanalysis. It strengthened the sense of belonging to the Psychoanalytic International, because those who remained faithful could see themselves as those who were willing to face the difficult truth while others faltered. It gave the psychoanalytic group a sense of coherence and contempt for the dissidents. Less desirable were other aspects. For instance, psychoanalysis lived in a continuous fear of new dissidents emerging, and it was not easy to predict which of the followers who presented original ideas carried within him the seeds of becoming another Adler or Rank. Thus, orthodoxy became part of psychoanalytic teaching and certain ideas were not only not taught, but feared. Ultimately, the idea of one truth and many falsehoods echoed the idea of monotheistic religions. It was, however, in principle acceptable to nineteenth century science that science is continuously coming ever closer to one veiled truth.

The founding of the International Psychoanalytic Association and the founding of the secret committee of seven ringleaders in 1912 were efforts to guarantee the stability of psychoanalysis in opposition to hostile pressure from without and heresies from within. The effort failed when one of the ringleaders, Otto Rank, in 1924 became himself a dissident. Freud failed to recognize that such methods must lead to orthodoxy and that they would be appropriate for a secret group of conspirators but not easily compatible with the aims of a scientific organization.

As this work was nearing completion, I had a feeling that recalled Einstein's famous statement, "Cunning is the Good Lord, but Evil he is not." The Lord's cunning may have bestowed upon Freud most of the truth, but some of the truth he put in the knapsack of the dissidents.

A well-known distinction I learned long ago came to my mind:

According to Aristotle, poetry is "more philosophic and of graver import" than history, because poetry is concerned with what is pervasive and universal, while history is addressed to what is special and singular. Aristotle's remark is a possible source of a widely accepted distinction between two allegedly different types of sciences: the nomothetic which seeks to establish abstract general laws for indefinitely repeatable events and processes, and the ideographic, which aims to understand the unique and the non-recurrent. [Nagel 1961, p. 547]

The therapeutic philosophy of every psychoanalytic school is by definition nomothetic in nature since it is applied to repeatable events, but every case and every analyst gives it an ideographic stamp. What emerges from the interaction between an analyst and his or her patient is also an unique event. Some therapists are attracted to the discipline because of its nomothetic nature while others find it interesting because of its ideographic nature. To me the combination of the two is so fascinating. Since the publication of Freud's *Interpretation of Dreams* (1900), most psychoanalytic schools have mastered the art of inference from manifest to latent interpretation. Nomothetic psychoanalysts hope that eventually universally accepted canons of correspondence between the latent and the manifest will be established. Ideographic therapists feel that the individuality of both analyst and analysand will never permit this to happen. Because I am submitting this essay for a conference in the ninetieth year of my life, I wish to cite a secular prayer by Goethe: "Holy Destiny bringeth it about that this work of my hands reacheth a conclusion." I have known Wilhelm Reich, Karen Horney, and Erich Fromm personally, and I have attended the Eranos Jungian meetings in Ascona, Switzerland. Two of my friends, the anthropologist Paul Radin and the founder of the study of Jewish Mysticism, Gershom Scholem, knew Jung well. Dissidence was in the air when I was a young analyst. I feel grateful for the opportunity to rethink and relive the content of this chapter.

ALFRED ADLER (1870–1937)

Alfred Adler was among Freud's earliest adherents, one of the first four members of Freud's Wednesday group. The minutes of the Vienna

Psychoanalytic Society (Nunberg and Federn 1906–1918) offer an opportunity to study in detail the transformation of the relationship between Adler and Freud. Freud was trying to break out of his professional isolation. With few exceptions, the members of the society were awed by Freud, but they had never been trained or analyzed, and their comprehension of psychoanalysis was limited. Among them, Adler is the most independent thinker and the one furthest away from Freud.

The first recorded meeting where Adler presented took place on November 7, 1906. The topic was the organic basis of neurosis. Other presentations not recorded have preceded this one. In 1907, Adler published a book entitled *Studies on Organ Inferiority*. Organ inferiority was not a discovery that Adler made. Under the Latin name, *Locus Minoris Resistentiae*, the term was a familiar medical concept, but Adler elevated it into the main cause of neurosis (Ellenberger 1970). The idea of organ inferiority was by that time familiar to all participants. Adler postulated hereditary tendencies influencing various organs. Organ inferiority heightens the sensitivity of these organs and gives rise to feelings of inferiority. The inferiority feelings can in turn be counterbalanced by cerebral activity. Examples cited are Beethoven's deafness, Mozart's misshapen ears, and Robert Schumann's auditory hallucinations.

For a time, no one realized that Adler's ideas were significantly different from those of Freud. Adler spoke again on March 6, 1907, this time presenting a psychoanalytic case. The patient was introduced as "a man with an inferior alimentary tract." From the many data of childhood presented, Adler emphasized the feeling of inferiority associated with the father's larger penis. When we read Adler's case presentation today we realize how psychoanalysis advanced in the presentation of a case. Adler enumerated the symptoms presented by the patient with the expectation natural to medicine that this enumeration would lead to diagnosis and to a technique of cure. The term *infantile neurosis* and its differentiation from *adult neurosis* had not yet been created. The group, including Freud, lacked the tools necessary to comprehend the case. When the capacity to collect data is not yet available, *organ inferiority* is a term both easily available and of great appeal to the synthetic function of participants. The lecture is of historical interest because it shows how Adler was conducting an analysis based on very different assumptions from those of Freud. Freud was friendly but noted that "the patient's development is not in accord with Adler's conceptions;

the patient was first an orator and only later did he begin to stammer." Speaking, Freud explained, is associated with exhibitionistic wishes, and stammering is the inhibition of exhibitionism. Adler attributed the neurosis to feelings of inferiority brought about by the father's bigger penis, while Freud found it in the inhibition of exhibitionistic wishes. We are still at a very beginning of psychoanalysis but already the decision between two alternate interpretations is not easy to make. In retrospect one can also see that two issues were debated: first, what is the correct causal sequence in the structure of neurosis; and second, which kind of interpretation would have the greater healing effect. That the discovery of the historical truth is curative was an implicit assumption never stated or tested.

In the next presentation, on January 29, 1908, Adler spoke on paranoia, which, now following Freud, he saw as suppressed exhibitionism. He noted the absence of fear in paranoia. Freud used the occasion to explain to Adler the nature of projection. He noted that a reformer is considered a paranoid until he acquires followers who protect him from being declared as ill. One asks oneself in view of the history of psychoanalysis whether what was seen as true of the reformer did not also become true of the future dissident.

The first Psychoanalytic Congress took place on April 27, 1908. There, Adler presented a paper titled, "Sadism in Life and Neurosis." The paper was discussed by the Vienna group on June 3, 1908. In that paper, the term *aggressive drive* appeared for the first time. Adler stated that anxiety emerges when the transformed aggressive drive is turned against the subject himself. In the discussion, Freud maintained that what Adler called the aggressive drive is in fact "our libido" and anxiety results from ungratified libido. Freud (1908) ended on a conciliatory note, although he was well aware of the difference between the two of them.

> Adler's description of the instinctual life contains many valuable and correct remarks and observations. Adler has taken notice only of the instinctual drives in normal psychology; the pathological has escaped his attention. He has made an attempt to explain illness in terms of normal psychology; this was the viewpoint of the *Studies on Hysteria*. [vol. I, p. 408]

What Freud meant by "normal psychology" is a psychology that does not take unconscious wishes into account. Adler's next presentation, a case of compulsive blushing, took place on February 3, 1909. Freud used the opportunity to give Adler another psychoanalytic lesson. Erythrophobia occupies a middle position between anxiety and paranoia. The patient blushes because he or she is ashamed for reasons that remain unconscious. What one usually finds behind the erythrophobia is repressed shame over premature sexual knowledge and shame over masturbation. Freud went on to explain to Adler that neurosis cannot be explained in terms of a single emotion, but can result only from a pair of opposite emotions. In this case, the conflict is between shame and rage. Adler's rejoinder confirmed that the lesson Freud attempted to teach him fell on deaf ears.

On March 9, 1909, Adler spoke once more. This time, the topic was the psychology of Marxism. Adler was deeply impressed by the achievements of Marx. Freud, on the other hand, emphasized that as civilization goes on, repression of instinct is continuously increasing. However, Freud conceded that the "enlargement of consciousness" operates in the opposite direction, opposing a steady rise of repression. Freud did not, at this juncture, elaborate on what he meant by "enlargement of consciousness," but from other contexts we surmise that he meant the great writers like Shakespeare and Dostoyevski and philosophers like Nietzsche and finally psychoanalysis itself. They all can be cited as examples of "enlargement of consciousness." On June 2, 1909, Adler presented on the topic of "oneness of the neurosis." In the lecture, Adler repeated what he said earlier about organ inferiority and aggression, and now added a major component of neurosis, which he called "oversensitivity." At this lecture, Freud was tactful but more distant. He criticized Adler for eliminating sexuality, and suggested that Adler's psychology is a psychology of consciousness, a portion of psychology that Freud had deliberately neglected. It was now clearer to Freud that Adler could not acknowledge the role of the unconscious.

On February 23, 1910, Adler spoke on "Psychic Hermaphrodism." He quoted Freud's former friend Wilhelm Fliess, that man falls ill because of his feminine tendencies and woman because of her masculine tendencies. Every neurotic shows bisexual traits. Adler argued that the disposition that belongs to the opposite sex is doomed and must atrophy or be sublimated. Neurotic men consider everything feminine in them as evil. Hermaphrodism breeds inferiority feelings. The wish to be the other gender leads to organ inferiority. Freud did not participate in this discussion. On October 19, 1910, Adler reported "a small contribution to the subject of hysterical lying." Lying to the psychoanalyst is to Adler also the result of inferiority feelings. It is also an expression of aggression. A case of a girl with "masculine protest" was cited. She had to be on top in every sexual intercourse. She was also enuretic, and the enuresis was another expression of her masculine protest. In this presentation, Freud objected to Adler's idea that every hysterical symptom and every dream is based on a bisexual conflict.

On January 4, 1911, Adler presented "Some Problems of Psychoanalysis." It is in this session that we can foresee the break coming, as Adler now insisted that libido cannot be regarded uniformly as the driving force in neurosis. He considered masculine protest as more important. Similarly, he insisted that Freud's wish-fulfillment ideas in dreams be subordinated to Adler's "safeguarding tendency." Adler here emphasized the importance of safety that Sandler would stress in 1960. Incest fantasies, while present, are not at the core of neurosis. Sexuality itself is stimulated through organ inferiority. The debate in this session was more vehement and Adler interrupted other speakers. Members of the group, alarmed by the growing disagreement, tried to bridge the gap.

Adler spoke again on February 1, 1911 under a more audacious title: "The Masculine Protest as the Central Problem in Neurosis." Defiance of Freud had moved to the center of Adler's argument. In Adler's view, the neurotic girl gives herself to a man in defiance of the mother; *ejaculatio praecox*, impotence in neurotic man, is a "safeguard" against sexuality. The wish to possess all women in neurotic men is to protect themselves from dependency on one woman. Freud was more critical. He admonished Adler because he gave new names to ideas that Freud had previously expressed; for example, his bisexuality was transformed by Adler into psychic hermaphrodism. It was in this session that the crucial moment occurred. Freud exclaimed, "This is not psychoanalysis!" Instead of presenting psychology of the unconscious, Adler advocated "surface ego-psychology." Freud now predicted that Adler's view would do much harm to psychoanalysis. Instead of psychology of the libido or sexual psychology, Adler offered general psychology. Freud predicted that Adler would make use of the latent resistances to psychoanalysis still alive in every psychoanalyst, that his views would do harm and yet remain sterile. Freud insisted that neurosis is the ego's fear of the libido. The denial of the unconscious was elevated by Adler into a theory. Freud spoke at greater length than was customary, and at the end of the session Stekel sided with Adler. A day later, on February 2, 1911, Freud informed Abraham, "I have completed the purge of the society and sent Adler's seven followers packing after him." What became evident was that Adler himself was reenacting with Freud the very theories that he was developing. He was overcoming his inferiority feelings toward Freud by compensating and trying to subordinate Freud's ideas to his own. That transference reenactment was taking place, neither Freud nor Adler was aware of. What added to the interest in this debate was that many of Adler's observations contained a kernel of truth and many of his observations would reenter psychoanalysis under different names.

The musicologist Max Graf (1942), the father of Little Hans and a member of the original Wednesday group, compared Freud and Adler:

> Adler possessed clarity, poise, and a fine psychological feeling; he went along his path in slow steps, ever testing. He remained on the surface of the earth. Unlike Freud, he never rose into the air in a flight of imagination, nor did he ever dig deep shafts into the bowels of the earth. But I was unable and unwilling to submit to Freud's "do" or "don't"—with which he once confronted me—and nothing was left for me but to withdraw from his circle. [p. 475]

The sociological difference between Freud and Adler has been pointed out by Ellenberger (1970). Freud aimed at conquering the interior of man's psyche for natural science, while Adler in his book of 1926 entitled *Menschenkenntnis* wanted to know how people function in society. (I read Adler's book in 1930, when I was 17; it made a powerful impression on me.) When World War I ended, Adler at 48 was young enough to profit from the rise of the Social Democratic Party and he presented a psychology of great social appeal to this new political group. Adler's patients were recruited from lower social strata than were those of Freud. To Freud, the Oedipus complex was central. In Adler's psychology, sibling rivalry played a greater role. At this point, I may add that Adler's psychology is closer to the spirit of Genesis, in which sibling rivalry plays the dominant role, while Freud's is closer to Greek tragedy, where the Oedipus complex is central.

In retrospect Freud's outburst against Adler is understandable. Adler threatened the edifice Freud had attempted to build, but even so it was unfortunate that Freud did not take the opportunity to explain to the bewildered group why this was not psychoanalysis and what, in contrast to Adler, psychoanalysis really is. With Adler's expulsion an irrational force of loyalty to Freud entered into psychoanalysis; it was a force that could not be dislodged. Since we are at this point dealing with the first controversy in the history of psychoanalysis, it may be useful to realize that we are dealing with two schools of therapy, very different in their basic assumptions of human nature and technique of treatment, without an objective way of comparison.

In the analysis of a phobia in a 5-year-old boy, Freud (1909) referred to Adler twice. There he used Adler's term *confluence of instinct* (p. 106) and once again when he referred to Adler's aggressive instinct. He admitted that the phobia of little Hans could be explained as being due to the repression of Little Hans' aggressive propensities. What Freud said on the occasion is interesting in light of subsequent events:

> I am nevertheless unable to assent to it, and indeed I regard it as a misleading generalization. I cannot bring myself to assume the existence of a special aggressive instinct alongside of the familiar instincts of self-preservation and of sex, and on an equal footing with them. [p. 140]

We are witnessing at this point, for the first time in the history of psychoanalysis, a disagreement about the origin of anxiety. We are also confronted with the problem that the psychoanalytic process itself cannot answer this question. It has been held against Freud that he rejected Adler's aggressive drive in 1908, but embraced the idea in 1920. In Freud's defense, one can say that a creative thinker must follow his own path, and in 1909 the evidence for the destructive drive or the death instinct was not yet available to him. The significance of the aggressive drive could be appreciated by Freud only after he recognized the role of the repetition compulsion and the negative therapeutic reaction in the lives of neurotics.

It seems that Adler never understood Freud's ideas, but learned from him the technique of listening to patients speak freely and recite their life history. What he heard he translated into his theory of organ inferiority, overcompensation, inferiority feeling, and psychic hermaphroditism. Adler did not uncover unconscious ideas but organized preconscious ideas. Can such an explanation be helpful? If our answer is yes, we have to accept that many diverse explanations can be given by different therapists and all of them will be helpful to a degree, raising the question of the role of truth in the treatment process. It follows that any therapeutic organization of what was previously disorganized can be used by the ego for relief. In that case, Adler's ideas could lead to some psychic reorganization and hence relief. Did Adler's individual psychology do harm to psychoanalysis, as Freud feared? It seems that Freud exaggerated its social and political dangers. There was much that was of value in Adler's ideas, but his competitive wishes stood in his way. On Freud's side there was a fear that what he created would be lost. What requires emphasis in order to balance the picture is that Adler, two decades before Freud, recognized the role of the aggressive drive as well as the greater role that the ego plays in psychic structure.

One more irony of history should be mentioned. One of the accusations Freud directed at Adler was

> psycho-analysis has never claimed to provide a complete theory of human mentality in general, but only expected that what it offered should be applied to supplement and correct the knowledge acquired by other means. Adler's theory, however, goes far beyond this point; it seeks at one stroke to explain the behaviour and character of human beings as well as their neurotic and psychotic illnesses. [Freud 1914, p. 50]

After World War II, Hartmann and his coworkers would attempt to do what Freud criticized in Adler: to transform psychoanalysis into a general psychology.

In his "New Introductory Lectures on Psychoanalysis" (1933), Freud took revenge on Adler. The popular writer Emil Ludwig had written a biography of Wilhelm the Second, Germany's last Kaiser. The biography was based on Adler's idea of organ inferiority because the German Kaiser had a withered arm. Freud transformed the same event into a mother–child relationship, emphasizing that it was the mother's withdrawal of affection from her handicapped child that was responsible for the Kaiser's feelings. Thus, Adler's inferiority feelings were recast in terms of disturbance of the libido in the relationship between infant and mother.

I have described Adler's departure in some detail because only the details can convey the events as they actually took place. Adler's dissidence helped Freud formulate what is and what is not psychoanalysis. It took some time, but eventually Freud recognized that Adler's formulation, because it did not include the unconscious, could be given to the patient early and did not require the same attention to the individuality of the patient that psychoanalysis required.

Was Adler ever a disciple of Freud? Adler himself always denied any indebtedness to Freud. I agree with Ellenberger's (1970) evaluation that Adler did not take anything from psychoanalysis (except listening to the patient), and therefore did not destroy anything. He had his own ideas before he met Freud, during their relationship, and after his departure. His system remained largely uninfluenced by Freud.

CARL JUNG (1875–1961)

The psychiatrists of the famed Mental Hospital Bergholzi in Zurich, Bleuler and his assistant, Carl G. Jung, were the first converts to psychoanalysis at the heart of the medical establishment, the first to apply Freud's idea to the treatment of psychosis. Unlike Freud's early followers, they were respected psychiatrists, and, what meant as much or even more to Freud, they were gentiles.

To Freud, it also seemed that Jung had the kind of winning personality that he felt he himself lacked. It was not long before Freud appointed Jung as his heir, his "Joshua" who would enter the "promised land," while Freud, identified with Moses, would die in the "wilderness," with the "promised land" only seen from afar. With the tools that Freud himself put at our disposal it is not difficult to predict that the meeting between a father eager to abdicate and an ambitious son with powerful oedipal wishes is not going to end well. Freud's Rome dreams containing the prohibition of entering Rome, which always appears far away, suggest that the identification with Moses had taken place in Freud before he met Jung. Jung only supplied the hitherto missing "Joshua."

Strange as it may seem, it was not mental illness that was at the center of Freud and Jung's controversy; it was mythology that the two wished to conquer. As Abraham summarized in 1909, myth is a collective dream and dream is a private myth. Just as the dream was deciphered by Freud, now the myth will yield its secret to Jung. The correspondence between Freud and Jung finds both of them eager to reinterpret myths from a psychoanalytic point of view, to throw over the traditional way myths were interpreted. Both have contempt for the traditional students of the myth.

When in 1914 Freud published his explanation of the departure of the two first dissidents, he had no premonition that the protocols of the meetings of the Vienna Society (Nunberg and Federn) between 1906 and 1918 would eventually be published. As to Jung, Freud did not expect that his prolonged personal correspondence with Jung would see the light of day (McGuire 1974). Freud's biographers, Jones (1955) and Gay (1988), and other historians of the Freud and Jung disputes such as Eissler (1982) all tended to exonerate Freud and blame Jung for the rift between them.

We have two ways of understanding Jung. From the correspondence with Freud between 1906–1914 (McGuire 1970), he emerges as a Romantic, a follower of Nietzsche, brash, arrogant, self-confident, eager to join Freud as an idealized father figure to help him throw over the burden of his own clergyman ancestors, until, disillusioned with Freud, he turns on him and on psychoanalysis. Jung's autobiography, published in 1961, is a diary of inner events, a deeply religious document. Jung himself saw his life as a life of self-realization; he would write his biography during his 85 years of life as the myth of his life, uncertain whether he would tell fable or truth. He knew he was different from many other men but he did not know who he really was. As a young man he was convinced that he would be destroyed. His dreams and his fantasies were real to him. In keeping with psychoanalytic precepts he began with childhood recollections but made no effort to differentiate screen memories from real memories; what he remembered were experiences of awe. Only gradually through many religious experiences does the psychoanalytically informed reader recognize that Jung had a childhood psychosis.

Already the correspondence shows that increasingly Jung was engrossed in the study of myth, and eventually the myth led the way to a break with Freud. There is much talk about the significance of incest in the correspondence but it is not easy to understand what the conflict was about. The biography makes the difference clear. Incest was to Jung only rarely a personal issue; it was to Jung a religious subject. That is why incest plays such a role in myths. Freud is found incapable of understanding the cosmic mystery of the incest idea.

It was Winnicott (1964) who played the crucial role in a reevaluation of what happened between Freud and Jung. Winnicott read Jung's *Memories, Dreams, and Reflections* (1961) and concluded that Jung suffered from a childhood schizophrenia. Jung could not accept Freud's help because Freud at that time had nothing of significance to offer to Jung in his struggle against the return of schizophrenia. Eventually, Jung had to discover his own self-cure, and because he succeeded in the difficult task of self-cure, he felt convinced that he, like Freud, could help others by the techniques that saved him. Jung's theory and technique were in essence the application of his self-cure to others. Freud's cures stopped short of psychosis; they demanded a psychosis-free ego capable of giving the analyst's assistance. Jung's method demanded less. Like Kohut, two generations later, it spoke to persons with a fragmented sense of self. The encounter with Freud and Freud's emphasis on infantile sexuality, the Oedipus complex, and the interpretation of dreams had a disorganizing effect on Jung, undermining the defenses Jung had built up, exposing him to the danger of the return of his childhood psychosis.

The break with Freud resulted in an identification with him and, like Freud, Jung embarked upon a self-analysis. In his self-analysis, Jung created Philemon, a wise mythical figure who offered assistance in his self-analytic work. In Greek mythology, Philemon was an equivalent to the biblical Noah, because he and his wife Baucis were the only ones to show hospitality to Zeus and Hermes, and were warned by the gods of a forthcoming flood. The couple escaped, climbing a mountain. It is understandable that an early mountaineer became Jung's patron saint. I assume that Philemon was a combination of Freud and Jung's stern Protestant clergymen ancestors. This beneficial figure enabled Jung to find a new self with a sense of mission and a technique of treatment that he could consider as superior to Freud. The fact that Jung could use a fantasy figure as an auxiliary psychoanalyst while Freud used Fliess in a similar capacity may explain why Jung remained a believer in God while Freud continued to be an atheist. On Jung's door hung the Latin proverb *Vocatus atque nonvocatus deus aderit*—called or not called for, God will attend.

The fact that Jung's ideas became increasingly reactionary and anti-Semitic to the point where he became acceptable to the Nazi regime as its leading psychologist should not obscure for us the fact that his self-analysis was not a matter of luxury but a matter of psychological survival. On the ship in 1909 in the famous visit to the United States, Jung, like Ferenczi later, tried to engage Freud in a mutual analysis, but according to Jung, Freud feared risking his authority, which Jung resented greatly. It is likely that at this point the de-idealization began, and following a period of *"Nachtraglichkeit"* of four years it broke out. If one follows the Freud/Jung correspondence, one asks oneself: How did the disagreement between the two come about? In retrospect, making use of insights that Freud made available to us, the coming break is foreshadowed in two episodes: In December 1908, Jung's son Franz Carl was born and Jung had a masculine equivalent to a postpartum depression, feeling superfluous after the birth of his son. This feeling of inadequacy was rationalized by the supposed Oedipus complex of the son. Misunderstanding psychoanalysis, Jung thought that the ideal father of the hero was embodied in Wagner's Siegfried whose father begets a child and dies promptly. Freud comforted Jung (McGuire 1974, letter 118, p. 186): "The child will find you indispensable as a father for many years, first as a positive and then in a negative sense." Freud did not realize that the fatherless Siegfried was Jung's ego ideal (Rycroft 1985), and what was even more relevant, that Siegfried's father was named Siegmund.

The second emotionally important event took place on February 11, 1910, only days after the break with Adler. At a time when the relationship was not yet clouded. Jung made the following suggestion to Freud:

> At present I am sitting so precariously on the fence between the Dionysian and the Apollonian that I wonder whether it might not be worthwhile to reintroduce a few of the older cultural stupidities such as the monasteries. . . . The ethical problem of sexual freedom really is enormous and worth the sweat of all noble souls. But 2000 years of Christianity can only be replaced by something equivalent. An ethical fraternity, with its mythical Nothing, not infused by an archaic-infantile driving force, is a pure vacuum and can never evoke in man the slightest trace of that age-old animal power which drives the migrating bird across the sea and without which no irresistible mass movement can come into being. [McGuire 1974, pp. 293–294]

The reference to Apollonian and Dionysian shows that Jung is under the influence of Nietzsche's "The Birth of Tragedy Out of the

Spirit of Music" and Nietzsche's "Ecce Homo." Jung yearns to convert psychoanalysis into a sect intoxicated by the god of wine. This is a different Jung than anyone would gather from reading his biography. Freud's reply to Jung was a model of sobriety:

> But you mustn't regard me as the founder of a religion. My intentions are not so far-reaching. . . . I am not thinking of a substitute for religion. This need must be sublimated. I did not expect the fraternity to become a religious organization any more than I would expect a volunteer fire department to do so. [p. 295]

Freud's rational reply could not meet Jung's emotional needs, and Freud's refusal to head such a fraternity was dangerous for Jung's mental stability, for it left him open to the temptation to anoint himself as the head of such a sect, a dangerous addition to the already existing feelings of megalomania. The final break in their personal relationship came two years later, in January 1913. But the origins of the break are already present in 1910.

Jung states that he was impressed by Freud's mechanism of repression that he found in *The Interpretation of Dreams*. Repression explained much of what he himself was struggling with in his association experiments. Jung maintained later that throughout his relationship with Freud, he remained unconvinced that sexuality is the force behind repression. He mentioned only sexuality as such, without reference to infantile sexuality or incestuous wishes. Historically, Jung raised the question: What if someone accepts one part of the analytic package, in this case repression, and not the other, the fear of castration, infantile sexuality, and the Oedipus complex? Freud felt that a mere recognition of repression would leave Jung holding an empty bag.

In the 1912 paper "The Dynamics of Transference," Freud spoke highly of Jung's term *introversion* for that part of the libido that is withdrawn from gratification in reality and forced to find satisfaction in fantasy. Introversion became a crucial concept for Freud because introverted libido enters "a regressive course and revives the subject's infantile images" (p. 102). It becomes the task of the psychoanalyst to track down this libido, make it accessible to consciousness and thus more serviceable for reality.

My own reading of Jung's memoirs led me to conclude that after the departure from Freud, Jung lapsed into a competitive identification with Freud. Like Freud, he attempted a self-analysis based on his childhood memories and his dreams. Jung reached the conclusion that until his ninth or eleventh year, he was an inwardly alive child, and at that age spent a great deal of time building little cities out of pebbles that he collected at the edge of the lake. At this point, Freud would have asked himself what the frenzy to build such cities was about, what defensive needs were fulfilled by it. But Jung approached his self-analysis differently. He resumed his childhood play, spending hours building such a city, hoping that by the resumption of the play of childhood, his inner aliveness and creativity would once more emerge, and he was not disappointed in the results. What Jung discovered was that a partial regression to a childhood constructive play can have a curative effect. Jung retained Freud's method, telling patients to free-associate, listening to their fantasies and dreams, but what he heard and gave back to his patients was very different.

In Winnicottian vocabulary we can say that Jung found a way back to his true self that was overwhelmed by a false self at the age of eleven. Unlike Adler, Jung did not reject the unconscious but gave it a different meaning. To Jung the unconscious was not the place where unacceptable wishes continue their subterranean life but a deposit of ancestral wisdom that was repressed in times of cultural upheavals. Two terms were of special significance in Jung's psychology: *collective unconscious* and *archetype*. The collective unconscious enabled Jung to claim that the religious mysteries of antiquity, Chinese and Indian yoga, medieval alchemy, and the anguish of modern man were all expressions of the same need. This collective unconscious is inhabited by great figures or archetypes—figures who, throughout history, were worshiped, honored, and feared. To early man, unconscious archetypes were projected as theophany. During analysis these archetypes are modified and can be counted upon to be of help. For modern man, they live inside of men and women, manifesting their power in mental illness as well as in creativity—the only difference being that ancient man ascended to revelation, while modern man descends into his unconscious.

Jung's psychology was closer to the prevalent religious sensibility. Jung believed that in the unconscious of Catholics, Jewish stirrings could be detected; in Protestant patients, Catholic residue can be found; and Jews showed pagan inclinations in their unconscious. Particularly powerful is the archetype of the great mother goddess. But much mischief is created by the archetype Puer Eternus, the youth who will not grow into man. Dreams were to Jung a dialogue between ego consciousness and the unconscious. Where Freud postulated a "dream censor," Jung created the "editor of the dream." It is the task of this editor to compose a meaningful text out of the endless material of individual life. When the editor is successful, great dreams emerge. He also translated bisexual conflicts into the conflict between accepting and rejecting the archetype anima in men and animus in women. Jung's analyses tended to reconcile the patients to their ancestral roots.

Jung will turn tables on Freud, and declare that Freud's emphasis on sexuality is more akin to a religious experience. Resorting to Latin vocabulary, Jung called Freud's interest in sexuality *Res religiosa observanda*. Sexuality was to Freud, according to Jung, *Numinosum*, that is, a spiritually elevated subject. Whether naively, or with malice, at this point Jung replaced Freud's enthusiasm for the discovery of the role of sexuality in psychoanalysis with the accusation that Freud had a spiritually elevated sexuality. Freud (1914) responded to Jung's denial of the importance of sexuality:

> These people have picked out a few cultural overtones from the symphony of life and have once more failed to hear the mighty and primordial melody of the instinct. [p. 62]

Jung saw Adler as nothing but a stand-in for Nietzsche, and Freud's emphasis on sexuality was interpreted as a covert attack on Nietzsche's will to power. The Jungian heresy can be seen as a revenge of the irrational forces dormant in the psyche against Freud's attempt to tame them in the service of rational aims.

For a time, Jung defended himself against anti-Semitic accusations, but in a way that was never entirely convincing. In 1914, a year after the break with Freud, Jung published "The Role of the Unconscious," in which he wrote:

> Christianity split the Germanic barbarian into an upper and a lower half, and enabled him, by repressing the dark side, to domesticate the brighter half and fit it for civilization. But the lower, darker half still awaits redemption and a second spell of domestication. . . . As the Christian view of the world loses its authority, the more menacingly will the "blond beast" be heard prowling about in its underground prison, ready at any moment to burst out with devastating conse-

quences. . . . The Jew has too little of this quality—where has he his own earth underfoot: The mystery of earth is no joke and no paradox. . . . I can understand very well that Freud's and Adler's reduction of everything psychic to primitive sexual wishes and power-drives has something about it that is beneficial and satisfying to the Jew, because it is a form of simplification. [Maidenbaum and Martin 1991, pp. 362–363]

This passage contains an interesting prediction of German National Socialism in 1914. Striking is how soon the language of the Enlightenment has been abandoned for the language of Romanticism that differentiates German "barbarians" from Jews who have no earth under their feet. This philosophy did not prevent Jung from working with world-renowned sinologists, anthropologists, and physicists, and writing introductory essays for Chinese ancient text. It only barred Jews from ever understanding the Germanic soul. In 1934 Jung wrote:

The Jew, who is something of a nomad, has never yet created a cultural form of his own and as far as we can see never will, since all his instincts and talents require a more or less civilized nation to act as host for their development. . . . The "Aryan" unconscious has a higher potential than the Jewish; that is both the advantage and the disadvantage of a youthfulness not yet fully weaned from barbarism. This suspicion emanated from Freud. He did not understand the Germanic psyche any more than did his Germanic followers. Has the formidable phenomenon of National Socialism, on which the whole world gazes with astonished eyes, taught them better? [Maidenbaum and Martin 1991, p. 217]

Between 1914 and 1934, the climate of opinion in the German-speaking world had become markedly more anti-Semitic, and so are Jung's remarks. It comes as a shock that Jung, a man of considerable culture and wide reading, can claim that 2,500 years of Jewish history and culture, including the Bible, be dismissed as "never created a cultural form of his own."

The German barbarian, who is split into upper and lower parts, mentioned by Jung is actually taken from Freud's idea of repression. However, reference to a lower part that awaits redemption is taken from the vocabulary of religion, and in Jung's case even more likely from a Wagnerian opera. What is implied is that the second redemption would undo the split between higher and lower conscious and unconscious in some utopian state. This is followed by the strange idea that the Jew, unlike the German, has no unconscious because he has no soil under his feet. In spite of many logical contradictions, Jung's statement mixing psychoanalysis with religious vocabulary has a powerful appeal. Jews are not yet caricatured as they will be in the Nazi literature, but they are described as intellectually arid, and therefore damned by faint praise.

Jung's anti-Semitism was of the Romantic type, not the paranoid type of Adolf Hitler and Nazi Germany. He did not wish for a Jewish annihilation, only for a cultural isolation. Nevertheless the 1934 statement shows how easily one type of anti-Semitism could get him to admire Hitler. Thomas Kirsch (1991), a Jungian analyst who is a Jew, described the dilemma:

> Let us move away from the past and ask how the issue of Jung's alleged anti-Semitism affects us today. How is it when I am with a patient? Does it make me feel that I might be less a Jungian because Jung had some complex, perhaps terribly negative feeling toward Jews? No. It makes absolutely no difference, and the thought never crosses my mind. On the other hand, I am often reminded in a session that I am Jewish, and there is a debt of gratitude that through Jung and my analysis, by which I mean the understanding of complexes in a transpersonal archetypal sense, I have come to a deeper understanding of my Jewish roots and their relationship to other cultures and religions. [p. 350]

Regaining through Jungian analysis one's Jewish or Christian roots may bring relief from isolation, but the salvation offered by Jung was achieved by the Romantic and counter-Enlightenment attitude that ancestry creates a gulf between people that cannot be bridged.

While still a psychoanalyst, Jung began a sexual affair with a young Russian Jewish woman, Sabina Spielrein, who later became a Freudian psychoanalyst and perished in the Holocaust. That Jung asked her mother for money in order to break off that relationship constitutes a dark chapter in Jung's biography. It has been argued that because many of Jung's friends and patients have been Jews, and particularly since his mistresses were Jewish women, his anti-Semitism should not be taken seriously. To this may be added the fact that in 1938, after the annexation of Austria by Hitler, Jung sent an emissary to Freud offering him financial help. Freud indignantly refused the offer. In my interpretation, Jung's behavior showed a wish for resumption of contact, but with himself in the stronger position.

What can be learned from the history of ideas from the Freud–Jung controversy? Adler misunderstood Freud and tried to erect a competing psychology. Jung's defection has a deeper significance, for in him became embodied not ordinary resistance to Freud's ideas but a kind of revengeful attack on what Freud had discovered. To adopt for a moment a Jungian way of thinking: in Jung, the collective unconscious revenged itself on the man who for the first time exposed the unconscious to understanding. It is as if the irrational forces dormant in the psyche revolted against Freud's attempt to tame them. Freud concluded the 1914 discussion of Jung with this statement:

> I can only express a wish that the future may grant an agreeable upward journey to all those who have found their stay in the underworld of psychoanalysis too uncomfortable for their tastes. [p. 66]

Reading Jung's autobiography (1961) made me believe that for Jung himself, fortune granted this wish.

OTTO RANK (1884–1939)

The next major figure to break ranks was Otto Rank, after he published *The Trauma of Birth* (1929). An episode from Rank's adolescence reported by Taft (1958) may shed some light on the course of Rank's life. His father was an alcoholic and had a violent temper. When Rank was 16, he and his brother, who was (unfortunately) named Siegmund, decided to break off their relationship with their father. They continued to live in the house but stopped talking to him. Rank came across Freud's work in 1904 and felt that his eyes had been opened and he could see everything clearly. Through Adler, Rank met Freud personally. Freud, who as a student often accepted money from what he called his "private bankers," now supported Rank and helped him get a university education. In 1907, Rank's first book *The Artist* appeared, and whatever the book may have been before Rank met Freud, when it was published it was an extension of Freud's 1904 essay "The Poet and Daydreaming." In this book Rank maintained, like Freud, that the artist spares himself repression by his creative work, and vicariously the same process takes place in the reader. Rank's second book, *The Myth of the Birth of the Hero* (1909) was introduced by Freud's essay, "Family Romance." In 1912, Rank received his doctoral degree and published *The Incest Motive in Poetry and Saga*. The book illustrated the ever-presence of the Oedipus complex in literature. Rank's next paper, "Nakedness in Saga and Poetry" (1913), continued the same theme. By that time, Rank was the editor of two psychoanalytic journals. In 1913, Rank also published, together with Hans Sachs, "The Significance of Psychoanalysis for the Mental Sciences." In 1914, Freud allowed Rank to contribute a section to the fourth edition of *The Interpretation of Dreams*. In "Mourning and Melancholia," Freud (1917) credited Rank for the insight that if a love object is given up for a narcissistic identification with the lost object, the love relationship was already narcissistic in nature. Only narcissistic love relationships end up in narcissistic identifications. What is striking is that Rank's extensive work is entirely in Freud's shadow. Individuation came to him only after the break.

In 1924, Ferenczi and Rank published a joint book, *The Development of Psychoanalysis*, in which they emphasize the propensity of analysands to live out their unconscious conflicts in action. This "acting-in" and "acting-out" can become the main subject of the analysis, making the psychoanalysis less dependent on childhood memories, and more alive and shorter. When *The Trauma of Birth* first appeared it was dedicated to Freud, and neither Rank nor Freud thought that it would lead to a break between them. Rank believed that he was only expressing clinical observations when he thought to have discovered the universal and major trauma of humanity, the trauma of birth:

> One day, in a specially obvious case, it became clear to me that the strongest resistance to the severance of the libido transference at the end of the analysis is expressed in the form of the earliest infantile *fixation on the mother*.
>
> The freeing of the libido from its object, the analyst, seems to correspond to an *exact reproduction* of the first separation from the first libido object, namely of the newborn child from the mother. [Rank 1924, p. 4]

It is of historical interest to note that the difficulty of resolving the transference was the origin of the idea of the trauma of birth.

Taft (1958) cites a letter of Freud's to Rank after the publication of Rank's *Trauma of Birth*.

> My observation has, as yet, not permitted me to make a decision, but up to now has furnished nothing that would correspond to your interpretation. . . . Your experiences are different; do they therefore cancel mine? We both know that experiences permit of many explanations, hence we have to wait for further experiences.
>
> After all, the right to have an opinion of one's own prevails for me, too. I have endeavored to respect it with each of my friends and adherents, as long as we could preserve a common ground. [cited in Waelder 1963, p. 637]

I find Freud's remarks of great interest precisely because they contain a contradiction. Freud knows that experience permits many explanations and yet he counts on experience to solve the problems. We know that this is beyond the capacity of experience to accomplish. The tone in which Freud writes is friendly and intimate. The Freud that Rank encountered was very different from the one Adler and Jung met. Rank is not experienced as a threat to psychoanalysis; there is plenty of time to test hypotheses. In the ten years that elapsed between Jung and Rank, Freud had become much more secure.

Freud further wrote:

> It is a long time since you have tried to interpret one of my dreams in such a powerful analytical way. Since then much has changed. You have grown enormously and you know so much about me. . . . I cannot confirm everything you write . . . but I do not need to contradict you anywhere. . . . The super-ego merely says to this process: "All right you old jester and boaster. This is not true at all! . . . You (the dreamer) are not David, you are the boasting giant Goliath, whom another one, the young David will slay." And now everything falls into place around this point that you [Rank] are the dreaded David who with his *Trauma of Birth* succeeds in depreciating my work. [Waelder 1963, p. 638]

Waelder cited these letters in response to the accusation that Freud exerted tyrannical power over his disciples.

At first, Rank did not even claim credit for this discovery, attributing it to Freud. He did, however, shift the emphasis from the role of the father to that of the mother and from the centrality of the Oedipus complex to the centrality of trauma of birth. What was even more disturbing, first to Freud's followers and then to Freud himself, was the conclusion Rank reached about how the analytic process should come to termination:

> When the analyst succeeds in overcoming the primal resistance, namely the mother-fixation, with regard to his own person in the transference relation, then a definite term is fixed for the analysis, within which period the patient repeats automatically the new severance from the mother (substitute) figure, in the form of the reproduction of his own birth. [Rank 1924, p. 9]

The quotation from Rank contains a contradiction: if the analyst has really succeeded to overcome a mother fixation—and the mother fixation is the root of the neurosis—then the patient himself should wish to terminate at this point, for nothing else should bind him to the analyst. That at this point an arbitrary decision to end the analysis in nine months had to be introduced shows that the birth trauma for Rank lost its metaphorical position and had to be repeated concretely in the nine months of pregnancy.

In our current language we would say that Rank discovered a pre-oedipal fixation on the mother. For the first time, the inability of the psychoanalyst to bring a psychoanalysis to termination is given as a reason behind dissidence. Freud had fixed a termination date for the Wolf Man (1918), but that was an emergency measure because the Wolf Man could not be brought to bring the analysis to a conclusion. Rank elevated this emergency mechanism into the cardinal point of his technique.

What matters in a historical perspective is the fact that Rank's dissidence is so very different from that of Adler and Jung. It comes, as it were, from within psychoanalysis itself, from its inability to reach termination. A quarter of a century after the discovery of the Oedipus complex a hitherto loyal disciple can discover a new trauma and return to the Breuer/Freud (1895) traumatic view of neurosis.

The correspondence between Freud and Abraham gives us a unique opportunity to be in touch with the spirit at that time and see how the two men reacted to Rank's growing alienation from psychoanalysis. On March 4, 1924, Freud wrote to Abraham:

> Let us assume the most extreme case, and suppose that Ferenczi and Rank came right out with the view that we were wrong to stop at the Oedipus complex, and that the really decisive factor was the birth

trauma, and that those who did not overcome this later broke down also on the Oedipus complex. Then, instead of our sexual aetiology of neurosis, we should have an aetiology determined by physiological chance, because those who became neurotic would either have experienced an unusually severe birth trauma or would bring an unusually "sensitive" organization to that trauma. Further, a number of analysts would make certain modifications in technique on the basis of this theory. What further evil consequences would ensue? We could remain under the same roof with the greatest equanimity, and after a few years' work it would become plain whether one side had exaggerated a useful finding or the other had underrated it. [Abraham and Freud 1907–1926, pp. 352–353]

In view of the importance of the Oedipus complex to Freud, this is an astonishing statement.

Those who consider Freud narrow-minded and closed off to other people's ideas should become familiar with these lines. Abraham replied to Freud's letter on March 8:

It is not at all difficult for me to assimilate new discoveries if they have been arrived at in a legitimate psychoanalytic manner. My criticisms are not directed at the results achieved by Ferenczi and Rank but against the methods they used. These seem to me to lead away from psycho-analysis and my criticisms will refer solely to this point. [Abraham and Freud 1907–1926, p. 354]

As the correspondence indicates, Freud was patient with Rank, and willing to wait. But Rank, possibly traumatized by the appearance of Freud's cancer, tried to, but could not, return to the psychoanalytic movement. A simpler and shorter technique of therapy gained dominance over him.

In 1937, in "Analysis Terminable and Interminable," Freud returned once more to Otto Rank:

A particularly energetic attempt in this direction was made by Otto Rank, following upon his book "The Trauma of Birth" (1924). He supposed that the true source of neurosis was the act of birth, since this involves the possibility of a child's "primal fixation" to his mother not being surmounted but persisting as a "primal repression." Rank hoped that if this primal trauma were dealt with by a subsequent analysis the whole neurosis would be got rid of. Thus this one small piece of analytic work would save the necessity for all the rest. And a few months should be enough to accomplish this. It cannot be disputed that Rank's argument was bold and ingenious; but it did not stand the test of critical examination. [p. 216]

What Rank tried to achieve was an oversimplification; he was the first dissident to have become impatient with the pace of psychoanalysis and the uncertainty of its result. Looking back at that controversy after eighty years, one is struck by the fact that Rank was drawing attention to issues that would become important later in the history of psychoanalysis, namely the role of separation anxiety preceding the Oedipus complex and castration anxiety.

Once more, as in Adler's case, a dissident drew attention to issues that eventually in a different form would reenter into the mainstream of psychoanalysis, in this case under the heading of the preoedipal phase of development. What has been rejected at one phase in analytic history is readmitted in a different form in the next phase.

SANDOR FERENCZI (1873–1933)

In the psychoanalytic pantheon, Ferenczi ranks second only to Abraham in the magnitude of his contribution to psychoanalysis. In "On the History of the Psycho-Analytic Movement" (1914), Freud referred to Ferenczi thus: "Hungary provided only one collaborator, S. Ferenczi, but one that indeed outweighs a whole society" (p. 33). When Ferenczi met Freud in 1908 or 1909, he was already 35 years old. A neuropsychiatrist with some sixty works to his name, Ferenczi accompanied Freud on the famous trip to the United States in 1909, when the Clark University lectures were given. In 1910, Freud and Ferenczi traveled to Palermo via Paris, Rome, and Naples, but the trip was not a success. Freud resented Ferenczi's feminine tendencies and Ferenczi felt reduced to the role of secretary. Nevertheless, Freud hoped Ferenczi would become his son-in-law by marrying his daughter, Matilde (Haynal 1946). Unlike Rank, who met Freud at a young age and was molded by Freud, Ferenczi always maintained a degree of independence. The two differed significantly and at their best they complemented each other's character. Eventually, however, these differences became irreconcilable. In 1976, as an introduction to the chapter on psychoanalytic technique (Bergmann and Hartman 1976), I made the following observation:

> Freud's papers on technique laid down the basic principles or the grand strategy of the procedure. Ferenczi's papers deal with more specific subjects. They resemble reports to headquarters from the front line. [p. 89]

Ferenczi's unsatisfactory analysis with Freud has become part of the psychoanalytic history because it was one of the motives that made Freud write his 1937 paper, "Analysis Terminable and Unterminable." Because the Freud/Ferenczi correspondence has appeared, we know the situation that made Ferenczi enter into analysis with Freud. It is a chapter that could have been written by Maupassant, in which he describes a man falling in love with the daughter of his mistress. Like a Maupassant hero, Ferenczi was analyzing the daughter of his mistress, Gisela Palos, when he fell in love with his patient. In this dilemma, the young woman was sent to Vienna to be analyzed by Freud. Freud was not neutral in this situation and used his influence to persuade Ferenczi to choose the mother. The choice meant that Ferenczi would have no children of his own. This may have left a residue of resentment in Ferenczi that emerged in due time.

To Ferenczi goes the credit for having written the first clinical paper based on Freud's dual instinct theory, "The Unwelcome Child and His Death Instinct" (1929b). Ferenczi concluded that "children who are received in a harsh and unloving way die easily and willingly" (p. 105). Perhaps still under Rank's influence he wrote:

> A child has to be induced by means of immense expenditure of love, tenderness, and care, to forgive his parents for having brought him into the world without any intention on his part. [p. 105]

Anticipating André Green's dead mother, Ferenczi said:

> There remains of course the task of ascertaining the final differences in neurotic symptom between children maltreated from the start and those who are first received with enthusiasm, indeed with passionate love but then dropped. [p. 106]

The implications of that paper, not immediately recognized, are far-reaching. Homo sapient is born devoid of the instinct for survival. The human infant needs love to be persuaded that life is worthwhile. Those who did not obtain this welcome will be depressed and suicidal. Ferenczi's paper raised new questions. Can love given by others, namely therapists, make up for such an early deficit? Even more pertinently, can the therapist, barred from expressing love directly and dependent on therapeutic work that requires the capacity for symbolization, undo the damage?

Ferenczi's first paper that could be described as a dissident paper was delivered at the Oxford Congress in 1929, entitled "The Principles of Relaxation and NeoCatharsis" (1929a). After a tribute to Breuer and Freud, Ferenczi described his own beginning work as a psychoanalyst. He met his first patient in the street and took him into his consultation room, and gave him Jung's association test. The test plunged the patient into the analysis of his early life. Ferenczi then went on to describe his efforts at active therapy, artificially producing an accentuation of tension [for detailed discussion of this phase of Ferenczi's work, see Bergmann and Hartman (1976)]. Ferenczi then describes his and Rank's setting a term for the ending of the analysis, and his efforts to follow Freud's recommendations and analyze the conflict between the ego, id, and superego. But in Ferenczi's hands, this method led to unsatisfactory results, resembling a relationship between teacher and pupil. Ferenczi felt that the application of ego psychology only leads to the repression of negative feelings toward the psychoanalyst. In many cases Ferenczi found it necessary to introduce indulgence, the very opposite of Freud's abstinence (1919). Under the heading of indulgence, Ferenczi included analyzing without a remuneration, letting the patients stay in bed and visiting them at home, prolonging the analytic hour as long as necessary. One can imagine how shocking this paper was at the Oxford Congress, and Ferenczi failed to become president of the association.

On the theoretical level, Ferenczi introduced the idea that there is a psychotic core behind every neurosis. At this point, Ferenczi acknowledged his indebtedness to "our colleague Elizabeth Severn": from Ferenczi's clinical diary, we learn that Severn was not a colleague but a patient of Ferenczi who, in Ferenczi's last years, succeeded to induce him to enter into a mutual analysis with her. Eventually she won the therapeutic battle and Ferenczi became her patient. The Oxford paper ends with a discussion with Anna Freud, in which she remarked that Ferenczi treated his patients as she treated children, obliterating the difference between child analysis and adult analysis. The next paper that almost precipitated a break was entitled "Confusion of Tongues Between Adults and the Child" (1933). It was presented at the Wiesbaden Congress. Eitingon, who presided over that congress, would not allow Ferenczi to present his paper; it took the personal intervention of Freud for Ferenczi to be allowed to present it.

In that paper, Ferenczi emphasized again the necessity of encouraging patients to express their negative feelings toward the analyst. His language, however, was more critical. He spoke of the "professional hypocrisy" of the analyst who remains undisturbed by whatever he hears, showing no emotion. Ferenczi felt that this coldness merely repeated for the patient the unconcerned parent and was of no therapeutic value. He also went back to the seduction theory, stating that many parents mistake the sexual play of children for the desires of a sexually mature person and respond sexually to the playful seductive behavior of the child. After the sexual experience has taken place, the child introjects the guilty feelings that the adult had or should have had, while the seducer often becomes moralistic and blames the child.

In the unwelcome child paper (1929b), Ferenczi stressed the need of the infant for love if he is to survive. He thus anticipated Spitz's paper on hospitalism by a decade and a half. In the confusion of tongues paper (1933), he added that the infant and child need not only love to thrive, but also the right kind of love. Unhappy parents, starved for love themselves, turning toward the child for their own frustrated needs for loving, are not likely to give to the child the kind of love the child needs.

Among the indulgences that Ferenczi allowed and that did not appear in print but reached Freud nevertheless, was allowing his women patients to kiss him. This became a subject of a scathing letter by Freud to Ferenczi reproduced in Jones's biography in which Freud expressed the fear that younger analysts will go further than Ferenczi, and "Papa Ferenczi" will be responsible for starting mischief he could not control.

Ferenczi's loneliness and bitterness in his last years emerges sharply from an entry in his diary, dated August 4, 1933:

The advantages of following [Freud] blindly were: (1) membership in a distinguished group guaranteed by the king, indeed with the rank of field marshal for myself (crown-prince fantasy). (2) One learned from him and from his kind of technique various things that made one's life and work more comfortable: the calm, unemotional reserve; the unruffled assurance that one knew better; and the theories, the seeking and finding of the causes of failure in the patient instead of partly in ourselves. The dishonesty of reserving the technique for one's own person; the advice not to let patients learn anything about the technique; and finally the pessimistic view, shared with only a trusted few, that neurotics are a rabble, good only to support us financially and to allow us to learn from their cases: psychoanalysis as a therapy may be worthless. [Ferenczi 1985, p. 186]

One further criticism of Freud I found of particular interest: "His brilliant ideas were usually based on only a single case, like illuminations as it were, which dazzled and amazed" (p. 185). I agree with Ferenczi but do not see it as a criticism of Freud. In psychoanalysis, major discoveries can be made on one particular case. The transformation of the "ideographic" into the "nomothetic," motivated by our need to make psychoanalysis a science, is often the weaker link.

Ferenczi died of pernicious anemia; Jones believed that he also succumbed to a psychosis before he died. But Balint, Ferenczi's pupil and executor, denied this accusation; a literature has grown around the subject (Benomi 1999).

Out of Ferenczi's emphasis on the infant need to be loved, Balint (1935) developed the concept of "passive love," in which a person does not love but wishes to be loved and gratified instantly and completely. This need for immediate gratification is experienced as a matter of life and death. Balint's passive love is a major contribution to the literature on love (Bergmann 1987). It is excellent as far as it goes but it fails to take aggression into account. The person desiring passive love says to his or her partner something like the following: "Because I have a history of childhood deprivation, you must allow me to be aggressive towards you. I have the right to attack you mercilessly, and criticize you when you fail to meet my needs. I still expect you to love me as much as ever." Passive love is narcissistic, but this narcissism lacks the defensive armor that Reich emphasized. It is a dependent kind of narcissism. The phenomenon that Balint described is familiar to all psychoanalysts. Eventually it led him to see psychoanalysis as a two-person psychology and libido as object seeking.

In retrospect one can conclude that Ferenczi was Freud's most important dissident, who had an enormous influence on subsequent events. Freud assumed that neurotic constellations in childhood are the result of an intrapsychic conflict with the child's instincts. Ferenczi assumed that the child became ill as a result of the parents' inability to love the child properly. Ferenczi, therefore, saw the source of the neurosis of the child coming from without—a return to the Breuer–Freud early hypothesis of the traumatic rather than intrapsychic origin of the neuroses. In the life of an individual, traumatic and intrapsychic conflicts interact in a complex way, but since Ferenczi one may overemphasize one at the expense of the other, and dissenting schools emerge.

CONTROVERSIES IN THE EARLY HISTORY OF PSYCHOANALYSIS

The Vienna Symposium on Masturbation

The first recorded discussion in the history of psychoanalysis was the 1912 symposium on masturbation conducted by the Vienna Psychoanalytic Association in which fourteen contributors took part. The discussion appeared in a special book published in 1912, a book that was never translated. However, the contribution of Victor Tausk, which I consider the most important one, was published in 1951.

A few remarks on Freud's writing on masturbation are a prerequisite for an appreciation of that discussion. In his prepsychoanalytic writings, Freud believed that, as an incomplete form of sexual discharge, masturbation causes physiological damage to the sexual apparatus and leads to a combination of symptoms designated as neurasthenia, in which headaches, constipation, and fatigue play a role. The term *neurasthenia* was introduced by Beard in 1867 to describe a hypothetical condition in which nerve cells were exhausted through depletion of stored nutrients. While masturbation led to neurasthenia, Freud believed that abstinence and *coitus interruptus* led to anxiety neurosis. Both neurasthenia and anxiety neurosis were called "actual neurosis" and distinguished from psychoneurosis because a direct and satisfactory sexual relationship was the natural cure to these psychological conditions.

In 1905, Freud differentiated three periods of masturbation: (1) masturbation in the earliest infancy, (2) masturbation taking place in the fourth year of life, and (3) pubertal masturbation (1905b). He noted that some children continue to masturbate without interruption. Masturbation often follows overstimulation caused by the seduction by an older person. Girls, Freud believed (unlike Horney and many other analysts), are capable only of clitoral masturbation, with the vagina remaining an unexplored sexual organ until puberty or later. Freud looked upon masturbation as "the executive agency of the whole infantile sexuality" (p. 189). Because masturbation is so central, it takes over guilt feelings previously associated with other psychic events. In his contribution to the 1912 symposium, Freud defended his differentiation between actual neurosis and psychoneurosis and suggested a new metaphor: "the nucleus of the psychoneurotic symptom—the grain of sand at the center of the pearl—is formed of a somatic sexual manifestation" (p. 248). He added that masturbation does not cause neurosis, but may well be a symptom of neurosis.

In the discussion of 1912 Ferenczi and Sachs connected anxiety during masturbation to castration anxiety. Ferenczi emphasized that fore-pleasure, expressed in fondling, looking, and kissing, is essential for the whole body to become sexually excited. Since fore-pleasure is missing in masturbation, it leads to a damming up of the libido. Paul Federn emphasized that the unsatisfactory nature of masturbation leads to further masturbation. Federn also felt that genital masturbation can protect the child from regression to pregenital sexuality.

By far the most important paper in that symposium was that of Victor Tausk (1912), who in many ways was ahead even of Freud. It is an astonishing paper, reminding us of the great loss to psychoanalysis that was caused by Tausk's early suicide.

Tausk defined masturbation as the sexual manipulation of the genitals without a partner. When sexual fantasies without manipulation are used, Tausk spoke of "psychic onanism." The continuation of masturbation into adulthood is a prolongation of childhood. Children who do not give up masturbation during the latency period are difficult to educate, difficult to manage, spiteful, and moody. Adolescence is a difficult period because it offers no compensation for sexual abstinence. Moderate masturbation Tausk considered as harmless, and even helpful. However, excessive masturbation will lead to the weakening of the secretory and nervous systems, and may contribute to impotence. In keeping with Freud's ideas, Tausk thought that inadequate and incomplete sexual discharge leads to sexual tension. It is during adolescence that longing without gratification first emerges. This state of ungratified longing is the birthplace of lyricism.

I come now to the point where Tausk was ahead of Freud. Tausk raised the question of whether masturbation can ever lead to a full discharge. Tausk believed that it depends on a person's sexual development. If a person's libido is still functioning on an infantile stage and is autoerotic in aim, masturbation can offer an adequate discharge. However, if the person already reached the stage of development where object love is important, masturbation contributes to anxiety. The disadvantages of continuing masturbation are that the masturbator has no reason to compete with others for the possession of a sexual object and thus fails to develop the aggression necessary to obtain a love object. Even if a love object is found, the masturbator is not strongly related to the love object, and any dissatisfaction or shortcoming of the love object throws him back to masturbation. Masturbation also has a tendency to fixate perverse tendencies, and it operates against the subordination of homosexual wishes to heterosexual ones. Tausk further noted that in prolonged masturbation the genitals acquire the characteristic of another person, so that the penis is referred to as "he" who does not want to become erect, or the vagina becomes an independent "she" that refuses to lubricate or have an orgasm. The supposed psychic independence of the genital organs makes frigidity and impotence more likely. A further danger is that only the genitalia of the other person are important, leaving the relationship as existing only between two genital organs, without participation of the persons themselves. If masturbation damages potency, it will also damage self-esteem. Finally, masturbation is the expression of an unconscious rebellion against the father, the masturbator saying, "I masturbate in spite of him, and if I suffer as a result, it will be his fault." In psychoanalysis one can often observe that masturbation often stops when hostility toward the father becomes conscious. To Tausk goes the credit for having moved the topic of masturbation from the physiological realm to the realm of object relations.

In 1951 Annie Reich summarized the Vienna symposium. She still upheld the distinction between psychoneurosis and actual neurosis.

In a danger situation the ego may give an anxiety signal, which stirs up defenses and leads to the formation of psychoneurotic symptoms. Or a traumatic situation may arise that brings about automatic discharges, that is, actual-neurotic phenomena. The inability to provide discharge is caused by psychic conflicts. It also often results from an ego regression that deprives the ego of adult methods of handling the demands of the id. She concluded, "We no longer see masturbation and neurasthenia as a direct and simple sequence" (p. 83).

Annie Reich then went on to point out what progress was made on the subject of masturbation since 1912. Psychoanalysts have recognized that certain activities like reckless driving and dangerous acrobatics are masturbatory equivalents, as are also the tantrums of children. She also quoted Anna Freud (1949): "Children can fight against the physical activity of masturbation by substituting other activities which may then become exciting, like masturbation once was. Or the battle can be directed against the masturbatory fantasies, resulting in modification of the fantasies." Annie Reich also noted that in the United States the pendulum has swung: Educators now stress the harmlessness of masturbation while psychoanalysts do not believe that masturbation is toxic as such; its retention becomes an obstacle in the capacity to love.

The Marienbad Symposium

In 1923 Freud introduced the structural point of view, dividing the personality into id, ego, and superego, without realizing that this division will give rise to important differences in the technique of psychoanalysis. In 1936 the clouds of war were gathering in Nazi Germany. The Fourteenth International Psycho-Analytic Association Congress was held in Marienbad, a resort town in Czechoslovakia. There, in response to the structural theory, a symposium on the theory and therapeutic results of psychoanalysis took place. The symposium was restricted in scope. Edward Glover and James Strachey represented London, while Fenichel, Bergler, Bibring, and Nunberg represented the German-speaking contingent. No American or French psychoanalyst participated in this symposium. However, despite its restricted scope, this symposium is of historical interest.

Among the participants, Herman Nunberg most closely represents Freud's own point of view. In Nunberg's view, "The task of therapy consists in resolving the conflict between the psychic institutions, thereby reducing psychic tensions" (Marienbad Symposium 1936). Free association allows the repressed unconscious to become conscious. The process is assisted by the synthetic functions of the ego. The derivatives of the unconscious become absorbed into the organization of the conscious ego. As long as the repetition compulsion serves exclusively the needs of the id, it remains outside the sphere of the ego. When it comes under the domination of the ego, the passive experience is turned into an active one and the repetition compulsion can be combated by the ego. As the analysis proceeds, repressed derivatives of the id enter consciousness; as the patient becomes conscious of the variety of his aggressive and sexual wishes, the danger of punishment from the superego also grows. To counteract this danger the patient identifies himself or herself with the analyst, taking over the analyst's superego. At the end of an analysis the superego becomes modified, and the ego becomes reconciled to the superego, the id, and the external world. Instincts are released from their fixation points and are accepted within the organization of the ego. These processes taken together achieve cure.

In contrast to Nunberg, Strachey emphasized the role of the superego. Neurotic illness interferes with the normal growth, and if this interference is removed normal growth can be expected to resume. "Analysis enables the half-child, half-dwarfed mind of the neurotic to grow toward adult structure" (Marienbad Symposium 1936, p. 139). Only transference interpretations are mutative and only they alone can bring about psychic change:

> For the prime essential of a transference-interpretation in my view is that the feeling or impulse interpreted should not merely be concerned with the analyst but that it should be in activity at the moment at which it is interpreted. Thus an interpretation of an impulse felt towards the analyst last week or even a quarter of an hour ago will not be a transference-interpretation in my sense unless it is still active in the patient at the moment when the interpretation is given. The situation will be, so to speak, a dead one and will be entirely without the dynamic force which is inherent in the giving of a true transference-interpretation. [p. 141]

Following Melanie Klein, Strachey believed that the nature of the superego is determined by the character of the internalized object relations. As long as they function on a punitive level, the patient will continue to be punitive toward other people. The effort of the analyst must be directed toward separating the patient from his or her archaic objects. In the course of analysis the analyst is interjected piecemeal, gradually modifying the severity and the sadism of the superego.

The recently developed ego psychology was represented by Otto Fenichel:

> Since it is only the ego which is accessible to our therapeutic intervention, there are, in principle, two modes of attack. We may try to strengthen the ego with a view to enabling it to put up a more successful defense against the instincts. Or we may induce it to desist from its defense or to replace that defense by one better adapted to the purpose. [p. 133]

Fenichel believed that the most useful interpretations are transference-resistance interpretations. When we show the patient how he or she is setting up a defense, we are also training the patient to tolerate instinctual derivatives without defending against them. Analysis always starts from the surface, what is active at the moment. Following Wilhelm Reich, Fenichel stressed that interpretations of resistance should always precede interpretation of content. In his presentation, Fenichel raised an interesting question. Since neurotics in their instinctual life remain fixated on an infantile level, and treatment diminishes the domination of the superego as well as the defenses of the ego, the patient should now, according to psychoanalytic theory, become perverse. Indeed, many patients fear such a possible outcome. Fenichel went on to point out that as a rule this does not happen, because the perverse wishes retained their power only because they were warded off. If they are admitted into the ego and into the whole personality, they adapt themselves to the genital supremacy reached by the patient. As a result, the patient becomes healthy and not a pervert. Fenichel found that the traditional formula of making the unconscious conscious, in this symposium defended by Nunberg, is only topographically conceived and fails to do justice to the economic and dynamic points of view.

What makes the Marienbad Symposium historically important is that Freud's structural point of view was by its very nature conducive to different approaches that psychoanalysts could adopt in their work, thus breaking the unity of method that had previously existed. Both the symposium on masturbation and the Marienbad symposium demonstrated that controversy as such does not lead to dissidence.

KAREN HORNEY (1885–1952)

The first woman of this series of dissidents and only one year younger than Rank, Karen Horney played a prominent role in the history of psychoanalysis long before she became a dissident. She was the first of a long line to battle with Freud and Abraham's portrayal of female psychology. By 1977, when Harold Blum published *Female Psychology*, all the contributors to this book had accepted Horney's revision of Freud's idea about female development; but this was twenty years after Horney's death. What is less known and may constitute my contribution, is that Karen Horney was not only the successful warrior in this war, but also a victim because of her failed analysis with Karl Abraham. While this conclusion is my own, I wish to acknowledge the help I received from Susan Quinn's (1988) superb biography of Horney. The biographer was in turn helped by a diary that was kept by Horney.

In 1909, newly married to a successful industrialist, expecting her first child, and still a medical student, Horney arrived in Berlin. While working in a mental hospital, she began in 1910 her analysis with Abraham, an analysis that lasted one year. Abraham himself had arrived in Berlin from Burgholzi in Zurich, where he was won over to psychoanalysis by Jung and Bleuler. He was the first psychoanalyst in private practice in Berlin.

Horney's view on feminine psychology not only clashed with that of Freud, it was also a criticism of Abraham's 1920 paper, "Manifestations of the Female Castration Complex." In 1924, Horney's first paper entitled "On the Genesis of the Castration Complex in Women" appeared. A few lines from this paper became famous. She stated that Freud's assertion that

> one half of the human race is discontented with the sex assigned to it
> and can overcome this discontent only under favorable circumstances

is decidedly unsatisfactory, not only to feminine narcissism but also to biological science. [p. 5]

It is likely that we hear in this remark not only Horney's view but also the reason why the analysis with Abraham failed; their views about female sexuality had to clash. In Horney's view there is first a "urethral eroticism," girl's envy of the way boys urinate. The girl also envies the right of the boy to touch his organ while he urinates because this is interpreted as a permission to masturbate and to look at the penis, rights that are denied to the girl. However, this envy of the boy's urination does not lead directly into the much later penis envy, which takes place only after the girl is disappointed in her oedipal love. With benefit of hindsight, this paper can also be read as a self-analysis with some reconciliation toward both Horney's father and Abraham.

When Horney published her next paper, "The Flight from Womanhood" in 1926, Abraham was already dead. Now she emphasized men's envy of pregnancy, of childbirth, and of the breast as well as the capacity of the woman to suckle. Horney questions Freud's belief that girls masturbate only clitorally and pointed out that women's fear of an excessively large penis producing pain shows that the little girl estimates correctly the differences in the size of the paternal phallus and her genitalia. Horney also noted that the wish to be a male is usually not difficult to obtain in the analysis of women so that penis envy is often a defense against the oedipal wishes of the girl. Horney felt that inadequacy feelings are easier to bear than guilt feelings. The fact that the debate between Horney and Freud could not be reconciled by clinical experience shows that the data do not favor one or the other hypothesis. We are faced with the next question, that if the truth is not obtainable by the psychoanalytic method, which of the two is more likely to yield favorable therapeutic results, and here at least I feel that Horney's approach is more encouraging and more likely to be helpful than Freud's (1937a) idea that penis envy is rock bottom.

Between 1922 and 1935, Horney wrote fourteen papers. She was one of the first analysts to study marriage. Freud, except for a few anecdotal remarks—such as "A wife is like an umbrella. Sooner or later one takes a cab" (1905a, p. 78), or that second marriages are less disappointing for women than the first—avoided dealing with marriage as a cultural institution. Like the dream, marriage is within the realm of normal psychology. The fact that we know from Horney's biography that she had a problem with promiscuity adds interest to what she wrote about marriage. In 1927, she wrote a paper on "The Problem of the Monogamous Ideal," which was read at the Tenth International Congress in Innsbruck. It opened with an assertion: "There is hardly another situation in life which is so intimately and so obviously related to the Oedipus situation as is marriage" (p. 318). What drives most men and women to matrimony is the expectation of the fulfillment of all desires arising out of the oedipus situation in childhood. To have him or her as the exclusive possession and bear or give him or her children seems like the fulfillment of oedipal wishes. Marriages end in disappointment because they cannot meet the oedipal expectations. Marriage is threatened from the side of the id because in reality becoming father or mother is not the picture left in our minds from childhood. Horney quoted Freud that husbands and wives are only oedipal substitutes. The bitterness and disappointment in marriage depend on the degree of discrepancy between the original wish and the substitute found.

Marriage is also threatened from the side of the superego. In resuscitation of the incest taboo, the incest taboo forces sexual desire to yield to the inhibition of parent–child relationships. Karen Horney knew only one case in which sexuality did not diminish markedly after marriage and that was the case of a woman who, in childhood, had sexual relations with her father—certainly a new way of looking at childhood seduction! Just as the child has to repress hostility toward the parents, so must the marital partners. Sexuality favors polygamy while the cultural ego ideal demands fidelity. The desire for monogamy Horney placed in the oral phase—the wish to possess is derived from the desire to eat up. It is supported by narcissistic wishes and fantasies of prestige. Fidelity, she argued, has no prototypes in infantile experiences. It is a restriction of instincts. The fact that in masturbation the parents are often replaced by other figures was taken by Horney as proof of infantile faithlessness. These ideas were not personal to Horney; Reich expressed similar thoughts. They represent the thinking and feeling of the first generation of psychoanalysts. During the Hartmann era an infantile prototype to fidelity was discovered in the term *object constancy*. That marriage can also be the fulfillment and not only the awakening of oedipal wishes was not an option considered by Horney.

In 1937, Horney published her first American book, *The Neurotic Personality of Our Time*. It was her first book as a dissenter. It became a popular book, going through thirty printings in its first decade. In 1960, when her books appeared in paperback (then a new invention), they sold over 500,000 copies [Quinn (1988), based on the publisher's information]. The sale of Horney's books showed an immense hunger for psychoanalytic information on the eve of World War II.

Horney characterized neurotics as permanently in need of being loved regardless of from where this love comes. At the same time they are incapable of loving. This discrepancy makes them dependent on the others and is responsible for feelings of inadequacy. Neurotics live in a permanent state of fear, and this fear in turn depends on a need to ward off all aggressive impulses. While this aggression must be repressed, repression cannot alone accomplish the task, and the aggression has to be projected, the projection increasing the fear. Ultimately the cause of all this fear is the insufficient warmth and love that these neurotics received from their parents. The Oedipus complex, to Horney, is not inevitable, not even in our culture; unloving parents drive the child into the Oedipus complex. The child who is not adequately responded to can respond in four ways or in combinations of them: love, submission, quest for power, or withdrawal. Instead of a capacity to love, the neurotic seeks safety based on feelings of living permanently in a world where enmity prevails. The will for power emphasized by Adler was to Horney not a basic event but a defense against fear of abandonment. Horney's book tended to play down the role of the superego and of guilt feelings. She emphasized the wish to remain a child and not to be responsible for one's own actions. The personality of our time is lonely and therefore in search of being loved even though it cannot love. Neurotics suffer more from contradictions in our culture, the quest for success against Christian morality, the conflict between freedom of the individual and deep dependency needs.

The book was reviewed by Franz Alexander (1937). He recognized the following deviations from Freud's concepts.

1. Neurotic conflicts are not repetition of infantile situations.
2. Cultural forces are more important than biological ones.
3. Although Horney's emphasis on anxiety is not new, the way she described the impact of the basic anxiety was perceived as "fruit of rich clinical experience" (p. 536).

4. "Horney's presentation of this oscillation between competitive hostility, fear, and love seeking passive subordination" (p. 538) was praised as most comprehensive.

Fenichel, in the circulating letter dated May 15, 1942 (collected and published in 1998), summarized Horney's agreement with Freud. I have abbreviated each listing:

1. Every psychic event is determined.
2. There is an unconscious.
3. Emotions are in conflict with each other.
4. Dreams are wish fulfillments.
5. The relations of patient and analyst is typical of the patient's interpersonal relationships.

Horney believed that the following issues must be changed in Freud's theory:

1. The libido theory
2. The role of the Oedipus complex
3. The concept of narcissism
4. The psychology of women
5. The theory of instincts
6. The role of infantile sexuality
7. The nature of transference
8. The theory of anxiety
9. The role of the superego
10. The significance of guilt feelings
11. The concept of masochism
12. The mode of operation of psychoanalytic therapy

What was not recognized at the time was that this was a new form of dissidence fundamentally different from that of Adler, Jung, and Rank. It was an attempt at a fundamental revision of Freud's work, and from now on this would be the fundamental form of all future dissidence. Each dissident would keep some parts of Freud and eliminate others.

Already in her European papers on female sexuality, Horney attributed more weight to culture, but the atmosphere at the New School for Social Research in New York at that time strengthened and her conviction that culture matters more than biology.

That the book appealed to my generation (I was 24 when it was published) is not surprising. More surprising is that notable figures like Franz Alexander and John Dollard also succumbed to the book's appeal. Anthropologists and sociologists were delighted that finally a psychoanalyst was emphasizing culture. The introduction of cultural factors into the psychoanalytic debate added new complications to the psychoanalytic discourse, and with it came a new potential for dissidence.

What Horney presented was a simplified version of Freud, a general description that every reader could see herself or himself mirrored in. This also accounted for the success of the book. Freud was still alive when the book came out, but the book's criticism of Freud was the first of a series of revisions that would characterize the next phase in the history of psychoanalysis. Other popular books followed, including those by Erich Fromm and Theodor Reik.

Like Ferenczi, Horney (1937) was particularly critical of Freud's later theories, the superego and the repetition compulsion. Nevertheless, she continued to appreciate Freud:

> I found that the more I took a critical stand towards a series of psychoanalytical theories, the more I realised the constructive value of Freud's fundamental findings and the more paths opened up for the understanding of psychological problems. [p. 8]

As the main reason for her dissatisfaction, Horney explained:

> My desire to make a critical re-evaluation of psychoanalytic theories had its origins in a dissatisfaction with therapeutic results. I found that almost every patient offered problems for which our accepted psychoanalytical knowledge offered no means of solution and which therefore remained unsolved. [p. 6]

Horney, like Fromm later, attempted to solve what psychoanalysis could not do by a new moral tone:

> It is so much easier for a woman to think that she is nasty to her husband because, unfortunately, she was born without a penis and envies him for having one, than to think, for instance, that she has developed an attitude of righteousness and infallibility which makes it impossible to tolerate any questioning or disagreement. It is so much

easier for a patient to think that nature has given her an unfair deal than to realize that she actually makes excessive demands on the environment and is furious whenever they are not complied with. [p. 108]

Reversing Freud's priorities, Horney stated, "It is necessary to bear in mind the possibility that the wish to be a man may be a screen for repressed ambition" (p. 109).

Naively, Horney believed that emphasizing security needs and blaming culture could bring about a significant difference in therapeutic results. The moralizing tendency that Freud worked so hard to keep out of psychoanalysis returned in Horney's work. She claimed not to wish to start a new school but to build on Freud's foundations. But how this was to be accomplished if not everyone agreed with her remained unclear. Horney understood Freud's libido theory as Wilhelm Reich did in terms of "real neurosis." The fact that a person can function well sexually and yet be neurotic she considered as proof that the libido theory is mistaken.

Together with fourteen followers, Horney resigned from the New York Institute. Susan Quinn's chapter on this split makes painful reading. According to Quinn, in Horney's last years, she was drawn to William James's "varieties of religious experiences": to Kirkegaard, "sickness unto death," to Aldous Huxley, the "perennial philosophy," and to Paul Tillich, who was then writing *The Courage to Be*. She was influenced by Zen Buddhism through Suzuki. One of Horney's devoted patients was Cornelius Crain, an American industrialist, who arranged for a triumphant visit for Horney to Japan's monasteries, where she spoke about the similarities between her method and the Japanese ways of cure.

Ten years later, under more modest circumstances, my wife and I also spent some weeks in Kyoto and Nara, getting to appreciate the beauty of the Japanese temples. We also had contacts with psychiatrists using the Zen method; however, I came to the opposite conclusion, namely that Zen masters never ask a pupil a single question about himself or his past. A vast gulf about the importance of the individual's biography separates psychoanalysis from all approaches coming from the East. Karen Horney occupies a unique position in the history of psychoanalysis. In the debate on female sexuality she won over Freud and is the first to have advocated "primary femininity."

Her later emphasis on culture led to a superficial approach to the problems psychoanalysis had to face. We are still struggling with the role of culture in determining mental illness.

WILHELM REICH (1897–1957)

By the time Wilhelm Reich graduated from medical school in 1922, he was already a member of the Vienna Psychoanalytic Society. From 1924 to 1930, Reich conducted his well-known seminar on character analysis. The seminar concentrated on stalemated analyses and analytic failures. Reich was a prolific writer who authored twenty-six books and one hundred papers. Dissatisfied with the therapeutic achievements of psychoanalysis, Reich saw character as an armor that the analyst must pierce. Analysis is not completed until genitality is free from guilt and free from attraction to incestuous objects. The character armor prevents the discharge of sexual energy. The analyst must draw the attention of the patient to artificial mannerisms in the patient's speech, such as the way he greets or parts from the analyst. The analyst should show the patient how inhibited his posture and mannerisms are. When the patient is confronted this way, he will either leave the analysis or establish a negative transference. This negative transference will last until the character armor is dissolved, and this way a stalemated analysis can be avoided.

Although Reich is best know for his emphasis on character analysis, the term did not originate with Reich, but rather with Freud in his 1916 paper, "Some Character-Types Met with in Psycho-Analytic Work":

> When a doctor carries out the psycho-analytic treatment of a neurotic, his interest is by no means directed in the first instance to the patient's character. He would much rather know what the symptoms mean, what instinctual impulses are concealed behind them and are satisfied by them, and what course was followed by the mysterious path that has led from the instinctual wishes to the symptoms. But the technique which he is obliged to follow soon compels him to direct his immediate curiosity towards other objectives. He observes that his investigation is threatened by resistances set up against him by the patient, and these resistances he may justly count as part of the latter's character. This now acquires the first claim on his interest. [p. 311]

Freud singled out three character types that are commonly encountered. The "exceptions," those wrecked by success and "criminals out of a sense of guilt," emphasize the relationship between character and fixation on one of the pregenital phases of the libido. The paragraph reflects Freud's reluctance to enter into character analysis, and the overcoming of that reluctance was an important moment in the history of psychoanalysis. With character analysis, the psychoanalyst moved a step further away from the medical model. Freud's paper was followed in the early 1920s by three papers on character written by Abraham, and other contributions followed. Reich, in turn, developed a systematic, easy-to-follow approach to character analysis, achieved by a confrontational attitude on the part of the psychoanalyst. Reich's confrontations usually created a negative feeling in the analysand, but Reich did not consider that a significant loss, since all positive feelings based on a character that has not been analyzed are hypocritical in nature. One of the merits of Reich's point of view was the curative value of negative transference if allowed full expression.

For Reich (1945), the reaching of genitality was equivalent to mental health. In his technique, Reich emphasized that there should be no interpretation of content without interpretation of character resistance. Reich became convinced that neurotic character formation underlies every symptom neurosis, so that the distinction between symptom and character lost its meaning.

In 1927 Reich published his revolutionary book *Die Funktion des Orgasmus* [the English *The Function of the Orgasm* published in 1942 is not an exact translation of the German book], in which he postulated that all neuroses were accompanied by a disturbance of genitality. Neuroses are nourished by undischarged libido. It is of great historical interest that this claim went back to Freud's 1898 work, "Sexuality in the Etiology of the Neuroses," in which he stated, "The most significant causes of every case of neurotic illness are to be found in factors arising from sexual life" (p. 263). This view was called "the Theory of the Sexual Etiology of the Neuroses." In this paper Freud differentiated between psychoneuroses, in which origins go back to traumatic events of early childhood, and "actual neuroses" (meaning present-day neuroses), which are due to lack of sexual discharge in adulthood. Reich extended the concept of actual neuroses as applying to all neuroses; therefore, the capacity to discharge libido in orgasm was the sign of health, and difficulties in achieving orgasm the cause of all adult neuroses. Orgasmic potency became the cure of neuroses. This orgasm had to be heterosexual and obtained without the help of fantasies.

While Reich spoke of genitality and the importance of sexual orgasm there was no emphasis on love, concern, and abiding relationships. The sexual drive was isolated from the other human needs; as a result the Reichian men and women remained isolated from each other in spite of both having an orgasm. In the absence of deep personal connections a shared ideology counteracted this loneliness.

Reich was at that time both a committed psychoanalyst and a committed Communist. However, as he developed his own ideas, he became alienated from both and eventually was expelled by the two movements he tried to bring together.

Combining psychoanalysis with Marxism, Reich believed that capitalism is responsible for the massive sexual inhibition in current society, and that this inhibition gives rise to mental illness. Reich's original three papers on character analysis were later transformed into his book *Character-Analysis* (1945). The original essays were published in the anthology of Robert Fliess in 1947. Among the dissidents, Reich was unique in going back to an early Freud, seeing all neuroses as actual neuroses. To Reich, undischarged libido became the cause of all mental illnesses.

Paul Robinson and colleagues (1969) aptly remarked that Reich maintained that his character analytic therapy was only the necessary prologue to traditional psychoanalytic work based on free association. However, in fact he did not get past this preliminary phase. The dissolution of the character armor became an aim in itself. As to Reich's attitude toward Freud, in *The Function of the Orgasm* (1942), Reich wrote:

> [Freud's] manner of speaking was quick, to the point and lively. The movements of his hands were natural. Everything he did and said was shot through with tints of irony. I had come there in a state of trepidation and left with a feeling of pleasure and friendliness. That was the starting point of fourteen years of intensive work in and for psychoanalysis. At the end, I experienced a bitter disappointment in Freud, a disappointment which, I am happy to say, did not lead to hatred or rejection. On the contrary, today I have a better and higher estimation of Freud's achievement than in those days when I was his worshipful disciple. I am happy to have been his pupil for such a long

time without premature criticism, and with a full devotion to his cause.
[p. 17]

After these laudatory remarks Reich admitted, "At the end I experience a bitter disappointment with Freud (p. 17)."

Among the views that Reich expressed, the belief that the death instinct is the product of the capitalistic system was particularly irritating to Freud. After leaving psychoanalysis, Reich developed what he called vegetotherapy, which included a metal (orgone) box that a person sat inside of and that Reich believed helped to accumulate life energy. He considered the orgone box to be effective also against cancer. For transporting this box across state lines, Reich was jailed for two years and died in jail. There is a moving account by Reich's son Peter on this chapter in Reich's life that leaves no doubt that paranoia gradually won the day.

Ernst Kris, in 1951, pointed out that Reich's attack on character was prestructural in that the analyst does not analyze the defense mechanisms of the ego but attacks them. The same problem will appear in Lacan's work. In the Anglo-Saxon world of ego psychology, Anna Freud, Otto Fenichel, and Heinz Hartmann won the battle against Wilhelm Reich. The historian, however, must note that Reich represented a possible extension and logical conclusion to what the early Freud stood for.

FENICHEL'S CIRCULAR LETTERS

In 1998, there appeared in German 119 circulating letters that Otto Fenichel wrote to a special group of coworkers between 1934 and 1945. Within the current context they throw new light on Wilhelm Reich's last months as a member of the International Psychoanalytic Association, but they also add significantly to our understanding of dissidence in the history of psychoanalysis. The first of these circular letters was written in March 1934 from Oslo, where Fenichel found asylum from the persecution of Jews in Nazi Germany. The letter opens with the following declaration:

We all are convinced that the future of the dialectical-materialistic psychology will grow out of Freud's psychoanalysis. . . . The harsher the realities of real experiences become, the easier it is to succumb to neurotic illnesses. . . . This can be observed even in successful analyses, and occurs even more frequently after unsuccessful analyses. Harsh reality can bring about the reactivation of old resistances and lead as it did with Rank to the forgetting of the analytic knowledge. [p. 35, my translation]

The circular letters have a conspiratorial structure. There is an inner circle of those who receive them and should destroy them after reading them; the very existence of the group should be secret. There is also a larger group of sympathizers who are not part of the conspiratorial group. Those who belong to the inner circle were Edith Jacobson, George Gero, and Wilhelm and Annie Reich. The wide range of mainly young psychoanalysts is asked to help the group to present its case in the psychoanalytic congress and the psychoanalytic periodicals. What they are fighting for are the following:

1. The right of the German Jewish refugees to belong to the International even if they resign or are expelled from the now Nazi-dominated German Psychoanalytic Society, as well as opposition to the Nazi takeover of the German Psychoanalytic Society.
2. The prevention of the expulsion of Wilhelm Reich from the International.
3. The continued battle for lay analysis so that psychoanalysis can influence sociology, anthropology, and similar humanities disciplines. Psychoanalysis has revolutionary implications for society as a whole, and should not be limited to the therapy of individuals.
4. Most significantly within the context of dissidence, an opposition to Freud's death instinct as a sign of capitulation to capitalism. The paper of Freud's that this group favored was the 1908 paper, "Civilized Sexual Morality and Modern Nervous Illness," in which Freud stressed the conflict between the sexual wishes of the child and the repressive forces of civilization. The group therefore championed the early Freud against the later Freud of the dual instinct theories (Fenichel 1935).

These Marxist psychoanalysts were convinced that psychoanalysis could thrive only when left-wing governments were established and

never where right-wing governments ruled. They believed that Freudian psychoanalysis would form the kernel of a future dialectic—materialistic psychology. They also saw a close connection between the
inevitable deterioration of life in capitalist society and the increase in
neurotic misery. They understood neurosis as a conflict between the
natural drive endowment of humans and the demands on renunciation
of instinctual gratification made by culture. Because the group's existence was kept secret, it never became a dissident group, but in a historical account it must be regarded as such a group.

The circular letters also illuminate the last phase of Reich's membership in the International. The German Society expelled Reich, and
at the Luzern congress the president, Ernest Jones, asked representatives of the other societies if any were willing to admit Reich to membership; no society volunteered. Reich was gaining adherents to his
view in the Norwegian Psychoanalytic Group, which was not yet a
member of the International; the leadership of the International therefore decided to postpone the Norwegian group's admission. Reich was
in danger of being expelled from Norway by the Norwegian govern-
ment, and Freud refused to interfere on his behalf. The danger of psychoanalysis being equated with total sexual freedom on one hand and
becoming associated with Bolshevism on the other represented a real
danger to the International. Since the expulsion from Germany was not
contested and no analytic society wanted Reich, he could not continue
to be a member. Reich was not opposed to his expulsion because he
felt that he carried the findings of the early Freud beyond what organized psychoanalysis was willing to tolerate.

No one examining the data at a distance of eighty years will side with
Ernest Jones. His behavior is reminiscent of Pontius Pilate in the New
Testament, washing his hands of the blood he spills. On one hand to claim
that no society wanted Wilhelm Reich and on the other to fail to admit
the Norwegian Society because it was too much under Reich's influence
seems hypocritical, but Reich's insistence on the unity between psychoanalysis and Communism together with the oversimplified view that
neuroses are caused by conflict between sexual needs and oppressive
culture did at that time seem to endanger the position of psychoanalysis
in the Western democratic countries. Thus a significant rift took place.

There is a statement by Fenichel in these circular letters that seems
to me particularly relevant to this symposium. He said discussions do

not have to lead to consensus as long as they illuminate the differences with greater precision.

SANDOR RADO (1890–1972)

Born in Hungary, Rado first studied law before he became interested in Freud. While still a student he became secretary of the Hungarian Psychoanalytic Society in 1913, and received his medical degree in 1915. In 1923 he left for Berlin and became secretary of the German Psychoanalytic Society. A year later Freud appointed him editor of the *Internationale Zeitschrift fur Psychoanalyze* and a few years later as manager of the second psychoanalytic publication, *Imago*. In 1931 he was invited to New York to organize the Analytic Institute there. Rado was appointed professor of psychiatry and founded the first psychoanalytic society, associated with Columbia University.

Rado thus had all the credentials to become an orthodox psychoanalyst. In his first dissenting paper, published in the *Psychoanalytic Quarterly* in 1939, he still acknowledged Freud as a pioneer but thought he had found a better way of analyzing than Freud had. By 1956 he was actively attacking Freud. Rado's point of departure was Freud's second theory of anxiety (1926); Rado wrote, "Freud astonishingly drew no conclusions for the technique of treatment" (p. 429). Rado defined neuroses as disorders of the integrative functions of the ego, and called his new technique "adaptational psychology." The normal ego has to learn to differentiate between the fear reflex and the anxiety reflex; the neurotic fails in this task, and as a result of this failure the ego dreads the resurgence of the anxiety attacks. Because of this fear the abnormal ego reacts as if a danger were threatening even when there is none. In a more advanced stage of anxiety the ego employs the "riddance principle." To get rid of the anxiety the ego now avoids all situations that could evoke this anxiety.

Had Rado consented to conduct a controlled experiment in which some anxiety-ridden patients would have been treated by the traditional psychoanalytic method and another group by his ego-building technique, new data would have become available, but instead he presented his view as a new development in psychoanalysis superior to that of Freud. By 1956 Rado regarded the whole psychoanalytic quest to establish a connection between the present neuroses and the childhood neuroses as unproductive.

Within the context of this presentation Rado's dissidence is interesting because unlike Horney he did not start by questioning some clinical facts like feminine sexual development; he carried ego psychology a step further than Freud had, deciding to eliminate first the id and then the significance of infantile sexuality and transference in favor of a technique built only on teaching the ego to behave rationally.

MELANIE KLEIN (1882–1960) AND ANNA FREUD (1895–1982): THEIR CONTROVERSIAL DISCUSSIONS

The controversy between Melanie Klein and Anna Freud began during Sigmund Freud's life. On May 16, 1927, the controversy entered into the correspondence between Ernest Jones and Sigmund Freud. In his letter to Freud, Jones expressed his satisfaction in the analytic work done by Melanie Klein with his children:

> Though we had brought them up as wisely as we knew how, neither child escaped a neurosis, which analysis showed, as usual, to be much more serious than appeared. The symptoms of moodiness, difficulties with food, fears, outbursts, and extensive inhibitions seemed to make it worthwhile, and now I am extremely glad. [Paskauskas 1993, p. 617]

Jones went on to say:

> It is a pain to me that I cannot agree with some of the tendencies in Anna's book, and I cannot help thinking that they must be due to some imperfectly balanced resistances. [p. 617]

In his reply on May 31, 1927, Freud expressed his happiness about the success of the analysis of Jones's children. He also felt that the differences between the two should not be overemphasized and asserted his own neutrality, but then added what to me seems a new attitude toward dissidents.

> I will make only one comment on the polemical part of your letter. When two analysts have differing opinions on some point, one may be fully justified, in ever so many cases, in assuming that the mistaken

view of one of them stems from his having been insufficiently analyzed, and he therefore allows himself to be influenced by his com-
plexes to the detriment of science. But in practical polemics such an
argument is not permissible, for it is at the disposal of each party, and
does not reveal on whose side the error lies. We are generally agreed
to renounce arguments of this sort and, in the case of differences of
opinion, to leave resolutions to advancements in empirical knowledge.
[p. 619]

Freud's reply to Jones is of interest because it states clearly Freud's
belief that the insufficiently analyzed analyst is influenced by his com-
plexes, while the fully analyzed follows the dictates of science. It is also
of interest because now, contrary to what he claimed earlier, Freud is
ready to abandon the argument as to who is resisting.

While World War II continued to rage, the controversial discussions between Anna Freud and her followers and Melanie Klein and
her disciples took place between 1941 and 1945. Now that these controversial discussions have been published (King and Steiner 1991), we
have the opportunity to follow the wealth of ideas that both groups
presented and see the clash as contributing to our deeper understanding of the nature of psychoanalysis. When these discussions took place,
Melanie Klein had been a prominent child analyst in England and her
book, *The Psychoanalysis of Children*, had already been published. She
enjoyed the prestige of having analyzed Ernest Jones's children and
the children of other prominent analysts. Anna Freud had in addition
to Freud's name already published *The Ego and the Mechanisms of Defence*. Her next important book *Psychology of Childhood* was to appear
in 1965.

The controversial discussions present an important example of
dissidence averted, because the British Psychoanalytic Society refused
to give Anna Freud the privileges her father had. That Melanie Klein
did not become a dissident represents her political victory over Anna
Freud. Thus a new chapter in the history of dissidence opened with
Klein.

Klein was the heir to Freud's dual instinct theory, and she carried
concerns with the aggressive drive further than Freud did. Klein's famous exclamation, "I am a Freudian but not an Anna Freudian," suggested a possible split between the father and his loyal daughter; I
showed elsewhere (Bergmann 2000) that in spite of her proverbial loy-

alty to her father, at times Anna could not help but represent the views of her generation, at variance with those of her father.

In her analysis of children, Klein, by contrast to Anna Freud, developed a technique of child analysis free from educational endeavors. She let a child play and interpreted the symbolic meaning behind that play directly, with little regard to timing. Klein believed that transference is at its height at the very beginning of analysis. It is when the child enters analysis that his fantasy about the analyst is at its very height. Klein stressed introjection and projection rather than identification in the emergence of the superego, and thus dated the superego much earlier than Freud did. Klein also believed that paranoid and depressive anxieties are far more common in early infancy than Freud had assumed. Later in her life, Klein laid more stress on envy and particularly on the envy of the maternal breast. The infant projects on the breast wishes to hoard the milk and to withhold the good milk from being given to the infant. The withholding bad breast feeling of the infant is at the core of the paranoid position. Introjection of the mother takes place first as a part object, the breast, and only later becomes amalgamated into a complete image of the mother. Processes of projection and introjection are the source from which unconscious fantasies emerge. By contrast Anna Freud stressed that the child's dependence on the parents limits the child's capacity to form transference. For her, the child analyst was also an educator. The interpretations she offered were carefully worded depending on the ego and on the child's capacity to absorb them.

The controversial discussion began with the question of whether one can speak of fantasy already in the first year of life. In Klein's view, the battle between the libido and the death drive goes back to early infancy, oral sucking being the expression of libido and oral sadism being the expression of the destructive drive. If destructive impulses predominate, a bad mother is introjected by the infant, which then the child will attempt to balance by introjecting the good penis of the father. The homosexual is forever looking for this "good penis" to counteract the introjected bad breast and the bad paternal penis. While Freud stressed identifications and repressions, Melanie Klein emphasized introjection and projection when the original objects cathected with aggression turned into bad objects after they were introjected and now have to be gotten rid of by being projected back into the outside world.

These defense mechanisms in turn create an earlier superego than Freud had anticipated. They create the schizoid and paranoid positions. Only under favorable conditions brought out by maternal love can the infant reach the depressive position. When the depressive position is reached, the infant develops a need for "reparation" to undo the earlier fantasies of destruction. Reparation wishes lead to ethical behavior and to the wish to create works of art and to fight for social causes. In the depressive position, the split between good and bad objects can be overcome. Developmental questions were under dispute but even more important was the question of which camp represent Freud's own thinking faithfully.

Only five years elapsed between the Marienbad symposium and the London controversial discussion, and yet the number of topics upon which psychoanalysts disagreed had increased to an amazing extent. The issues psychoanalysts disagreed on were the following:

- Can children be analyzed by interpreting the symbolic meaning of child's play?
- Is fantasy present in the infant in the first year of life?
- Is transference at its height at the onset of analysis, or does it grow as the analysis deepens?
- What is the relative importance of introjection and projection as opposed to repression?
- Is aggression at its height during infancy, and must the infant go through the paranoid position and then the depressive position?
- When is the superego established?
- How early does the oedipal phase take place?
- Is the need for reparation of earlier aggression the background for creativity?

Behind this controversy looms another question: Did psychoanalysts wait for Freud to die to let all these controversial issues come into the open?

It was during these controversial discussions that Anna Freud expressed the point of view I had cited at the beginning of this chapter. For Anna Freud, the two main foundation stones of psychoanalytic technique after Breuer's period were the substitution of free association for hypnosis and the reduction to a minimum of the real relationship between analyst and patient. In Anna Freud's view, controversies took place because different analysts emphasize different pathogenic factors as causing the neurosis. Thus, the concept of the dammed-up libido was responsible for the active therapy by Ferenczi and Rank. While Rank's birth trauma aimed at a planned termination of the analysis, Ferenczi's emphasis on the indulgent attitude of the analyst was designed to reproduce the mother–child relationship between analyst and patient. Reich, who attributed neurosis to the failure in the reaching of the genital position to an earlier repression of the aggressive drive, evolved a technique designed to reproduce the aggressive scenes between analyst and patient. Anna Freud felt that Melanie Klein had not as yet developed her own variation on technique, but such a development she felt was bound to take place. Anna Freud's prediction came true and Kleinian psychoanalysts often give massive interpretations early in the analysis with a greater emphasis on the transference.

The role that Anna Freud played subsequently in the history of psychoanalysis continued to be conservative. In a 1954 debate on the widening scope of psychoanalysis, Anna Freud expressed her regrets that so much energy was withdrawn from the classical neurosis, which could have been more profitably spent on intensifying and improving our techniques in the original field of neurosis. Psychoanalysts, she said, should confine their efforts to neurotic patients with sufficiently healthy egos to profit from psychoanalysis. She singled out children who lost contact with their mother before object constancy was reached; these children remained superficial in all their object relationships, including to the therapist. Such children demand a radical deviation from classical technique, which in her opinion can never be converted into a psychoanalysis. The same ideas were expressed in her 1976 paper presented at the London Congress in opposition to André Green (1975a, see also Bergmann 1999). Anna Freud contrasted the foreboding picture that Green presented about the crisis within psychoanalysis with the optimism and excitement the psychoanalytic pioneers experienced about the idea that they were the first human beings privileged to witness and understand the significance of instinctual forces emanating from the unconscious. Thus the question of who can profit from psychoanalysis moved to the center of the controversy.

That the method of inquiry is identical with the method of therapy was one of the main assumptions of classical psychoanalysis. Strictly speaking it was not an empirical discovery but an article of faith that Freud inherited from the Enlightenment. In the London debate of 1976 Anna Freud restricted this connection to the neuroses. It is only within the neurotic realm that inquiry is identical with the method of cure. Only neurotics can be cured by knowing their unconscious.

Melanie Klein not only worked with more disturbed patients, but she also believed that many, if not all, neurotics have a psychotic kernel that usually escapes the attention of the psychoanalyst.

In the Klein–Freud controversy the role of Edward Glover is of particular interest (Baudry 1998). Glover changed sides from being Klein's ardent supporter to being a bitter opponent. What makes Glover's role so significant is not only his prominence as a psychoanalytic writer, but also that at the time he was analyzing Melitta Schmideberg, Klein's daughter. The two formed an alliance against the mother, a kind of mutual acting out of the oedipal drama. Glover's animosity toward Klein crossed the Atlantic, and this in turn contributed to the hardening of the anti-Kleinian position in American psychoanalysis (Glover 1945).

CLASSICAL AND POSTCLASSICAL PSYCHOANALYSIS

The death of Freud in September 1939, the defeat of Hitler, and the migration of psychoanalysts from the continent of Europe to England and the United States all contributed to the end of the period that I call classical psychoanalysis. One can say that the era ended gloriously in the publication of Fenichel's classic in 1945. In Bergmann (2000) I explained at some length why I consider the Hartmann era to be a new era in the history of psychoanalysis and not just a continuation of classical psychoanalysis. Here I will only enumerate what in my opinion are the most important differences between classical and post–World War II psychoanalysis:

1. The sea change brought about by object relations theory, transforming a one-person psychology with the neutral observer assisting the analysand to know herself or himself into a two-

person psychology based on interaction between analysand and analyst.

2. The abandoning of Freud's idea that the child is born narcissistic and transforms narcissistic libido into object libido, into a paradigm that object libido is there from the beginning and only disappointment in the caregiver brings about narcissistic withdrawal.

3. The significance of Winnicott's "holding environment" as a major contributor to the transformation psychoanalysis, which can bring about, as an equal partner, the achievement brought about by the work of interpretation. Not every patient is capable of using the standard analytic situation as a port of safety from which to launch the journey into the unconscious. Many patients require a long period of preparation before the analysis proper can begin.

4. A systematic effort to widen the scope of analysis by extending it beyond the confines of neurosis (Green 1975a, Stone 1954).

5. The recognition that these less privileged diagnostic categories may not have the Oedipus complex as their kernel and that castration anxiety is their main anxiety, but suffer from two contradicting anxieties: the anxiety of abandonment and the anxiety of annihilation by intrusion.

6. The classical psychoanalysis emphasis on the diagnostic differentiation between analyzable and nonanalyzable. André Green introduced the concept of listening and trying to understand the patient without any reference to intrapsychic change. This listening of itself has an ameliorative if not curative impact. Most of these patients never had anyone trying to listen and understand them.

DISSENTION AFTER FREUD'S DEATH

We have seen how Karen Horney disagreed with Freud's ideas on feminine sexuality, but she became a dissenter only after Freud's death. We also noted that the Anna Freud–Melanie Klein controversy began during Freud's lifetime but reached its culmination point after his death.

The dissenters after Freud's death that will be discussed in this section are Fromm, Lacan, Kohut, and Fairbairn.

ERICH FROMM (1900–1980)

Erich Fromm grew up in an Orthodox Jewish home and until the age of 27 planned to become a Talmudic scholar. At 26 he married Frieda Reichmann, a psychiatrist, and his interest turned to psychoanalysis. Fromm was analyzed by Wilhelm Wittenberg, and Karl Landauer (one of the few psychoanalysts to perish in the Holocaust), and between 1928 and 1930 he was in analysis with Hans Sachs in Berlin. The analysis with Sachs apparently ended with strong negative feelings, which may account, at least in part, for the critical attitude Fromm adopted toward psychoanalysis.

Like Karen Horney, Fromm is classified as an interpersonal psychoanalyst. There is a close affinity in their views, and according to Quinn, Horney's biographer, the two were also lovers for some time. This love was Horney's happiest relationship with a man.

Unlike the previous dissidents, Fromm had no personal connections to Freud. His dissidence is based on purely ideological and political grounds. Fromm came from the Institute of Social Research in Frankfurt, the home of the Frankfurt School, a group of thinkers who tried to use psychoanalysis to understand, and influence, the social and political turmoil in Germany after World War I. In 1930, Fromm's book on the dogma of Christ appeared. It was an attempt to understand the rise of Christianity from a Marxist point of view. I had occasion to deal with that book at some length in my book, *In the Shadow of Moloch* (Bergmann 1992), but it is of no interest in the present context. In Europe, Fromm wrote only two articles in *Imago*, the journal dedicated to applied psychoanalysis. In 1936 Fromm published in France a German book under the title *Authority and Family*. It was a pioneering work dealing with the psychology of authority. It dealt with the interaction between the psychic structure, which is the domain of psychoanalysis, and the social background that fosters the formation of the authoritarian character. This interaction is accomplished through the formation of the superego, which in turn enforces repression. This left Fromm to assert that the Oedipus complex itself could arise only under certain

cultural conditions. In every authoritarian society dependency is established upon those who are above in the social hierarchy and sadism
toward those below, including women, children, animals, slaves, war
captives, and minorities. The authoritarian society in turn creates the
masochistic personality. The authoritarian character may be heterosexual, but the structure of submission has a homosexual quality. The
authoritarian character is incapable of loving. In the United States
Fromm together with Karen Horney, Harry Stack Sullivan, and Clara
Thompson formed what was known as the neo-Freudian group.

In 1941, Fromm's famous book *Escape from Freedom* appeared. The
book today may seem as if it were written by an intellectual of little
originality, but that was not the way my generation felt when this book
came out. It appeared to us then as a major contribution to our understanding of society. The very idea that freedom can be hated seemed
astonishing. World War II was raging and victory still far away. The
book was also an astounding commercial success. In the foreword to
that book, Fromm stated:

> It is the thesis of this book that modern man, freed from the bonds of
> pre-individualistic society, which simultaneously gave him security
> and limited him, has not gained freedom in the positive sense of the
> realization of his individual self; that is, the expression of his intel-
> lectual, emotional and sensuous potentialities. Freedom, though it has
> brought him independence and rationality, has made him isolated and,
> thereby, anxious and powerless. . . . The understanding of the rea-
> sons for the totalitarian flight from freedom is a premise for any ac-
> tion which aims at the victory over the totalitarian forces. [p. viii]

The book's first and last chapters deal with Freud. Since Fromm deals
with the problem of human freedom, why an attack on Freud? Freud was
not one of the enemies of freedom. In the first chapter, Fromm singled
out for criticism Freud's belief that man is antisocial and that society must
domesticate him and check man's basic instincts, and only after this repression has been successful "something miraculous happens" (p. 10).
The repressed drives become socially valuable through sublimation. In
the last chapter, Fromm delineated his differences from Freud. The pessimistic appraisal of human nature made Freud in Fromm's view an en-
emy of freedom. In my view this is a grave logical flaw, as if realizing
difficulties in the path of freedom is the same as opposing freedom.

We believe that man is *primarily* a social being, and not, as Freud assumes, primarily self-sufficient and only secondarily in need of others in order to satisfy his instinctual needs. . . . The problem of what happens to man's instinctual desires has to be understood as one part of the total problem of his relationship toward the world and not as *the* problem of human personality. Therefore, in our approach, the needs and desires that center about the individual's relations to others, such as love, hatred, tenderness, symbiosis, are the fundamental psychological phenomena, while with Freud they are only secondary results from frustrations or satisfactions of instinctive needs. [p. 290]

Freud's psychology is a psychology of want. . . . Freud saw in sex only the element of physiological compulsion and in sexual satisfaction the relief from painful tension. The sexual drive as a phenomenon of abundance, and sexual pleasure as spontaneous joy—the essence of which is not negative relief from tension—had no place in his psychology. [p. 295]

It seems as if Fromm learned from Freud only that there is an id and that society's function is to repress the id, which then miraculously reemerges in sublimation. The existence of intrapsychic conflict and the concepts of ego and superego seem to have passed Fromm by. This truncated image of Freud was then attacked by him. Fromm read into Freud ideas of Nietzsche and Jung and to some extent those of Wilhelm Reich. Fromm's *Escape from Freedom* was reviewed by Saul in the *Psychoanalytic Quarterly* in 1942. The review was respectful of Fromm but deplored the fact that Freud was set up as a straw man to be knocked down.

In 1951, Fromm published *The Forgotten Language*. He advocated the teaching of dream language in college, so that students will be capable of interpreting their own dreams. One shudders at the thought of a young borderline student not in psychoanalytic treatment being taught to interpret her or his own dreams. This is how Fromm described dreams:

Dreams express any kind of mental activity and are expressive of our irrational strivings as well as of our reason and mortality, that they express both the worst and the best in ourselves. . . . What is important is to understand the texture of the dream in which past and present, character and realistic event, are woven together into a design which tells us a great deal about the motivation of the dreamer, the dangers he must be aware of, and the aims he must set himself in his effort to achieve happiness. [n.p.]

To Fromm, as to the ancient interpreters of dreams, the dream offers wise counsel. This idea has appeal to all who find unacceptable Freud's idea that in dreams the repressed returns in a disguised and acceptable form. Like Rank, Fromm saw birth as "the expulsion" from the maternal paradise. Object relations were to him an attempt to regain this lost connection to the maternal paradise. It is of interest that the same idea will appear also in Lacan. If separateness is faced and acknowledged, new relationships can develop. If separateness is denied, the illusory connection to the maternal body will continue. Human passions are based not on Freud's drives but on the need to overcome loneliness. The denial of the basic loneliness leads to strategies of self-protection and therefore to neurosis and the search for magical saviors in the realm of politics.

In 1956 Fromm published *The Art of Loving*, a book that was widely read. In it Fromm differentiated between mother's love, which is unconditional, all-enveloping, and all-protecting, and father's love, which makes demands and establishes discipline. These ideas of Fromm resemble Lacan who speaks of the "law of the father." But Lacan's observations are more comprehensive. Fromm's idea of maternal love is an idealized love. Any clinician who ever analyzed a mother's hatred for her daughter, or a mother's disappointment when her son marries, will have difficulty in sharing Fromm's idealization of maternal love.

In 1959 Fromm published *Sigmund Freud's Mission: An Analysis of His Personality and Influence*, in which Freud is described as an oral receptive person with passive dependence on his mother. Freud is further accused of an ambition to conquer the world and create a church of his own with priests and laity. Psychoanalysis became to Fromm a surrogate religion for the urban middle and upper classes. Until now, only Freud's ideas were under attack; in this book Fromm used psychoanalytic ideas to attack Freud's character. The book was reviewed by Waelder in 1963, who described Fromm as an evangelist, a harsh but apt description.

In 1973 Fromm published *The Anatomy of Human Destructiveness*, in which he came close to Freud's dual instinct theory. He differentiated between defensive or benign aggression in the service of survival of the individual and the species, and malignant aggression, unique to man, whose only purpose is the satisfaction of the aggressive drive itself.

In 1996, a group of Fromm's coworkers and students published a tribute to his memory (Cortina and Maccoby 1996). It is a moving but also a sad book. There is something noble about a group of students getting together fifteen years after an author's death to rescue his memory from oblivion. Nevertheless, ambivalences can be read between the lines. The contributors would probably say that this ambivalence reflects Fromm's democratic ideas. The authors are aware of an inner conflict in Fromm and describe it as a conflict between his analytic voice and his prophetic voice. Marianne Eckardt (Karen Horney's daughter) rightly, in my opinion, points out that for the neo-Freudians, neurosis became a moral problem. Neurosis interferes with man's naturally given striving for self-realization. Neuroses become an inimical force to be eradicated. We thus come to an unexpected conclusion. The humanist attitude toward psychoanalysis with its emphasis on morality is in the service of the superego, which in turn is likely to interfere with the capacity of the psychoanalyst to listen to the inner conflicts of his patients with a reasonable degree of neutrality. According to Eckardt, Fromm listed six theories in psychoanalysis that are in need of revision: the theory of drives, the theory of the unconscious, the theory of society, the theory of sexuality, the theory of the human body, and the theory of psychoanalytic therapy—a broad order. The dissidents who were also social reformers were all attracted to the Breuer–Freud emphasis on trauma, and downplayed Freud's ideas on intrapsychic conflict.

JACQUES LACAN (1901–1981)

There are special subjective and objective difficulties in discussing Lacan as a dissident. With many of the dissidents previously discussed— Wilhelm Reich, Karen Horney, and Erich Fromm—I had personal contact. With Jungians I became familiar in the Eranos meeting in Switzerland. Personal friends such as the anthropologist Paul Radin and Gershom Scholem were in contact with Jung. Lacan appeared on my professional horizon much later, when contact was established with

French psychoanalysts André Green, Janine Chasseguet-Smirgel, and Joyce McDougall. None of them were Lacanians, but Lacan's influence on them was palpable, above all in their opposition to Hartmann's ego psychology, my own home ground. That Lacan's thought and language are difficult to grasp is well known even to those who can read him in the original. I had to learn about him in translation. I found Benvenuto and Kennedy (1986), Etchegoyen (1991), and Sass (2001) helpful.

Lacan's language is rich in connotation, but frequently more or less deliberately vague. His language, while irritating to many Anglo-Saxon readers, is much admired among European intellectuals, particularly those raised on existential literature. I cite one example:

> The symptom is here the signifier of a signified repressed from the consciousness of the subject. A symbol written in the sand of the flesh and on the veil of Maia, it participates in language by the semantic ambiguity that I have already emphasized in its constitution. [Lacan 1966a, p. 380]

Anyone who read Schopenhauer will rejoice to rediscover "the veil of Maia," but strictly speaking in sober language, the paragraph has little meaning.

With Lacan psychoanalysis came close to the cult of personality that was so characteristic of the twentieth century. All dissidents were charismatic because the capacity to surround oneself with admiring students is a sine qua non for a successful dissident. But with Lacan it reached proportions of legend. All we need is to imagine a waiting room full of patients, each waiting for hours for his or her turn for a session that would at times last only a few minutes. Or we can imagine Lacan's seminar filled to overflowing so that one had to come an hour early to find a seat (Clement 1983).

Like Melanie Klein, Lacan saw himself as a Freudian and like her he went beyond Freud. There are ample reasons to doubt Lacan's sincerity in his claim to go back to Freud but even if he were sincere, could he have gone back to Freud? Roads lead in many directions but never back. Italian Renaissance never went back to Athens, although Athens influenced it a great deal. Freud was the child of nineteenth century science. Brücke's oaths that only chemical and physiological forces are operating in biology was part of Freud's faith. Lacan was the child of the twentieth century. Heidegger, Husserl, Lévi-Strauss, Saussure's linguistics, and surrealism were influences in his life. Freud was an emancipated Jew at home in German culture; Lacan was Catholic and French. The two would have had great difficulty in understanding each other.

Before France was overrun by the Nazis, Lacan was in psychoanalysis with Rudolph Loewenstein. When Loewenstein had to flee France, Lacan's analysis remained incomplete. There is a belief that this interruption was traumatic for Lacan, and that Lacan's animosity toward Hartmann's ego psychology has its roots in his interrupted analysis by Loewenstein, who was prominent in psychoanalytic ego psychology. At the time when in the United States Margaret Mahler was developing her ideas about the separation–individuation phases, Lacan went back to Freud's 1920 "Fort Da" play. But in his reading of that famous scene, Lacan made the father responsible for the dissolution of the tie between mother and infant. Where Mahler saw gradual development within a slowly developing ego eventually resulting in separation–individuation, Lacan postulated the traumatic interruption of the mother–infant relationship brought about by the "law of the father." There is a continuity between Rank's trauma of birth and Lacan's separation by the father of the mother–child union, which ushers in both the reality principle and the Oedipus complex.

Lacan was the first important dissident to appear on the analytic stage after Freud's death and after World War II. In the 1950s and 1960s, he was one of the best-known European analysts and the major counterweight to the Heinz Hartmann and Anna Freud school of ego psychology. Lacan denounced Hartmann because the latter gave the psychoanalyst the right to differentiate between reality and fantasy and between transference neurosis and working alliance. That Lacan belonged to a new generation of psychoanalysts becomes evident when we note other influences besides Freud on his concepts and formulations. While a traditional psychoanalyst sees transference as a prominent example of the repetition compulsion, where the past reappears in the relationship between analyst and analysand, to Lacan it is an original relationship in which both analyst and analysand participate.

Lacan's doctoral thesis, *Paranoid Psychosis and Its Relations to Personality*, appeared in 1932, and Lacan became a member of the Paris Psychoanalytic Society in 1934. At the first international congress after World War II (1949) he spoke about the mirror stage, which is generally considered his first original contribution to psychoanalysis. The idea of studying the infant's relationship to his mirror image came from the gestalt psychologist Köhler (1925), who studied the responses of chimpanzees to their mirror image. Lacan found that the infant becomes aware of his mirror image at about 6 months and falls in love with that image. Lacan, however, was not what in the United States is called an infant observer. The mirror stage became to him a way of formulating theoretical concepts. The ego emerges from the mirror stage as an imaginary relationship. The result is *méconnaissance*, the refusal to accept the truth. To Lacan, the ego plays mainly a negative role. Lacan opposed the efforts to make psychoanalysis part of natural science and situated it within language. The realm of psychoanalysis is not reality but psychic reality, that is, what is true for the subject. We can understand Lacan better if we keep in mind that his doctoral thesis was based on an attempt to understand the psychic reality of a paranoid woman who stabbed an unknown actress, while living in a delusional world. To understand Lacan, it might be useful to imagine that Freud came upon the Schreber case before the *Studies on Hysteria* and *The Interpretation of Dreams*.

Lacan's dissidence illustrates that the cultural atmosphere in which one grows up has a greater effect on psychoanalytic thinking than we would like to imagine. By its very nature psychoanalysis is influenced by nonpsychoanalytic thinkers.

Lacan introduced a new reading of Freud's famous Dora case. Reversing the customary order, he postulated that Dora's transference began as a result of Freud's countertransference. Freud felt excluded by Dora and could not accept the homosexual tie between Dora and Frau K. Desire was first evoked in Freud by his feeling excluded from their relationship. According to Lacan, Freud could not accept that Dora, fixated on Frau K., could not love Herr K. Identifying himself with Herr K., Freud attempted to persuade Dora that she was in love with Herr K. Thus, in Lacan's order, transference followed countertransference. In Lacan's view, Freud should have confronted Dora with her homosexual feelings; had he done so, he would have resolved Dora's neurosis. This was indeed a radically new reading of Dora's case. In Lacan's view, the relationship between Frau K. and Dora took place in the mirror stage. She wished to be her mother's penis and displaced this feeling on Frau K. Freud should have imposed "the law of the father" and separated Dora from Frau K. Only if she had accepted the law of the father would she have developed from the imaginary stage to the symbolic stage. Lacan criticized Breuer's relationship to Anna O. (Bertha Pappenheim) along similar lines. There, too, he believed that Breuer's countertransference sexualized their relationship. He sees Anna O.'s pseudocyesis as Breuer's desire. It was he who wished to impregnate her.

Lacan saw the unconscious as structured like a language and therefore borrowed some basic terms from linguistics. He introduced into psychoanalysis the concept of signifier and signified, which he took from Ferdinand Saussure and Roman Jakobson. From Heidegger, Lacan took the difference between *Gerede* (empty speech/*parole vide*) and *Rede* (speech that is alive/*parole pleine*). The subject begins analysis by talking about himself without talking to the analyst or by talking to the analyst without talking about himself. When he can talk to the analyst about himself, the analysis in Lacan's view will be finished. One can also trace the influence of Hegel, Schopenhauer, and Nietzsche in Lacan's work.

Lacan connected his own views that the unconscious is written like a language to Chapter VI in *The Interpretation of Dreams*, in which Freud described the dream content as a pictographic script, a picture puzzle structured like a rebus. Lacan was aiming to bring Freud closer to Lévi-Strauss (1949, 1951). For Lévi-Strauss the unconscious consists of an aggregate of structural laws by which the individual's experiences are transformed into a living myth. The social sciences should not emulate the natural sciences because of the distorting effect of the observer. Structural linguistics offers a better scientific model for the social sciences. Lacan differentiated between language, ("*le langage*") and speech ("*la parole*"). Language is a system of signs, social and arbitrary in nature, existing only within the confines of a language. To Saussure, the signs are composed of a relationship between signifier and signified. At this point Lacan introduced an original idea of his own. When the patient free-associates, he goes from one signifier to another—without reaching the signified. When the signified is reached, the process of free association comes to an end. Lacan also differentiated between condensation, which he saw as a form of substitution and therefore like a metaphor, and displacement, which works by contiguity and combination and therefore like metonomy.

In 1953, Lacan was president of the Paris Psychoanalytic Society when he was expelled from the International. The expulsion had little to do with the theorizing I have so far discussed, but was caused by a radical change that he introduced into psychoanalytic technique. As Lacan constructed the psychoanalytic hour, the analysand first speaks only to himself. It is the analyst who facilitates the discourse between them. There is the "other" (with a small "o") to whom the analysand consciously is addressing his speech, but unconsciously he is addressing the "Other" (with a capital "O") behind whom looms the father. Speech moves constantly on both conscious and unconscious levels. In conscious speech, unconscious messages are communicated as the analyst deciphers the message while at the same time communicating directly with the unconscious of the patient. The relationship between analyst and analysand is forever in danger of becoming empty speech. To retain its vitality, Lacan advised that the analyst interrupt the hour whenever he felt that deadness has taken place. As a practical measure, Lacan's hours at times lasted only a few minutes. It was this innovation in technique that was unacceptable to the International. Only because Lacan gave up the analytic hour as a basic instrument did he officially become a dissenter. If Lacan had not changed the length of the hour, he would have ranked with Hartmann and Klein as a modifier but not as a dissenter (Bergmann 1993).

The Rome discourse of 1953 was Lacan's declaration of war on American ego psychology. The man who started by studying a classical paranoid patient now saw Freud as betrayed by his own disciples, and at times even the later Freud as betraying the earlier one. This seems to be a characteristic of many dissenters; they do not say that Freud changed his mind but that he betrayed the cause. The vocabulary of betrayal indicates that dissent has something irrational about it and so often comes close to paranoia. Freud is not only disagreed with, he is accused. As Lacan understood, psychoanalytic history was not a matter of development or change in which one can agree or disagree but a matter of conspiracy. Lacan sees himself as opening windows to throw daylight on Freud's idea.

It was in the Rome discourse that the differentiation between the symbolic, the imaginary, and the real was formulated, which is one of the best known of Lacan's contributions. The imaginary emerges early in the life of the infant, during the "mirror" stage between 6 and 18 months, when the infant discovers his image in the mirror, a discovery that will in due time lead to self-reflection. The mirror stage is dyadic in nature. Sibling rivalry may take place already in the mirror stage, when the wish to be near the mother and loved by her encounters rivalry. The mirror stage initiates a split between unconscious discourse and conscious discourse. It is the realm of the imaginary that the desire for completion and the desire to obtain or become the phallus are played out. By contrast to the imaginary, the symbolic represents the structure of the unconscious, where the "law of the father" reigns supreme. It is in this realm that castration anxiety and the oedipal taboo become established. It is in the symbolic realm that the impossibility of becoming mother's phallus is eventually accepted by the infant. Freud's reality principle is included in the symbolic. The work of analysis consists of transforming the imaginary into the symbolic. It is through the symbolic use of language that the unconscious reveals itself to us. The third category comprises the "real." Contrary to what one would expect the word *real* to mean, the "real" is what is left over, what cannot be symbolized. It is the realm of psychosis. The real is close to what is sometimes referred to as "concretization of the metaphor," in the famous example cited by Searls, where a psychotic patient is told, "You cannot have your cake and eat it too," and answers, "I have stopped eating cake long ago." In the realm of the real, things and words are no longer separated from each other. In the realm of the real, *jouissance* reigns. The *jouissance* of the other means being for the other an object of enjoyment, which includes the masochistic desire to be the object of abuse. *Jouissance* is not identical with being the object of desire because to Lacan desire always means the lack of something. For *jouissance* nothing needs to be lacking. By *jouissance*, Lacan means a sense of total enjoyment linked to illusory attainment, a pleasure brought about by the erasure of all differences, the kind of pleasure perverts and drug addicts attempt to reach. *Jouissance* includes the pleasure of orgasm but it is also pleasure in the realm of excess. It is the essence that gives life its highest value and is often associated with death. Wagner's *Tristan and Isolde* is the opera of *jouissance*, but deaths in other operas also embody it. Lacan's tripart division is competitive with Freud's own tripart division into ego, id, and superego, but it deals with a realm unknown to classical psychoanalysis.

From Hegel, Lacan took the centrality of desire. According to Hegel's (1807) phenomenology of the mind, man is basically self-conscious when for the first time he says "I." At that point, he has a desire distinct from the object. The "I" receives its positive contents from the negated object desire. "I exist because I am different from my mother." The desire is directed toward another self-conscious object. Eventually we learn to desire not only another body but the other's desire. When that happens, the wish to be loved becomes paramount. The phallus for Lacan represents to the child the signifier of mother's desire.

Lacan differentiated between wish and desire. A wish can at times become fulfilled, at least temporarily, but desire remains forever ungratified. To cite an example, the anorexic adolescent girl refuses to eat, first because she was overfed. But then her very refusal of the mother's wish becomes her desire. She must diminish the mother's desire for her, so that she can come to feel her own desire. Desire depends on the "other" for its existence. Narcissism is a desire to be desired by the other. If desire were ever gratified, it would lead to the undoing of father's law and the separation from the other. This is humanity's tragic state—desire must forever seek the object, but the aim can never be reached. It is this search that constitutes the essence of desire, and its lack of fulfillment creates individuality.

Lacan differentiated between *jouissance* and *plaisir*. The latter deals with wishes and pleasure. *Jouissance* is what Tristan and Isolde are looking for after they drink the love potion and cannot find this side of the grave. *Jouissance* knows no fear of death since only the ego knows and feels death. In his 1959 paper, Lacan used the concept of *jouissance* to see Hamlet in a new way. According to Lacan, Hamlet has lost his way to desire and therefore lives according to the time of the others. His whole behavior becomes understandable if we see him as a man without *jouissance*. The phallus is to Lacan much more than a part object. It is what the mother lacks and desires, and the child, be it male or female, cannot give her. It is the missing half that Aristophanes in Plato's symposium speaks of. For Lacan, however, it was Bernini's statue of Santa Teresa in Rome that embodied *jouissance*. To ordinary tourists, she embodies a woman in a state of orgasm.

In the Rome discourse Lacan, like Freud, grappled with feminine psychology and feminine sexuality. To Lacan sex exists outside of language. Sexual relationships involve an unspeakable enjoyment; the signifier "love" is the substitute for what cannot be verbally communicated.

The analytic patient prefers loving the analyst to understanding himself or herself. The psychoanalyst's aim is to bring this "love" into the symbolic realm; when a woman enters the symbolic realm she enters it not whole, but lacking the phallus. Lacan, therefore, at this point makes no concessions to feminist movements. By contrast to women, man is identified with the phallus at the expense of sexual enjoyment. I had some difficulty in following Lacan at this point until I recalled a patient telling me that when he was an adolescent, a girl pointed to his penis and asked, "What do you have there?" He recalls answering, "It is mine." In my own vocabulary I designated the patient as having reached the phallic but not yet the genital phase. It seems to me that Lacan in his own way is speaking about this phase.

The sexual experience of the woman cannot be put into words and cannot be integrated into language. It seems to me that Lacan here shares Freud's sense of mystery before the feminine. Femininity can for Lacan be defined only negatively. The woman often feels a double castration, not having the phallus and not having her own sexuality. To be decent, she had to keep her genitalia hidden so as not to disturb man's ignorance about her sexuality. Instead she shows him the beauty of her whole body that veils her genitalia. Unlike Freud, Lacan doesn't assign all these theories to infantile sexuality, which is overcome during the genital phase. So far as I could determine, Lacan's psychology stops short of the genital phase.

What Lacan did understand, and what he had an excellent ear for, was the many contradictions that had emerged within psychoanalytic work. He recognizes the contradictions within the psychoanalyst between listener and interlocutor. Meaning does emerge in the analytic situation, but it is not logical secondary process meaning; it is a meaning that merges through ambiguities after massive denial and when intentions are ignored. It is when the patient stumbles that the analyst gets the message.

Lacan presents a strange mixture of some brilliant insights, some original formulations, and a great deal of material that was borrowed from others. Lacan's place in the future history of psychoanalysis, in my opinion, will depend on the place ego psychology will occupy. If it continues to remain central and survives the special reformulation that Hartmann and his generation gave to it, it is likely that Lacan will be forgotten. Should, however, the battle against ego psychology gain in importance, Lacan will be remembered as the first to declare war on the dangers of ego psychology, which European psychoanalysts were acquiring from United States psychoanalysts and from Anna Freud's work in London. It was only after my study of Lacan was coming to an end that I realized that the difficulty in understanding him is not only the language but also that he represents a qualitatively different kind of dissident. Like Melanie Klein, he does not oppose Freud but modifies him to become a kind of Freud useful to himself. Consciously, the dissenter only argues with Freud, but when we enter the language of the dissenters we can hear them talking to each other.

HEINZ KOHUT AND SELF PSYCHOLOGY

Except for Jung's psychology, no other school of psychoanalysis represents as radical a break from Freud's theory, philosophy, and technique of treatment as does Heinz Kohut's self psychology. Whether one agrees or disagrees with it, it remains an astonishing fact that self psychology could have grown out of Freudian psychoanalysis and taken root in it. What is central to Kohut is not intrapsychic conflict, but the defect of the self structure, and what cures is not one of the factors enumerated either in the Marienbad Symposium (1937) or in the Edinburgh Symposium (1961), but a completely new idea, namely that the therapist as a new selfobject by his empathy corrects the failures of the original parents as selfobjects, and thus enables the analysand to resume growth. Unlike Freud, Kohut counted on a drive to be cured in the patient himself or herself. Given the "actualizing matrix" of the psychoanalytic situation, the defective self of the patient with a narcissistic personal disturbance will mobilize strivings to complete development (Kohut 1984).

Even the Oedipus complex is embedded in an oedipal selfobject disturbance (Kohut 1984). It may be argued against Kohut that his description of classical psychoanalysis may reflect 1910, but not 1984. But what matters in this historical review is that Kohut, like other dissidents, does not regard the Oedipus complex as the nucleus of the neurosis. Kohut did not believe that the attainment of unambivalent, heterosexual relations is necessary or even a possible goal of treatment. Kohut made self psychology more hospitable to homosexuality as an adequate solution to the search for a productive new selfobject.

Kohut developed his ideas in a series of stages. His first book on narcissism, entitled *The Analysis of the Self*, published in 1971, was a book that most analysts would consider a valuable extension of psychoanalysis into the difficult sphere of analysis of narcissistic pathology. I recall vividly the deep impression Kohut's book made on me, but also the feeling that Kohut's ideas were somehow familiar. I realized that they were anticipated in Thomas Mann's novel *Joseph in Egypt*, where Joseph's narcissism undergoes the kind of transmutation that Kohut had in mind.

After the publication of *The Analysis of the Self*, Kohut was accused of neglecting the aggressive drive. In 1973, he responded by publishing his essay on narcissistic rage. In it, Kohut stated that human aggression is at its most dangerous when it is attached to the "grandiose self" and the "archaic omnipotent object" (p. 378). Narcissistic rage expresses itself in an inexhaustible need to take revenge. It can never be forgiven and what remains unforgivable is the sense of shame, a defeat in the realm of the omnipotent grandiose self. It is for that reason that the evil stepmother in *Snow White* cannot tolerate that someone else is fairer than she is. The need for psychoanalytic help can become such a narcissistic injury. For such analysands the very fact that they must seek help is a narcissistic injury. They will try to make the treatment as short as possible or try to prove to the therapist that he or she is really not needed, or even turn the tables on the therapist and try to analyze her or him.

It was his second book, *The Restoration of the Self*, published in 1977, that revealed Kohut as a dissenter. Freud in his 1914 paper "On Narcissism" stressed the possibility of narcissistic libido becoming converted into object libido, a process common in the state of falling in love. Conversely, disappointment in loving can transform object libido back into narcissistic libido. By contrast, Kohut suggested that narcissistic libido and object libido have two different lines of development and are not convertible into each other. Narcissistic libido can cathect selfobjects, that is objectively another person who is experienced as part of the self, but it cannot undergo transformation into object libido.

For Kohut, narcissistic pathology became a specific pathology different from both borderline pathology and neurosis. Being fundamentally different, it also required a different technique of treatment. In a deeper sense, self psychology belongs to the object relations point of view because the narcissistic pathology is attributed to failures in the original selfobject, that is mother or father, to respond appropriately to the needs of the child. The analytic relationship offers an opportunity both to repeat the past failure and offer cure because the analyst as a new selfobject attempts to mend, and when analysts fail in their efforts to correct the failure of the original selfobject, they admit their failures and do not attempt to deny their shortcomings. Going further, the self psychologist apologizes for the inability to be the ideal selfobject. It is the actual behavior of the psychoanalyst and not the recovery of the past that is at the core of the cure. In the course of treatment, the Kohutian therapist permits and does not interfere with the needs of the patient to resume an idealization that was prematurely interrupted in the relationship to the early selfobject. In Kohut's (1977) view, it is not the interpretation that cures the patient, but the new relationship. This Kohut eventually believed to hold true not only for narcissistic personality disorders but also in patients suffering from structural neurosis. Kohut coined the term *transmuting internalizations* to describe the slow process through which a new psychological structure is built. In Kohut's view, classical psychoanalysis attempts to reach the deepest level of the patient's experience by uncovering his impulses, wishes, and drives. It aims to make the patient aware of his archaic sexual lust and hostility. Following Kohut's line of thought, it is not the aim of the psychoanalyst to confront the patient with newly discovered drive representation that the patient then can learn to suppress, sublimate, or integrate into his or her life. The self-psychologically informed psychoanalyst, by contrast, addresses the defects in the self brought about by the early unempathic selfobjects. Rather, the function of the analyst is to uncover the threat to the organization of the self (Kohut 1977).

Kohut defined psychoanalysis as a study of complex mental states, which can be comprehended by empathy and introspection. Empathy Kohut saw as vicarious introspection, becoming aware of another person's complex mental state. Psychoanalysis he saw as the science of these subjective states. The sense of self, central to Kohut's psychology, is both an independent as well as interdependent center of initiative. The degrees of separateness and interdependence fluctuate. Empathy in general and the empathy of the mother in particular were elevated by Kohut to humanity's deepest need, and its absence became the source of most mental suffering. Kohut, like Ferenczi, saw the baby as pre-adapted to respond to an empathetic caregiver. Where this need of the baby meets the expected response, a cohesive sense of self will develop. Empathic failures, on the other hand, lead to defensive patterns. Among dissidents, Kohut stands out as advocating a profound change in the aims of psychoanalytic therapy. It was Socrates who first elevated self-knowledge into an ideal. And it was Goethe who said, "The greatest happiness of humanity is the personality." In this tradition, individuation was always an implicit ideal of the Enlightenment period and of psychoanalysis. This emphasis on individuation and personality development was no longer central to Kohut. What he was interested in was the productive relationship between a person and his major selfobjects. The term *selfobject* was coined by Kohut to designate a relationship in which another person becomes part of the self and the relationship between the two is essential for development and happiness.

It is by now commonly accepted knowledge that Kohut's paper, "The Two Analyses of Mr. Z" (1979), represents a record of his orthodox psychoanalysis with Ruth Eissler (Baudry 1998) and what followed later, his own self-analysis. I recall that this fact was conveyed to me in the strictest confidence by one of Kohut's closest collaborators, and I had kept the promise never to mention it to anyone. However, as time went on, I realized that the fact had become common knowledge, so that it need no longer be regarded as confidential information. It says something about the state of our profession that Kohut, instead of acknowledging the success of his self-analysis and proclaiming it with pride as his own creative achievement, felt obliged to disguise it into a form of a double analysis of Mr. Z. Whether one agrees with Kohut's self-analysis or not, I do not see how anyone can deny that the second analysis of Mr. Z was a major psychological achievement. I will not recapitulate the data themselves since they are well known, but only draw attention to the fact that Mr. Z's first and orthodox psychoanalysis was, by ordinary standards, successful, both as judged by life goals and analytic goals (Bergmann 2001c, Ticho 1972). The masturbatory, masochistic fantasies of total enslavement to a powerful woman receded, and heterosexual relationships were made possible for Mr. Z. He moved into his own apartment. Mr. Z's Oedipus complex was analyzed, including ambivalence and hostility toward the father as an oedipal rival. Mr. Z even went through the appropriate mourning period about the ending of the analysis, and the gains held for five years, but something basic, the child's need for a father, was not recognized. The second analysis of Mr. Z, or the self-analysis that Kohut did, became the answer, and, as in the case of Jung, the triumph of the self-analysis over the official analysis became the foundation stone for a new dissidence.

Outwardly, in Kohut's life, those five intermezzo years between 1966 and 1971 were the years between the publication of the paper "Forms and Transformation of Narcissism" and the publication of the book *The Analysis of the Self*. It was during those years that the gains of his analysis were gradually eroded. The five-year period may not have been an accidental one, since when Mr. Z or Kohut was five, the father who had established a relationship with another woman came back into the house and put an end to Mr. Z's blissful period in which he as a child was the oedipal victor and the sole possessor of his mother. The reasons Mr. Z gave for returning to the analysis, or the reason that prompted Kohut to undertake an extensive self-analysis, were that in spite of establishing heterosexual relationships, Mr. Z experienced no pleasure in them, and in order to counteract a feared premature ejaculation, he felt compelled to reawaken within himself the masochistic image of the woman that demands sexual performance. But what really brought about the need for a reevaluation was an external factor, the steady deterioration of the mother who, in those intervening years, developed paranoid delusions. It was only now that Kohut recognized how disturbed the mother was, and what in the first analysis seemed a victory over the oedipal father was transformed into a conviction that during the years of infancy the father had abandoned him to a very disturbed mother. It was at this point of his self-analysis that Kohut came to an insight that forced him to go beyond the confines of traditional analysis. He found that the loss of the mother as an "archaic selfobject" was so threatening that a "disintegration anxiety" set in. Kohut's self-analysis also led him to recognize the pivotal role in all analyses of narcissistic personalities of the "idealizing transference." Kohut felt strongly that the need for an idealizing transference should be supported rather than analyzed away by the analyst. When left to play its productive role, the idealizing transference eventually becomes transformed into a "mirror transference." During this phase, the patient becomes self-centered and demanding, and insists on perfect empathy. Such patients tend to become enraged at the slightest out-of-tuneness of the therapist; that is, they insist that the analyst do nothing else but reflect back to the patient what the patient is conveying. Utmost empathy and patience is demanded from the psychoanalyst to work out this phase. To me it seems that the stage that Kohut called "mirror transference" is similar to the stage Balint called "passive love."

In the posthumously published book *How Does Analysis Cure?* (1984), Kohut returned to reflect further on the two analyses of Mr. Z. In the first analysis, the emphasis was on faulty psychic functioning, while in the second analysis, a faulty psychic structure was discovered. The crucial dream in which the father attempts to return and the son slams the door the father is trying to open was interpreted in the first analysis as an oedipal dream. In the second analysis, it was interpreted as a "self-state" dream dealing with the child's need for paternal presence in order to build psychic structure. Kohut now became convinced that no analyst not trained in self psychology would have been capable of making such a shift. If indeed Mr. Z was Kohut himself, then the self-analysis gave him back the need for a father that his first analysis did not succeed in giving him, but only a psychoanalytically trained person could arrive at this distinction. In my experience most creative psychoanalysts must carry on a self-analysis that goes beyond what their own analysis achieved, but this leads to dissidence only when the hostility toward one's own analyst, projected on Freud, is greater than the gratitude for what the analyst, with all her or his shortcomings, did achieve. If Kohut's narcissism and his anger had not interfered, he could have followed Winnicott's example, enlarging the horizon of psychoanalysis without creating a new dissidence. What matters in the current context is that the same dream can be subjected to two very different interpretations.

Baudry (1998) has drawn attention to a number of troubling issues raised by the way Kohut introduced his new method. If Kohut was Mr. Z and Mr. Z's dominant masturbation fantasy was one of total submission to a powerful woman, was his first analysis then a reenactment of that fantasy? Baudry's paper leaves us with the disturbing thought that self psychology represented Kohut's second attempt to overthrow the powerful mother-psychoanalyst and establish his own place under the sun. We are left with another question: Assuming that Baudry was right in summarizing the individual and pathological roots behind Kohut's creation, does it invalidate self psychology as a psychoanalytic theory? To what extent are usefulness and validity of a theory dependent on and independent of its unconscious origins within the founder?

Kohut then came to a conclusion important beyond the confines of self psychology, namely that an analysand can perceive the pathology of the original object, in this case the mother, only when the analyst is not again exposing him to the pathological milieu of early life. When the self-analysis of any analyst leads to conclusions that go significantly beyond the conclusions reached in the analysis itself, the temptation to become a dissident and start a new school of one's own becomes powerful. To put it in the language we owe to Ernst Kris's 1956 paper, "The Personal Myth," the orthodox analysis failed to pierce the myth of the loving mother, and left intact the basic fantasy. Because of Kris's work, we know that the danger of not uncovering aspects of the personal myth is a permanent danger in many analyses. To Kohut, the success of his orthodox analysis appeared to be a transference cure based on the analysand trying to live up to the requirements of the analyst as he once complied with the expectations of his sick mother. As a result, Mr. Z settled for "the joyless pleasure of a defeated self—via self-stimulation" (1979, p. 17). Masturbation was to Mr. Z not a quest for pleasure, but a reassurance that he is alive. It was only after the pathology of the mother was worked through that the yearnings for a strong father gained center stage.

Because Kohut chose to present a clinical case, debate started immediately. In a letter to the editor in the same volume in which the "Two Analyses of Mr. Z" appeared, Mortimer Ostow (1979) argued that the first analysis did not represent classical technique at its optimal capacity:

> Dr. Kohut chose to interpret the anger as a response to his efforts to show the patient that he was still craving, in the transference, his mother's single-minded admiration and commitment. It seems to me that the analyst might have been impressed by the contrast between the idyllic relation the patient described, and the hostility he exhibited in the transference. The contrast alone suggests that the manifest account covered repressed hostility. [p. 531]

Kohut, in Ostow's view, also failed to understand the masochistic masturbation fantasy of Mr. Z as indicating the patient's enslavement to the mother. Ostow argued that a Freudian analysis better conducted would have made the second analysis unnecessary.

The failure of the orthodox analysis to maintain the progress gained was due to two forces interacting with each other. The first was external to the analysand's mother's deterioration that made the reexamination of their relationship urgent, and the second was the failure of that analysis to penetrate the personal myth of the loving mother. Had Kohut been an ordinary person, a second analysis might have achieved what the first one failed to do. But Kohut was by that time a well-known figure in the analytic world, and such figures, when they are in need of further analysis, have difficulty in finding a personal analyst. Had Kohut found a psychoanalyst capable of breaking through the personal myth of Kohut's childhood, self psychology might never have emerged. As it turned out, all psychoanalytic schools learned something essential from Kohut, even those that do not regard refinding of a selfobject as essential for growth, creativity, and even happiness. The second analysis of Mr. Z contains the important observation that the boy needs a good internalized image of the father in order not to experience the woman as dangerous and castrating.

RONALD FAIRBAIRN (1889–1964)

The earliest representative of object relation theory as a dissident school was Fairbairn. His book (1941) began with a special interest in schizoid personalities, schizoid processes, and hysterical disassociations. Schizoid personalities, Fairbairn emphasized, are notorious for their struggle against libidinal investments in others. They fear that their love will not be accepted by the other—that loving will empty them out. They avoid genitality and are addicted to part objects. Convinced that any attempt at deeper human relationships is futile, they have lost even the hope of oneness with libidinal objects. Aggression is prominent as well as fear of always killing whatever they love. They also stifle creativity.

Scharff and Birtles (1994) have suggested that the debate between Freud and object relations theory goes back to the famous debate between Plato and Aristotle, with Freud following the platonic division between mind and body, which can be extended to the conflict between sex and aggression, life and death instinct, id and ego, and individual and society. In contrast to that platonic dualist point of view is the Aristotelian, Kantian, and Hegelian emphasis on integration and reciprocity. In the Aristotelian philosophy humans are animals naturally endowed to form a society.

Unlike Freud, Fairbairn did not see repression as directed at an unacceptable idea but, following Melanie Klein, as directed against internalized bad objects. Fairbairn (1941) understood dreams as portraying the splitting brought about schizoid mechanisms. Dreams and fantasies deal with relationships between ego structures and internalized object relationships, and between ego structures themselves. The mother is internalized by three separate affective experiences, resulting in three separate mothers: the "exciting mother," the "rejecting mother," and the "ideal mother." The splitting enables the child to maintain control. The "central ego" was to Fairbairn an impoverished residue left over after the frustrating and exciting objects were split off. In dreams he saw antilibidinal objects and antilibidinal ego structures affecting and interacting with the central ego, which clings to ideal objects. The interaction between those subpersonalities are analogous to Freud's superego and id, but they are not so much concepts as vivid actors in the dream drama.

Internalized object relations are reenacted in the transference, which usually begins with the central ego relating to the analyst as an ideal object. During this phase, the analysand is struggling to prevent a negative transference from emerging, but the negative transference will emerge when the bad object asserts its power. Fairbairn saw the superego as "a moral defense" also in terms of object relations theory. The superego attempts to maintain a good object relationship with the bad object, trying to mitigate the bad object's aggression by shifting the blame to the self.

In his later work Fairbairn (1958) saw resistance as an effort to maintain the internal world as a closed system while the analyst's efforts are to make this inner world accessible to inter-reality. Fairbairn differed from Freud in another important way: in his view, it is the pleasure derived from good objects that fosters the reality principle, whereas to Freud, it was the frustration of gratification that leads the infant to awaken from the world of hallucinatory wishful feeling, to a gradual painful acceptance of the reality principle. This difference is fundamental because Freud's view (1919) leads to an emphasis on abstinence as a central treatment concept. This is not true, for either Ferenczi or Fairbairn.

There is a utopian aspect in Fairbairn's thinking that should be noted because it is characteristic of many dissenters: like Horney, he also sees the sexuality of the Oedipus complex as a breakdown of the libidinal relationships of the child to his parents. If the child is loved, the relationships remain desexualized; only under conditions of frustration does the sexualization of the Oedipus complex take place. What emerges for me when I compare Fairbairn to Freud is that Freud remains the observer, telling his patient what he sees, while Fairbairn, like Saint Michael, enters the battle and is engaged in combat with the bad objects.

DONALD WINNICOTT (1897–1971)

No psychoanalyst of the post–World War II generation had as powerful an impact on psychoanalysis as Winnicott did, and yet Winnicott cannot be classified with the dissenters. The very fact that innovation does not necessarily lead to dissent is of interest. Winnicott's first contribution was his recognition of the significance of the transitional object in the life of the infant. The transitional object is a blanket or teddy bear to which the infant gets attached; it is the first "me" and "not-me" possession. This discovery alone would have made Winnicott a respectable "extender"; he became a significant modifier when he metaphorically enlarged the transitional object into the concept of transitional space, which is the space between therapist and patient where the analytic process takes place. The "good-enough mother" creates for the infant a holding environment where the infant can grow and develop. Holding is followed by handling and eventually by "object presenting." The mother is first perceived subjectively and only gradually when separation between self and object takes place is the object also experienced objectively. Difficulties in smooth transitions fosters the creation of a false self that corresponds to the mother's desires, while the true self is kept isolated and secret. Analysis miscarries if the analyst accepts this false self as the real self, the necessary regression does not take place, and the analysis will not come to an end. To reach the true self the analyst must tolerate periodic destruction. Winnicott emphasized especially the role of playing in the analysis and also to be alive in the presence of the analyst as the child is playing in the presence of the mother. The aim of analysis is not resolution of conflict but resumption of growth. All this addition and transformation of psychoanalytic ideas was accomplished without any criticism of Freud. Winnicott showed how a second floor could be built without transformation of the first floor built by Freud.

OBJECT RELATIONS THEORY

If object relations theory has a discernible origin, I would suggest that it began in 1937, the year Michael Balint published his paper on primary object love. It was in that paper that he introduced the idea that the libido is not pleasure seeking but rather object seeking; narcissism is already the result of disappointment. Balint (1937) defined this primary object love as "I shall be loved and satisfied, without being under any obligation to give anything in return" (pp. 898–899). It is with amazement that we note that so seemingly small a change had so vast an impact on the subsequent history of psychoanalysis.

To discuss object relations theory from the point of view of dissidence is complicated by problems of boundary, already discussed by Kernberg (1995). In addition to Fairbairn and possibly Winnicott, if we extend the boundary to include ego psychology as belonging to the object relations point of view, psychoanalysts such as Erikson, Edith Jacobson, Mahler, Loewald, Sandler, and Kernberg will be included. If we extend the boundaries further, interpersonalists like Greenberg and Mitchell will also be included.

If we approach the problem historically, object relations theory as a different way of conceptualizing psychoanalysis began in the 1930s. Laplanche and Pontalis observed that object relationships as an idea plays no part in Freud conceptual scheme. In the *Three Essays* (Freud 1905b) the mother was viewed from the point of view of the hypothetical infant. She is only an object insofar as the infant drives are directed toward her. It is within such a context that terms like *object choice, love object*, and much later *object constancy* were formulated. Freud (1915) differentiated instinctual sources from "instinctual aim" and "instinctual object."

The roots of object relation theory can be traced back to Ferenczi's paper of 1909, "Introjections and Transference." From there it can also be further traced to Freud's "Mourning and Melancholia" (1917) with the famous quotation, "The shadow of the object fell upon the ego" (p. 249). Among those who can claim to have originated object relations theory, Michael Balint has a prominent place. Balint was Ferenczi's disciple, and Ferenczi, in his little book entitled *Thalassa* (toward the sea in Greek history), stated that object relations already predominate in the earliest layers of the infant. He saw object relationships as decisive in determining a person's fate.

The most important change brought about by the object relations point of view was the transformation of psychoanalysis into a two-person psychology with analyst and analysand in perpetual interaction. Object relations theories did not conceptualize the individual as developing in isolation but in and through a permanent interaction with significant others.

John Bowlby's work (1958, 1960a,b) also contributed to the advancement of object relations theory. Bowlby observed that when young children are separated from their mother and placed with strangers, they go through three typical phases: protest, despair, and detachment. Bowlby's work helped bring about the realization of the total dependence of the infant on interaction with the main caregiver. At the time when these papers were written, the Hartmann era dominated psychoanalytic thinking in the United States and Bowlby was severely criticized by Anna Freud, Max Schur, and Rene Spitz in the 1960 issue of the *Psychoanalytic Study of the Child*. No rejoinder by Bowlby appeared in that issue.

Mechanisms of introjection and projection play a larger role in object relations theory than in classical psychoanalysis. Some object relations theorists emphasize particularly the revision in Freud's drive theory, while others see it primarily as a shift in emphasis. Melanie Klein, with her emphasis of early projection and introjection, is included as an object relations theorist by some, while others deny this place to her because she remained loyal to Freud's dual instinct theory. In its extreme form, object relations theory can be little more than an attack on Freud's dual instinct theory. In Greenberg and Mitchell's book (1983), psychoanalysts are graded by their distance from Freud's instinct theory, and as they put it, "A theorist attitude towards the drives determines his place in psychoanalytic circles" (p. 304). Looking at the history of psychoanalysis from this angle, Edith Jacobson receives a positive evaluation "for her attempt to merge relational with classical metapsychological explanations" (p. 306). Kernberg, who has retained Freud's drive theory, does not fare as well: to me, the fact that Kernberg is an object relations theorist without being a dissident implies that object relations theory is a modification of many of Freud's ideas, but modification and dissidence are not synonymous.

DISCUSSION

If the publication of Freud's *The Interpretation of Dreams* (1900) is considered the birth of psychoanalysis, then psychoanalysis is now over one hundred years old. The record I put together in the preceding presentation is open to many interpretations but one seems to me most compelling: there were many creative psychoanalysts who for a time contributed to the development of psychoanalysis but ultimately did not find their home in it and sought other solutions. Psychoanalysis is not every psychoanalyst's ultimate home. History did not confirm Freud's hope that it was his good fortune to discover the hidden truth behind neurosis and devise the method for curing it. And yet with the one exception of Jung, who sequestered psychoanalysis as applicable only to Jews, all dissenters paid homage to Freud as the pioneer discoverer, wishing only to amend him in a variety of ways. The other major conclusion I draw is that psychoanalysis is not a hermetically sealed discipline but in constant contact with and influenced by other currents influential in society. Psychoanalysis was, to begin with, a child of its time, trying to apply the rational ideas of the Enlightenment to the irrational aspect of the human unconscious. Psychoanalysis united the strivings of nineteenth century science with what philosophers like Schopenhauer and Nietzsche contributed and writers like Dostoyevsky and Ibsen were discovering about the unconscious. The amalgam was a relatively weak gestalt that many other subsequent workers could aim to modify. It may be useful to keep in mind that the very term *scientist* did not come into use until the second half of the nineteenth century. Even Darwin did not see himself as a scientist, and for Freud to be considered a philosopher rather than a scientist would have meant defeat of all his endeavors. It may also be useful to keep in mind that theory building was one of the characteristics of the Enlightenment, and Freud was certainly a great theory builder.

Although no one knew it at the time, in 1900, there were already two different psychoanalytic models that could be followed: the model of trauma that emerged from the *Studies on Hysteria*, and the model of repression and the return of the repressed in the form of symptoms or manifest dreams that emerged from *The Interpretation of Dreams*. Some psychoanalysts, like Ferenczi, would feel more attracted to the trauma model, while others would feel more at home within the regression model that would in time evolve into the model of intrapsychic conflict.

After the formulation of the dual instinct theory with its postulate of the death instinct, there was room for further controversies. Analysts like Otto Fenichel who were Marxists could not accept the death instinct and indeed within what is called orthodox psychoanalysis there was enough room for controversy and dissidence.

Jung's example is of particular interest. With Freud's support he set out to conquer the world of the myth for psychoanalysis but the appeal of the myth as understood by German Romanticism proved much stronger than the all-too-weak commitment to psychoanalysis, and Jung created a new therapy based on curing alienation by advocating a return to one's religious and national roots. With him psychoanalysis succumbed to the very phenomenon it sought to understand.

The reader of this presentation will have to judge whether I succeeded in conveying that the story of dissidence within psychoanalysis is a rich story worth knowing and a contribution to the history of ideas in the twentieth century. If I am on the right track, mastering this history should not only contribute to clarity but also increase the therapist's clinical capacity; the potential availability of different models of thought can be useful in working with difficult patients. If I have been successful, then the sense of shame that so many of us felt about the fragmentation of psychoanalysis will be mitigated by a sense of wonder over the wealth of ideas that psychoanalysis brought about.

A Talmudic story may serve as an introduction to the discussion. One of the learned rabbis, Elisha, the son of Avuya, was converted to Hellenism and stopped observing all the Jewish laws. He had a disciple, Rabbi Meir, who refused to break with him and continued to discuss the law with him. In response to the indignation he said, "I found a pomegranate. I ate the inside of it and threw out the outer shell." I am asking for Rabbi Meir's blessing in this discussion.

Instead of deploring the controversies I am searching for a way for them to deepen our understanding of the nature of psychoanalysis. I have shown elsewhere that Freud and Socrates had much in common. Both attempted to teach us to look not so much at the outer world but rather into the interiority of man. Like Freud, Socrates too was the originator of mutually recriminatory philosophies: Plato's Academy, Aristotles' Peripatos, the School of Stoics, and Cynics. Their disagreements have remained unreconciled, but generations of Western thinkers have profited from studying their disagreements. Dare we hope for a similar fate?

Going back to a Greek source, I might cite Sextus Empiricus, active around 200 A.D., who was both a therapist and an empirical philosopher. In his book "Outline of Pyrahonism" he compared arguments to medicines, some being stronger than others; just as a medicine can heal one individual and not another, so an argument may be persuasive to one person and not to another. He than added what we might call a psychoanalytic insight: that the persuasiveness of an argument depends on one's antecedent beliefs.

There is but a stone's throw from Sextus Empiricus to Grossman's 1995 paper stating that theoretical concepts represent unconscious fantasies. Because attachment to theories can be based on infantile transferences, controversies over theories become moral issues; at the same time Grossman recognizes that theory-free observations are not possible. There is no way of organizing data except through a theory, and this very same theory blinds us to data not encompassed by the theory. Rangell (1982) recognized the same process when he spoke of transference to theory.

Charles Rycroft, according to Peter Fuller (1985), applied this skepticism to Freud's own thinking. Why did Freud assume that there were two groups of instincts and not three or four, and why did he assume that they were opposed and not complementary to one another? Was it really because the clinical facts compelled him to make these assumptions, or was it perhaps because linguistic habits of thought impelled him to follow Hegel and construct a dialectical theory?

There is a classical explanation of the dissident phenomenon in Freud's history of the psychoanalytic movement (1914), and as reported in Jones's biography of Freud (1955, vol. 2, Chapter V, and 1957, vol. 3, Chapter II). According to this view, two forces are operating in every psychoanalysis: transference and resistance. These two forces operate not only in the analytic situation but also in the relationship between Freud and his dissident coworkers. Freud commented in 1914:

> I had always myself maintained that everyone's understanding of it [psychoanalysis] is limited by his own repressions (or rather, by the resistances which sustain them) so that he cannot go beyond a particular point in his relation to analysis. But I had not expected that anyone who had reached a certain depth in his understanding of analysis could renounce that understanding and lose it. [p. 48]

Freud's surprise in what he called relapses is of interest. It shows once more that he was the child of the Enlightenment and more at home in the historical or genetic point of view than in the dynamic one that believes that intrapsychic conflict can always potentially flare up once more. Freud employs regression as an explanation for dissidence. If we accept the Freud/Jones point of view, dissidence is a pathological phenomenon based on resistance or a relapse from a painful truth. In that case, there is little to be learned about dissidence except the price psychoanalysis had to pay for this phenomenon.

In circular letter 50 (September 10, 1938), Fenichel, perhaps the leading psychoanalyst of the second generation, raised the question of why dissident psychoanalysts use some of Freud's ideas against others; he wondered why they did not have ideas of their own. My own survey has shown that Fenichel was wrong. Adler, Jung, Ferenczi, and Lacan, to name only a few, did not lack originality. Based on the analogy of resistance, Fenichel pointed out that the resisting patient does the same thing: he or she accepts some analytic interpretations and uses them as resistance against other unacceptable ideas. As an example he cites Reich's emphasis on genitality as a sign of health because in this respect he considered himself healthy and therefore could deny his neurosis in other places. One can add that Reich's followers probably did the same. Therefore, the role of resistance in dissidence should not be dismissed, but neither should it be allowed to be the total explanation.

In the circulating letters, Fenichel offered a psychoanalytic interpretation for this supposed behavior of dissidents, saying they tried to castrate the father with the father's own penis. Paradoxically Fenichel also found that this effort to use Freud against Freud brought out the hidden positive tie to him. Examining Fenichel's arguments I came to the hypothesis that this kind of ambivalence was experienced by all analysts and that it is likely that the nature of Freud's discoveries were such that they had to evoke various degrees of ambivalence towards him.

I will now submit some reflections that seem pertinent to me.

The Determination of Dissidence

The material presented, if we exempt Lacan, shows that it is not the differences with Freud that determined dissidence. It is the basic attitude of gratitude or criticism. According to Melanie Klein, interjection of the good object leads to gratitude, while interjection of the bad object leads to an attempt to expel the object. Applying this idea to the history of dissidence we can say that any of Freud's findings can be questioned without the questioner becoming a dissident. Only if the struggle with Freud ends in disappointment or hostility to him is dissidence necessary. Great men like Freud evoke hostility not only because of envy and not only because the ideas of psychoanalysis evoke resistance, but also because great men evoke the wish that they should have been greater, and that they should not have been in any way limited by their time and culture.

The Incomplete or Unsuccessful Analysis as a Source of Dissidence

It was this work that led me to the realization that an incomplete or unsuccessful analysis plays an important role in dissidence. Ferenczi was unhappy with his analysis with Freud and so was Karen Horney with her analysis with Abraham. Lacan's analysis with Lowenstein was interrupted, and Kohut had described in the two analyses of Mr. Z highlighting the different conclusions reached in his analysis and his self-analysis. There are many people who are happy with their analysis and some even say that psychoanalysis saved their life. But there are others who had to continue in a painful self-analysis the work that was left incomplete in their analysis. Dissidence takes place when self-analysis leads to discoveries that could not have been discovered in the analysis. Dissidence is a phenomenon of hubris due to the success of self-analysis. It is not disagreement with Freud as such that leads to dissidence, but disappointment in him. We can assume that behind every dissident lurks a disappointment in Freud that continued to fester.

The Incomplete Nature of Psychoanalytic Knowledge

Psychoanalysis, like medicine and other disciplines, cannot answer many of the questions that emerge in the course of its inquiry. Many personal concerns and theoretical questions remain unanswered. Some of the questions that could not be answered surfaced time and again in the history of psychoanalysis. To face the unknown and admit ignorance is a difficult task. That is the reason why myth and religion were called upon to explain what could not find explanation. Dogma was all too often the answer to the unknown—and dogma creates controversy. A successful personal analysis should increase our capacity to live with the unknown. But in real life, psychoanalytic theory was often called upon to play the same role as religious or political beliefs did for their own true believers. To cite some of the common examples, we know that neurosis is shaped by outer traumatic events affecting development as well as by intrapsychic conflict. But how much weight is to be assigned to either one of those is often difficult to determine and therefore a source of dissidence.

Freud himself shifted the relative importance from the traumatic to the intrapsychic belief around 1900; Ferenczi, on the other hand, as well as Rank, remained loyal to the traumatic theory. Within the traumatic point of view, differences remained. Is the basic trauma, that of birth (Rank) or is it the lack of the kind of love that a child needs (Ferenczi)? Within the conflict theory, there were also differences in opinions. Is early childhood relatively conflict-free until the Oedipus complex is reached (Freud)? Or is it the infant already in great jeopardy because of excessive aggression at birth (Klein)? Is the oedipal conflict fundamental (Freud)? or does it take place only when the child is not given the kind of love he needs (Horney and Kohut)? Is aggression or the death instinct a basic drive (Freud) or is aggression a response to frustration (Horney)? Is the need for safety the primary need (Horney from Adler) or secondary to the need to have libidinal wishes gratified (Freud)? Is penis envy in women primary (Freud) or based on disappointment in obtaining the love of the father (Jones and Horney)?

Questions of another order emerge that go to the core of psychoanalysis. Is the aim of psychoanalysis to make the unconscious conscious with some time devoted to working through, as Freud thought, or is it the rediscovery of the capacity to play that Winnicott emphasized? Do we aim to change a less desirable equilibrium of forces for a better one, as Brenner (1982) suggested? Or is the emphasis on a new type of relationship with a new object, as Loewald (1960) thought essential? It is not easy to know whether these different aims are compatible with one another or whether the aim sought affects the very nature of the analytic process.

To these fundamental questions, a long list of problems of psychoanalytic technique can be added. But what remains crucial is that these questions did not find an answer once and for all within the framework of psychoanalysis. Psychoanalytic controversies arise at the point where psychoanalysis itself does not offer an answer. We became dogmatic when our method leaves us in the lurch.

The Psychoanalytic Point of View and the Psychoanalytic Situation

The history of dissidence forces us to conclude that psychoanalysis is a mixture of two components that do not necessarily demand each other. On the one hand we have Freud's findings: infantile sexuality, the Oedipus complex, transference and resistance, narcissism, female sexuality, the differentiation between reality and pleasure principle, and the structural point of view. But in addition, Freud also created the analytic situation—a way of obtaining new data and a way of communication between therapist and patient where the patient reports memories, dreams, personal feelings about the analyst, his loves and hates for other people, and much else. It turned out that this situation created by Freud opened the door to a power given to the therapist in the transference that enables him or her to influence the patient in more than one direction. All dissidents have used the psychoanalytic situation, but what they communicate is very different from what Freud did and thought useful.

No Road Leads Back

In my interpretation, classical psychoanalysis came to an end with World War II. Fenichel's (1945) psychoanalytic theory of the neurosis is both the culmination point and the end of classical psychoanalysis. After that date, creative analysts can be modifiers or dissenters according to how they internalize Freud. But no one can be a classical analyst. No more than any painter today can paint as impressionists did. Psychoanalysis was a human creation and all human creations are subject to perpetual changes.

The Role of Conviction and Reconstruction

Freud (1937b) believed in the curative powers of both convictions and reconstructions:

> The path that starts from the analyst's construction ought to end in the patient's recollection; but it does not always lead so far. Quite often we do not succeed in bringing the patient to recollect what has been repressed. Instead of that, if the analysis is carried out correctly, we produce in him an assured conviction of the truth of the construction which achieves the same therapeutic result as a recaptured memory. [pp. 265–266]

Since all dissidents were convinced that they were right, this study raises the question of how convictions are arrived at and how they are maintained. There is much to be said in favor of having convictions. They are the opposite of the inability to act that paralyzes many compulsives and suggests that no energy is lost on intrapsychic conflict. Convictions make it possible to attain goals that a less determined person would have given up. But there is another side to conviction where the mind is closed to new ideas, where aggression is directed toward those who hold other beliefs, and where a hindrance to further learning and development has taken place. This other side of conviction has not been studied by psychoanalysis. Furthermore, the fact that, under ordinary conditions, students of a given psychoanalytic institute acquire the convictions that their personal analysts and teachers hold suggests that psychoanalytic schools resemble religious schools more than universities (Kernberg 1986).

In Freud's mind, conviction was closely allied with reconstruction and working through, as the quotation above already indicates. The best case for psychoanalytic reconstruction was made by Waelder (1970). According to Waelder, any discipline that deals with the past must rely on reconstruction. Like Freud, Waelder compared psychoanalysis to archaeology. The famous Rosetta stone yielded the secret of Egyptian hieroglyphics only because a whole set of hypotheses were applied, such as that the Greek and the hieroglyphic text tell the same story. Then came the hypothesis that the hieroglyphics framed by a cartouche contained the name of a king. It was only because hypotheses were applied that the Egyptian hieroglyphics were deciphered. Another example cited by Waelder is the François vase in Florence successfully reassembled from two thousand shards. Waelder maintained that psychoanalysts do not differ from astronomers who reconstruct the history of the universe, and lawyers who reconstruct the scene of a crime. All such endeavors have limits, but they have to be undertaken in spite of the limitations. Waelder quotes the Austrian playwright Grillparzer: "It is difficult to know the future, but it is impossible to know the past because we can never emancipate ourselves from the knowledge of what came out of it in the meantime" (p. 658).

In the "New Introductory Lectures on Psycho-Analysis," Freud (1933) proudly asserted:

> Psychoanalysis has a special right to speak for the scientific Weltanschauung at this point, since it cannot be reproached with having neglected what is mental in the picture of the universe. Its contribution to science lies precisely in having extended research to the mental field. [p. 159]

In view of the various dissident schools that have emerged, we have to ask ourselves whether Freud's proud claim has withstood the test of history. Controversies of course occur in the natural sciences, but they are by their very nature temporary. Either a crucial experiment puts an end to them or further knowledge accumulates, leading to a decision, whereas the question of which of the psychoanalytic schools achieves the aim of mental cure most effectively is fought out in the form of public opinion, where skill of presentation and literary appeal count for more than the presentation of scientific data. For a few decades after World War II, the intellectual climate of opinion was favorable to Freudian analysis, at least in the Western cultures. This has changed in the last two decades. However, the popularity, or lack of it, says very little about the scientific validity of the psychoanalytic findings.

In the "Leonardo" (1910), Freud noted that science began in the Renaissance because nature could be looked at without metaphysical propositions. In a fragment written in 1938, a year before Freud's death, and entitled "Some Elementary Lessons in Psycho-Analysis," Freud wrote:

> Almost as much difficulty is created by the fact that our science involves a number of hypotheses—it is hard to say whether they should be regarded as postulates or as products of our researches. [p. 282]

It is evident that dissidents differ in what they reconstruct. Even Adler's interpretations of inferiority feelings and masculine protest turn out to be a variety of reconstruction. The Fund for Psychoanalytic Research and Development has devoted a great deal of energy to the question of reconstruction. Our efforts culminated in a book published in 1994 by Harold Blum, in which Blum made the valuable observation that Freud's firm belief in determinism reflected a point of view of science before the uncertainty principle was discovered, which stated that there could be "no objective, context-free observation, no avoidance of pre-established orientation, and thus no objectivity about historical actuality" (p. 140). He further concluded, "The past is not only not reconstructed in analysis, it can not be objectively reconstructed since there are multiple probable realities." This is as far as Blum went, and it was indeed rather far. But the material presented here forces upon me a further step. If the reconstruction does not flow directly from the material but is imposed upon the material by some preexisting postulates, and different schools grow upon a different set of postulates, we cannot claim in good con-science to be entirely in the realm of science. Psychoanalysis with all its schools may be on a road that will justify its claim to be a science, but at the moment we are not at that point yet. It is even conceivable that the task is beyond human capacity to achieve.

It becomes important to inquire why are reconstructions necessary in any psychotherapeutic work? Some reflection, I believe, will lead to the conclusion that most patients left to their own devices associat-ing freely will begin at a certain point to go in circles repeating what they just said without making new discoveries. It becomes the task of the therapist to break this chain by interpretation. The analyst has really only two techniques to break through his patient's circle: either he can use himself as a basis of data and tell the analysand what he thinks, or he can say nothing. The first technique is in essence a nonscientific method, where most people listening to complex events offer advice based on their own experience. I recall that Eissler gave an example of this method. If the physician found that a trip to Italy did him a great deal of good, he would then advocate to his patients a trip to Italy. Postulates of all schools are designed to prevent unproductive going in circles, and to present interpretations arising from the unconscious of the therapist.

There is always the possibility of saying nothing, a technique seized by many bewildered therapists. I will cite such an example. A man, uncertain as to whether to divorce his wife and marry his mistress, observes a mother nursing her baby in the park. He feels that his mother never nursed him like that, but preferred his brother. He develops the fantasy that he would like to suck at this woman's breast, but unlike the baby he would give her back her milk through his own semen. Thus united, they will nourish and satisfy each other forever. The therapist did not know what to say in response, and so she let the patient talk on. I choose to interpret that what the patient told her was a transfer-ence fantasy, basically oral in nature, that is mutually satisfying be-cause it excludes all rivals. What matters in the current context is not whether I was right in my interpretation but that to say nothing im-plies first not to condemn the communication and to allow the replace-ment of both brother and father by an oral-genital mother and child relationship. This wish in a disguised form is reenacted in the trans-ference. Silence when an interpretation is called for is bound to be interpreted by the unconscious of the patient and possibly also by the unconscious of the therapist as an approval. To say nothing in a case like this is equivalent to enactment. To interpret is to reconstruct either on the basis of the personal history of the analyst, or on a previously established psychoanalytic frame of reference. At this point, we face pitfalls unknown to archaeologists.

Freud's Responsibility for the Dissidence

The accusation that Freud was intolerant of any dissent has been refuted by Waelder, as my discussion of Rank has shown. However, this does not mean that Freud's character and point of view did not play a role in the emergence of dissidence. Freud was not rigid in the sense that he never changed his mind, but it is true that when he did change his mind he had a tendency to move from one certainty to another, not leaving enough room for what is yet unknown. Of course, Freud was right when he pointed out to Wilhelm Reich that abolishing private property would not put an end to the workings of the aggressive drive. But it is equally true that Freud, wanting to make psychoanalysis a part of natural science, did not give due consideration to the impact of culture on the kind of neurosis that becomes prevalent at any given time. Being a child of the static nineteenth century, he was not sufficiently alert to the implication of the ever-changing social and cultural map that characterized the twentieth century.

Prediction for the Future

Prophecies are dangerous, but hard to resist. We can disagree with Freud on any number of issues, but we can never lose our awareness of what we owe to him. I am in agreement with Kernberg but fear that the malaise goes deeper. Kernberg (2001) stressed the cross-fertilization that is taking place among different psychoanalytic schools, implying that time is working in favor of a unified approach that will emerge from the experiences of the various schools. I have written this communication because I do not trust history alone to achieve this aim. Kernberg (2000) suggested that one of the criteria to judge a psychoanalytic institute is: "Are multiple psychoanalytic theories and clinical approaches respectfully taught?" (p. 118). In most cases the answer will be no.

Psychoanalysis originated in medicine, but the medical model proved inadequate for the discipline of psychoanalysis. Neurosis is not an illness that can be cured without leaving traces behind. It is, and remains even after the analysis, part of the character. It may modify in significant ways the dictum that character is destiny, but only by modifying what there was; it cannot create a new structure.

Freud did not discover the "truth." He discovered a way of ameliorating psychic suffering, and alternate ways of achieving this aim have been discovered. Comparing the results has proven to be difficult. Understanding the history of psychoanalysis, as I have tried to do it, is by itself a fascinating endeavor. It enlarges our horizon, but it also contributes to making us better psychoanalysts. The more we recognize how much we still do not know, the more carefully we will listen to our patients. We can never be sure what patient will present the clinical data we need to understand one of the many puzzles to which we do not have the answer. The road upon which Freud started proved much longer and less of a royal road than Freud and his coworkers anticipated.

Freud wished his name to be associated with Copernicus and Darwin, who disturbed the narcissistic sleep of mankind, Copernicus by depriving us of the feeling that the earth is the center of the universe and Darwin by demonstrating that we were not created by God in his own image but evolved out of the animal kingdom. Freud thought that he would be remembered because he demonstrated that we are not even masters in our own inner world since we exert no dominion over our own unconscious. We are grateful to the great discoverers; however, it nevertheless remains true that if the discovery had not been made by this particular person, sooner or later someone else would have made the same discovery. But if Plato and Aristotle had not lived, the history of philosophy would have taken a very different path. And if Michelangelo had not lived, there would have been no Sistine Chapel. The same applies to Freud; psychoanalysis was not waiting to be discovered by a "Godless Jew" as Freud maintained. Other techniques of psychotherapy would have been discovered, but there would have been no psychoanalysis.

Both Copernicus and Darwin were discoverers, but is psychoanalysis a discovery or a creation by Freud? At the turn of the twentieth century, Freud discovered that meaning can be extracted from dreams, that derivatives of the unconscious emerge in slips and forgetting of words. He also discovered the technique of free association. Two more discoveries were added somewhat later, namely that infants are not devoid of sexual feelings and that most analytic patients will develop feelings of hate or love toward the analyst based on feelings they had for the early significant objects in their lives. In subsequent developments further discoveries were made, such as narcissism, the repetition compulsion, and the dual instinct theory. We owe to the dissidents the discovery that all these new findings did not by themselves constitute a strong gestalt. Some of them can be accepted and others rejected and most of them are subject to other interpretations. Freud was a child of his own time and as Thomas Mann well understood psychoanalysis was a reconciliation between the Enlightenment and Romanticism. In its totality, psychoanalysis was created and not discovered, and because it was a creation and not a discovery, dissidents had to play a major role in its history.

References

Abraham, H. C., and Freud, E. L. (1907–1926). *A Psycho-Analytic Dialogue: The Letters of Sigmund Freud and Karl Abraham 1907–1926*. New York: Basic Books, 1965.

Abraham, K. (1909). Dreams and myths. In *Clinical Papers in Psychoanalysis*. New York: Basic Books, 1955.

———— (1920). Manifestations of the female castration complex. In *Selected Papers of Karl Abraham*, trans. D. Bryan and A. Stachey, pp. 338–369. London: Hogarth Press, 1948.

———— (1924). A short study of the development of the libido, viewed in the light of mental disorders. In *Selected Papers of Karl Abraham*, trans. D. Bryan and A. Stachey, pp. 418–501. London: Hogarth Press, 1948.

Adler, A. (1908). Der Aggressionstrieb Im Leben und in der Neurose. *Fortschritte de Medizin* 26:577–84.

Alexander, F. (1937). Review of *The Neurotic Personality of Our Time*. *Psychoanalytic Quarterly* 6:536–546.

Alexander, F., Eisenstein, S., and Grotjahn, M., eds. (1966). *Psychoanalytic Pioneers*. New York: Basic Books.

Balint, M. (1935). Critical notes on the theory of pre-genital organization of the libido. In *Primary Love and Psychoanalytic Technique*, pp. 49–72. New York: Liveright, 1953.

———— (1937). Early development states of the ego: primary object love. In *Primary Love and Psychoanalytic Technique*, pp. 90–108. New York: Liveright, 1953.

Baudry, F. (1998). Kohut and Glover: the role of subjectivity in psychoanalytic theory and controversy. In *Psychoanalytic Study of the Child* 53:3–24. New Haven, CT: Yale University Press.

Benomi, C. (1999). Flight into sanity: Jones' allegations of Ferenczi's deterioration reconsidered. *International Journal of Psycho-Analysis* 80:507–542.

Benvenuto, B., and Kennedy, R. (1986). *The Works of Jacques Lacan: An Introduction*. London: Free Association Books.

Bergmann, M. S. (1987). *The Anatomy of Loving*. New York: Columbia University Press.

———— (1992). *In the Shadow of Moloch: The Sacrifice of Children and Its Impact on Western Religions*. New York: Columbia University Press.

———— (1993). Reflections on the history of psychoanalysis. *Journal of the American Psychoanalytic Association* 41:929–955.

———— (1996). The tragic encounter between Freud and Ferenczi and its impact on the history of psychoanalysis. In *Ferenczi's Turn in Psychoanalysis*, ed. P. L. Rudnytsky, pp. 145–159. New York: New York University Press.

———— (1997). Termination: the Achilles' heel of psychoanalytic technique. *Psychoanalytic Psychology* 14(2):163–174.

———— (1999). The dynamics of the history of psychoanalysis: Anna Freud, Leo Rangell, and André Green. In *The Dead Mother: The Work of André Green*, ed. G. Kohon, pp. 193–204. New York: Routledge.

———— (2001a). The conflict between Enlightenment and Romantic philosophies as reflected in the history of psychoanalysis. Freud Lecture presented at the New York Psychoanalytic Society, New York, April, 2000.

———— (2001b). The leap from the *Studies on Hysteria* to *The Interpretation of Dreams*. In *Storms in Her Head: Freud and the Construction of Hysteria*, ed. M. Dimen and A. Harris. New York: Other Press.

———— (2001c). Life goals and psychoanalytic goals from a historical perspective. *Psychoanalytic Quarterly* 70:15–34.

Bergmann, M. S., ed. (2000). *The Hartmann Era*. New York: Other Press.

Bergmann, M. S., and Hartman, F. R. (1976). *The Evolution of Psychoanalytic Technique*. New York: Basic Books.

Blum, H. P. (1994). The confusion of tongues and psychic trauma. *International Journal of Psycho-Analysis*. 75:871–882.

———— (1994). *Reconstruction in Psychoanalysis: Childhood Revisited and Re-created*. Madison, CT: International Universities Press.

Blum, H. P., ed. (1977). *Female Psychology*. New York: International Universities Press.

Bowlby, J. (1958). The nature of the child's tie to his mother. *International Journal of Psycho-Analysis* 39:350–372.

———— (1960a). Separation anxiety. *International Journal of Psycho-Analysis* 41:89–113.

———— (1960b). Grief and mourning in infancy. *Psychoanalytic Study of the Child* 15:9–52. New York: International Universities Press.

Brenner, C. (1982). *The Mind in Conflict*. New York: International Universities Press.

Breuer, J., and Freud, S. (1895). Studies on hysteria. *Standard Edition* 2, pp. ix–335.

Carotenuto, A. (1982). *A Secret Symmetry: Sabina Spielrein Between Jung and Freud*, trans. A. Pomerans, J. Shepley, and K. Winston. New York: Pantheon Books.

Clement, C. (1983). *The Lives and Legends of Jacques Lacan*. New York: Columbia University Press.

Cortina, M., and Maccoby, M., eds. (1996). *A Prophetic Analyst: Erich Fromm's Contribution to Psychoanalysis*. Northvale, NJ: Jason Aronson.

Dupont, J., ed. (1988). *The Clinical Diary of Sandor Ferenczi*. Cambridge: Harvard University Press.

Eckhardt, M. H. (1996). *Fromm's Humanistic Ethics and the Role of the Prophet: A Prophetic Analyst*. Northvale, NJ: Jason Aronson.

Edinburgh Symposium. (1961). The curative factors in psycho-analysis. Gitelson, M., Nacht, S., Segal, H., Kuiper, P., Garma, A., King, P., Heimann, P., participants. Twenty-second congress of the International Psycho-Analytical Association, Edinburgh, July/August.

Eissler, K. R. (1982). *Psychologische Aspekte des Briefwechsels zwischen Freud und Jung*. [*Psychological Aspects of the Correspondence between Freud and Jung*]. Stuttgart, Germany: Frommann-Holzboog.

Ellenberger, H. F. (1970). *The Discovery of the Unconscious*. London: Penguin.

Etchegoyen, R. H. (1991). *The Fundamental of Psychoanalytic Technique*. London: Karnac.

Fairbairn, W. R. D. (1941). *Revised Psychopathology of the Psychoses and Neuroses in an Object Relations Theory of the Personality*. New York: Basic Books.

———— (1958). *From Instinct to Self: Selected Papers*, ed. D. E. Scharff and E. F. Birtles. New York: Jason Aronson.

Fenichel, O. (1935). A critique of the death instinct. In *Collected Papers of Otto Fenichel*, first series, pp. 363–372. New York: W.W. Norton, 1953.

—— (1945). *The Psychoanalytic Theory of Neurosis*. New York: W.W. Norton.

—— (1998). *Rundbriefe*, vols. 1 and 2, ed. E. M. Ghlitner and J. Reichmayr. Frankfurt, Germany: Stromfeld.

Ferenczi, S. (1909). Introjection and transference. In *Sex in Psychoanalysis*, pp. 35–93. New York: Basic Books, 1950.

—— (1923). *Thalassa: A Theory of Genitality*. New York: Psychoanalytic Quarterly, 1938.

—— (1929a). The principles of relaxation and neocatharsis. In *Final Contributions to the Problems and Methods of Psychoanalysis*, trans. E. Moscbacher et al., ed. M. Balint, pp. 108–125. New York: Basic Books, 1955.

—— (1929b). The unwelcome child and his death instinct. In *Final Contributions to the Problems and Methods of Psychoanalysis*, trans. E. Moscbacher et al., ed. M. Balint, pp. 102–107. New York: Basic Books, 1955.

—— (1933). Confusion of tongues between adults and the child: the language of tenderness and passion. In *Final Contributions to the Problems and Methods of Psychoanalysis*, trans. E. Moscbacher et al., ed. M. Balint, pp. 156–167. New York: Basic Books, 1955.

—— (1949). Confusion of tongues between adult and child. *International Journal of Psycho-Analysis* 30:225–230.

—— (1985). *The Clinical Diary of Sandor Ferenczi*, ed. J. Dupont. Cambridge, MA: Harvard University Press.

Ferenczi, S., and Rank, O. (1924). *Entwicklungziele der Psychoanalyze* [*The Development of Psychoanalysis, Nervous and Mental Diseases*]. Monograph, 1925. New York: Nervous and Mental Disease Press.

Fliess, R. (1947). *The Psychoanalytic Reader*. New York: International Universities Press.

Frank, A. (1979). Two theories or one or none? *Journal of the American Psychoanalytic Association* 27:169–207.

Freud, A. (1949). Certain types and stages of social maladjustments. In *The Writings of Anna Freud*, vol. 4, pp. 75–94. New York: International Universities Press.

—— (1954). The widening scope of indications for psychoanalysis: discussion. *Journal of the American Psychoanalytic Association* 2:607–620.

—— (1976). Changes in psychoanalytic practice and experience. *International Journal of Psycho-Analysis* 57:257–260.

Freud, S. (1898). Sexuality in the etiology of the neuroses. *Standard Edition* 3, pp. 261–285.

—— (1900). The interpretation of dreams. *Standard Edition* 4/5, pp. xi–627.

———— (1905a). The technique of jokes. *Standard Edition* 8, pp. 16–89.

———— (1905b). Three essays on the theory of sexuality. *Standard Edition* 7, pp. 125–245.

———— (1908). "Civilized" sexual morality and modern nervous illness. *Standard Edition* 9, pp. 177–204.

———— (1909). Analysis of a phobia in a five-year-old boy. *Standard Edition* 10, pp. 3–149.

———— (1910a). "Wild" psycho-analysis. *Standard Edition* 11, pp. 219–227.

———— (1910b). Five lectures on psycho-analysis. *Standard Edition* 11, pp. 3–56.

———— (1910c). Leonardo da Vinci and a memory of his childhood. *Standard Edition* 11, pp. 59–137.

———— (1912a). Contributions to a discussion on masturbation. *Standard Edition* 12, pp. 239–254.

———— (1912b). The dynamics of transference. *Standard Edition* 12, pp. 97–108.

———— (1914a). On narcissism: an introduction. *Standard Edition* 14, pp. 67–102.

———— (1914b). On the history of the psycho-analytic movement. *Standard Edition* 14, pp. 3–102.

———— (1915). Instincts and their vicissitudes. *Standard Edition* 14, pp. 109–140.

———— (1916). Some character-types met with in psycho-analytic work. *Standard Edition* 14, pp. 309–333.

———— (1916–17). Introductory lectures on psychoanalysis. *Standard Edition* 15/16, pp. 3–496.

———— (1917). Mourning and melancholia. *Standard Edition* 14, pp. 237–258.

———— (1918). From the history of an infantile neurosis. *Standard Edition* 17, pp. 3–248.

———— (1919). Lines of advance in psycho-analytic therapy. *Standard Edition* 17, pp. 157–168.

———— (1926). Inhibitions, symptoms and anxiety. *Standard Edition* 20, pp. 77–174.

———— (1933). New introductory lectures on psycho-analysis. *Standard Edition* 22, pp. 3–248.

———— (1937a). Analysis terminable and interminable. *Standard Edition* 23, pp. 209–253.

———— (1937b). Constructions in analysis. *Standard Edition* 23, pp. 255–269.

———— (1938). Some elementary lessons in psycho-analysis. *Standard Edition* 23, pp. 279–286.

Fromm, E. (1936). *Autorität und Familie*. Paris: Librarie Felx Alcun.

———— (1941). *Escape from Freedom*. New York: Farrar & Rinehart.

———— (1951). *The Forgotten Language*. New York: Rinehart.

———— (1956). *The Art of Loving*. New York: Harper & Row.

———— (1959). *Sigmund Freud's Mission: An Analysis of his Personality and Influence*. New York: Harper.

———— (1973). *The Anatomy of Human Destructiveness*. London: Jonathan Cape.

Fuller, P. (1985). Introduction to Charles Rycroft. In *Psychoanalysis and Beyond*. Chicago: University of Chicago Press.

Gay, P. (1988). *Freud: A Life for Our Times*. New York: W. W. Norton.

Gill, M. M., and Holtzman, P., eds. (1976). *Psychology Versus Metapsychology: Psychoanalytic Essays in Memory of George. S. Klein, Psychological Issues*, vol. 4(4). New York: International Universities Press.

Glover, E. (1931). The therapeutic effect of inexact interpretation: a contribution to the theory of suggestion. In *The Technique of Psycho-Analysis*, pp. 353–366. New York: International Universities Press.

———— (1933). *War, Sadism and Pacifism*. London: Allen and Conwin.

———— (1945). Examination of the Klein System of child psychology. *Psychoanalytic Study of the Child* 1:75–118. New York: International Universities Press.

Gorlich, B. (1996). Psychoanalyse und soziologie: Erich Fromm. In *Psychoanalyse in Frankfurt*, ed. Plankers et al. Tubingen: Diskord.

Graf, M. (1942). Reminiscences of Professor Sigmund Freud. *Psychoanalytic Quarterly* 11:465–476.

Green, A. (1975a). The analyst, symbolization and the absence in the analytic setting (on changes in analytic practice and analytic experience). *International Journal of Psycho-Analysis* 56:1–22. Also in *On Private Madness*, ed. A. Green. Madison, CT: International Universities Press, 1986.

———— (1975b). Potential space in psychoanalysis. In *On Private Madness*, pp. 277–296. Madison, CT: International Universities Press.

———— (1980). The dead mother. In *On Private Madness*, pp. 142–173. Madison, CT: International Universities Press.

Greenberg, J. R., and Mitchell, S. A. (1983). *Object Relations in Psychoanalytic Theory*. Cambridge: Harvard University Press.

Grosskurth, P. (1987). *Melanie Klein: Her World and Her Work*. Cambridge: Harvard University Press.

Grossman, W. I. (1976). Nightmare in armor: reflections on Wilhelm Reich's contributions to psychoanalysis. *Psychiatry* 39:376–385.

———— (1995). Psychological vicissitudes of theory in clinical work. *International Journal of Psychology* 76:885–899.

Grossman, W. I., and Stewart, W. H. (1977). Penis envy from childhood wish to developmental metaphor. In *Female Sexuality*, ed. H. P. Blum. New York: International Universities Press.

Grubrich-Semitis, I. (1986). Six letters of Sigmund Freud to Sandor Ferenczi. *International Review of Psycho-Analysis* 13:259–277.

Hale, N. G. (1995). *The Rise and Crisis of Psychoanalysis in the United States, 1917–1985.* New York: Oxford University Press.

Handlbauer, B. (1990). *Die Adler-Freud-Kontroverse.* Frankfurt: Fischer, Taschenbuch, Verlag.

Haynal, A. E. (1946). Freud and his intellectual environment: the case of Sandor Ferenczi. In *Ferenczi's Turn in Psychoanalysis*, ed. P. L. Rudnytsky, pp. 25–40. New York: New York University Press.

———— (1988). *Controversies in Psychoanalytic Methods from Freud to Ferenczi and Michael Balint.* New York: New York University Press.

———— (1989). *Controversies in Psychoanalytic Method.* New York: New York University Press.

Hegel, G. (1807). *The Phenomenology of Mind*, trans. J. B. Baille. Mineola, NY: Dover.

Hook, S. (1959). *Psychoanalysis Scientific Method and Philosophy.* New York: New York University Press.

Horney, K. (1924). On the genesis of the castration complex in women. *International Journal of Psycho-Analysis* 5:50–65.

———— (1926). The flight from womanhood. *International Journal of Psycho-Analysis* 7:324–339.

———— (1927). The problem of the monogamous ideal. *International Journal of Psycho-Analysis* 9:318–331.

———— (1936). The problem of the negative therapeutic reaction. *Psychoanalytic Quarterly* 5:29–44.

———— (1937). *The Neurotic Personality of Our Time.* New York: W.W. Norton.

———— (1939). *New Ways of Psychoanalysis.* New York: W.W. Norton.

Jones, E. (1955). *The Life and Work of Sigmund Freud, Vol. 2: The Years of Maturity 1901–1919.* New York: Basic Books.

———— (1957). *The Life and Work of Sigmund Freud, Vol 3: The Last Phase 1919–1939.* New York: Basic Books.

Jung, C. G. (1961). *Memories, Dreams, and Reflections.* New York: Pantheon.

Kernberg, O. (1986). Institutional problems of psychoanalytic education. *Journal of the American Psychoanalytic Association* 34:799–834.

———— (1995). Psychoanalytic object relations theories. In *Psychoanalysis: The Major Concepts*, ed. B. E. Moore and B. D. Fine, pp. 450–462. New Haven, CT: Yale University Press.

———— (1996). Thirty methods to destroy the creativity of psychoanalytic candidate. *International Journal of Psycho-Analysis* 77:1031–1040.

———— (2000). A concerned critique of psychoanalytic education. *International Journal of Psycho-Analysis* 81:97–120.

———— (2001). Recent developments in the technical approaches of English language psychoanalytic schools. *Psychoanalytic Quarterly* 70:519–547.

King, P., and Steiner, R., eds. (1991). *The Freud-Klein Controversies, 1941–1945.* London: Tavistock/Routledge.

Kirsch, T. (1991). Jung and the Jews: personal reflections. In *Lingering Shadows: Jungians, Freudians, and Anti-Semitism,* ed. A. Maidenbaum and S. A. Martin, pp. 349–353. Boston: Shambhala.

Klein, G. S. (1976). *Psychoanalytic Theory: An Exploration of Essentials.* New York: International Universities Press.

Köhler, W. (1925). *The Mentality of Apes,* trans. E. Winter. New York: Harcourt, Brace.

Kohut, H. (1971). *The Analysis of the Self.* New York: International Universities Press.

———— (1973). Thoughts on narcissism and narcissistic rage. *Psychoanalytic Study of the Child* 27:360–400. New Haven, CT: Yale University Press.

———— (1977). *The Restoration of the Self.* New York: International Universities Press.

———— (1979). The two analyses of Mr. Z. *International Journal of Psycho-Analysis* 60:3–27.

———— (1984). *How Does Analysis Cure?* Chicago: University of Chicago Press.

Kris, E. (1951). Ego psychology and interpretation in psychoanalytic therapy. *Psychoanalytic Quarterly* 20:15–30.

———— (1956). The personal myth: a problem of psychoanalytic technique. In *Selected Papers of Ernst Kris,* pp. 272–300. New Haven, CT: Yale University Press, 1975.

Lacan, J. (1959). Desire and the interpretation of desire in *Hamlet.* In *Literature and Psychoanalysis,* ed. S. Felman. Baltimore: Johns Hopkins University Press, 1982.

———— (1966a). The Language of Alienation. In *Psychoanalytic Versions of the Human Condition,* ed. M. Oliner, P. Marcus, and A. Rosenberg. New York: New York University Press, 1998.

———— (1966b). Sole reflections on the ego. *International Journal of Psycho-Analysis* 34:11–17.

Lacan, J., and Granoff, W. (1956). Fetishism: the symbolic, the imaginary and the real. In *Perversions, Psychodynamics and Therapy,* ed. S. Lorand and M. Balint. New York: Gramercy Books.

Laplanche, J., and Pontalis, J. B. (1973). *The Language of Psychoanalysis.* New York: W.W. Norton.

Lévi-Strauss, C. (1949). *The Effectiveness of Symbols in Structural Anthropology.* New York: Basic Books.

——— (1951). *Language and the Analysis of Social Laws.* New York: Basic Books.

——— (1968). *Structural Anthropology.* New York: Penguin.

Loewald, H. (1960). On the therapeutic action of psychoanalysis. *International Journal of Psycho-Analysis* 41:16–33.

Maidenbaum, A., and Martin, S. (1991). *Lingering Shadows: Jungean Freudians and Anti-Semitism.* Boston: Shambhala.

Mann, T. (1933). Freud's position in the history of modern thought. *Past Masters.* New York: Knopf.

——— (1938). *Joseph in Egypt.* New York: Knopf.

Marienbad Symposium on the Theory of the Therapeutic Results of Psycho-Analysis. (1936). Glover, E., Fenichel, O., Strachey, J., Bergler, E., Nunberg, N., Bibring, E., participants. Fourteenth International Psycho-Analytical Congress, Marienbad.

Masson, J., trans., ed. (1985). *The Complete Letters of Sigmund Freud to Wilhelm Fliess, 1887–1904.* Cambridge: Harvard University Press.

McGuire, W., ed. (1974). *The Freud/Jung Letters: The Correspondence between Sigmund Freud and C. G. Jung,* trans. R. Manheim and R. F. C. Hull. Bollingen Series XCIV. Princeton: Princeton University Press.

Muller, J. P., and Richardson, W. J. (1982). *Lacan and Language.* New York: International Universities Press.

Nagel, E. (1961). *The Structure of Science.* New York: Harcourt, Brace & World.

Newman, E. (1970). Stages in religious experience and the path of depth psychology. *Israel Annual of Psychiatry* 8:232–254.

Nunberg, H., and Federn, E., eds. (1906–1918). *Minutes of the Vienna Psychoanalytic Society, 1906–1918,* vols. 1–4. New York: International Universities Press, 1962–1975.

Oliner, M. M. (1988). *Cultivating Freud's Garden in France.* Northvale, NJ: Jason Aronson.

Ostow, M. (1979). Letter to the editor. *International Journal of Psycho-Analysis,* 60:531–532.

Paskauskas, R. A., ed. (1993). *The Complete Correspondence of Sigmund Freud and Ernest Jones.* Cambridge: Harvard University Press.

Quinn, S. (1988). *A Mind of Her Own: The Life of Karen Horney.* Reading, MA: Addison-Wesley.

Rado, S. (1939). Developments in the psychoanalytic conception and treatment of the neuroses. *Psychoanalytic Quarterly* 8:427–437.

———— (1956). *Collected Papers, Vol. 1. Psychoanalysis of Behavior*. New York: Grune and Stratton.

Rank, O. (1907). *The Artist: The Beginning of Sexual Pathology*. Vienna: Heller.

———— (1909). *The Myth of the Birth of the Hero*. Nervous and Mental Diseases Monograph 18. English trans. pub. by Robert Brunner, New York, 1952.

———— (1912). *Das Inzestmotiv in Dichtung und Sage* [*Incest Motive in Poetry and Saga*]. Vienna: Deuticke.

———— (1913). Nakedness in saga and poetry. *Imago* 2:267–301, 409–446.

———— (1924). *The Trauma of Birth*. New York: Harcourt, Brace.

Rangell, L. (1982). Transference to theory: the relationship of psychoanalytic education to the analyst's relationship to psychoanalysis. *Annual of Psychoanalysis* 10:29–56.

Reich, A. (1951). The discussion of 1912 on masturbation and our present-day views. *The Psychoanalytic Study of the Child* 6:80–94. New York: International Universities Press.

Reich, W. (1928). On character analysis. In *The Psychoanalytic Reader*, ed. R. Fleiss, pp. 129–147. New York: International Universities Press, 1948.

———— (1929). The genital character and the neurotic character. In *The Psychoanalytic Reader*, ed. R. Fleiss, pp. 148–169. New York: International Universities Press, 1948.

———— (1930). Character formation and the phobias of childhood. In *The Psychoanalytic Reader*, ed. R. Fleiss, pp. 170–182. New York: International Universities Press, 1948.

———— (1942). *The Function of the Orgasm*. New York: Orgone Institute Press.

———— (1945). *Character Analysis*. New York: Orgone Institute Press.

Robinson, P., Roheim, G., Reich, W., and Marcuse, H. (1969). *The Freudian Left*. Ithaca: Cornell University Press.

Rubinstein, B. (1976). On the possibility of strictly clinical psychoanalytic theory. *Psychological Issues* 36:229–264.

Rudnytsky, P. L. (1985). Nietzsche's oedipus. *American Imago* 42(4):413–439.

Rudnytsky, P. L., Bókay, A., and Giampieri-Deutsch, P., eds. (1996). *Ferenczi's Turn in Psychoanalysis*. New York: New York University Press.

Rycroft, C. (1985). On ablation of parental images. In *Psychoanalysis and Beyond*. Chicago: University of Chicago Press.

Sandler, J. (1960). The background of safety. In *From Safety to Super Ego*, pp. 1–8. New York: Guilford, 1987.

Sass, L. A. (2001). The magnificent harlequin. *International Journal of Psycho-Analysis* 82:997–1018.

Saul, L. (1942). Review of *Escape from Freedom*. *Psychoanalytic Quarterly* 11: 245–248.

Schafer, R. (1976). *A New Language for Psychoanalysis*. New Haven, CT: Yale University Press.

Scharff, D. E., and Birtles, E. F. (1994). *From Instinct to Self: Selected Papers of W. R. D. Fairbairn*, vol. 1. Northvale, NJ: Jason Aronson.

Schimek, J. G. (1975). The interpretations of the past: childhood trauma, psychical reality, and historical truth. *Journal of the American Psychoanalytic Association* 23:845–865.

Segal, H. (1962). The curative factors in psychoanalysis. *International Journal of Psycho-Analysis* 43:212–17.

Soronoff, D. E., and Biztles, E. F. (1997). From instinct to self: the evolution and implication of W. R. D. Fairbairn's theory of object relations theory. *International Journal of Psychology* 78:1085–1103.

Stone, L. (1954). The widening scope of indications for psychoanalysis. *Journal of the American Psychoanalytic Association* 2:567–594.

Taft, J. (1958). *Otto Rank*. New York: Julian Press.

Tausk, V. (1912). On masturbation. *Psychoanalytic Study of the Child* 6:61–79. New York: International Universities Press, 1951.

Ticho, E. A. (1972). Termination of psychoanalysis: treatment goals, life goals. *Psychoanalytic Quarterly* 41:315–333.

Waelder, R. (1962). Psychoanalysis, scientific method, and philosophy. *Journal of the American Psychoanalytic Association* 10(1):617–637.

——— (1963). Historical fiction. *Journal of the American Psychoanalytic Association* 11:628–651.

——— (1970). Observation, historical reconstruction and experiment: an epistemological study. In *Psychoanalysis Observation Theory Application*, ed. C. Hanly and M. Lazerowitz, pp. 280–326. New York: International Universities Press.

Wallerstein, R. S. (1998). *Lay Analysis: Life Inside the Controversy*. Hillsdale, NJ: Analytic Press.

Winnicott, D. W. (1964). Memories, dreams, reflections. *International Journal of Psycho-Analysis* 45:450–55.

Edinburgh Symposium References

Garma, A. (1962). The curative factors in psycho-analysis. *International Journal of Psycho-Analysis* 43:221–224.

Gitelson, M. (1962). The curative factors in psycho-analysis. *International Journal of Psycho-Analysis* 43:194–205.

Heimann, P. (1962). The curative factors in psycho-analysis. *International Journal of Psycho-Analysis* 43:228–231.

King, P. (1962). The curative factors in psycho-analysis. *International Journal of Psycho-Analysis* 43:225–227.

Kuiper, P. (1962). The curative factors in psycho-analysis. *International Journal of Psycho-Analysis* 43:218–220.

Nacht, S. (1962). The curative factors in psycho-analysis. *International Journal of Psycho-Analysis* 43:206–211.

Segal, H. (1962). The curative factors in psycho-analysis. *International Journal of Psycho-Analysis* 43:212–217.

II

Prepared Contributions of the Participants Prior to the Conference

2

Dissidence—Disagreement and Alternate Hypotheses for the Foundation of Psychoanalysis: On the Importance of Examining the Underlying Meanings of Freud's Hypotheses

ANDRÉ GREEN

Once again, Martin Bergmann has put his immense knowledge, powerful reflection, and serene wisdom at our service, to help us clarify our thoughts on an important chapter of the history of psychoanalysis. Beyond the question of dissidence, implicitly, his essay deals with the question of the reference points of psychoanalytic thinking. This may allow us to understand the reasons that lead to the diversity of trends our vision has to encompass today in order to grasp explicit or implicit problems that upset the minds of the psychoanalysts, even without any threat of dissidence. I am grateful to Martin Bergmann for the work he has accomplished, but, unfortunately, I do not believe that a purely historical approach can fully explain the sources of the past and present disagreements. Of course, Martin Bergmann can argue on this and say this is not his topic, but there is no way in which we can avoid that question. I shall try to propose an explanation that seems to me necessary for having a working hypothesis that, appropriately discussed, could, I hope, guide us toward possible progress in our thinking about those matters.

I propose dropping the traditional point of view, considering Freud's theory, as dogma, a dissidence becoming a schism, wanting to correct its mistakes. Instead, I adopt a more neutral point of view: given a body of ideas, which acts as the starting point of the development of a practice and of a theory, what is the meaning of the disagreements of the other bodies of knowledge derived from it or, even, splitting from it?

Sometimes dissidence expresses a clear wish to part from Freudian psychoanalysis, because of a fundamental dissent on basic conceptions that give birth to alternate and independent disciplines that have gained their autonomy (Adler, Jung).

Other basic disagreements with Freud's fundamental options lead to new trends of psychoanalysis, forming subgroups, without wishing to split (Hartmann, Kohut, Melanie Klein, Lacan, etc.).

Between these two extremes, stands what has appeared in the course of history as adjunctions to the Freudian theory or different interpretations of basic notions or introduction of new views that, as time went by, led, willy-nilly, to a separation of the so-called classical Freudian mainstream of the discipline (Reich, Rank, Horney).

We are now in a position of having to consider the offspring of the subgroups within psychoanalysis. They only aim at modifying and improving Freud's basic concepts (Bion, Winnicott, Laplanche, Kernberg).

I agree with Martin Bergmann: "No one can be a classical analyst." Just as I would say an orthodox Freudian today is an abstraction. That is, even if some agree with Freud's basic hypotheses, these have to be necessarily modified and, by all means, reformulated and given a new content. As there are no more dissenters excluded from the analytic community, we are all dissenters, at some point, today. But we have to define what still links us to the Freudian theory.

FREUD

The roughly sketched categorizations I have presented are a preliminary step to circumscribe what I call the "Freudian core."

Freud had the intuition of the unconscious long before he described it. In the beginning, he tried different approaches, mostly clinical, and found himself in front of insolvable contradictions from, let's say, 1895 to 1900. We all know the decisive step he took with the exploration of dreams, mostly his own. *The Interpretation of Dreams* marks the beginning of psychoanalytic thinking. I would like to summarize what I consider important in the method and in the findings, as I think they still form the Freudian core.

Psychoanalysis has a triple aim:

1. To discover the basic structure of normal psychic functioning.
2. To apply the findings about it to the psychic understanding (and, if possible, cure) of the kind of pathology to which it can be applied and is the closest to normal functioning (neurosis). Bridges can be established in both ways (from normality to neurosis, from neurosis to normality), as, in fact, normality is always relative. The main idea is that the same principles could be found at play in normality and neurosis, with differences that will be defined. This implies that we address the aspects of normality that are the least under the control of consciousness, for example, dreams.
3. The investigation about the applications of the preceding principle to affections that do not belong to neurosis has brought new amendments required by their specific organizations. This extension produced additional basic concepts. In the end, many of the findings of Freud's late period concerning facts that do not belong to neurosis were, surprisingly, included in normal functioning (example: the splitting of the ego). So normality was also connected with psychosis. Three methods have evolved:
   a. The Freudian method always follows the same path; it goes from what is better known about psychic activity by the supposedly normal mind of the analyst trying to elucidate the most obscure part of his own psychic activity (dream), and extends his knowledge progressively to what is ignored in the disturbed patients, which seems to have little connection with normal functioning.
   b. During the history of psychoanalysis, another method was proposed that did the reverse of the preceding one. It consisted in starting from what analysts think as the most primitive (that is, the deeper, the earlier in development and the most disturbed) and to retrace the hypothetic evolution which leads to normality (Klein). Here, we start with

the most unknown or deeply uncovered, to reach the most apparent, which can be observed at the surface.

c. More recently, another method appeared. It consists in postulating, as Freud, what could be the normal structure of the mind (seen in interaction with another mind), giving up any concern about its links and its relationship to the different categories of pathology, which are supposed to be determined by specific mechanisms.

My preference is the first method, in which the starting point is the mind of the analyst, with the possibility of a topographical regression, in order to proceed in the task of defining its specificity for psychoanalysis, which does not appear in the simple descriptive approach, but follows the indirect path of an unconscious formation (dream, fantasy, transference, etc.).

It is important to note that Freud has chosen, from all the possible angles of normality, the one that escaped consciousness—the dream. He first came to the conclusion that the functioning of the dream evoked the better type of functioning that he observed in neurosis and, later, in psychosis. The conclusion he drew was that neurosis has its germ within normality. Psychosis was included later. Normality included and sometimes masked some parts of its own functioning because of a kind of censorship that, even during the day, could be released, in a small proportion (conscious fantasy). He then concluded that the refraining force was repression. Moreover, when thinking about the dream, he realized that there were connections between the dream thoughts and thoughts that were present during the day. At some point of his investigations, he felt that some kind of force seemed to oppose the progress of the associations on the dream (resistance), especially if the dream was told to some significant person (transference). He connected this inhibition, which seemed to oppose the progression of associations, with another force of opposite nature, where thoughts seemed to circulate more freely during the dream than during the waking state (primary process). Therefore, the dream was not only a special form of narrative, it was endowed with forces and undergoes unconscious work. Also, it conveyed a sense of reality that, by no means, was inferior to the one during our awake time (psychic reality).

Repression, resistance, primary process, transference, and psychic reality are present here, without even having to mention the most important one: the discovery of the unconscious. For him, this was the basis for a new theory of psychic activity. A central role has to be given to wish fulfillment. Moreover, comparing the findings of the dream with other psychic events, he had to conclude that there was a tendency to come back, again and again, to the same wishes, already a kind of compulsion. This finally was the explanation for transference. Not only the wishes were important, but, even more, their tendency to be transferred. About the nature of the wishes, he decided to root them in internal moves (drives) driven from inside. He labeled their guiding principles: pleasure–unpleasure principle, reality principle.

Nevertheless, what was even more important than everything else was Freud's discovery that all the characteristics that were drawn from the analysis of the dream could be found—with a proper method (free association, as dream-like thinking)—without any dreaming. Finally, this allowed for the building of the theory of the unconscious.

An important change took place, later, in Freud's work. Freud started by thinking that the dream could serve as an intermediary formation between normality and neurosis (everybody dreams: normal people, people from different cultures, patients of all kind, neurotics, psychotics, etc.). Later on, he changed his ideas about dreams. In the "Outline," Freud (1940) parallels the dream with psychosis: "A dream then is a psychosis" (*Standard Edition*, XXIII, p. 172), a benign and reversible one. The conclusion is in many ways in agreement with other Freud's views that this form of psychosis is also part of our normal functioning, especially when we are not awake. Our ego is potentially psychotic. It is unconscious of its own defenses. This modifies the Freudian core because it now has to include a psychotic nucleus. Modern writers deal differently with this observation (M. Klein, W. R. Bion, D. W. Winnicott, H. Searles).

From this core, we can orient ourselves in many directions, for instance, the wish fulfillment of the dream leads us through fantasy to desire. And from there to pleasure and eroticism. The concept of the drive and the pleasure-seeking object are seen as consequences. The core can also guide us toward the relationship to reality, the differences between the accomplishment of the wish fulfillment (in fantasy, reality, etc.) and the repression of reality in psychosis. It deals with the relationship of normality to neurosis, perversion, psychosis, etc. So we understand the core as a kind of roundabout, susceptible to orient us on different paths.

This observation may help in seeing the differences with the other main dissident hypotheses.

Freud's insistence is manifested not only on pleasure seeking, but also on the solutions the psychic apparatus can find when circumstances happen to oppose the ordinary solutions of the realization of the wish (reality, censorship, prohibition, etc.).

This is what I call the Freudian core with its historical variations. I believe it is still true today; I believe that any psychoanalytic theory of any kind has to show no disagreement with its value as the fundamental principle of psychoanalytic thought, whatever adjunctions or corollaries are called for. I will consider as real dissidence any theory, whatever it says, that is in disagreement with this core, explicitly or not. This is not a value judgment, just an observation.

Please note that I do not say that the Freudian core is the earliest mental functioning, neither do I deny the existence of other types of psychic functioning, nor do I even say it is normal functioning; I am only saying that it is the more fundamental setting of ideas to understand Freud's basic assumptions to build a new field of knowledge and to name it psychoanalysis. Because what is implied in this basic assumption is that there is a part of psychic activity that is animated by what is known as wish fulfillment, and that it is this part that is the center of psychoanalysis. What we have labeled wish fulfillment is a representative of a larger series, including pleasure seeking, eroticism, fantasy, satisfaction, drive functioning, etc. But not motivation, please; that's a concept good for rats.

This part has to be recognized as the core of the Freudian thought, because, as I see it, it is the most powerful part of the psychic activity, which raises our interest in life, keeps it the most alive, incites movements of curiosity, stimulates our intelligence, and, most of the time, increases the field of our investments and extends our relationships, though it can be neither operative nor fruitful unless an important part of it remains repressed. It is evaluated through the activation of the unconscious and, also, according to the emotional states associated with it.

In reviewing these well-known facts, I wish to say that I have tried without pedantry to propose a general statement: Every dissidence, open or hidden, stems from a disagreement with this Freudian core. Every dissidence always, in one way or another, refuses, partly or totally, this core. The disagreement is increased when we add Freud's explanations on the reasons, mechanisms, causes, and constructions of this basic model. In other words, a great portion of contemporary psychoanalysis is in more or less permanent, more or less complete, dissidence.

What I have defined as the Freudian core—if I cannot prove it is universal—was, at least, present in *all* the people who have come to me: patients, candidates, consultants, etc., with all kinds of pathology. Even with severely disturbed people who seem to display other prevalent features, the core is there, in a disguised or modified form that never completely covers it. The better a disturbed patient gets, the more visible the core becomes.

We have to avoid confusing the core with normality, because its presence can be found beyond the so-called normality. I would prefer labeling it as the conditions for a fruitful psychic functioning, in a way that the analyst can grasp it analytically and convey it to other analysts who share the same preoccupations of analyzing psychic activity with some common basic hypotheses related to an unconscious activity, whatever their disagreements are about the way they conceive it.

TOPICS OF DISSENT

The concepts Freud found to justify and explain this core stimulated important discussion about some of his postulates: the localization of the process (the inner world), the nature of the force (the drive), its qualification (libido and destruction), the causes that determine its activation (internal conflict), the guiding principles (pleasure–unpleasure, reality), the role of the object, the cause of anxiety, etc.

The more Freud became explicit about his thinking, the more the whole conception raised criticism and became unacceptable on some points, or on its global proposed understanding.

To understand the building of Freud's theory, one must notice that it took many years for Freud to succeed in giving a complete picture of what he was trying to say. The first period extends from 1900 (*The*

Interpretation of Dreams) to 1913 (*Totem and Taboo*). Freud, starting from the dream, had to progressively include the psychopathology of everyday life, the theory of sexuality (1905), language (*Jokes*, 1905), art (Gradiva 1907, Leonardo 1910), clinical applications (Dora in 1901, Hans in 1909, Rat Man in 1909, Schreber in 1911), technique (1911–13), anthropology (*Totem and Taboo*, 1913). In other words, Freud's theory encompasses normality, clinical and technical applications, art (sublimation), and the consideration of other (so-called primitive) cultures (anthropology).

Along the way, dissent became obvious, for more and more followers had opportunities to disagree on one point or another. I shall mention only two other phases after the completion: from 1913 to 1920, a period of progressive transition; and from the last phase starting in 1920 until the end. I consider this last period as the most important, and it is significantly different from what has been called structural theory. But it is interesting to see that, after the first period, dissidence seldom led anymore to exclusion, but rather to the progressive formations of subgroups destined to promote conceptions meant to improve psychoanalysis, however far from Freud's ideas.

In the present situation, the problem is not anymore to agree or disagree with Freud. Freud's theory, after having been scrutinized for what to retain from his work and what to abandon (M. Gill), is now marginalized. His work, for many, represents a sort of prehistory of our discipline. Freud is seen as a Neanderthalian psychoanalyst.

To summarize, I shall distinguish some major events in the history of psychoanalysis in view of our discussion:

1. The split with Adler, Jung, and some others around 1912.
2. The period of Ferenczi's last work (1929–1933).
3. The second breakthrough by Hartmann, Melanie Klein, and Lacan's revisions. From this date on, the unity of psychoanalysis becomes questionable because of the opposite factions that developed within it and spread over the world.
4. The relational perspective (and its multiple subgroups), which began after the Kohutian mutation.

I do not consider that the tolerance to a multiple conception of psychoanalysis is an acceptable condition. Fragmentation is a step toward death. Our task is to try to confront the main hypotheses, to discuss them at length, and to try to find a way of re-creating not a common ground, but rather an open unified conception of psychoanalysis.

A Special Case: Ferenczi

I would like to make a special case of the issue born in 1923 to 1924 with Rank and Ferenczi. I will not spend much time on Rank, because the issue is so contradicted by facts that it fails without even having to be argued. But an interesting case of dissent in the history of psychoanalysis is Ferenczi. It is not an easy conflict to settle. Ferenczi discussed traditional techniques. His criticism on that point is valid. It has not prevented psychoanalysts from holding on to their rather rigid attitude. But this is not the essential of his contribution. Ferenczi's true discovery was his description of severely disturbed patients (severely neurotic, nonneurotic, psychotic, or borderline). He has indisputably shown how these clinical pictures did not fit into the teachings of the so-called classical Freudian analysis, neither clinically nor technically. We owe him the description of some of the deepest mechanisms of pathology shown by these patients in his works between 1929 to 1933. His clinical diary is a most valuable document.

On the other hand, Ferenczi's technique was entirely wrong. Freud was wrong in his misunderstanding of Ferenczi, and Ferenczi was wrong in his innovations (mutual analysis). The contradictory solutions he adopted were not the answer. We are still in want of a valuable one. We are still searching for the proper technique. We still have a lot of work to do.

WHY FRAGMENTATION?

To understand the reasons for the fragmentation of psychoanalysis, and without mentioning personal factors, which everyone can claim to have, we have to consider different factors:

1. The unexpected revelation of difficulties in the cure of many patients, which were considered as good indications of analysis. Freud was very much aware of that until the end of his

life. His successive modifications of theory are linked to this fact.

2. The inclusion, in the analytic field, of a new category of patients for which the main concepts of theory were neither appropriate nor useful (borderline cases, nonneurotic structures).

3. The change of paradigms in the fields of science and epistemology. It is not easy either to ignore them, arguing about the specificity of analytic knowledge, or, for the same reason, to passively submit to them, ignoring the requirements of psychoanalysis. But the development of new concepts must enhance reflection in the analytic field and promote the appropriate guidelines that structure the development of analytic thinking.

4. The changes in the leading new concepts in psychoanalysis, which are the result of the combination of the three preceding factors. Still, there is resistance to change, not only by conservative trends, but also because the proposed changes do not seem always compatible with psychoanalytic thinking. It is striking to observe how, in the course of the evolution of psychoanalysis, little effort has been made to clarify what is the specificity of our thinking and how, in the psychoanalytic community, different central hypotheses have shaped our field of knowledge, giving birth to a plurality of trends. Our specific way of thinking can be testified in the comparison of our works with the works of contiguous disciplines (psychology, psychiatry, sociology, etc.).

I believe that, in order to progress in this direction, we need to focus on the core concept (starting with Freud, but proceeding to today) and to examine to what extent it is compatible with scientific thinking or with the other present trends of thought, as modern philosophy and epistemology (in their diverse aspects) invite us to examine.

THERE ARE MANY ROOMS IN THE HOUSE OF GOD

If we think of the present state of fragmentation of psychoanalysis, we can see how the present descriptions of some of the most important movements of our discipline have led to a progressive resignation about our differences rather than to a real acceptance, integration, and clear understanding of the fundamentals of the different trends. Looking at it, we will be struck by four factors:

1. The violence of the fights in the past between fractions of psychoanalysis (ego psychology vs. Kleinian psychoanalysis, classical French psychoanalysis vs. Lacanianism). I remember the time when Otto Kernberg was considered as a half-dissident. Finally, he won the battle against his opponents. One has forgotten the long ago battles when opponents treated each other in offending terms (Greenson–Rosenfeld, Rangell–Green), without any real attempts at understanding differences. Remember the International Psychoanalytic Association congresses of fifty years ago!

2. The present consensus is not less surprising. Superficial points of agreement have been found without really giving the feeling that the basic differences have been thoroughly discussed. It is interesting to note that the kind of cease-fire of the present situation is more dependent on a context of crisis (in the hope that the adoption of a conciliation may save psychoanalysis from the dangers threatening its existence). I still defend the idea that a true examination of the differences has not taken place. Debates are feared; shields are supposed to protect from narcissistic wounds.

3. If there are indisputable signs of mutual influences in some parts of the world (contemporary Freudians and Kleinians in Great Britain, Lacanians and non-Lacanians in France, etc.), in the overall picture some of the most original thinkers remain relatively isolated (Winnicott's influence, which is very important in France, is, on the whole, mostly ignored in the United States and limited in Latin America; Bion is largely undervalued in the United States, where Kleinianism is supposed to begin to be accepted; Bion's difference with the other Kleinians is underestimated). Searles, considered as an important thinker in France, is nearly ignored in the United States.

4. One of the most important factors in recent psychoanalysis has been the rise of a new objectivistic approach to child development, under the inspiration of Peter Fonagy, which brings research to the fore. This change of perspective leaning on developmental psychology neglects the methodological problems

of psychoanalysis, with insufficient criticism of the parameters of such a trend and of their compatibility with the psychoanalytic way of thinking.

FAREWELL TO DISSENTERS OF THE PAST AND TO THOSE OF THE FUTURE

I do not think a retrospective view on dissidence can help us in solving our present problems. It has shown us that superficial tolerance leads to an impasse.

Except for the *Controversies* of 1941–1945 in London, which led to an unique cross-examination with deep scrutiny of the divergences, there is no other real debate like this one.

Looking back at the history of dissidence, I cannot say that I would wish to apologize to any of the dissenters. The truth is that they form a polymorphous group. Adler and Jung could not stand Freud's psychoanalysis for different reasons. Both could not cope with the idea of libido. Adler was advocating factors belonging to reality. As a principle, I would say that any psychoanalytic conception, wanting to defend the idea of a direct influence of reality (and even more, social reality) upon psychic activity is wrong because it bypasses everything we know about inner structuralization. Jung believed in an inherited ancestral wisdom, and conceived the collective unconscious as a reserve that would provide the answers to the subject. A quick glance at religions, myths, and folktales gives us a vision where a happy end helps in forgetting the violence, the savagery, the work of the most harsh drives. And it is still going on in reality.

After Adler and Jung, the psychoanalytical movement was in turmoil, because it attracted all kinds of people, including some who were mentally ill (Reich), or whose honesty was suspected (Stekel). If some criticisms could be raised about the way these people have been excluded from the psychoanalytic community (Reich), I cannot say the decisions were wrong.

Other cases are more delicate. I am referring to the psychoanalysts whose aim was to criticize Freud's biological background and relative neglect of social influences. Here, too, I find myself on the side of Freud. The "culturalist movement" was, in fact, very poor. Having studied them, I do not regret the departure of H. S. Sullivan, Fromm, C. Thomson, and K. Horney. Again, we find the idea of a primary direct social influence on the mind and a negation of the significance of the Oedipus complex. How can identification come into play without including a social dimension? Didn't Freud speak of the "sexualization of social instincts" in the Schreber case? There is more to study on the topic (Berenstein, Puget).

It is not only because psychic factors come first and social ones later. It is mostly that the first ones take place at a more fundamental infrastructural level, and the second ones on a superstructural level. We have seen deeply rooted Marxist convictions, which sometimes led to important contributions, being dropped down in a phase of the evolution of a person without major changes in the structure of his/her personality. The changes were about the superficial aspects of the person. Otherwise, we have to examine Freud's discoveries from the angle of his bourgeois origins, which is a misunderstanding of his work (Marx, also, was a German bourgeois). The same idea applies, today, to the so-called brain factors. If they are not put in perspective and related to epigenetical factors, they are of little help.

MODERN TRENDS

All this leads to the consideration of these questions: What is psychic causality (Green 1995), and how do we interpret psychic events, considering their relationship to the unconscious or to the basic elements of theory? Once again, I will plead for an epistemological analysis of Freudian concepts. What is their meaning in Freud's terms? How do we understand them today? Is our present-day analysis in continuity with the psychoanalytic way of thinking, or are we shifting from this point of view to a new approach, closer to psychology, physiology, or sociology?

Today, the question is: What are the basic elements necessary to build a theory? We are split between different trends, which are usually seen as antagonistic:

- Drive theory (Freud)
- Object relationships (Fairbairn, M. Klein, Sandler)

- Attachment theory (Fonagy)
- Ego psychology (Hartmann)
- Self psychology (Kohut)
- Intersubjective and relational (Renik, Greenberg, and Mitchell)
- Theory of the signifier (Lacan)

Around these poles, other psychoanalysts have built very interesting constructions, sometimes richer than these extreme points of view. They are the result of a blending: Winnicott and W. R. Bion, derived from a double paternity—Freud and Klein. We can realize how far these theoretical constructs are from Freud, and I will not try to defend their orthodoxy. Both are original in their own way. Both seem to me very creative, and account for the more complex activities of the mind, born, most of the time, from the psychoanalytic experience with patients (children and adults), belonging more to borderline personality disorders, or even psychotic structures, than to neurosis. Though I am not strictly a follower of either of these theorists, I have been inspired, in my own work, by their theories. They provided me with the richness, the complexities, the diversity of psychic functioning in its different fields; they represent the psychoanalytic way of thinking, or what I have also called the psychoanalytic spirit.

CONCLUSION

There is no dissidence in present-day psychoanalysis, because there is a widespread dissent. Taking it too seriously would lead to minute splitting, war, and death. So we have found compromise: pretense of tolerance, search for willy-nilly common sharings that are not very convincing and appear as life jackets to avoid sinking. I am not pessimistic, just realistic. I prefer to stand on the side of those who pretend that the multiple points of view are not always compatible, because our postulates are different—not because I prefer disagreement to agreement or war to peace, but because, at least from this point, we are forced to confront our postulates, our axioms, our hypotheses, our results, our ways of thinking about problems that are partly common to all, and partly different. Cultural traditions seem more important than we thought.

The dissidence of the past, I am sorry to disagree with Martin Bergmann, is not of great help in understanding that of the present. It is too late for regrets. The best we can do is to look, without compromise, at the present, analyze it, discuss the matter between ourselves, and, when necessary, with others, and try to understand where the real differences are. There should lie the reason for our meeting or for a meeting to come.

3
"Dissidence" in Psychoanalysis: A Psychoanalytic Reflection*

OTTO F. KERNBERG

The present "age of pluralism" in psychoanalytic theorizing justifies a new look at the historical aspects of dissidence and change in the development of psychoanalysis during the past century. A conference on this subject organized around a fundamental contribution to this subject by Martin Bergmann (Part I, this volume) stimulated this contribution. What follows is a general reflection on dissidence in psychoanalysis.

"Dissidence" is defined (*Concise Oxford Dictionary*) as disagreement, especially with the religious doctrines of an established church. Dissidence within psychoanalysis thus implies an ideological or religious quality of psychoanalytic convictions, and implicitly raises questions about the scientific nature of psychoanalysis. Bergmann (this volume) quotes Freud as stating that disagreements regarding psychoanalytic theories should be settled with empirical evidence. Yet Freud, Bergmann goes on, also asserted that rejection of some basic psychoanalytic theories reflected psychologically motivated resistance to the truth of psychoanalysis, implying that the perfectly analyzed psychoanalyst would

---

*A chapter in *Power of Understanding*, a Festschrift honoring Veikko Tälikä, edited by Aira Laine, will be published by Karnac, London.

not present such opposition. Dissidence, according to this latter view, again has the connotation of opposing ideological or religious belief systems rather than of engaging in scientific discourse.

If one translates the question of dissidence into the question of the nature of scientific evidence in psychoanalysis, the focus shifts to the development of methods for empirical examination of controversial issues. I assume that, even in the current relatively immature stage of methodology of scientific research in psychoanalysis, some issues may be approached empirically. These might include the nature of the analytic relationship, the interaction of technique and process and between process and outcome, and the effectiveness of psychoanalytic treatment, for example. But many fundamental questions must remain open, and can only be resolved gradually, by means of the cumulative clinical experience of the profession, and the shared communication and evaluation of this clinical experience over time.

As Bergmann points out in his overview of the main contributions stemming from psychoanalytic dissidents, many of their theories, originally rejected by the psychoanalytic community, were eventually woven into the main fabric of psychoanalytic theory and method. Bergmann raises a fascinating question: What made some of these dissidents "dissidents," and what made some potential dissidents "modifiers" who enriched psychoanalytic theory with their contributions? His central thesis is that, at least in the early generation of dissidents, the personal relationship with Freud played a major role. It is an open question as to what extent the personal relationship to Freud's thinking continued having such a central role for the dissidents and modifiers who emerged after his death. While I am in essential agreement with the major proposal of Martin Bergmann, in what follows I shall take on the role of a "modifier," building on his rich contributions while focusing on the varying influence that personal, scientific, cultural, and institutional factors have on the emergence of dissidents.

THE PERSONAL RELATIONSHIP WITH FREUD

Bergmann describes convincingly the importance of the development of personal conflicts, particularly rivalries between Freud and his early disciples, with clear implications of oedipal conflicts and sibling rivalry as major contributors to the development of dissidents. Perhaps the most striking illustration of this dynamic is the gradual sharpening of the disagreements between Freud and Adler, and the eventual departure of Adler from the psychoanalytic group. But Adler is one among many, including Jung, Rank, Ferenczi, Horney, and Wilhelm Reich. All of these dissidents had personal relations with Freud, but at a certain point, when their contributions ran counter to Freud's convictions and the related boundaries of psychoanalytic formulations of the time, they met with sharp criticisms that reinforced their insistence on their particular views, finally leading to a split.

I agree with Bergmann that a personal disappointment either in their psychoanalysis or in the relationship with Freud played an important role. Obviously, behind that conflict were issues of the psychopathology of all participants, activated by the regressive effects of the personal psychoanalysis, and by the institutional reinforcement of such conflicts as these, which resonated with the psychoanalytic movement's relationship to its founder and charismatic leader. In fact, one might raise the question of whether what appeared on the surface as personal conflicts with Freud might not have been unconsciously stimulated by the innocent bystanders of the psychoanalytic movement. By "innocent bystanders" I am referring to the psychology of regressive group processes that enact profound ambivalence toward the leader, expressing the hostility by a selected opponent or subgroup, which permits the silent majority to deny its own aggression, acting as innocent bystanders. While these analysts admired Freud and followed him without questions, their unconscious hostility might have been enacted through fostering the conflict with Freud of a selected "representative" or scapegoat.

Freud was open to new ideas, and changed his views significantly in the course of time, but he was strongly assertive of them at any particular point. His efforts to integrate the thinking of his disciples when it did not correspond entirely to his own may at times have been facilitated by those closest to him. At other times the influence of his close friends may have increased the sharp differences between Freud's views and those of a young challenger. The personalized accentuation of the differences of their theoretical and technical formulations from those of Freud strongly suggests that the young challengers had intense feelings about these differences. Much of the more subtle dynamics of the early group probably is no longer available for scrutiny, but what we can assess is the influence of cultural factors on the different viewpoints that evolved, and the use of ideology to support and rationalize more personal struggles.

What was the influence of Freud's rigidity in asserting his viewpoints? In all fairness, the enormous scope of Freud's discoveries, the continuous broadening of the world of unconscious conflicts, and their consequences that he opened up would make it reasonable to think that it was difficult for the early group to absorb, in addition, the theoretical and clinical breakthroughs stemming from his disciples. When such contributions were presented with an aggressive assertion of revolutionary "uniqueness," like that of Adler, and, eventually, Rank, an impatient rejection of their ideas seems understandable. I believe, however, that what haunted the psychoanalytic movement, and continues to haunt organized psychoanalysis to this day, is that the clinical basis of psychoanalytic discoveries, the knowledge learned from psychoanalysis as an investigative tool, is fraught with methodological difficulties. The mutual influences of analysts' theories and patients' regressive deployment render decisions regarding alternative theoretical formulations very difficult to make. The inevitable subjectivity and uncertainty of the clinical process will be resolved (if ever) only after an entire generation of analysts has approached the problem from different viewpoints, and sufficient knowledge has been accumulated for the entire psychoanalytic movement to move on.

For example, Ferenczi's (1949) stress on the importance of the mother–infant relationship, and with it, the emphasis on preoedipal development turned out to be an extremely important advance in psychoanalytic understanding. It was elaborated later on by Melanie Klein, Winnicott, and Mahler, but it would take still another generation to establish a synthetic view that would integrate the preoedipal and oedipal stages of development in the concept of the archaic oedipal constellation. Similarly, Adler's stress on the importance of competitiveness and aggression would only later be integrated into the psychoanalytic mainstream, under the influence of newly accumulated information from the psychoanalytic treatment of severe psychopathologies, leading to Freud's discovery of the importance of repetition compulsion and superego pathology.

It might be argued, of course, that psychoanalysis as an institution might have been more open to new ideas had the leadership been more functional and less authoritarian. New ideas might then have been welcomed, studied, elaborated, and integrated, rather than having to undergo periods of dissidence and reencounter. But the enormous difference between Freud's creativity and the dependent attitude of his disciples probably constituted such a powerful dynamic that a more relaxed search for consensus might have slowed down the pace of Freud's own discoveries and contributions. Here the question of the extent to which it is functional that the psychology of the institution adapts to the personality of the creative leader becomes relevant. In other words, some degree of authoritarianism on the part of an extremely creative leader may represent a reduction in an organization's optimal functioning, but a price well worth paying for supporting such a leader. In all fairness, one also may grant the dangerous nature of experimenting with a new investigative tool, namely psychoanalytic exploration, as causative in bringing about the inappropriate aspect of the behavior of those early disciples.

THE IMPACT OF IDEOLOGICAL CROSS-CURRENTS ON THE DEVELOPMENT OF DISSIDENCE

Bergmann describes convincingly Jung's deep adherence to religion and mythology, with its linkage to German Romanticism, and ultimately to racist nationalism and anti-Semitism, and his irresponsible immersion in the Nazi culture. By the same token, Freud's profound identification with the rationalist and atheist culture of the nineteenth century may have contributed to Jung's rationalization of his departure from the psychoanalytic movement (McGuire 1974).

It is only in the last thirty years that various psychoanalytic contributors have reflected on the subtly militant atheism of psychoanalysis's ideological stance toward religion, expressed in the not infrequently heard statements in the 1950s and the 1960s that a well-analyzed person could no longer be a religious one. The concern over psychoanalysis becoming a "Weltanschauung" was first expressed by Chasseguet-Smirgel and Grunberger (1969), and has led in recent times to a meaningful reexploration of the relationship between psychoanalysis and religion, for example, in the Mainz seminars in Germany (Kernberg 2000b).

Marxism became the ideological crosscurrent that influenced the dissidence of Wilhelm Reich, was already a factor in Alfred Adler's partisan political stance regarding the social democratic party in Austria, and reemerged in Erich Fromm's critique of capitalist societies. Perhaps the most extreme representatives of this ideological development were Herbert Marcuse's (1955) utilization of psychoanalytic thinking as part of what might be called a Marxist theology of liberation, and Althusser's utilization of the superego concept, bringing together Lacan and Marx in analyzing the ideological superstructure of capitalism. The demise of Soviet Communism and the loss of popularity of Marxist ideology in general has brought about a curious disappearance of the psychoanalytic community's concern with the relationship between psychoanalysis and Marxism, but we must remember how it agitated the entire psychoanalytic generation in the 1960s and 1970s, leading, for example, to the splitting off of Marxist groups from the psychoanalytic societies in Argentina. Those Marxist groups have, in the meantime, disappeared entirely.

The most recent of these cross-cultural currents has been the feminist critique of Freud, expressed along a broad spectrum, from the thoughtful contributions of Melanie Klein and Edith Jacobson, correcting Freud's assumptions about early superego development in women, to the general critique of the primary nature of penis envy in women, and to the dissidence of Karen Horney (Benjamin 1986, Blum 1976, Horney 1967). The marginalizing of Horney is especially to be regretted in the light of the later integration of new understanding of early development in both genders, stemming from both the North American and European recent literature. Karen Horney's departure from the New York Psychoanalytic Society was probably determined less by the heretical nature of her ideas than by the internal conflicts of the then monolithic institution to which she belonged.

It is difficult to assess concurrently—rather than with hindsight— to what extent ideological currents infiltrate psychoanalytic thinking and codetermine the differential characteristics of psychoanalytic institutions in different countries today. When a general cultural agreement prevails in a certain region of the world, psychoanalytic institutions may not even be aware of those cultural influences on psychoanalytic development. For example, the strong adaptational stress on the part of American ego psychology, the assumed normal adaptation to an "average expectable environment" (Solnit 2000, p. 181), the Hartmann era emphasis on the positive functions of the ego in facilitating adaptation, and the tendency to reject the concept of a primary aggressive drive (let alone the concept of a death drive) all flourished in the optimistic cultural development of the United States after the end of World War II (Bergmann 2000). Meanwhile, predominance of concern over primitive aggression was strongly developed in Great Britain during and immediately after the war years.

The spread of Lacanian psychoanalysis, with its stress on philosophy and rejection of Anglo-American empiricism has had a strong impact on Latin American psychoanalytic societies living within a francophone cultural environment, while it has left only the merest traces in the humanities departments of American universities. It is interesting, furthermore, how the recent stress within the biological sciences on genetics and the revolution in neurosciences have prompted psychoanalysts to reexamine the relationship between mind and brain, an interest totally absent from the psychoanalytic culture of only ten or twenty years ago. It is significant, it seems to me, that the idolatrous attitude toward Freud of most of his followers during those years did not include recognition of his great interest in neurology and the relationship of mind and brain.

My point is that, during periods of rapid cultural shifts, when new ideological currents clash with traditional influences upon psychoanalytic thinking, that clash may contribute to the development of dissidence, eventually exaggerated as a system of rationalization for opposition that has deeper roots in psychoanalytic institutional dynamics.

INTRINSIC CHALLENGES OF PSYCHOANALYTIC THEORY AND TECHNIQUE TO THE CONVENTIONAL ASSUMPTIONS OF MASS CULTURE

Here I enter a problematic area of argument. One often hears, particularly in conservative psychoanalytic circles, that the hard times psychoanalysis is presently undergoing are related to the ongoing threat of Freud's findings to conventional assumptions of mankind. I believe that this argument tends to underestimate the serious problems that psychoanalysis has created for itself by accepting, indeed enacting, its reputation as isolationist, elitist, and biased against empirical research. However, I believe the argument holds in terms of the persistence, within conventional culture, at least of the Western world, of the myths of the sexual innocence of childhood, the basic goodness of human beings, and the positive consequence of any human encounter in which at least one of the two parties is attempting to help the other. As Max Gittelson put it simply, there are many people who believe in psychoanalysis, except sex, aggression, and transference.

These conventional assumptions are often called "resistance" to psychoanalytic concepts, an unfortunate misuse of a term whose specific meaning in psychoanalysis has to do with the manifestation of defensive operations in the psychoanalytic situation. This definition has particular implications for a contemporary theory of technique; more about this later.

The assumption of infantile sexuality, one of the most revolutionary discoveries of Freud, will probably be accepted in theory by every psychoanalyst. In practice, however, the ignorance or neglect of infantile sexuality shows up again and again in the theorizing of dissidents as well as in various technical approaches within the psychoanalytic establishment. Thus, Jung's stress on the collective unconscious and archaic archetypes pointedly neglected infantile sexuality, and, as Bergmann pointed out, Jung accused Freud of having elevated sexuality to the equivalent of a religious commitment. Rank's stress on the fundamental importance of the relationship of the infant to the mother likewise de-emphasized infantile sexuality, and even Ferenczi, in accentuating the devastating effects of sexual abuse and traumatization on the child, implicitly turned back to that innocent view of childhood.

Melanie Klein's formulations, although they incorporated the concept of the premature oedipalization as a defense against preoedipal aggression, in practice stressed preoedipal conflicts almost to the exclusion of the erotic quality of the relationship between infant and mother. Only in the last ten years, probably under the influence of contacts with French psychoanalysis, has the focus on oedipal conflicts again been accentuated in the work of Kleinian authors. Karen Horney, Kohut's self psychology, and the intersubjective and relational psychoanalytic schools evince an underemphasis of unconscious oedipal conflicts. It is as if the vissitudes of infantile sexuality have to be rediscovered, again and again, against this cultural trend influencing psychoanalytic practice and theorizing.

The rejection of Freud's dual drive theory of libido and aggression and its replacement by an object relations approach also reflect the tendency to underestimate both infantile sexuality and aggression (Kernberg 2001). This shows clearly in the clinical illustrations of intersubjective, relational, and self psychological case material, for example, in the symposium on "The Good, the Bad, and the Ugly," organized by all the New York–based IPA psychoanalytic institutions and the leading psychoanalytic journals in New York in 1991 (Kernberg 2003). Perhaps self psychology has been most outspoken in this regard, and Kohut's proposal that aggression derives from the traumatic fragmentation of the self may be the most specific formulation of that view. Erich Fromm's (1941) views imply that, in an optimally arranged society, the degree of aggression would decrease significantly. As Bergmann pointed out, Fromm was deeply critical of Freud because of his pessimistic stance in this regard.

The empirical research on attachment, of significant clinical as well as theoretical importance regarding early development, tends to focus primarily on the traumatic effects of mother's lack of normal responsiveness to the baby. Extrapolating from that research, the intersubjective and relational approaches have focused on the analyst's inevitable failures to understand these effects as traumatic, requiring repair via appropriate interpretation before the analytic process can go on. In this regard the approaches follow a path not dissimilar from the techniques of self psychology. As in the theories of Fairbairn, the emphasis on the traumatic origin of neurosis and unconscious conflict implicitly denies the central importance of the disposition to aggression.

In the light of contemporary affect theory, and the probability, as I have suggested, that the drives are supraordinate integrations, respectively, of positive and negative affects, one may question the primary nature of the drives, but not the primary nature of both negative and positive affects, the disposition to rage, anger, hatred, and disgust, as well as to joyful contact and erotic pleasure. The primary nature of both intense positive and negative affect states and their influence on structure building supports, I believe, Freud's basic dual drive theory (Kernberg

1992b). It may be argued that only under pathological circumstances may aggression become so dominant that the effort to destroy all relationships—including the self—may become the dominant motivation, thus crystallizing as a death drive in some severely psychopathological conditions. That is a far cry, however, from the systematic underemphasis on the importance of the conflict between libido and aggression at all levels of psychological development implicit in many dissidents' objections to Freud's dual drive theory.

Regarding the transference, the painful reality that unconscious negative dispositions from many sources are an important aspect of the unconscious relationship of the patient with the analyst, of the defensive object relations in the transference that we call resistance, and an important part of the technical challenges for the analyst, is another culturally supported source of denial. The stress on the "real" relationship between patient and analyst, not as a consequence of transference interpretation but as a precondition for transference analysis, has led to an ever-reemerging tendency to induce the patient's cooperation seductively with supportive interventions. The problematic trend in earlier ego psychological approaches to stress the "overcoming" of resistances and the misinterpretation of their functions only more recently corrected in the work of Paul Gray and Fred Busch also serve as rationalization for an "antiauthoritarian," implicitly supportive technical approach (Kernberg 2001).

Here I cannot resist the temptation to explore somewhat further the issue of resistance, and the culturally influenced questioning of the technical implications of this concept in the service of denial of the importance of the aggressive components of negative transference developments. Resistances should be analyzed in terms of the functions of the corresponding object relationship in the transference. Many years ago, Hanna Segal (1964) defined defensive operations, stating that resistances and the impulses against which they had been erected reflect, respectively, object relations activated defensively to deal with object relations activated by impulse. In this connection, I believe that the contemporary stress on a "two-person psychology," on the mutual influences of transference and countertransference, tends to undermine the more subtle aspects of transference analysis represented by a "three-person psychology," the analyst being split into one part responding in the countertransference to the patient's transference and into another part reflecting on that very development. The analyst's analysis of his countertransference as a preliminary step to analyze the transference–countertransference bind tends to be flattened by the premature utilization of countertransference by either adjusting to the patient's assumed reaction to an assumed stance of the analyst, or by communication of the countertransference to the patient. Under these conditions, the analytic dialogue shifts excessively into an analysis of the present interpersonal situation, to the detriment of the exploration of the deeper layers of the patient's unconscious conflicts around aggression and eroticism.

My point is that various dissidents, in their global reaction to psychoanalytic theory and technique, have incorporated an identification with conventional cultural assumptions, and that this identification is not necessarily related to any "unanalyzed" personal psychopathology. Such cultural adaptation may contribute to the development of dissident theories into a broad replacement of psychoanalytic theory in toto.

Perhaps the strangest dissidence in this regard, is Lacan's (Benvenuto and Kennedy 1986, Clement 1983). Leaving aside the problematic nature of his personality, his mystifying style of communication, and the question of to what extent he distorted some basic Freudian concepts while assuming that he was providing the most faithful clarification and development of Freud's thoughts, his most significant dissident approach was his complete neglect of transference analysis and of the actual transference–countertransference relationship. This attitude was reflected in the arbitrary shortening of the analytic session according to the analyst's assessment of whether meaningful communication was coming from the patient. The assumption that "empty talk" warranted ending the session meant brushing aside the analysis of unconscious defenses, and, in the process, returning to a truly "one-person psychology" (or rather, a one-person psychology being enacted simultaneously by two persons in the same room). To this day, one of the most problematic aspects of Lacanian psychoanalysis is the lack of presentation of clinical data that characterizes the entire Lacanian literature. There is no doubt that there are important theoretical contributions stemming from Lacan, particularly his proposals regarding archaic oedipal developments, the transformation of a dyadic relationship marked by the imaginary into a triadic one represented by the symbolic and its relation to the oedipal situation. So, returning once more to Gittelson's phrase, I believe it does summarize impressively, the nature of the attitude of major dissenters and "paradissenters" toward basic psychoanalytic theory and technique.

THE INFLUENCE OF INSTITUTIONAL DYNAMICS ON THE DEVELOPMENT OF DISSIDENCE

Returning to Bergmann's comments on the influence of the personal relationship with Freud on the thinking of the early dissidents, obviously those who had no direct relationship with Freud still evinced an intense conflictual attachment to his basic ideas. I believe that this apparent focus on Freud's thoughts may mask major institutional dynamics of psychoanalysis, in addition to the other causal factors of dissidence mentioned so far. Psychoanalytic institutions developed strongly authoritarian tendencies, perhaps culminating at the time of maximum cultural prominence and popularity of psychoanalysis in its major centers in London, the United States, Buenos Aires, and Paris.

I have referred to this issue in earlier contributions (Kernberg 1992a, 2000a), and only wish to summarize here briefly my main proposal, namely, that the carrying out of psychoanalytic treatment within an institutional context led to institutional structures intended to protect candidates and training analysts from massive acting out of transference and countertransference, but these structures in fact had some unfortunate effects. While psychoanalytic treatment was considered as a combination of a science and an art, it was taught within an institutional structure that resembled a combination of a religious seminary and a technical professional school. The dominant administrative distortion was the development of the training psychoanalysis system, with the concentration of all authority regarding teaching, supervising, analyzing, and administrative leadership in the hands of the training analysts. This created a privileged class and an underclass (the candidates), with chronic institutional aggression acted out in the form of transference splitting, idealization of some subgroups, and paranoid developments regarding other subgroups and outsiders.

An atmosphere of submission and rebelliousness, of monolithic theorizing and indoctrination while professing a flexible analytic understanding became a major characteristic of psychoanalytic institutions, particularly where their social prestige and influence assured the stability and legitimacy of their educational enterprise. Within this atmosphere, I believe, dissidence became an expression of rebelliousness against the status quo, affecting to various degrees both early and particularly later dissidents. The case of Karen Horney illustrates this problem, and so, more dramatically, does the fascinating summary of Rycoff's withdrawal from the psychoanalytic institution that Bergmann provided in the addendum to his paper. I believe that it is not a coincidence that Kleinian and Kohutian groups developed in the United States within the most conservative ego psychological institutions, and, at times, these same analysts then shifted from a Kleinian commitment to a self psychology or intersubjective one.

The controversial discussions in Great Britain (King and Steiner 1991) that prevented a split between the groups of Melanie Klein and Anna Freud may have unwittingly permitted the enormous development of psychoanalytic contributions of the British Psychoanalytic Society in the 1940s through the 1960s, by assuring an institutionalized tolerance of alternative ideas and implicit confrontations of those ideas in the context of evaluation of clinical material over time. Yet the fact that candidates trained by Kleinian psychoanalysts remained Kleinian and that candidates trained by analysts of the middle group and of Anna Freud's group remained within those respective groups points to the enormous pressure of institutionalized psychoanalytic ideology in distorting the psychoanalytic process, and in determining the position of the students regarding their respective training analyst's allegiances.

Authoritarian pressures in institutes may brand innovators as dangerous rebels, and force potential "modifiers" into an oppositional stance. Institutional splits or the development of dissidence can be the result if one of the mutually split groups represents officialdom and the other is expelled and declared "nonpsychoanalytic." This is what happened in 1949 with the group of Schultz-Henke in Germany, expelled from the International Psychoanalytic Association, not because of what many years later was assumed to be related to their past contamination by Nazi influences, but because of the rejection of the concept of the death drive by Schultz-Henke, and the determination of the International Psychoanalytic Association at that point that this position was incompatible with psychoanalytic theory. Little did the psychoanalytic community expect that large segments of it would reject the concept of a death drive, particularly in the United States, fifty years later.

Institutional dynamics typically show up as conflicts between groups that appear, on the surface, as conflicts between charismatic individuals in leadership positions of these groups. Charismatic leadership undoubtedly helps to crystallize groups around the leader, but the institutional dynamics leading to such mutually split off groups, described by Bion as the basic group assumption of "fight–flight," lie in institutional dynamics. Fortunately, the psychoanalytic community has painfully learned that the expulsion of individuals and groups because of differences in theory leads to dissidence and a potential weakening of the psychoanalytic movement, and that the containment of theoretical differences may have a beneficial effect on psychoanalysis as a whole. This principle operated already in the controversial discussions, and later on in the capacity of the American Psychoanalytic Association and the International Psychoanalytic Association to contain Kohut's self psychology—in spite of its rejection of basic psychoanalytic theories that earlier would have led to a split. I have recently been able to observe the surprising development of a strong and articulate "intersubjectivity" group in the Chilean Psychoanalytic Association that used to be rigidly Kleinian, a counterpart to the developments in Argentina, where the traditionally rigidly Kleinian Argentinean Psychoanalytic Association has experienced the development of a powerful Lacanian group.

I believe that a variety of controversial issues regarding psychoanalytic technique are influenced by these same institutional dynamics. The confusion of the concept of resistance as the clinical manifestation of defensive operations in the transference with opposition to the psychoanalytic treatment that has to be "overcome" outside as well as inside the consulting room seems to me a typical manifestation of an authoritarian influence of the psychoanalytic institution on psychoanalytic technique. The questioning of the authority of the psychoanalyst on the part of self psychology and the intersubjectivity and relational approaches seems to me equally an effort to react to institutional authoritarian pressures by injecting a political, democratic ideology into the analytic process. As another example, the transformation of the concept of technical neutrality into the anonymity of the psychoanalyst proposed both by ego psychological and Kleinian schools in the 1950s and 1960s seems to me a direct consequence of the efforts to protect the untouchable training analysts from contamination with the candidates' social body, rather than the alleged effort to protect the "purity" of the transference.

IMPLICATIONS FOR THE FUTURE
OF THE PSYCHOANALYTIC ENTERPRISE

It seems to me that, if the factors I have referred to are indeed fundamental contributors to the development of dissidence within psychoanalytic institutions, and if we are willing to learn from our history in considering the future development of psychoanalysis, we do have some major tasks at this time. First, the development of scientific research in the broadest sense, is an urgent task. It will include both the gradual development of psychoanalytic expertise through the analysis of the effects of alternative approaches to the clinical situation over time, and empirical research, in the sense of setting up experimental designs by which alternative theories can be tested and the field developed in this context.

It is obvious that there are enormous difficulties in the objective study of the psychoanalytic process, but we are gradually advancing in our capacity to carry out such studies. There are methods from other sciences that we may appropriate in addition to the use of the psychoanalytic situation per se as our major investigation of the unconscious. The dogmatic affirmation that only psychoanalytic treatment permits us to learn more about the dynamic unconscious and to resolve questions about alternative theories and techniques has been used to protect our institutions against the strengthening of psychoanalytic research in the broadest sense, in addition to isolating us from the surrounding world of science.

Second, we must tolerate the development of alternative approaches in our midst, both theories and methods, and see as our task to evaluate them systematically, not in order to absorb and integrate eclectically everything that comes along, but to develop our understanding in depth of what is essential about the psychoanalytic process and needs to be reaffirmed in the face of new developments. What has been called the "age of pluralism" only means that we have multiple theories and approaches, and not that all of them have to be accepted or integrated. They have to be used as challenges, as tests of our science, and they cannot be avoided, because they confront us with the influence of cross-cultural, ideological, and fundamental scientific discoveries occurring in fields at the boundary of psychoanalysis. The temptation to use neurobiological findings merely to affirm that Freud was right all along can be as destructive as the systematic ignorance of such findings. We have to be prepared to modify our theories and techniques in the light of controversies, and not as an effort to politically accept a bland pluralistic eclecticism.

Strengthening our scientific enterprise implies fundamental changes in psychoanalytic education, the development of an authentically scientific atmosphere where faculty and students jointly study our field, openly recognize and articulate areas of uncertainty and ignorance, and discuss how we can proceed to obtain new knowledge. I am aware that every time this challenge is formulated, there is an immediate response of "We are doing all of this anyhow," and it usually takes a long time to show that this may not be so at all.

If the proposed dynamics regarding ideological crosscurrents and consistent conventional cultural assumptions are true, there may be some battles that have to be fought again and again: the pendulum switch between genetic and intrapsychic versus environmental and traumatic determinants of unconscious psychic conflicts also may have to be elaborated again and again. In earlier work (Kernberg 2001), I pointed to the present development of a mainstream of psychoanalytic technique that combines fundamental contributions from ego psychology, Kleinian psychoanalysis, the British independents, and the French mainstream, while an alternative development has been the consolidation of a relational/intersubjective/self psychological approach. These developments may illustrate the extent to which Freud's basic discoveries regarding aggression, sexuality, and transference have to be worked through, again and again, in the process of the development of psychoanalytic knowledge.

Finally, one of the most astonishing blind spots in the development of psychoanalysis has been the neglect of the development of psychoanalytic psychotherapy for a broad spectrum of patients whose psychopathology does not respond to standard psychoanalytic treatment. The denial of this issue, on the one hand, and the development of significant breakthroughs in psychoanalytic psychotherapies, on the other, often outside the context of psychoanalytic institutions, present a major paradox. Veikko Tähkä's book, *Mind and Its Treatment* (1993), provides a helpful overview of these new developments. This paradox reflects, I believe, the ongoing insecurity of psychoanalysis regarding the survival of its science, and therefore the need to protect the mythical identity of psychoanalysis, on the one hand, and a self-destructive avoidance of full integration of some of the most important contributions of psychoanalysis to the field of psychotherapy, on the other. We may be at the beginning of the breakdown of this denial, and of the awareness that a broad spectrum of psychoanalytically derived techniques can be explored, applied, and scientifically evaluated, strengthening the contributions of psychoanalysis to society. The development of independent societies of psychoanalytic psychotherapy functioning in parallel and even in competition with psychoanalytic societies is one form of unrecognized institutional dissidence that has been very damaging to psychoanalysis and needs to be overcome. This is the subject for another paper.

References

Benjamin, J. (1986). The alienation of desire: women's masochism and ideal love. In *Psychoanalysis and Women: Contemporary Reappraisals*, ed. J. L. Alpert, pp. 113–138. Hillsdale, NJ: Lawrence Erlbaum.

Benvenuto, B., and Kennedy, R. (1986). *The Works of Jacques Lacan: An Introduction*. London: Free Association Books.

Bergmann, M. S. (2000). *The Hartmann Era*. New York: Other Press.

Blum, H. P. (1976). Masochism, the ego ideal, and the psychology of women. *Journal of the American Psychoanalytic Association* 24:157–191.

Chasseguet-Smirgel, J., and Grunberger, B. (1969). *L' Univers Contestationnaire*. Paris: Petite Bibliothèque Payot.

Clement, C. (1983). *The Lives and Legends of Jacques Lacan*. New York: Columbia University Press.

Ferenczi, S. (1949). Confusion of tongues between adult and child. *International Journal of Psychoanalysis* 30:225–230.

Fromm, E. (1941). *Escape from Freedom*. New York: Farrar & Rinehart.

Horney, K. (1967). *Feminine Psychology*. London: Routledge & Kegan Paul.

Kernberg, O. F. (1992a). Authoritarianism, culture, and personality in psychoanalytic education. *Journal of the International Association for the History of Psychoanalysis* 5:341–354.

——— (1992b). *Aggression in Personality Disorders and Perversion*. New Haven, CT: Yale University Press.

——— (2000a). A concerned critique of psychoanalytic education. *International Journal of Psycho-Analysis* 81:97–120.

——— (2000b). Psychoanalytic perspectives on the religious experience. *American Journal of Psychotherapy* 54(4):452–476.

——— (2001). Recent developments in the technical approaches of English language psychoanalytic schools. *Psychoanalytic Quarterly* 70(3):519–547.

——— (2003). Editorial comments on the symposium "The Good, the Bad, and the Ugly." Clinical perspectives of the question: how does treatment help? *Journal of the American Psychoanalytic Association* (in press).

King, P., and Steiner, R., eds. (1991). *The Freud-Klein Controversies, 1941–1945.* London: Tavistock/Routledge.

McGuire, W., ed. (1974). *The Freud/Jung Letters: The Correspondence Between Sigmund Freud and C. G. Jung,* trans. R. Manheim and R. F. C. Hull. Bollingen Series XCIV. Princeton: Princeton University Press.

Segal, H. (1964). *Introduction to the Work of Melanie Klein.* New York: Basic Books.

Tähkä, V. (1993). *Mind and Its Treatment: A Psychoanalytic Approach.* Madison, CT: International Universities Press.

4

Some Implications for Learning Psychoanalysis in Martin Bergmann's "Rethinking Dissidence and Change in the History of Psychoanalysis"

ANTON O. KRIS

Martin Bergmann has once again challenged us to consider the implications of his earlier work (1993, 1997) on heretics, modifiers, and extenders. His invention of the concept of the Hartmann era (2000) proved enormously fruitful at our previous meeting. On the present occasion, in which he focuses on dissidence, my first reaction was to regard the term itself as out of date. Is there not a widespread and deep ecumenical movement among psychoanalysts? Does anyone still believe that there is one single psychoanalysis from which dissident views and practices can be distinguished, let alone Freud's psychoanalysis, which, with all its contradictions and complexity, remains Bergmann's touchstone for measuring dissent? Bergmann's division of dissenters into those who came before Freud's death and those who came later no doubt reflects the modern lack of unanimity. From another angle, will anyone disagree with Bergmann's view that valuable observations and theoretical innovations are contained in the work of even the heretics but certainly of the modifiers and extenders?[1]

---

1. Bergmann's welcome emphasis on Freud's tolerance of disagreement, throughout his monograph, for example, in his comments on the 1912 symposium on masturbation and the 1936 Marienbad symposium, might be an exception to uniform agreement.

A second look reveals another purpose. Bergmann seeks to influence individual analysts in developing their own psychoanalytic approach and their theoretical views and practices. His historical method opens an avenue for understanding the process of learning and practicing psychoanalysis. The motivations for the various modifications and heresies can be seen as special cases of enduring the problems and dilemmas of becoming and being a psychoanalyst. In this response I shall spell out some of the implications of Bergmann's historical survey, as they apply to the technique of psychoanalysis.[2]

How does one begin learning psychoanalysis? Bergmann assumes—and I share his assumption—that Freud so completely established the core of psychoanalysis that, however one approaches the field, those fundamental contributions necessarily become the starting point. I have in mind the invention of the psychoanalytic situation[3] and the requirement that the analyst devote himself to understanding the patient and to conveying that understanding in words to help the patient gain understanding, the use of free association (meaning the patient's relative diminution of conscious control), the inference that unconscious mental life profoundly influences behavior (including thought and speech in the psychoanalytic situation), the recognition of resistance and transference, and so on. No matter the theoretical perspective with which the learner approaches the task, these basic components of psychoanalysis will play a significant role. More to the point, however, theoretical perspective must be learned, modified, and integrated in a never-ending personal task of acquisition. So, Bergmann's review of the history of dissident psychoanalytic theoretical perspectives—"All dissidents have used the psychoanalytic situation, but what they communicate is very different"—offers an opportunity to recognize some principles of the learning process.

---

2. Although I shall not take up the theoretical disputes and points of view, I take it for granted that there can be no technique without theoretical perspective, explicit or implicit.

3. I differ on this point from Friedman (1994), whose discussion magnificently illuminates the psychoanalytic method but who refers to it as a discovery. Bergmann writes that "Freud created the analytic situation" but also that he "discovered the technique of free association."

Bergmann could as well have taken Freud himself as the first dissenter, as he changed his views over nearly half a century. With one important exception, the results would have been the same. That is, every new formulation (always bearing some relationship to observation, but hardly the idealized notion that new observations required new theoretical views) produced a confrontation and coordination with the hitherto established positions that Freud, at every turn, expressed with certainty. He differed from the dissidents, however, in the degree of his attachment to earlier formulations. That is, in Bergmann's terms, Freud was mainly an extender of Freud.[4] Bergmann's strategy, however, is to focus on the heretics and modifiers, not only because they provide a livelier target, but also because they illustrate current questions both for established analysts and for those at the beginning of the learning process.

In the discussion of Alfred Adler, Bergmann shows us the first heretic. How does it help us understand the problems of the learner? Passing over Adler's tendentiousness, born of competition, let me turn to Bergmann's conclusion: "Adler's formulation, because it did not include the unconscious, could be given to the patient early and did not require the same attention to the individuality of the patient that psychoanalysis required. . . . Adler did not take anything from psychoanalysis" (p. 15). Adler's emphasis on inferiority has the same quality as countless psychodynamic case formulations, based on external views, no matter how complex and subtle, that fail to take into account the patient's psychic reality. This essential concept, one of the crucial lessons of *The Interpretation of Dreams*, is hard to learn. It requires a commitment to drawing inferences from the data generated by use of the psychoanalytic method.[5]

"The Jungian heresy," Bergmann tells us in his rich interpretation, "can be seen as a revenge of the irrational forces dormant in the psyche against Freud's attempt to tame them in the service of rational aims"

---

4. Bergmann's conclusions regarding the Marienbad symposium could support the view of Freud as modifier.

5. There are as many psychoanalytic methods as there are varying psychoanalytic perspectives, but all of them, so far as I understand, take as essential the exploration of psychical reality through its derivatives.

(p. 29). Does this apply to learning psychoanalysis? Unfortunately, I believe it does, though the instances that concern me most might more properly be regarded as the forgetting of what one has learned. Boundary violations on the part of mature analysts, candidates, and therapists of many persuasions fall into this unhappy category. It seems unlikely that learning (including the analyst's analysis) alone can ever be sufficient to safeguard analysts and patients from this disastrous eventuality. It is, nonetheless, a crucial matter for those learning psychoanalysis to address and readdress.

Bergmann's discussion of Otto Rank readily allows generalization to all learners of psychoanalysis. "What Rank tried to achieve was an oversimplification; he is the first dissident to have become impatient with the pace of psychoanalysis and the uncertainty of its result" (p. 34). It embodies what Anna Freud used to call "this-only or that-only" analysis. Both impatience and one-sidedness confront every analyst, again and again. In the quiet of contemplation they can easily be conquered by adherence to first principles, but in the heat of analytic work, especially under conditions of personal stress, the analytic stance is often hard to hold. It must be buoyed up, not only by training but also by consultation.

The case of Ferenczi differs from the previous three. Ferenczi not only has become a hero of the whole psychoanalytic community, in its attempts to wrestle with Freud's legacy, but also he attempted to make critical assessments of his own experiments (even rejecting some of them, e.g., mutual analysis). Many of his radical observations and ideas have been confirmed, but fewer of his specific technical measures. Here, too, I believe, a generalization may be made for learning psychoanalysis: it is very difficult to maintain passionate beliefs when they differ from prevailing views, and even harder to assess the motives that lead to them—all the more so when something of great value is at stake on both sides. Innovation and conservation are equally necessary for the psychoanalytic profession as well as for the creative psychoanalyst. No formula is likely to resolve the problem of that divergence.

Bergmann's discussion of Karen Horney and Erich Fromm brings into play a number of interesting themes, especially the influence of culture on development. For the learner it is hard to remember that to gain a psychoanalytic understanding of the influence of culture, it must be understood through its effect on the patient's psychical reality. I want to focus, however, on Bergmann's "unexpected conclusion. The humanist attitude toward psychoanalysis with its emphasis on morality is in the service of the superego which in turn is likely to interfere with the capacity of the psychoanalyst to listen to the inner conflicts of his patients with a reasonable degree of neutrality." This problem presents a serious challenge to the learner. It arises frequently in analysis, and it is not easy to resolve, even with our new, greater attention to our own contributions to the analytic process, especially when the patient's narcissism and the analyst's come into conflict. The difficulties it regularly presents, not only for learners but also for experienced analysts, played a most unfortunate part in the treatment of narcissistic patients in the postwar decades of psychoanalytic ascendancy, when new power in the hands of analysts was not matched by a sufficient understanding of either the narcissistic disorders or the analysts' actions.

Wilhelm Reich, extender and heretic, rightly saw that the defenses represented a crucial problem, which stimulated the whole Viennese analytic community, but wrongly supposed that an attack by the analyst was necessary. He accepted the patient's gambit that the durable defenses represent an absence of conflict. Accordingly he substituted counteraction to conflict-analysis. This error recurs frequently in psychoanalytic training and in practice. Stubborn denial, masking anxiety, is too often read as implacable hostility. Entitlement is still sometimes seen as the total position of the narcissistic patient. In developing an analytic attitude, it is important to keep in mind that patients who seek analytic help may go to great defensive lengths to avoid the painful experience of internal conflict or of involvement with another person.

"Only because Lacan gave up the analytic hour as a basic instrument did he become a dissenter. If Lacan had not changed the length of the hour he would have ranked with Hartmann and Klein as a modifier but not as a dissenter" (p. 86), Bergmann notes ironically. His intention is to emphasize that Lacan's complex formulations present not only valuable, stimulating rereadings of Freud but also significant ideas and syntheses of his own.[6] He sums up Lacan's heresy in the "changed length of the hour." The most important change, it seems to me, is that Lacan takes action beyond the ordinary action of the analytic dialogue,

---

6. In my view, however, they are marred by unnecessary and provocative ambiguity.

ending the hour rather than interpreting the emptiness of the experience. To modify the procedure so far as to give the analyst the authority to terminate the session prematurely, however, runs into conflict with a number of elements of the core of psychoanalysis, such as the conditions for free association and the analyst's obligation to use words to convey his understanding. This heresy focuses our attention on the temptation to take action, which is an inevitable part of the analyst's experience. It may be enacted in giving comfort, advice, or a host of other well-intentioned but noninterpretive acts. On balance, some of these may be justified. Learning to make the shift from reaction and directive action to interpretation, especially under the influence of significant transference and countertransference, remains a perennial task for student and established practitioner.

In the discussion of Ronald Fairbairn, Bergmann notes that Freud regards "abstinence as a central treatment concept. This is not true, either for Ferenczi or Fairbairn" (p. 103) or, I want to add, for Kohut. It seems to me that the idea of abstinence in technique is, on the one hand, illusory, and, on the other, essential. That is, there are numerous gratifications built into the analytic method, without which analysis could not proceed—for example, the opportunity to be the focus of the analyst's attention; the experience of satisfying transferences; being understood and, even more, understanding oneself; and the relief of symptoms and recovery of lost freedom of affect, memory, and desire. On the other hand, interpretation, while it may lead the way to new gratification, serves to frustrate and, at least temporarily, to create a condition of abstinence. For the learner and for the practitioner of psychoanalysis it is always necessary to keep in mind the balance between gratification and frustration, a major element in the analyst's timing.

To summarize, Bergmann has opened a window through which we may view in exaggerated form a number of issues fundamental to learning the technique of psychoanalysis. His discussion and mine follow historical sequence, but in this brief restatement I shall group the observations functionally. Foremost among them are the focus on psychical reality and the limitation of action in favor of interpretation and understanding within the analysis. Next come issues related to the maintenance and development of the analytic situation: the balance between frustration and gratification, the taming of irrational forces, the mastery of impatience, and the avoidance of moralizing. The task of recognizing that some patients attempt to obliterate all evidence of internal conflict and others attempt to avoid all but the most superficial involvement with the analyst continues to demand attention from learners and practitioners. Finally, as much as we value creativity and must make strenuous efforts to promote new observations and ways of looking at them, a balance must be struck between conservation and innovation.[7]

References

Bergmann, M. S. (1993). Reflections on the history of psychoanalysis. *Journal of the American Psychoanalytic Association* 41:929–955.

——— (1997). The historical roots of psychoanalytic orthodoxy. *International Journal of Psycho-Analysis* 78:69–86.

Bergmann, M. S., ed. (2000). *The Hartmann Era.* New York: Other Press.

Friedman, L. (1994). Ferrum, ignis, and medicina: return to the crucible. *Journal of the American Psychoanalytic Association* 45:20–36.

---

7. In my view creativity and innovation require room for excess and for one-sidedness. So it is up to the field as a whole to strike a favorable balance.

5

The Wise Baby and the Wild Analyst

Harold P. Blum

Having long been in eclipse for several generations of psychoanalysis after his death in 1933, Sandor Ferenczi's formulations on such important topics as object relations, countertransference, empathy, and psychic trauma have stimulated and advanced contemporary psychoanalytic thought. Theoretical and technical controversies Ferenczi engendered have filtered into current disagreements and debate. Ferenczi has returned from the suppressed past with posthumous honors. Has the pendulum swung to idealization in an opposite reaction from the earlier devaluation and dismissal? This chapter considers not only Ferenczi's innovative and valuable contributions, but also his regression and divergence, his confused and confusing ideas, and his wild psychoanalysis. Ferenczi's depiction of the wise baby is further elaborated. I particularly discuss problems in Ferenczi's propositions concerning psychic trauma, transference–countertransference regression and enactment, his clouding certain aspects of hysteria and trauma in terms of conscious dissimulation and deception, and his presumption of the inborn innocence and primary love of the child.

Ferenczi attributed this conscious deception to early traumatization by, and then unconscious identification with, hypocritical and deceitful parents. Where does the truth lie? What is unconscious fantasy versus conscious confabulation? What does the lie reveal? In his ceaseless inquiry and reflection on this problem, Ferenczi remained conflicted and uncertain, profoundly perplexed, and oscillating concerning the significance of reality versus fantasy. In the course of this communication, I shall compare and contrast some of the viewpoints of Ferenczi and Freud, adding current psychoanalytic thought.

Sandor Ferenczi was Freud's most brilliant and favorite disciple, and at the same time, the self-proclaimed "enfant terrible of psychoanalysis" (Ferenczi 1927, p. 77). Ferenczi was the wise baby who was sometimes wise, sometimes a lost child, a loyal disciple, and a challenging rebel. Yet, Ferenczi was wise enough to know that "the idea of a wise baby could be discovered only by a wise baby." (Ferenczi 1932, p. 274). Ferenczi was a very precocious pupil of Freud who could readily exchange novel ideas with his mentor while being emotionally dependent on and entreating recognition from his master (P. Hoffer 2001). I do not believe that the problem that arose between Ferenczi and Freud concerning the importance of actual trauma and the reality of child abuse was a traumatic experience for the psychoanalytic community (Balint 1968). It was, however, painfully disturbing to both Ferenczi and Freud, and traumatic to a then very vulnerable Ferenczi. The relationship between Freud and Ferenczi involved a wealth of analytic and intellectual exchanges, "an intimate community of life, feelings and of interests" (Freud letter to Ferenczi January 11, 1933).

What is traumatic for some persons is not necessarily traumatic for others. What was probably noxious for the development of psychoanalysis was the silent suppression of controversy and debate, the whole problem of fixation to past positions, and idealization of Freud and his genius to the point of hero worship and near deification. Actual traumatic experience ensued in the disruptions in the psychoanalytic community immediately after Ferenczi's death and during Freud's final years, such as the Nazi persecution and the horrors of the Holocaust and World War II. The possible trauma of the Freud–Ferenczi controversy pales by comparison with the traumatic experience of Nazism and the war years. In the postwar period many analysts fled from considering the impact of massive trauma. This avoidance was not because of the Freud–Ferenczi controversy, but because of their own traumatic or stressful experience. With notable exceptions, the in-depth exploration of the Holocaust and the reevaluation of the psychoanalytic theory of psychic trauma had to await recovery and distance from a massive traumatic situation, and the magnitude of the historic tragedy (Bergmann and Jucovy 1982).

The first generation of psychoanalysts after World War II generally avoided confronting the war and Holocaust issues. The next generation removed from the direct traumatic experience was able to begin the analytic examination of this massive trauma, and its special effects within the world of psychoanalysis. Escalating interest in war neuroses and the Holocaust, and then new attention to the sexual abuse of children, converged in a major shift toward the psychoanalytic investigation of trauma. Unconscious fantasy and intrapsychic conflict remained vital, but not to the exclusion of horrifying and horrible experience. These issues contributed greatly to the Ferenczi revival. Traumatic reality returned to the fore of contemporary psychoanalysis. I refer to real trauma, the prevalence of child abuse and neglect, the effect of ubiquitous countertransference, and the analysts' influence as a real object, with a real character, values, and theoretical convictions. The analyst's subjectivity and the patient's realistic perception as well as transference reactions to that subjectivity are at the forefront of contemporary controversy concerning the analytic process. Ferenczi tried to learn from his technical experiments and analytic adventures, believing they could be subject to rigorous analysis and self-analysis. He was thus bound to search for success in analytic failure, attempting to find solutions for his own disturbance. His experiments were related to his three brief two- to three-week analytic experiences with Freud in 1914 to 1916. Ferenczi's analysis continued episodically in their correspondence, along with obscured transference and countertransference, and their enmeshed friendship.

The coalescence of their analytic and personal relationship, the blurring of boundaries, the interweaving of conscious suggestion with transference and countertransference are now evident in the extraordinary quadrangle of Freud and Ferenczi, Ferenczi's mistress Gizella, and her daughter Elma. Ferenczi took Gizella into analysis, and when her analysis stopped in 1911 she recommended that Ferenczi analyze Elma. He proceeded to "analyze" this future stepdaughter in a set of relationships further complicated by the marriage of Elma's younger sister to one of Ferenczi's younger brothers. Ferenczi fell passionately and actively in love with Elma, who was young, fertile, and seductive.

He could not decide between his love for mother and daughter. Gizella was maternally and sacrificially willing to abdicate in favor of her daughter. Freud reluctantly complied and analyzed Elma for the first three months of 1912, while carrying on a private correspondence with both Ferenczi and her mother. Boundary crossings and indiscretions by all parties reverberated among all concerned, and supposedly confidential information and letters were shown to another party.

Leaving Freud, Elma briefly returned with Freud's apparent approval, for more analysis with Ferenczi during which they ambivalently discussed marriage. Elma finally decided to part, married an American, and settled in New York. Freud had also notified Gizella of his preference for her, and had simultaneously advised Ferenczi to marry her. Ferenczi had been fond of his sister, also named Gizella, and perhaps there is reminiscence of Freud's puppy love for Gizella Fluss.[1] Freud had repeatedly informed Ferenczi about his "resistance" to marriage, but particularly to his marrying Gizella. After years of hesitation, Ferenczi asked Freud to propose his marriage to Gizella! Freud complied and seemingly denied his role, writing to Ferenczi, March 25, 1917, "Your will be done"! It is of interest that toward the end of his life the slowly dying Ferenczi (clinical diary, note of October 2, 1932) wrote, "Is the only possibility for my continued existence the renunciation of the largest part of one's own self, in order to carry out the will of that higher power to the end (as though it were my own)?" This fascinating and perplexing group process might also be depicted as a tragicomic operetta. The manifold complications would have further stimulated Ferenczi's interest in countertransference, technical experiments in deprivation and indulgence, and mutual analysis imbricated with nonanalytic interpersonal interaction.

Freud's concepts of psychic trauma and its treatment have remained fundamental, and were to be both questioned and expanded by Ferenczi. Similar to medical trauma, Freud found that the traumatic memory was walled off through repression, but could continue to exert a pathogenic influence. The trauma was revived in a return of the repressed, and thus "hysterics suffer from reminiscences" (Breuer and Freud 1895, p. 7). Freud had initially stated, "We invariably find that

---

1. To clarify, Gizella was Ferenczi's mistress and later wife. Ferenczi also had a sister named Gizella. Freud, as an adolescent had fallen in love with a Gizella Fluss.

the memory is repressed but has only become a trauma by deferred action" (Breuer and Freud 1895, p. 356). It was necessary for the patient to recapture and recall the traumatic experience from its forgotten state, to abreact the buried strangulated affects such as terror and rage, and to integrate the formerly repressed memory with cognitive reevaluation of the traumatic experience. The experience of the trauma as belonging to the past was essential for recovery.

However, Freud and Ferenczi both presented several models of psychic trauma, which were theoretically interrelated but not entirely consistent. As a result, the notions of trauma today have remained somewhat blurred and indistinct. It is necessary to define the concept of trauma and which concept is being used in a particular context and framework (Haynal 1989). For example, in one of Freud's preanalytic formulations, a childhood seduction trauma first became traumatic at puberty. In a subsequent formulation of *après coup* or deferred action, a traumatic event is not traumatic at the time it is experienced, but is given a traumatic meaning and becomes traumatic at a later date. This formulation was given its most potent expression by Freud (1918) in the Wolf Man case, when the trauma of the primal scene at 18 months was first experienced as traumatic in the dream of the Wolf Man on his fourth birthday. Thus, a developmental reorganization at age 4 resulted in a fresh trauma, a proposition that contributed to Ferenczi's later controversial discourse with Freud. The term *primal scene* was first introduced in the Wolf Man case, as a preoedipal experience, which became a phase-specific oedipal seduction trauma. The trauma was then analytically understood from an internal as well as a psychic reality perspective, although Freud considered that fantasy always contained elements of reality (Martin-Cabre 1997). Laplanche and Pontalis (1973) actually redefined deferred action: "Experiences, impressions and memory traces may be revised at a later date to fit in with fresh experiences or with the attainment of a new state of development" (p. 111). Different from Freud, this remodeling of memory in the course of development did not tie deferred action to trauma.

Freud had also proposed partial traumas "which have only been able to exercise a traumatic effect by summation" (Breuer and Freud 1895, p. 6), anticipating later concepts of strain trauma and cumulative trauma (Khan 1963, Kris 1956). Freud (1917) described psychic trauma as resulting from "an increase of stimulus too powerful to be dealt with or worked off in the normal way, and this must result in permanent disturbances of the manner in which energy operates" (p. 275). Although using energic terms, Freud referred to the overwhelming of the ego, with ensuing global regression, and obligatory tendencies to repeat the traumatic experience. His theoretical conceptualizations were distant from the clinical discourse of Ferenczi, more of a strategic overview than Ferenczi's tactical therapeutic focus (Bergmann, Part I, this volume).

Freud never relinquished the importance of trauma, and Ferenczi never entirely disavowed the importance of unconscious fantasy (Martin-Cabre 1997). Ferenczi, however, both elaborated and diverged from Freud's views. He differed from Freud in placing emphasis on the frequency of external trauma across sequential developmental phases. Rather than strain trauma and deferred action, he highlighted pathogenic object relations and identifications. Considering retraumatization through the analytic relationship, he was interested early in the analysts' own emotional responses to the patient, the "dialogues of the unconscious" and countertransference. Ferenczi called attention to the analytic or parental abuse of power while often being insensitive to his own suggestive influence and manipulation of patients.

Little recognized was Ferenczi's additional focus on conscious deception and lies. Viewing one of the major effects of trauma as a dissociation, splitting, or even more severe fragmentation of the personality, he enigmatically asserted,

> In an earlier paper, I offered the suggestion that in infancy all hysterical symptoms were produced as conscious fictional structures. I recalled also that Freud used to occasionally to tell us that it was . . . a sign of approaching cure, if the patient suddenly expressed the conviction that during the whole of his illness he had really been only shamming. . . . What in the light of morality and of the reality principle we call a lie, in the case of an infant and in terms of pathology we call a fantasy. [Ferenczi 1927, pp. 78–79]

Ferenczi's patient had completely forgotten a session and had amnesia for the events of the day of the missed session. Ferenczi felt he had obtained incontrovertible evidence of the patient's conscious mendacity and then stated in a footnote, "I have no hesitation in generalizing this single observation, and interpreting all cases of so-called split personality as symptoms of partially conscious insincerity which forced those liable to it to manifest in turn only parts of their personality" (1927, p. 78). For Freud the feeling that symptoms were regarded as a sham once the patient was fully conscious of what he had been previously unconscious, represented major psychoanalytic progress. For Ferenczi, the patient was engaging in deliberate deception or possibly a compromise formation between conscious simulation and unconscious fantasy. Two years earlier, in "Psycho-Analysis of Sexual Habits," habits about which adults often lie, Ferenczi (1925) observed "that the illness which tormented and incapacitated them so much was after all only a pretense (or simulation), is quite sound in the sense that they have produced in adult life symptoms which during childhood they aimed at and sought after in play" (p. 284). Ferenczi thus proposed to alter the psychoanalytic understanding of the unconscious fantasy behind such symptoms. Instead, Ferenczi proposed that a patient was rationalizing conscious fabrication. Unconscious fantasy, and possibly preconscious fantasy, in Ferenczi's formulation, became self-serving conscious fabrication. Fantasy was turned into conscious fiction (Leys 2000), and though Ferenczi would explore the consequences of actual confabulation, he retreated from psychic reality.

There are similarities in Ferenczi's (1928) uncertainty and confusion regarding what was conscious and unconscious in trauma, to his recognition of the role of iatrogenic suggestion and "forced fantasies" in a patient's fabrications. A patient might both consciously and unconsciously desire to please or placate the psychoanalyst and forcing fantasies might engender a form of confabulation. Iatrogenic influence through his technical experiments blurred the difference among feigning, fabrication, and fantasy. The question of reality versus fantasy and truth versus fiction, were subtle problems that influenced Ferenczi's theoretical investigations. Honest, adventurous, yet often misguided technical experiments and recommendations were in his last years probably also reactions to the advancing reality of his fatal illness. The unconscious denial and dissociation about which he wrote were not remote from himself. At the same time, his creativity was served by his striving for analytic independence within his ambivalent relationship to his beloved mentor, colleague, and close friend, Freud (Blum 1994a, Haynal 1993). Since Ferenczi was dying at the time he wrote the clinical diary, his independent thrust was also fueled by defending against his dependent wishes and needs. Ferenczi's conflicts included magical wishes for repair and rescue by Freud, as well as anxiety that Freud had deserted him and had become a punitive object identified with Ferenczi's illness.

When Ferenczi described the continuing conflicted pathogenic relationship between the child abuser and the abused child, he transcended the primary intrapsychic processes that Freud elucidated in psychic trauma. Clarifying the caregiver's influence in the child's confused and distorted sense of reality, Ferenczi placed object relations at the center of the traumatic situation. The complicated relationship between adult perpetrator and abused child could now be elaborated with attention to the importance of the adult's denial, deception, and hypocrisy. Ferenczi believed the silence, lies, and hypocrisy of the caregivers were the most traumatic aspects of the abuse. However, this emphasis diminished the importance of the narcissistic mortification, and particularly of the sexual and aggressive abuse imprinted in the child's mind and body. For Ferenczi, the sincerity and honesty of the analyst counteracted the past hypocrisy to which the patient had been subjected. He did not explain how analytic candor would alter the patient's unconscious defenses, or substitute for analysis of the patient's unconscious conflicts and trauma. Writing to Freud, October 12, 1910, just after their Sicily vacation and the Palermo incident, Ferenczi asserted: "There is certainly much that is infantile in my yearning for honesty—but . . . not everything that is infantile should be abhorred; for example, the child's urge for truth, which is only damned up by false educational influences" (1929, p. 224). Here Ferenczi again refers to conscious education in falsehood rather than internal unconscious conflict. The child's sense of reality and the child's curiosity may be blunted by unconscious conflict and traumatic regression. The child's need for parental love and approval and fears of punishment are powerful incentives to conform with the parent's silence and falsified reality. Moreover, children have wishful fantasies, and readily deny and distort reality.

The overt and unspoken dialogue of Freud and Ferenczi led to an enriched and enlarged understanding of psychic trauma consonant with contemporary psychoanalysis (Rachmann 1993). Ferenczi dissected the parent–child interaction beginning with the parent's abuse of the child as a sexual object and abuse of the child's need for love and protection. The adult's reactions often encompass a panoply of efforts to conceal and rationalize the abuse. The adult abuser projects his own unconscious sexual desires, shame, and guilt onto the child, while being unempathic and unattuned to the child's actual needs. The child's sense of reality is undermined as the parent acts as if nothing has happened, attempts to enforce silence, intimidates the child with punitive threats, bribes the child with presents and promises, imposes and insists on an altered version of the actual experience, or indicates that no one would believe the child. Some abused children do not trust others or their own perceptions. Like Ferenczi, the child is left in a state of doubt, of belief and disbelief, often externally submissive and internally rebellious.

The confusion of the child is also an identification with the parent who is at one point abusive and at another point overly solicitous and indulgent with remorse. The splitting within the child may be related to contradictory attitudes and behavior displayed by the parent. The preservation of the good affectionate object is paramount, so that a split-off idealized all-good object serves survival, in concert with the denial of reality. Ferenczi's concepts followed from Freud's purified pleasure ego and anticipated this Kleinian form of splitting with all-good and all-bad objects. Adding to Freudian splitting in which the ego both denies and recognizes reality, Ferenczi noted the child's identification with the contradictory attitudes and feelings of the parents. Ferenczi indicated a malignant form of splitting characterized by fragmentation of the self, foreshadowing later concepts of ego dissolution and loss of self-cohesion.

Ferenczi must have been aware of Freud's (1896) attention to parental abuse of power, "the adult, who cannot escape his share in the mutual dependence necessarily entailed by a sexual relationship, and who is yet armed with complete authority and the right to punish" (p. 215). Ferenczi's sensitivity to parental neglect and threats may have been facilitated by his own childhood experience, including his being the eighth of twelve siblings, his father's death when he was 15, and having a depleted, rigid mother who complained to him and about him (Haynal 1993). He competed with Freud's other disciples for Freud's love and approval, and correctly inferred Freud's irritation with his regression and whining for attention.

In many respects, "The Confusion of Tongues" (1933) paper can be read as a personal document about himself, as well as a plea to and protest against Freud. It can also be read as Ferenczi's demand for independence from Freud, and as an effort to master his own traumatic confusion. However, considered as a paper independent of its author, it proved to be of historic significance and a controversial catalyst of theoretical change. The paper was delivered in September 1932, in Wiesbaden, Germany, at the Twelfth International Psychoanalytic Association Congress. I will not review here the personal interplay of Freud and Ferenczi at that time, the near censorship of Ferenczi's paper, and the cold reception that the paper received (A. Hoffer 1991). Ferenczi's conclusions on the child's identification with the aggressor, the guilt of the aggressor, the aggressor's shame, and current fear of discovery and prosecution have been accepted into current psychoanalytic thought. However, Ferenczi's concepts of identification with the aggressor differed in form and content from Anna Freud's (1937) later formulation. Ferenczi described a primitive form of identification as fusing with the aggressor, and/or being totally submissive to the aggressor. Submission and sacrifice of the self or ego functions represents a masochistic adaptation to a sadistic object. The aggressor is incorporated so that the child will not be abandoned and abused, and the aggressor may be split off and reprojected onto another object.

The seduced or traumatized child's selectively adapting to the aggressor, for example, in the child's attachment style, would represent a higher level of identification and organization than fusion. Fusion or merger is a global identification in contrast to the selective identification Anna Freud described. For her, the child identifies with the aggression and power of a differentiated aggressor, and the form in which the aggression is expressed. The child becomes the active aggressor rather than the passive victim. The child who has had a tooth extracted repeats his trauma by symbolically extracting the tooth of a playmate. While the abused child may later enact masochistic self-injury, the child could become an abusive parent. With regard to seduction trauma within the family, issues of power, aggression, and submission, although important, do not attend to actual incest. The child may be left in a heightened state of sexual arousal or a defensive numbing of excitement and affect. The numbing and doubting are fortified through identification if an insensitive aggressor appears calm and complacent as though nothing happened. Affect dysregulation and obsessive doubting may be a sequel to such deception and evasion. However, Ferenczi did not discuss identification with the aggressor in the perpetuation of abuse, and the child's becoming a bully or a cruel parent. Becoming submissive and masochistic is the reverse of becoming the aggressor and sadistic. Ferenczi did not take up the question of the seduction of the aggressor, identifying with the aggressor's seduction, or of masochism as a defense against the aggressor's rage and the child's own rage and hate. Ferenczi's perspectives, however, on the parent–child interaction, the childish parent, and the parentified child foreshadowed the current concept of the intergenerational transmission of trauma.

Though Ferenczi enacted infantile narcissistic and oedipal conflicts in his relationship with Freud, his "Confusion of Tongues" paper departs from the child's own sexual and aggressive impulses. Ferenczi (1933) refers to the abused child who "until then, felt blissfully guiltless" (p. 164). He further remarked that the abuser's hatred traumatically surprises and frightens the spontaneously and innocently playing being into a guilty love-automaton imitating the adult anxiously, self-effacingly. Ferenczi's formulation here is remarkably unanalytic, and disregards the child's own impulses and unconscious fantasies. He knew but denied the knowledge that abused children may have intense guilt and shame consequent to unconscious complicity as well as identification with the feelings of the abuser. They often irrationally blame themselves for the abuse. The child is not a tabula rasa or empty container to be simply a pawn of the adult through robotic imitation and obedience (Furer 1998). Childhood sexuality, incestuous conflicts, the violent fantasies and aggressive behavior of children, and the readiness with which children regress when frustrated and disappointed are overlooked. The rich fantasy life of children, in which menacing figures may be mercilessly eliminated and narcissistic injuries magically avenged and erased, are all essentially overlooked in Ferenczi's evocation of "innocent play."

If submission represented a major aspect of Ferenczi's unconscious relationship with Freud, the "Confusion of Tongues" paper demonstrated an infantile rebellion. The wise child, who Ferenczi described in his 1923 paper, "The Dream of the Clever Baby," attempted to offer solace, comfort, and protection to the dissociated traumatized child. In reversal of roles, the wise child also demonstrates that his suffering led to precocious caregiving and a precocious sagacity, with an advanced capacity to mother others including the childish parent.

But Ferenczi still needed the love and understanding of his master and mentor, whom he simultaneously proceeded to alienate. While advancing psychoanalytic thought, Ferenczi simultaneously resurrected the fantasy of a pure and innocent childhood disturbed by external trauma, and by exogenous objects and their internalizations. If this derived from a view of himself as an innocent victim, it may well have been related to the fact that Ferenczi was dying in 1932. His "Confusion of Tongues" paper and some of his remarks in his clinical diary at the time would indicate that to a degree Ferenczi saw himself as the innocent victim of a pernicious persecutory object, his pernicious anemia. Ferenczi felt he had been assaulted without cause, provocation, or ability to defend himself. The wise baby became the terribly sickly child. The fatal illness intensified his zeal to heal, but despite his best dedicated efforts he was unable to maintain an analytic process with his own patients or to succeed in the searching self-analysis of his escalating traumatic experience.

The rebellious and submissive trends in Ferenczi's personality, as well as the regressive and progressive crosscurrents, were present long before the slowly progressive disease process of pernicious anemia. But these trends were exacerbated by Ferenczi's illness and his response to Freud's oral cancer (Blum 1994a, Hoffer 2001). Ferenczi had rebelled against serving as what he regarded as Freud's secretary in the Palermo incident in 1910, when they were traveling together in Sicily. Although Ferenczi and Freud had been discussing the psychodynamics of paranoia, Freud then proceeded to write the Schreber case during their Sicily vacation in his own hotel room and Ferenczi missed the opportunity to be a coauthor. Freud regarded Ferenczi as whining for attention, and Freud then wished he was with a real woman. Freud and Ferenczi were traveling together while Freud was writing about repressed homosexuality as a major determinant of paranoia. Ferenczi lamented that Freud had not analyzed his negative transference. He was frustrated and disappointed, having unconsciously wanted child analysis in his scant adult analysis. Freud wrote to Eitingon, November 1, 1931, about Ferenczi: "He didn't find the love among his colleagues that he demands out of infantile need, and for that reason is determined to be loved by his patients, thus uses transference and countertransference to that end" (Jones 1957).

At the 1929 Oxford Congress, Ferenczi presented a paper, "The Unwelcome Child and His Death Instinct." Stemming from his own clinical and personal experience, this paper can be read as a demonstration of Ferenczi's burgeoning interest in parental neglect and in lack of parental empathy. The shift in theoretical emphasis was from internal psychic fantasy to the pernicious developmental effects of external inappropriate parenting and environmental failure. Ferenczi's paper provided incipient descriptions of developmental arrest, failure to thrive, and marasmus leading to infant death. Since pernicious anemia usually has a slow, insidious onset, the child's death instinct may have unconsciously referred to an early stage of his own fatal illness. Self-scrutiny of his own childhood fixations and regression continued with valuable reflections on the treatment of infantile adults in "Child Analysis in the Analysis of Adults" (1931). His writing of his fascinating clinical diary, which he began early in 1932, was soon concurrent with his writing "The Confusion of Tongues" during the same final year of his life.

In his clinical diary, Ferenczi was inwardly preoccupied with his relationship to Freud and his psychoanalyst siblings. He again returned to the importance of countertransference, and to the analytic necessity of honestly admitting analytic errors to oneself, and when appropriate, to the patient. His pioneer exploration of countertransference, of bilateral unconscious communication in the analytic process, and of problems of self-disclosure addressed and anticipated later developments and current controversies. Considering the history and fate of psychoanalytic ideas, none of the major papers that shaped new concepts of countertransference in the 1950–1960 decade cited Ferenczi.

Alongside his valuable contributions, his self-disclosure in the clinical diary revealed egregious and mutually destructive acting out of transference and countertransference. This is evident in the two cases of mutual analysis with Clara Thompson at the beginning of the clinical diary, and Elizabeth Severn at the end of the clinical diary. Freud admonished Ferenczi for engaging in a technique that permitted kisses, caresses, and intimate physical contact. Ferenczi observed his own regressive enactments and was amazingly able to contribute to the contemporary theory of technique, despite and possibly because of his countertransference disturbance and technical departures. During the period in 1932 that the "Confusion of Tongues" paper was formulated and written, the clinical diary shows unequivocally that Ferenczi was erratic and alternately a wild analyst and a creative analyst. Ferenczi recognized the analyst's position as participant observer. The analyst was not the completely neutral, totally objective analyst who was simply a mirror who reflected the patient's unconscious fantasies back to the patient with an accurate and appropriate interpretation. The analyst needed to explore his/her own emotions, to refine their own perceptive and affective resonance (Borgogno 1999). Countertransference was no longer limited to the analyst's own internal resistances and blind spots but also to the analyst's lack of empathy, sensitivity, and attitudes toward the patient, as well as his/her personal interest and values. For Ferenczi, countertransference was as continuous as transference, and a potential source of analytic insight rather than only resistance to understanding the patient. The analyst as only mirror and blank screen was exposed as myth. However, recognition of the analyst's participation in the analytic process was a prelude to later extreme proposals to abandon technical neutrality and objectivity.

Ferenczi allowed for two participants and two interpreters, but he did not emphasize the asymmetry that is a necessary part of the analytic situation. The analyst has an expertise and experience that the patient lacks, the analyst does have superior analytic knowledge, and the analyst learns about the inner life and life history of the patient in a depth that the patient cannot possibly know about the analyst. The patient's capacity to interpret the analyst is limited, distorted by transference, though at times almost uncannily insightful. There is bilateral unconscious communication in the analytic process, and many colleagues would evoke the concepts here of projective identification and projective counteridentification. Nevertheless, the patient is no more capable of extended analysis of the analyst than a wise baby, and the wise baby is still a baby.

On his side, Ferenczi admonished analysts to avoid hypocrisy. But in his own efforts at objective self-observation of his feelings about his patients, he could not really appreciate the regressive pull of his own increasing illness. We are now far more aware of the problems of the infirm and impaired analyst. Ferenczi could not readily distinguish what was valuable and progressively innovative in his own ideas and formulations from blatant errors and countertransference departures into blind alleys, and the destructive behavior he deplored. His therapeutic zeal, was connected with a genuine wish to help very ill patients. However, sickly and dependent, his extreme healing efforts were also unconsciously a wish for his own rescue and his need to enact self-rescue fantasies. He wanted to receive loving care from his analyst and patients, craving the tenderness and comforting desired by the ill, neglected, and suffering child. A revival of childhood and transference seduction and depression may be inferred (Bokanowski 1993).

If Ferenczi did not realize the suggestion and manipulation inherent in his own mutual analysis experiments, his confusion and sense of his patients' confusion and disappointment are evident at the end of the clinical diary. Having initially reported the sexual abuse of Clara Thompson by her father at the beginning of the clinical diary, at the end Ferenczi noticed that Thompson was convinced she had overestimated her father's and Ferenczi's importance. Apparently in a new reconstruction of her own, Thompson stated that everything comes from the mother. The eight-year relationship of Ferenczi with Elizabeth Severn had a sad and almost bizarre ending in late 1932, just before Ferenczi's own death. After Severn's treatment had stalled, he more than redoubled his efforts by seeing the patient twice a day, sometimes for four to five hours, not excluding weekend sessions and night sessions, and continuing her analysis during vacations. Analytic sessions had been held at home (Fortune 1994). For nine months until December 1932, Severn manifested ambivalent extremes of love and hate toward Ferenczi. Who would go first on the couch in mutual analysis; who should pay whom? Ferenczi had occasionally treated this patient without fee, and at one point agreed to suspend her analysis until she completed his analysis with her as analyst. While Severn was apparently solely analyzing Ferenczi, he had completed and presented his paper, "The Confusion of Tongues." Confusion abounded between the regressive reactions and role reversals of analyst and patient and between florid transference and countertransference. It is not surprising that Ferenczi inferred the developmental importance of regression, and its differentiation from developmental lag and arrest.

Freud disapproved of some of Ferenczi's experiments and departures in theory and technique, but his deep attachment to Ferenczi remained. He proposed Ferenczi in 1932 for the presidency of the

International Psychoanalytic Association, which indicates that Freud did not then appreciate the gravity of Ferenczi's illness. However, if their relationship began with reciprocal respect as an important determinant, the final phase was characterized by reciprocal ambivalence. They spoke in a "confusion of tongues" and could not understand or empathize with each other. Ferenczi had commented in the clinical diary that his mother had thought he would be the death of her. Had she retaliated by unconsciously causing his fatal illness? Had he unconsciously fantasized that he was the cause of Freud's cancerous illness, that each would be the cause of the other's death? Ferenczi felt deserted by the "higher power"—Freud.

In March 1933 Ferenczi told Groddeck that he believed Freud's deceit was responsible for his declining physical condition. Yet he concurrently acknowledged that his ill health had left him near a mental collapse or breakdown. Ferenczi did not then question his blame of Freud for his deteriorating physical and mental condition. His animosity toward Freud was dissociated from his enduring affection and respect, a form of splitting that Ferenczi had inferred in traumatized patients. The reason for the ambivalence was not solely based on transference, but also derived from the real intimate relationship and behavior of the two friends. Ferenczi's attribution or designation of Freud's deceit may again have been related to his assumption of deceit in the psychodynamics of hysteria. However, in the quadrangular relationship of Freud, Ferenczi, Elma, and Gizella, there had been numerous indiscretions, secret communications, and breaches of confidentiality. Both Freud and Ferenczi were involved in a very complicated relationship with each other, including an anlage of mutual analysis through Elma. The enactment in which Freud participated may have represented a new edition of the Freud, John, and Pauline triangle of Freud's Irma dream and "Screen Memory" (1899) paper. Ferenczi's experiments in mutual analysis may have been first enacted aboard ship when Freud, Ferenczi, and Jung analyzed each other's dreams en route to and from Clark University in 1909.

Ferenczi was clearly ahead of Freud and other colleagues when he had the foresight to recognize the new menace of Nazism. Alongside his own self-deception, Ferenczi could maintain clear awareness of traumatic reality. Ferenczi's attention to conscious deception and a conspiracy of silence was seen as a flight from the unconscious at the 1932 International Psychoanalytic Association Wiesbaden Congress. In retrospect it also brought new attention to the importance of the surface and conscious or preconscious defense. The Freud–Ferenczi controversy can be appreciated as a stimulus for the exploration of the role of the interplay of fantasy and reality in psychoanalytic theory and practice. In Ferenczi's clinical work with very disturbed patients, he focused on the infantile quality of their mental life. These patients had regressed to preoedipal levels or to commingled disorganized states involving all developmental levels. They were in many respects overgrown babies, and Ferenczi wondered if they needed analytic parenting in the form of a strict father or indulgent mother. He preceded Winnicott (1965) and Balint (1968) with the notion that the developmentally arrested internal baby could have a new analytic beginning. Balint's concept of the preverbal impairment of the "basic fault" followed from some of Ferenczi's ideas. Ferenczi suggested that the psychoanalysis of psychotics would be possible if it were not for the resistance of the analyst (Young-Bruehl Chapter 8, this volume). Emphasizing the importance of the analytic experience of the patient, complementary to and perhaps as important in very infantile patients as verbal insight, Ferenczi explored that experience as a bilateral process. More than any other pioneer analyst, Ferenczi initiated the study of the analyst's experience, the analyst's mind, and the analyst's noninterpretive influence on the analytic process.

Ferenczi assumed, apart from his own experience, that usually the analyst flexibly regressed and more or less objectively observed during analysis. The analyst regressed to the wise baby, who Ferenczi proposed could parent the regressed or developmentally arrested patient to the developmental level required for effective analytic interpretation and reconstruction. In these propositions Ferenczi engendered much of contemporary psychoanalytic thought and controversy. Commemorating Ferenczi, Freud (1933) observed that he had made all analysts into his pupils, and asserted, "It is impossible to believe that the history of our science will ever forget him" (p. 229). Ferenczi (1928) had called attention to the revision of emotional experience in the course and termination of analysis, and stated, "In the course of this revision, it is from a certain distance and with much greater objectivity, that he looks at the experience. With the benefit and limitations of history and hindsight we continue to analyze our analytic past" (p. 97).

References

Balint, M. (1968). *The Basic Fault: Therapeutic Aspects of Regression*. London: Tavistock.

Bergmann, M., and Jucovy, M. (1982). *Generations of the Holocaust*. New York: Basic Books.

Blum, H. (1989). Punitive parenthood and childhood trauma. In *The Psychoanalytic Core: Essays in Honor of Leo Rangell*, ed. H. Blum, E. Weinshel, and F. Rodman, pp. 167–186. New York: International Universities Press.

———— (1994a). The confusion of tongues and psychic trauma. *International Journal of Psychoanalysis* 75:871–882.

———— (1994b). *Reconstruction in Psychoanalysis: Childhood Revisited and Recreated*. New York: International Universities Press.

Bokanowski, T. (1993). La depression de transfert de Ferenczi. *Etudes Freudiennes* 34.

Borgogno, F. (1999). *The Analyst's Emotional Involvement. Sandor Ferenczi's Contribution to Contemporary Psychoanalysis*. Milano: Franco Angeli.

Breuer, J., and Freud, S. (1895). Studies on hysteria. *Standard Edition* 2.

Dupont, J. (1912). *The Clinical Diary of Sandor Ferenczi*. Cambridge, MA: Harvard University Press.

Falzeder, E., and Brabant, E., eds. (2000). *The Correspondence of Sigmund Freud and Sandor Ferenczi, vol. 3, 1920–1933*. Cambridge, MA: Belknap Press of Harvard University Press.

Ferenczi, S. (1923). The dream of the clever baby. In *Further Contributions to the Theory and Technique of Psycho-Analysis*, pp. 349–350. London: Hogarth, 1955. New York: Brunner/Mazel, 1980.

———— (1925). Psycho-analysis of sexual habits. In *Further Contributions to the Theory and Technique of Psycho-Analysis*, pp. 259–297. London: Hogarth, 1955. New York: Brunner/Mazel, 1980.

———— (1927). The problem of the termination of psychoanalysis. In *Final Contributions to the Problems and Methods of Psycho-Analysis*, pp. 77–86. London: Hogarth, 1955. New York: Brunner/Mazel, 1980.

———— (1928). The elasticity of psychoanalytic technique. In *Final Contributions to the Problems and Methods of Psycho-Analysis*, pp. 87–101. London: Hogarth, 1955. New York: Brunner/Mazel, 1980.

———— (1929). The unwelcome child and his death instinct. In *Final Contributions to the Problems and Methods of Psycho-Analysis*, pp. 102–107. London: Hogarth, 1955. New York: Brunner/Mazel, 1980.

———— (1931). Child analysis in the analysis of adults. In *Final Contributions to the Problems and Methods of Psycho-Analysis*, pp. 126–142. London: Hogarth, 1955. New York: Brunner/Mazel, 1980.

———— (1932). *Final Contributions to the Problems and Methods of Psycho-Analysis*, p. 274. London: Hogarth, 1955. New York: Brunner/Mazel, 1980.

———— (1933). The confusion of tongues between adults and the child. In *Final Contributions to the Problems and Methods of Psycho-Analysis*, pp. 156–167. London: Hogarth, 1955.

Fortune, C. (1994). A difficult ending: Ferenczi, R. N., and the experiment in mutual analysis. In *100 Years of Psychoanalysis*, ed. A. Haynal and E. Falzeder, pp. 217–224. Geneva: Cahiers Psychiatriques Genevois.

Freud, A. (1937). *The Ego and the Mechanisms of Defense*. New York: International Universities Press, 1946.

Freud, S. (1896). The aetiology of hysteria. *Standard Edition* 3.

———— (1899). Screen memory. *Standard Edition* 3.

———— (1917). Introductory lectures on psychoanalysis. *Standard Edition* 18.

———— (1918). From the history of an infantile neurosis. *Standard Edition* 17.

———— (1921). Group psychology and the analysis of the ego. *Standard Edition* 18.

———— (1933). Sandor Ferenczi. *Standard Edition* 22.

Furer, M. (1998). Changes in psychoanalytic technique, progressive or regressive. *Journal of Clinical Psychoanalysis* 7:209–235.

Haynal, A. (1989). The concepts of trauma and its present meaning. *International Review of Psychoanalysis* 16:315–321.

———— (1993). Ferenczi and the origins of psychoanalytic technique. In *Legacy of Sandor Ferenczi*, ed. L. Aron and A. Harris. Hillsdale, NJ: Analytic Press.

Hoffer, A. (1991). The Freud/Ferenczi controversy: a living legacy. *International Review of Psychoanalysis* 18:465–472.

Hoffer, P. (2001). The wise baby meets the enfant terrible: the evolution of Ferenczi's views on development. The Sperling Lecture, presented to the Psychoanalytic Association of New York.

Jones, E. (1957). *The Life and Work of Sigmund Freud*, vol. 3. New York: Basic Books.

Khan, M. (1963). The concept of cumulative trauma. *Psychoanalytic Study of the Child* 18:286–306. New York: International Universities Press.

Kris, E. (1956). The recovery of childhood memories in psychoanalysis. *Psychoanalytic Study of the Child* 11:54–88. New York: International Universities Press.

Laplanche, J., and Pontalis, J-B. (1973). *The Language of Psycho-Analysis*. New York: W.W. Norton.

Mahler, M., Pine, F., and Bergman, A. (1975). *The Psychological Birth of the Human Infant*. New York: Basic Books.

Martin-Cabre, L. (1997). Freud-Ferenczi: controversy terminable and interminable. *International Journal of Psycho-Analysis* 78:105–114.

Rachman, A. W. (1993). *Ferenczi and Sexuality in the Legacy of Sandor Ferenczi*, ed. L. Aron and A. Harris. Hillsdale, NJ: Analytic Press.

Winnicott, D. (1965). *The Maturational Processes and the Facilitating Environment*. New York: International Universities Press.

6

The British Object Relations Theorists: Fairbairn, Winnicott, Balint, Guntrip, Sutherland, and Bowlby

JILL SAVEGE SCHARFF

DEGREES OF DIVERSITY AND CONTROVERSY AMONG CONTRIBUTORS IN OBJECT RELATIONS THEORY

British object relations theory comprises various, related, complementary ideas about development, motivation, personality structure, and relationships in life and in analysis. The founding contributors were British psychoanalysts working from the 1930s to the 1980s—Ronald Fairbairn, Donald Winnicott, John Bowlby, Michael Balint, Harry Guntrip, and John Sutherland. Their ideas belong in the independent group of the British Psychoanalytic Society (Kohon 1986, D. Scharff 1996, Sutherland 1980). They preferred that affiliation rather than creating a school because they valued autonomy and independent thought.

American psychoanalysts may have been taught that the theories of Melanie Klein qualify for inclusion as British object relations theory. True, Klein also wrote her major papers in Britain, and, like the object relations theorists, she was concerned with the effect of infants' relationships with their mothers on the development of psychic structure. Unlike the object relations theorists, however, she valued Freud's instinct theory, elaborating especially on the force of the death instinct in coloring the infant's perceptions of the early months of life. Lumping

Klein with the British object relations theorists does not do justice to the major difference between the theory of Klein, which accepts drive theory, and British object relations theory, which refutes it.

This chapter focuses on the British object relations theorists, and thus not on Klein, but it refers to her ideas in passing, as they are highly relevant to the development of British object relations theory, and they offer a gloss on the degrees of diversity we are discussing. I emphasize the work of Fairbairn, Winnicott, and Sutherland, and I briefly discuss Balint, Guntrip, and Bowlby.

Classical psychoanalysts accepted Freud's assumptions that human beings are motivated by the need to discharge the tension of unconscious impulses arising from instincts, culminating in the murderous rivalries and sexual longings of the Oedipus complex. Until Freud made the major shift to structural theory featuring psychic regulatory structures based on identification with lost objects, he thought that these impulses were kept in check by opposing instincts. Freud could maintain his confidence in a particular theory like that and yet change it radically some years later and espouse the new theory with equal confidence. As Bergmann wrote in Part I of this volume, when Freud's followers did the same, Freud could not accept their challenges and excluded them from the inner circle of psychoanalysis. Bergmann suggested that Freud's being hurt by his challengers' ingratitude and disloyalty colored his response to their new ideas and led him to banish them from the inner circle. I imagine that Freud also simply wanted to dominate the field that he had invented and keep it his way. Freud seemed to fear that the ideas of others would dilute the potency of the psychoanalytic way of thinking and threaten its acceptance worldwide. Adler, Jung, and Rank, Freud's major challengers in Europe, and Horney, Fromm, and later Kohut, Sullivan, and Mitchell in the United States went on to found alternative schools of psychoanalysis, all of them viewed as dissident or nonanalytic from the vantage point of classical theory.

More germane to my topic is the late-life dissidence of Ferenczi, described by Bergmann as the mother of the psychoanalysis of which Freud was the father. It is sometimes said more specifically that Ferenczi is the mother of object relations theory, in that he focused on the relationship between the analyst and analysand and recognized the pathogenic effects of traumatic family relationships. Ferenczi (1933) deviated from Freudian principles to develop a nonhierarchical, interactional, relational field for mutual examination by patient and analyst. He took his research on the analytic relationship to extremes of role reversal, which challenged the classical technique of therapeutic neutrality and abstinence, and he continued to value the explanatory power of Freud's seduction hypothesis, which appears to have been experienced as a threat to acceptance of Freud's later theory about the mind-blowing force of oedipal fantasies. Prior to being discredited at the end of his life, Ferenczi had quite an influence on psychoanalysis, being the analyst of Balint and of Abraham who analyzed Klein, thereby affecting directly and indirectly both British object relations and Kleinian thinking.

Freud's assumptions were challenged by object relations theory in which the relationship between mother and infant and between analyst and analysand, rather than the individual analysand, took center stage, and the sexual and aggressive instincts colored the infant's internalization of experience with the mother and father, separately and as a couple, rather than being energies to release or tame. Winnicott ended the fiction of the infant as a totally separate being; Klein, on board with the instinctual basis of development, advanced the Oedipus complex to the first year of life; and Fairbairn replaced drive theory altogether with a purely object relations perspective on motivation.

Klein and Winnicott did not want to be seen as dissidents. Klein saw herself as going along with Freud's views on the instinctual basis for development and developing his interest in identification, while Winnicott avoided seeming oppositional by not separating his brilliant intuitions from accepted Freudian theory. Unlike the discursive Klein and poetic Winnicott, Fairbairn was philosophically sophisticated and academically rigorous. His systematic approach led to a fully elaborated theory based on his premise that the libido was directed at being in relationship—a direct challenge to Freud's intensely biological, drive-oriented view of motivation. In contrast, Winnicott's ideas stand separately as brilliant insights or techniques, but at the theoretical level did not accumulate to confront the need for fundamental change. Winnicott viewed Fairbairn's radical concept of the endopsychic situation as an affront, rather than a new way of thinking appropriate to the current intellectual climate.

To this day the psychoanalytic establishment in London—even those in the independent group—remains somewhat ignorant of

Fairbairn's theory of the endopsychic situation. This is less true in the United States, where Sutherland's teaching influenced junior and senior staff, including Kernberg, whose elegant insertion of object relations into the ego psychology model reached many American psychotherapists. Fairbairn's work may have been relatively ignored in Britain because he worked in Edinburgh, eight hours distant from London, and rarely made the journey there because of his discomfort about being neurotically unable to urinate when in a train (Sutherland 1989). Other factors suppressing interest in Fairbairn were the diversity and individualistic nature of the other object relations theorists of the independent group, the charismatic appeal of Winnicott, and the dominance of the Kleinian group, whose members referred to each other's papers, used the same language, molded a coherent Kleinian point of view, and built a group with considerable political influence.

I think that Fairbairn and Winnicott were responding to the effects of shifts in the culture of scientific thinking away from the theory of thermodynamics that was the background to Freud's thinking and toward a theory of relativity. I see them as innovators, bringing diversity and richness to the psychoanalytic sensibility. Yet I agree with Bergmann that they have been viewed as dissidents, so defined by their deviation from the Freudian mainstream, especially in the United States where the male, medically dominated American Psychoanalytic Association kept a monolithic grip on psychoanalysis until the lawsuit of the 1980s.

OBJECT RELATIONS THEORY AND THE DEGREE OF DISSIDENCE IN MY WORK

In my work I integrate concepts from the Kleinian group, such as Klein and Bion, with those of the British independent group, despite, but not in disregard of, the theoretical inconsistency between the groups (J. Scharff 1992). I feel that my doing this has probably been viewed as somewhat dissident by both schools as well as by the classical Freudians. (As an aside, Bion's studies of group relations, which have been extremely useful in demonstrating the interpersonal expression of internal object relationships, did not meet with Klein's approval.) In the American psychoanalytic world, I've been somewhat suspect in that I've applied psychoanalysis to family and couple therapy and I've developed an alternative institutional model based on object relations principles for the teaching and learning of psychoanalytic concepts (D. Scharff and J. Scharff 1987, 1991, J. Scharff and D. Scharff 1992, 2000). In the British psychoanalytic world, I am now seen as an American who has not declared for either the Kleinian or the British independent group. In the family therapy world I've been seen as a dissident in that I do work with resistance, defense, anxiety, unconscious fantasy, and dreams, and do not give behavioral and paradoxical instructions that supposedly bypass unconscious resistances. I have a mid-Atlantic point of view on British psychoanalysis and I'm on the edge of the psychoanalytic mainstream in the United States. At the same time, I'm on the boundary between individual and family therapeutic modalities. It's an uneasy place to sit.

The dissident position is a familiar one to me. As a Scot, I've always been part of a national identity that is distinct from my British citizenship. As a psychiatric resident, I was supervised by an individual therapist/Freudian analyst in charge of the inpatient unit and a social psychiatrist head of the day hospital, each of whom disliked the other's methods. I could either (1) operate in one arena wholly devoted to one point of view in the morning and then switch in the afternoon, or (2) integrate. I did not like the split that the supervision arrangement produced in my thinking, and yet I found it impossible to integrate such disparate theories, or to bridge from the individual to the social dimension. That is what led me first to study family therapy, since I saw the family as the link between the individual and societal dimensions, and second to embrace object relations theory, an individual psychology that applies well to understanding family and group dynamics. I came to this in Edinburgh while working for and studying with Jock Sutherland, a Fairbairn scholar and integrator of psychoanalytic viewpoints, in the city where Fairbairn had lived and died. In that environment, object relations theory was not taught as such but was simply the prevalent psychodynamic viewpoint. In fact I didn't hear the term *object relations theory* until I emigrated to the United States, where it was probably taken from the American title of the (1954) reprint of Fairbairn's (1952) book.

My training analyst was analyzed by a Freudian, but she was influenced toward a more eclectic approach by the nature of her child analytic supervision and exposure to the developmental approach of Anna Freud. Perhaps the diversity between my analyses and my supervision experiences is another factor in my liking to see myself as an integrator, one who applies psychoanalysis widely across the therapeutic modalities, in teaching models, and in building an institution as an open system (D. Scharff and J. Scharff 1987, 1991, J. Scharff 1992, J. Scharff and D. Scharff 2000). Unfortunately, I have often felt regarded as a dissident. I am extremely grateful for Martin Bergmann's compassionate, broad perspective on dissidence in Part I of this volume and Robert Wallerstein's (2002) vision that is enabling me to see myself within the context of an international, pluralistic psychoanalysis instead.

FREUD'S USE OF THE OBJECT

To pay respect to Freud's vision even while disagreeing with him on crucial points, Fairbairn (1944) derived the term *object relations* from Freud's concepts of the object and the ego's relation to the object. Freud used the term *object* to refer to the need-satisfying place that the sexual instinct aimed at for gratification and tension reduction, and to the object of the drives, whereas in object relations theory it is the object of attachment. Freud used the phrase *ego's relation to the object* when describing the ego's defensive attitudes toward the aim and target of the sexual and aggressive instincts that derive from the id, an unconscious physically based source of energy that must seek discharge. In Fairbairn's object relations theory, the infant is born with a whole ego looking for an object to relate to—for feeding, holding, comfort, security, and a sense of personal significance and belonging. In relation to various experiences with that object, the pristine infant ego differentiates. Freud retained a physiologically based theory in which the human personality was thought of as deriving from the management of drive tension and the resolution of conflict between the ego, aided by the superego, and the disruptive forces of the id. It fell to Fairbairn, Klein, Winnicott, and others of the British independent or Kleinian traditions to develop a psychological theory of the relations between ego and objects.

THE BRITISH INDEPENDENT GROUP

Balint

Unlike the other British object relations theorists, Balint (1952) continued to favor an instinct theory model alongside his object relational model. He believed that the libido was seeking sexual satisfaction as well as relatedness with the object. His writing on the need to work at preoedipal levels by allowing therapeutic regression to reach and heal the basic fault in the personality (Balint 1968) informed clinical practice especially in its application to the doctor–patient relationship (Balint 1957). His sensitive description of the differences in personal style between those patients who were philobatic (those who gained a sense of security from open space because they were fearful of being trapped in close proximity to an object) and those who were ocnophilic (those who avoided the spaces between objects because they felt more secure when clinging to an object) was helpful to clinicians and has found its modern equivalent in the work of nonanalytic marital therapists who talk in terms of pursuer–distancer spousal conflicts. Despite the usefulness of his work and his tremendous influence on the clinical acumen of the medical and mental health professions, his work did not constitute a major challenge to classical psychoanalytic theory.

Bowlby

Bowlby (1969, 1973, 1980) developed a theory based on ethology. Drawing on studies of animal behavior across species, Bowlby found common elements governing the behavior of the young and their mothers. He found that all primate infants seek and need attachment to their mothers in order to survive; all infants show fear and aggression when not protected by their mothers; and all infants in all higher species show specific attachment behaviors that result from and reinforce their mothers' nurturing behaviors. Bowlby saw that the infant–mother relationship is crucial and is secured by built-in behaviors that may be regarded as instinctual, but that focus on securing survival, not on gratifying sexual or aggressive drives (Bowlby 1958). He observed that the purpose of instinctual behaviors, such as rooting, crying, smiling, clinging, following with the eyes, and seeking proximity, was to secure the infant's relationship with the caregiving figure—the primary influence on development. Pleasure seeking is entirely secondary to the main goal of securing attachment and survival, and aggression results not from the death instinct, but from fear when the child is unprotected.

Curiously, Bowlby's theory has been read as one that is instinct based, focusing on the importance of the actual behavior of the object of the drives (Greenberg and Mitchell 1983). On the contrary, Bowlby's is a research-based alternative to classical drive theory and it is supportive of object relations theories. David Scharff, who studied in Bowlby's seminar, thinks that Bowlby (1988) believed that the analytic theory closest to his work was that of Fairbairn (D. Scharff, personal communication). Holmes (2001) wrote that Bowlby insisted that his research was "a scientifically based variant of object relations theory" (p. xii). But Bowlby's absorption in the actual, concrete experience of the object and his relative inattention to the child's modification of the internal world limited his own theories from amounting to a thoroughly analytic view of the human experience and led to his being ignored by many analysts (Slade 1996). His line of thinking pursued by Main and Ainsworth, however, gave rise to the field of attachment theory research, which is extremely influential in clarifying the object relational view of human development (Ainsworth et al. 1978, Main and Goldwyn, in press). It is the prolific writing and excellent presentation skills of Peter Fonagy and Mary Target, analysts and researchers, that have brought attachment research back into the realm of psychoanalysis and given it a degree of acceptance unrealized in Bowlby's lifetime.

British object relations theory and Bowlby's attachment theory have in common the belief that human beings are motivated not by instincts but by the need to be in relationships, that a person can't be understood separate from the social context, and that the inner sense of security derives from the experience of early care. So both theories make a connection between inner and outer worlds. Attachment theory deals with internal reality as a collection of internal working models; object relations theory deals with a self as a dynamic system of internal object relationships. Attachment theory uses systematic observation and narrows its focus to the research study of separation and reunion behavior; object relations uses free-form observation and intuition to study and interpret complex, subtle shifts in behavior in the therapeutic relationship. Both theories focus on observable behavior and take account of defense, anxiety, and motivation. Object relations theory deals with the concept of unconscious fantasy and unconscious communication by projective and introjective identification to elaborate on the connection between internal and external reality. Attachment theory has followed suit by showing that the mother's capacity for mentalizing influences the child's attachment style (Fonagy et al. 1995).

Many psychoanalysts rejected attachment theory as antianalytic in that it diverted attention from the power of unconscious fantasy and drives during development and refocused it on the external reality of child-rearing experiences. But object relations analysts accepted Bowlby's findings from research because they fit with ideas emerging from clinical practice about how the infant took in experience to build the structures of the self.

Winnicott

Winnicott agreed with Bowlby about the importance of secure attachment to the mother, but he did not remain rooted in the actualities of the environment, even though of all the object relations theorists he was the most aware of the influence of the parents on the growing child (Winnicott 1958, 1960a, 1965, 1971). He focused equally on the internal life of the child, drawing on the rich child-analytic tradition and especially the Kleinian concepts of unconscious fantasy. He admired both Freudian and Kleinian theories, but he did not preserve their integrity when he assimilated them. Distorting and playing with them as he was taking them in, he created his own ideas out of the creative mix into which he dropped the essence of his clinical wisdom. Many of Winnicott's concepts, such as the transitional object (Winnicott 1951), are most evocative in their enigmatic quality, which makes it difficult and even pointless to pin him down to precise formulations. He seems to have intended this, believing that it is from uncertainty that growth and creativity occur.

Winnicott neither followed nor challenged Freud's description of the structure and function of ego, superego, and object. In fact, he downplayed his departures from classical views. He preferred to think in terms of true and false self, each of them responsible for transactions with reality that drive/structural theory had earlier attributed to ego, superego, or id (Winnicott 1960b). Ignoring his radical divergence from classical theory, he claimed a connection between the true self and the sexual instinct and between the false self and the ego's adaptation to social reality. Where Freud was talking about the need to control the drives, Winnicott was trying to establish the primary importance of forming a self with meaning, value, and integrity. However, Winnicott did not refute drive theory; he simply crowded it out (Greenberg and Mitchell 1983). In other words Winnicott soared above classical, energic, and mechanistic considerations of structure and function to express concern for the whole person. He made spurious, deferential links between his own relational concepts and Freud's instinct/structural theory concepts to minimize difference, and so he bypassed the real problem of articulating his concepts with those of Freud. He did not want to be seen as dissident, but he did not want to be pigeon-holed either. He was influenced by Klein's ideas of unconscious phantasy, projective and introjective identification, but he rebelled against the constraints of subscribing rigidly to those views and becoming a formal member of her group. It seemed to him that the Kleinians valued the child's phantasy to the detriment of understanding the whole world of the psychosomatic partnership of the mother and infant, while to the Kleinians he seemed too involved in physical aspects, child-rearing realities, and gratifying activities.

For Winnicott, the adequacy of the maternal caregiving activity is what secured the child's psychological development. In conceptualizing children's responses to inadequate mothering, where Klein described projection, and Fairbairn emphasized the child's splitting and repression in response to frustration, Winnicott put developmental failure and the growth of the false self at the top of the list: Just as the "good-enough mother's" functioning facilitated development, so mothers' failures could be expected to handicap children's maturational processes.

This has led some to imply that Winnicott's contribution is no more than a deficit model of psychopathology, one that suggests that what is wrong with troubled children comes solely from deficiencies in their treatment by others, inadequate supplies, or lack of security. Winnicott's contribution does apply to understanding the way shortcomings in the enviromental provisions for a child are translated into psychic difficulty, in contrast to Klein, who largely ignored this area, and to Fairbairn, who did not supply any details about it. But it is inaccurate to say that Winnicott did not appreciate the child's own contribution to the development of a self. He thought that the beginning of the self has twin origins at the core of the infant self as it reaches out to the world. It derives from (1) the external world of objects in and out of reach and (2) the infant's own spontaneous gestures at the core of its being. The baby begins in itself and in its mother. As the mother becomes the first external object for the child, the child finds a self in her reaction and in her handling. And at the same time, the child internalizes the experience with her; that is, she becomes the material out of which the internal world is populated.

Winnicott (1971) conceives of psychotherapy and psychoanalysis as an experience of play in the area of the gap between patient and therapist. The child must be able to play to be healthy. The adult must be helped to play—with ideas, with significant others, with aspects of a relationship, and with the therapist—for healing to occur.

Because of his background as a doctor to children with physical ills, Winnicott did some unconventional things as an analyst, such as encouraging some patients to get off the couch and walk around, placing a child outside the door during a temper tantrum (1947), and physically holding some patients in states of regression. Some of these acts, especially physical contact, are unacceptable to most modern analytic therapists, and account for some skepticism toward his views in the United States. Yet, it is from the ideas conveyed in these actions that Winnicott's most important clinical contributions have come. It is with the clinical concepts of holding in the mind, relating and mirroring, and playing in the potential space of therapy that the modern object relations therapist works.

Fairbairn

Fairbairn's (1952, 1963) theory of personality development is the most systematic of the object relations school (Birtles 1996, Grotstein and Rinsley 1994, Scharff and Birtles 1994). Trained as a philosopher prior to becoming a physician, Fairbairn was a rigorously logical thinker. Although preserving his medical awareness of bodily symptomatology, Fairbairn did not subscribe to a highly biological approach. Influenced more thoroughly by his training in mental philosophy, Hellenic studies and theology—especially Hegel's (1807) writings on self and other, spirit and desire—Fairbairn took a philosophical view of the human infant, its desire for the other, and its needs for growth (Birtles 1996, Birtles and Scharff 1994). In his clinical experience with children who were being sexually and physically abused (Fairbairn 1943a), military personnel with war neuroses (Fairbairn 1943b), and patients with schizoid defenses against trauma and loss (Fairbairn 1940), he repeatedly noticed their need to use splitting and repression to maintain their integrity of their psychic functioning. These observations led to his theory of the endopsychic situation (Fairbairn 1944), designed to explain the development of hysterical neuroses (Fairbairn 1954) and schizoid personality.

Fairbairn admired Freud's classical theory, studied it closely, and taught it faithfully to the medical students at the University of Edinburgh, but, as his early lecture notes show, he simply couldn't agree that the infant is driven by instinctual energy to seek gratification and that there is no ego at birth, only an id—a far too impersonal concept for him (Birtles and D. Scharff 1994). He did not, however, fully outline his differences with Freud and the reasons for them until the late papers, only recently published (D. Scharff and Birtles 1994). Meanwhile, in his clinical reports written as early as 1927, Fairbairn considered the relationship of the patient to her family and others to be of central clinical importance, but without yet having a theoretical framework that differentiated such a perspective from the standard Freudian point of view.

Taking a dispassionate, intellectually critical approach to Freudian theories, Fairbairn found inconsistencies, and those together with his clinical findings therefore called for a complete revision of Freudian theory. Colleagues were uncomfortable with Fairbairn's intellectual honesty, because it challenged their beliefs and their professed loyalty to Freud. Fairbairn viewed his informed criticism of Freud as a mark of intellectual respect, but to others he seemed anarchic. Fairbairn did not see himself that way, and he must have been hurt by Winnicott and Khan's (1953) scathing review of his book *Psychoanalytic Studies of the Personality*.

The revision that was regarded as dissident was Fairbairn's argument that the infant is motivated by the need to be in a relationship, not propelled by instincts, and that at birth there is no id, but only a pristine, unstressed, unspoiled, undifferentiated ego. Only in dealing with the inevitable frustrations of actual existence in relationship to another person would this ego be stressed to greater or lesser degree, depending on the constitutionally determined strength of the ego and the responsiveness of the mother. Out of respect for Freud, Fairbairn retained the rather impersonal terms *object* to refer to the infant's experience of the mother and *libidinal* to refer to the tendency to seek the satisfaction of being in a relationship. In other words, in Fairbairn's theory, the object is intimately connected to the libido. It is not merely an object that the sexual drive alights upon for gratification, as in Freudian terms. In Fairbairn's view, the libido is primarily object seeking, not gratification seeking. And, far from simply happening to be there, the object participates in evoking the libidinal behavior. The object is essential for experience, which then gives the ego the material for building psychic structure. Only excessively frustrating mother–infant relationships that excite painful levels of longing in infants who are seriously rejected incite behaviors that aim at sexual and aggressive discharge. In other words, Fairbairn viewed such evidence of drive activity as a relational breakdown product, not a primary motivational, instinctual energy.

In Fairbairn's view, pleasure is the affect accompanying and signaling the successful mother–infant relationship. Similarly, displeasure is an affective sign of a mismatch in the relationship, not evidence of the dominance of the death instinct. When the level of frustration is intolerable, Fairbairn thought, the young ego defends itself by splitting of the object, splitting of the ego itself, and repression of the unsatisfactory parts of object, ego, and the associated affects. Thus he saw frustration as the motivation, and splitting and repression as the mechanism, for personality formation.

Fairbairn also invoked the mechanism of splitting at the later oedipal phase of development to explain the phenomenon of the family romance. He thought of the reorganization of internal structure during the oedipal phase as a creation by the child in response to ambivalence about both mother and father. The child tries to organize and simplify this complex situation, he said, by using the familiar technique of splitting the object, in this case by making one parent the good object and one the bad, organized along gender lines. Klein, on the other hand, dated the Oedipus complex much earlier, and based the infant's rage and envy of the parental couple in the infant's inborn awareness of the parents' intercourse from which the child was excluded.

In Fairbairn's theory, the unconscious is formed from repressed precipitates from the original ego and its objects connected by the relevant affects. In consciousness, there are the central ego (inheritor of the original pristine ego), the ideal object (a structure reflecting the internal experience of having had a good enough object), and feelings of satisfaction, pleasure, and joy in living and loving. In the unconscious, there are the libidinal and antilibidinal egos tied by feelings of neediness and rage to their exciting and rejecting objects, respectively. These repressed libidinal and antilibidinal internal object relationships are in dynamic relation inside the self, and they tend to press for reemergence and inclusion in the central ego. Fairbairn showed how this dynamic situation inside the self is portrayed in dreams, which he saw as short movies about the parts of the self in action, rather than as displays of conflicts over wishes.

Unlike Freud, who focused on the intrapsychic life of his patients, Fairbairn studied the relationship between his patients' internal worlds and their experiences with each parent and with the analyst. Unlike Kleinian theory, Fairbairn's object relations theory takes account of the actual nature of the object, as well as the infant's perceptions and misperceptions of object experience. With further good-enough object experience, earlier impressions can be modified and repression need not be so severe. With frustrating object experience, further splits in the ego occur. In this way, as the infant matures, social learning in the family context modifies or cements intrapsychic structure.

From distant Scotland, Fairbairn followed the work of Melanie Klein and her group in London on the experience of the infant in relating to the mother. As his writing progressed, he incorporated some of Klein's ideas that fit well with his own, but he did not accept her ideas without question. Fairbairn suggested that Klein's concept of unconscious phantasy as the fundamental link between the drives and reality was not more than one aspect of the life of the internal object. Phantasy colors the experience that is then internalized as an internal object, which exerts its influence over future experience, determining perceptions of, and creating unconscious phantasy about subsequent versions of, the external object.

Fairbairn's model emphasizes that the internal world is organized by internalizing experience with the outer world. He is specific about the growing psyche's input in creating a distinctive inner world that is not simply a carbon copy of the outer experience. Fairbairn's model of mind is one that is capable of blending outer influence with inner structuring throughout development. This balance makes his the most flexible of models, able both to consider the full influence of external reality and of inner forces that determine and modify development. For instance, Fairbairn's model of endopsychic structure can accept and understand the full force of external trauma such as physical or sexual abuse or the loss of a parent, but it also allows for the rich elaboration of the child's inner distortions and modifications of outer experience.

David Scharff (1992b) has expanded Fairbairn's theory as a model for a general psychology and for the development of the self, not only as an explanation of pathology. In his view, libidinal and antilibidinal constellations affect the ego's way of relating in both health and disease. The libidinal ego pulls toward the object both pleasantly and in a clinging way, and the antilibidinal ego distances from the object both to express angry rejection and to seek autonomy within the context of relationships. Object seeking and autonomy preserving are the dominant trends in relating, and it is only when the trends are not in balance that they become pathological. The exciting object and rejecting object normally color the object-seeking and autonomy-preserving functions of the central ego, and only the excesses in their repression or de-repression create pathological ways of relating. All aspects of the self—both ego and object, central and repressed internal object relationships—are in dynamic internal relationship with each other, influencing and being influenced by external object relations.

Fairbairn's contribution has often been misread as focusing solely on the effect of the external object on the developing ego. In fact he takes account of the constitutional weakness of the ego and its need for defense against unpleasant experience, and regards these as the main factors that influence the developing ego structure, modified however by actual experience. He goes beyond structuring the unconscious to give a theory of the functioning of the ego as a system of interconnecting parts that operate in conscious and unconscious areas. The crucial point about Fairbairn's theory is not just that ego is repressing unpleasant content or feeling, but that ego represses ego as well. Now the ego is truly executive, not just as a structure in charge of mediating reality, but as the active manager of the development of the self (Sutherland 1994). The ego forms its own psychic structure from its experience with the object and it grows in relation to the original and subsequent objects. A radical element in Fairbairn's theory is the idea that the psyche at birth is whole and capable of organizing itself, both in response to external experience and in accord with constitutional givens. This inherent self-organizing capacity of mind is fundamental to growth and to the potential for therapeutic change.

Guntrip

Guntrip (1961, 1969) followed Fairbairn in thinking of human motivation as interpersonally derived (Hazell 1994). He extended and popularized Fairbairn's object relations theory in personal terms for understanding and communicating about the human self and soul. His writing reached beyond psychoanalysts to psychotherapists and especially pastoral counselors. Guntrip thought that the core of psychopathology is the schizoid self, a part of the ego that has undergone yet another level of splitting than the levels that Fairbairn postulated. In despair and hopelessness, this regressed ego returns to a state of objectlessness. These views on regression within the ego led him to a departure from Fairbairn's concepts, because Guntrip was raising the possibility that the pristine ego at birth is objectless, unlike Fairbairn who thought that the ego at birth is primarily object seeking. But like Winnicott who wanted his ideas to derive from Freud, Guntrip wanted to view his work as an extension or minor revision of Fairbairn for which he wanted acknowledgment from Fairbairn. At the end of his life, Fairbairn conceded the point, but it is not clear why he would do so, because it introduced a fundamental misunderstanding of the difference between their ideas as to whether the pristine ego was object seeking or not.

Personally analyzed by both Fairbairn and then by Winnicott, Guntrip was in a position to observe both analysts at work. Guntrip (1975) said that in practice he found Fairbairn's technique to be quite classical while his theory building was radical, whereas Winnicott's technique was radically different from classical technique, although he refused to challenge classical theory.

Sutherland

As Fairbairn's major expositor, biographer (Sutherland 1963, 1989), and chronicler and editor of the British object relations theorists (Sutherland 1980), Sutherland spent the first seventy years of his life fostering and promoting the ideas of others, building bridges between their different psychoanalytic orientations, and moving easily between various levels of complexity and dimensions (Kohon 1996). Sutherland's work of this period is well known in London and in the United States because of his positions as director of the Tavistock Clinic in London, annual visiting Sloan professor at the Menninger Clinic in Kansas, and editor of the *International Journal of Psycho-Analysis*. After a successful late-life self-analysis (Sutherland 1990), in which he analyzed the functioning of various split-off parts of his self, he healed his tendency to identify with his parents one at a time, allowed himself to experience them as an internal couple, and then enjoyed the creative pairing of ideas and aspects of himself that he had previously avoided. The result was that in his late seventies and eighties he became capable of highly original abstract thinking about the nature of the self, how it develops and maintains its structures, and is sustained in interaction with others and with society's institutions. He defined the self as a dynamic organization of purposes and commitments whose behavior is governed by conscious and unconscious motives and whose development and functioning are inseparably linked to the social environment and at the same time autonomous and self-renewing. His posthumously published paper on the autonomous self is the final statement of his thinking. The rest of his original work on the self is lost because it was communicated orally in his mid-eighties and not written up by his students as far as I know.

Like Fairbairn, and unlike Klein, Sutherland insisted that instincts are not external to the structures of the self or of subselves but are inherent in, and subordinate to, them and to the fundamental human drive to be in a meaningful relationship (Padel 1995). He found the attachment research of Bowlby (with whom he had shared a house for their families in London) to be highly relevant to his views on development, but unlike Bowlby he thought that attachment was not an end in itself, but simply a necessary gestalt for the gestation of the self. Sutherland found Klein's vivid descriptions of the ego's fantasied object relationships useful, but he criticized her for not giving enough theoretical attention to the structuring of the self. He conceived of the self as a dynamic structure from the moment of birth, a holistic ego that structures itself by splitting and repression in response to experience with its objects. More than Fairbairn, he emphasized the internalization of the good object in consciousness, perhaps influenced by Kleinian concepts of life-affirming introjective identification. Going beyond Fairbairn, and not unlike Sullivan, he talked in terms of processes rather than structures so as to emphasize the dynamic, changing quality of the personality over the life cycle.

The terms that Sutherland used—*processes* and *subsystems*, rather than *structures*—were suited to describing the internal object relationships and their external versions in which the self engaged over time in daily life (Padel 1995). Influenced by open systems theory models that were not available to Fairbairn (Bertalanffy 1950, Miller 1965, Prigogine 1976), Sutherland specifically refuted Freud's principle of entropy—the organism's motivation to return to the non-excited, resting state—on the grounds that organisms do not remain static and their behavior predictable. In modern times of rapid change and adaptation, organisms as a whole do not appear to return to the resting state. They are not organized by negative feedback aimed at conserving energy. In fact, they do not seem to operate on the principle of homeostasis at all. Rather they aspire to ever higher levels of organization. Sutherland thought that parts of the organism might resist change, but that as a whole the organism tends to seek change. It responds to positive feedback by entering a state of disequilibrium that is not totally unpleasant. This state of chaos is generative and leads to the development of new forms, not a return to the resting state. The organism tends to seek higher levels of organization in psychological, social, and cultural structures.

Sutherland was influenced by Kohut's work on the self and Joseph Lichtenstein's contributions on identity to think more about the self in his last few years. He took Stern's (1985) infant research as a confirmation of his view that the self at birth is capable of, and driven toward, autonomy and integrity, which if frustrated, led to a noticeable protest by the infant self.

Sutherland thought that aggression was not only the reaction to the frustration of the need for attachment (as Bowlby thought), or the frustration of the need to be in a satisfying relationship (as Fairbairn thought), and certainly not the desperate attempt to protect the self from the death instinct (as Klein thought). Sutherland (1994) postulated that aggression results from the self's struggle for its autonomy, which it is competent to pursue, but which is inevitably frustrated by having dependent needs as well—even when these are met in an entirely satisfactory manner.

CONCLUSION

Fairbairn and Winnicott believed that average infants find average mothers to be reasonably good and yet inevitably somewhat frustrating, and so the infants respond with aggression to alert their mothers to what is needed. Where Fairbairn saw infants filled with rage because they were frustrated by the inevitability of being let down or rejected by their mother some of the time, Klein saw infants filled with rage because they were reacting against the threat of annihilation emanating from the constitutionally derived death instinct. On occasion Klein admitted that the mothers' behaviors contribute to the situation too, but she emphasized the role of the infants' innate aggression. Neither of them thought much about the impact of fathers. Only now are there attempts at taking account of the child's processing of experiencing two parents and their relation to each other from birth (Beebe and Lachmann 2002, Fivaz-Depeursinge and Corboz-Warnery 1999).

Whereas Klein held that the trauma of birth subjects the infant to the impact of the death instinct and so contributed to the *fear of annihilation of the self*, for Fairbairn it raised the issue of *fear of loss of the object*. In Klein's view infantile anger stemmed from the projection of the death instinct to protect the self from annihilation by it. In Fairbairn's view, at birth the infant loses the state of uterine bliss in which need has been met automatically and physiologically and there has been no perceived need of an object. After birth, there is total dependency on the primary object, and this leads to frustration of autonomous strivings and anger at the object. No matter if there are differences; each is useful in one setting or another. The human condition is far too complex for any single theory to suffice.

Fairbairn died in 1963, and Winnicott in 1971. Even before their deaths, other contributors had picked up the threads of the rich tapestry they began. In the last two decades, the work has continued, increasingly on both sides of the Atlantic, throughout Europe and in North and South America. Object relations no longer resides solely in the British Isles. The relational paradigm first described by Fairbairn, Winnicott, and the other object relations theorists, augmented by the ideas of Klein and Bion, has become the organizing set of ideas in modern psychoanalysis worldwide. Object relations theory has been applied to couple and family therapy, group therapy, organizational consultation, medical practice, and pastoral counseling, and it has influenced literature and philosophy.

Once excluded from discussion, object relations theory is now featured at both psychoanalytic and family therapy association meetings. When I coauthored *Object Relations Family Therapy* in 1987, object relations theory was on the fringe. In the recent *Handbook of Family Therapy* (Sexton et al. 2003), my chapter on object relations theory was listed as one of five *traditional* approaches! Clinical adaptations used in brief therapy, attachment research extended to adults and couple relationships, clinical study of sexual and societal trauma, and contemporary Kleinian ideas have validated and enriched object relations therapy. Principles from chaos theory of nonlinear dynamic systems are now pushing object relations theory toward another paradigm shift.

From Classical Freud to Contemporary Object Relations Psychoanalysis

Now we have a psychoanalytic theory of development in which the infant is motivated to be in multiple actual relationships in a dynamic system, which gives security and meaning to the self and knowledge of the other, and in which the human personality is conceptualized as continuing to grow throughout life with a nuclear family group, an extended family group, and important individual relationships, as well as a host of unconscious internal object relationships interacting dynamically through projective and introjective identification—all influencing each other and the person's development (D. Scharff and J. Scharff 1987, Shapiro et al. 1975). We have come far from Freudian instinct-based tripartite structural theory to a contemporary object relations theory that includes an integrated consideration of the biological, constitutional givens of the ego and a systemic view of the individual in the relational context, subject to organizing and disorganizing forces.

In the twenty-first century, object relations theory continues to evolve. Analysts of different schools are listening both to their own theories and to other theories from which they incorporate whatever makes sense. Self psychologists are now studying intersubjectivity (Stolorow and Atwood 1992), Freudian theorists referring in Sandler's terms to role relationships are applying the principles of projective identification in their discussions of clinical enactments of transference–countertransference phenomena (Chused 1991, Jacobs 1991), and object relations theorists are focusing more thoroughly on the experience of the self (Bollas 1987, 1995, Ogden 1994, D. Scharff, 1992a). Adding the ideas about the self-regulating, self-renewing, and self-transforming autonomous self, and research findings on neural development, attachment, affect regulation, and transgenerational transmission of trauma, we find that object relations is building a broader base from which we can look forward to further developments in adapting theory so that psychoanalysis, informed by twenty-first century philosophy and science, will be a sensitive, flexible, and muscular method for studying and treating the various conditions of human experience.

References

Ainsworth, M. D. S., Blehar, M. C., Waters, E., and Wall, S. (1978). *Patterns of Attachment: A Psychological Study of the Strange Situation*. Hillsdale, NJ: Lawrence Erlbaum.

Balint, M. (1952). *Primary Love and Psychoanalytic Technique*. London: Tavistock, 1965.

————— (1957). *The Doctor, His Patient and the Illness.* London: Tavistock.

————— (1968). *The Basic Fault: Therapeutic Aspects of Regression.* London: Tavistock.

Beebe, B., and Lachmann, F. (2002). *Infant Research and Adult Treatment: Co-Constructing Interactions.* Hillsdale, NJ: Analytic Press.

Bertalanffy, von, L. (1950). The theory of open systems in physics and biology. *Science* 111:23–29.

Birtles, E. F. (1996). The philosophical origins of Fairbairn's theory of object relations. Presented at the Fairbairn conference of the International Institute of Object Relations Therapy, New York, October. In *Fairbairn Then and Now*, ed. N. Skolnick and D. Scharff. Hillsdale NJ: Analytic Press, 1998.

Birtles, E. F., and Scharff, D. E., eds. (1994). *From Instinct to Self: Selected Papers of W. R. D. Fairbairn*, vol. 2. Northvale, NJ: Jason Aronson.

Bollas, C. (1987). *The Shadow of the Object.* New York: Columbia University Press.

————— (1995). *Cracking Up.* New York: Hill and Wang.

Bowlby, J. (1958). The nature of the child's tie to his mother. *International Journal of Psycho-Analysis* 39:1–24.

————— (1969). *Attachment and Loss*, vol. 1. New York: Basic Books.

————— (1973). *Attachment and Loss*, vol. 2. *Separation, Anxiety, and Anger.* New York: Basic Books.

————— (1980). *Attachment and Loss*, vol. 3. *Loss, Sadness and Depression.* New York: Basic Books.

————— (1988). *A Secure Base: Clinical Applications of Attachment Theory.* London: Routledge.

Chused, J. (1991). The evocative power of enactments. *Journal of the American Psychoanalytic Association* 39:615–639.

Fairbairn, W. R. D. (1940). Schizoid factors in the personality. In *Psychoanalytic Studies of the Personality*, pp. 3–27. London: Routledge, 1952.

————— (1943a). Phantasy and inner reality. In *From Instinct to Self: Selected Papers of W. R. D. Fairbairn*, vol. 2, ed. E. F. Birtles and D. E. Scharff, pp. 293–295. Northvale, NJ: Jason Aronson, 1994.

————— (1943b). The repression and return of bad objects (with special reference to the war neuroses). In *Psychoanalytic Studies of the Personality*, pp. 59–81. London: Routledge, 1952.

————— (1944). Endopsychic structure considered in terms of internal object relationships. In *Psychoanalytic Studies of the Personality*, pp. 82–136. London: Routledge, 1952.

————— (1952). *Psychoanalytic Studies of the Personality.* London: Routledge.

(Reprinted as *An Object Relations Theory of the Personality*. New York: Basic Books, 1954.)

———— (1954). The nature of hysterical states. In *From Instinct to Self: Selected Papers of W. R. D. Fairbairn*, vol. 2., ed. E. F. Birtles and D. E. Scharff, pp. 13–40. Northvale, NJ: Jason Aronson, 1994.

———— (1963). Synopsis of an object relations theory of the personality. *International Journal of Psycho-Analysis* 44:224–226. Reprinted in *From Instinct to Self: Selected Papers of W. R. D. Fairbairn*, vol. 2., ed. E. F. Birtles and D. E. Scharff, pp. 155–156. Northvale, NJ: Jason Aronson, 1994.

Ferenczi, S. (1933). Confusion of tongues between the adult and the child. In *Final Contributions to the Problems and Methods of Psychoanalysis*, pp. 156–167. London: Hogarth, 1955.

Fivaz-Depeursinge, E., and Corboz-Warnery, A. (1999). *The Primary Triangle: A Developmental Systems View of Mothers, Fathers, and Infants*. New York: Basic Behavioral Science–Basic Books.

Fonagy, P., Steele, M., Steele, H., et al. (1995). Attachment, the reflective self, and borderline states: the predictive specificity of the adult attachment interview and pathological emotional development. In *Attachment Theory: Social, Developmental and Clinical Perspectives*, ed. S. Goldberg, R. Muir, and J. Kerr, pp. 233–279. Hillsdale, NJ: Analytic Press.

Greenberg, J., and Mitchell, S. (1983). *Object Relations in Psychoanalytic Theory*. Cambridge, MA: Harvard University Press.

Grotstein, J., and Rinsley, D., eds. (1994). *Fairbairn and the Origins of Object Relations*. London: Free Association Books.

Guntrip, H. (1961). *Personality and Human Interaction*. London: Hogarth.

———— (1969). *Schizoid Phenomena, Object Relations and the Self*. New York: International Universities Press.

———— (1975). My experience in analysis with Fairbairn and Winnicott. *International Review of Psycho-Analysis* 16:145–156.

Hazell, J. ed. (1994). *Personal Relations Therapy. The Collected Papers of H. S. Guntrip*. Northvale, NJ: Jason Aronson.

Hegel, G. W. F. (1807). *The Phenomenolgy of Spirit*, trans. A. V. Miller. London: Oxford University Press.

Holmes, J. (2001). *The Search for the Secure Base: Attachment Theory and Psychotherapy*. East Sussex, England, and Philadelphia: Brunner/Routledge.

Jacobs, T. (1991). *The Use of the Self*. Madison, CT: International Universities Press.

Kohon, G., ed. (1986). *The British School of Psychoanalysis: The Independent Tradition*. London: Free Association Books.

———— (1996). Book review of *The Autonomous Self: The Work of John D.*

Sutherland, ed. J. S. Scharff. *Journal of the American Psychoanalytic Association* 44:1261–1262.

Main, M., and Goldwyn, R. (In press). Interview-based adult attachment classification: related to infant–mother and infant–father attachment. *Developmental Psychology*.

Miller, J. G. (1965). Living systems, basic concepts. *Behavioral Science* 10:337–379.

Ogden, T. (1994). *Subjects of Analysis*. Northvale, NJ: Jason Aronson.

Padel, J. (1995). Book review of *The Autonomous Self: The Work of John D. Sutherland*, ed. J. S. Scharff. In *International Journal of Psycho-Analysis* 76(1):177–179.

Prigogine, I. (1976). Order through fluctuation: self-organization and social system. In *Evolution and Consciousness: Human Systems in Transition*, ed. C. H. Waddington and E. Jantsch, pp. 93–126, 130–133. Reading, MA: Addison-Wesley.

Scharff, D. E. (1992a). *Refinding the Object and Reclaiming the Self*. Northvale, NJ: Jason Aronson.

——— (1992b). *The Sexual Relationship: An Object Relations View of Sex and the Family*. London: Routledge & Kegan Paul. Northvale, NJ: Jason Aronson, 1998.

Scharff, D. E., ed. (1996). *Object Relations Theory and Practice*. Northvale, NJ: Jason Aronson.

Scharff, D. E., and Birtles, E. F. (1994). *From Instinct to Self: Selected Papers of W. R. D. Fairbairn*, vol. 1. Northvale, NJ: Jason Aronson.

Scharff, D. E., and Scharff, J. S. (1987). *Object Relations Family Therapy*. Northvale, NJ: Jason Aronson.

——— (1991). *Object Relations Couple Therapy*. Northvale, NJ: Jason Aronson.

Scharff, J. S. (1992). *Projective and Introjective Identification and the Use of the Therapist's Self*. Northvale, NJ: Jason Aronson.

Scharff, J. S., and Scharff, D. E. (1992). *The Primer of Object Relations Therapy*. Northvale, NJ: Jason Aronson.

——— (2000). *Tuning the Therapeutic Instrument. Affective Learning of Psychotherapy*. Northvale, NJ: Jason Aronson.

Sexton, T. L., Weeks, G., and Robbins, M. (2003, in press). *Handbook of Family Therapy*. New York: Guilford.

Shapiro, E., Zinner, J., Shapiro, R., and Berkowitz, D. (1975). The influence of family experience on borderline personality development. *International Review of Psycho-Analysis* 2(4):399–411 and in *Foundations of Object Relations Family Therapy*, ed. J. S. Scharff, pp. 127–154. Northvale, NJ: Jason Aronson.

Slade, A. (1996). Attachment theory and research: implications for the theory and practice of individual psychotherapy. *Handbook of Attachment Theory and Research*, ed. J. Cassidy and P. R. Shaver. New York: Guilford.

Stern, D. (1985). *The Interpersonal World of the Infant: A View from Psychoanalysis and Developmental Psychology*. New York: Basic Books.

Stolorow, R., and Atwood, G. (1992). *Contexts of Being: The Intersubjective Foundations of Psychological Life*. Hillsdale, NJ: Analytic Press.

Sutherland, J. D. (1963). Object relations theory and the conceptual model of psychoanalysis. *British Journal of Medical Psychology* 36:109–124. Reprinted in *The Autonomous Self: The Work of John D. Sutherland*, ed. J. S. Scharff, pp. 3–24. Northvale, NJ: Jason Aronson.

———— (1980). The British object relations theorists: Balint, Winnicott, Fairbairn, Guntrip. *Journal of the American Psychoanalytic Association* 28(4):829–860. Reprinted in *The Autonomous Self: The Work of John D. Sutherland*, ed. J. S. Scharff, pp. 25–44. Northvale, NJ: Jason Aronson.

———— (1989). *Fairbairn's Journey into the Interior*. London: Free Association Books.

———— (1990). Reminiscences. In *The Autonomous Self: The Work of John D. Sutherland*, ed. J. S. Scharff, pp. 392–423. Northvale, NJ: Jason Aronson.

———— (1994). The autonomous self. In *The Autonomous Self: The Work of John D. Sutherland*, ed. J. S. Scharff, pp. 303–330. Northvale, NJ: Jason Aronson.

Wallerstein, R. S. (2002). *From dissidence to pluralism—and onto what?* Unpublished paper presented at the conference Understanding Diversity and Controversy in Psychoanalysis, Psychoanalytic Research and Development Fund, New York, February 14–15, 2003.

Winnicott, D. W. (1947). Hate in the countertransference. In *Collected Papers: Through Paediatrics to Psycho-Analysis*, pp. 194–203. London: Hogarth, 1975.

———— (1951). Transitional objects and transitional phenomena. In *Collected Papers: Through Paediatrics to Psycho-Analysis*, pp. 229–242. London: Hogarth, 1975.

———— (1958). *Collected Papers: Through Paediatrics to Psycho-Analysis*. London: Hogarth, 1975.

———— (1960a). The theory of the parent-infant relationship. In *The Maturational Processes and the Facilitating Environment*, pp. 37–55. London: Hogarth.

———— (1960b). Ego distortion in terms of true and false self. In *The Maturational Processes and the Facilitating Environment*, pp. 140–152. London: Hogarth.

———— (1965). *The Maturational Processes and the Facilitating Environment.* London: Hogarth.

———— (1971). *Playing and Reality.* London: Tavistock.

Winnicott, D. W., and Khan, M. (1953). A review of Fairbairn's *Psychoanalytic Studies of the Personality. International Journal of Psycho-Analysis* 34:329–333.

7

From Dissidence to Pluralism in Psychoanalysis—and Onto What?[1]

ROBERT S. WALLERSTEIN

Martin Bergmann in Part I of this volume has offered us a comprehensive overview of a most important aspect of psychoanalytic history over its span of now more than a century—how it has dealt with innovative conceptions and new theoretical perspectives that have differed from whatever has been its consensually accepted mainstream, which for most of Sigmund Freud's active professional lifetime was what Freud himself created and espoused—granted that he enlarged and altered his own conceptualizations over time, and at times quite drastically, and granted also that he welcomed contributions from his adherents so long as they were fully compatible with his own positions, and usually just extensions or amplifications of them.

Freud and those around him, in the first years a very small band, in Vienna, in Zurich, and a little later in Berlin and Budapest, from the beginning felt threatened and beleaguered, kept outside the scientific academic and medical worlds, partly due to the shocking nature of the central psychoanalytic doctrine of infantile sexuality—in the dominantly Victorian age of the time—and partly due to the more or less

---

1. This paper is adapted from another (Wallerstein 2002b) manuscript that has been modified for the purposes of this symposium.

official anti-Semitism of the Austro-Hungarian Empire, which precluded ready access for Freud and his followers to academic positions and respectability. And so those who arose from within psychoanalytic ranks with decidedly different emphases and/or new overarching theoretical perspectives were experienced as threats to the very integrity of the discipline, and it was felt that they had to be extruded from its ranks. Freud's 1914 monograph, "On the History of the Psycho-Analytic Movement," was, at once, a historical unfolding of the development of psychoanalysis to that time, a spirited exposition of what Freud conceived to be the central unifying psychoanalytic doctrines to which psychoanalysts were expected to adhere, and a detailed account of his reasons for parting with, or pushing out, Breuer, Bleuler, Stekel, and, written at greatest length, Adler and then Jung, as no longer to be counted as coworkers, as part of the evolving psychoanalytic movement.

In accord with these needs, or perhaps better, these conceptions, Freud and his followers established the International Psychoanalytical Association (IPA) at the Second International Psychoanalytical Congress, held in 1910 in Nuremberg,[2] and two years later, in 1912, Freud created the secret committee of the seven ring holders, himself and six of his most devoted and cherished followers. Both of these moves were efforts to guarantee the stability of his central psychoanalytic doctrines against fractious divisiveness from within, and against diluting or hostile pressures from without—thus trying to ensure the enduring capacity and loyalty of those who carried the psychoanalytic imprimatur. Those who, during Freud's lifetime, were expelled from the IPA or who left it—and Martin Bergmann has provided us a detailed accounting of the four best known, Adler, Jung, Rank, and (almost) Ferenczi—were labeled dissidents who would each be free to follow his own psychological bent, but should, in all honesty, no longer call it psychoanalysis. Thus, the initial circling of the wagons, the early categorization of proper psychoanalysis vis-à-vis dissidence and those extruded as dissidents.

---

2. In "On the History of the Psycho-Analytic Movement" (1914), Freud wrote: "I considered it necessary to form an official association because I feared the abuses to which psycho-analysis would be subjected as soon as it became popular. There should be some headquarters whose business it would be to declare: 'All this nonsense is nothing to do with analysis; this is not psycho-analysis'" (p. 43).

This feeling of being a beleaguered discipline, constantly needing to define its parameters and to protect its integrity, has been an almost constant aspect of the psychoanalytic landscape worldwide over the century since those early beginnings, with the single major exception of the first post-World War II decades, and then only in America, the period in which I was trained analytically—actually in the decade of the 1950s—a period now looked at nostalgically as the halcyon days. This was of course the period of great psychoanalytic popularity in America, and of the almost monolithic hegemony within American psychoanalysis of the ego psychology paradigm architected by Heinz Hartmann and his many collaborators, and systematized by David Rapaport, all declared to be the direct line of descent from Freud's ego psychology articulated in "The Ego and the Id" (1923), and "Inhibitions, Symptoms, and Anxiety" (1926), and then expanded by Anna Freud's landmark elaboration of the defensive functions of the ego, *The Ego and the Mechanisms of Defence* (1936), an eightieth birthday presentation to her father, and Heinz Hartmann's counterpart elaboration of the adaptive functions of the ego, *Ego Psychology and the Problem of Adaptation* (1939).

This was also the period of the capture of American psychiatry by the psychoanalytic idea, with psychoanalysts being avidly sought by medical schools to chair their departments of psychiatry, with psychoanalysis installed, under the banner of psychodynamics, as the psychological theory of psychiatry, and with psychoanalytic psychotherapy developed as the adaptation of psychoanalytic conceptions and techniques to the clinical exigencies of the more severely ill psychiatric patients crowding the teaching hospitals and associated outpatient clinics of the academic medical centers—more severely ill, that is, than the putatively classically neurotic patients around whom the technical precepts of psychoanalysis had been originally formulated. This was also, concomitantly, the period of the full analytic practices of those trained within the rapidly burgeoning institutes of the American Psychoanalytic Association, and of an ebullient optimism of an ever-expanding future for the practitioners of this psychoanalytic mainstream, the self-proclaimed carriers of the authentic unitary and unifying Freudian legacy.

But we also know that Freud's strenuous efforts to establish and maintain such a unitary, and consensually accepted, structure of psychoanalysis—which the American ego psychologists long felt that they could successfully enshrine—in the end failed, with the rise within organized psychoanalysis of an alternative metapsychology and its linked differing technical precepts, that is, the Kleinian movement that would not let itself be extruded—and this actually occurred even in Freud's lifetime.

It was in fact the Kleinians who insisted on their even more impeccable psychoanalytic credentials, with their unswerving adherence to Freud's death instinct theory as a central theoretical building block, when the Viennese, who were closer to the persona and mind of Freud, split so sharply on the value to psychoanalysis of this particular theoretical turn of Freud's. This particular history has of course been chronicled in magisterial detail, both personal and scientific, in the 1991 volume edited by Pearl King and Riccardo Steiner, *The Freud-Klein Controversies, 1941–45*. Although these controversial discussions took place in the early 1940s, in wartime Great Britain, when the central protagonists on both sides, Anna Freud and Melanie Klein, and their strongly committed followers were all in London, sharing in, and striving for control over, the British Psychoanalytical Society, the controversy itself originated a good deal earlier, in the late 1920s and through the 1930s, when Melanie Klein was already established in London and had gained substantial support from the British analysts (together constituting the English school), and Anna Freud and her central supporters were still in Vienna (constituting the Viennese school), and when the two schools were vigorously arguing the proper theoretical and technical dimensions of the then nascent precepts that should govern the emerging arena of psychoanalytic work with children.

At the time there were vigorous—and at times, contentious—exchanges of letters between Freud and Ernest Jones (a member of the favored group of closest adherents, the secret committee of seven ring holders) in which Freud strongly backed his daughter Anna, and chided Jones for giving comfort and support to Melanie Klein. There were exchange lectures in the mid-1930s between London and Vienna in which Jones and Joan Rivière from London and Robert Waelder from Vienna aired the scientific differences between the two schools [see the King-Steiner volume (1991) for a detailed account]. In the end, neither group succeeded in delegitimizing the other psychoanalytically, and an administrative compromise was effected by the British Society in which both groups, the (Anna) Freudian and the Kleinian, would exist side by side, educationally and scientifically, under the same British Society umbrella, along with a third, called the middle group (and in more recent years renamed the independent group) which did not subscribe to the strict precepts of either of the arrayed opposed forces. Each of the three groups would be free to elaborate its own governing theoretical perspective (its own metapsychology), and its own technical precepts, each one claiming, of course, to be a comprehensive and sufficient understanding of mental functioning, and a competent, fully adequate, guide to the amelioration of mental disorder. It was at this point, and still in Freud's lifetime, that the Kleinians successfully fought off the label of dissident—and the implied threat of extrusion—and, in its place, psychoanalytic theoretical diversity, or pluralism, as we have come to call it, was born.

With this beginning of the theoretical diversification of institutional psychoanalysis, organized within the IPA—except, as already stated, in the United States—the succeeding decades saw the rise of Bion's extensions of Kleinian thought; of the crystallization of the British object-relational school grounded in Fairbairn, Winnicott, and Balint emerging as the middle group, and therefore neither (Anna) Freudian nor Kleinian; of the philosophical/linguistic framework of Lacan in France; of the hermeneutic emphasis spearheaded by Ricoeur in France and Habermas in Germany; and ultimately of others still, all claiming their accepted place within the house of psychoanalysis.

Not a few commentators have stated their conviction that, had the deviations of Adler and Jung occurred within the more recent decades of an accommodating pluralism in psychoanalytic ranks, they too might now represent alternative theoretical perspectives within the framework of the IPA, not psychological movements outside of it. Indeed, many of their central tenets, once the basis for a declared departure and extrusion, have come back to an accepted place within the main corpus of psychoanalysis, almost across the board; for example, Adler's emphasis, long before it was incorporated by Freud, on the aggressive drive (and concomitant sibling rivalry, masculine protest, compensatory mechanisms, etc.) and on the centrality of ego functioning in psychic equilibration (again, before Freud), or Jung's emphasis on the importance of continuing adult psychological development, later elaborated into psychosocial stages across the entire life span by Erik Erikson, albeit in a different way.

Finally, even in the American Psychoanalytic Association (APsaA), where Freud's vision of a unified theoretical structure for psychoanalysis had long seemed to take root and succeed, this seeming theoretical hegemony of ego psychology ultimately gave way, with the growth within the American's ranks of Heinz Kohut's self psychology, with its alternative theoretical constructions of the bipolar self, of Tragic Man rather than Guilty Man, of deficit and its restoration, rather than of conflict and its resolution. Alongside Kohut, there was Margaret Mahler's developmental emphasis, and Roy Schafer's action language built around the agency of the self, and of course the major paradigm shift of the past two decades exploding in America outside the American's ranks, away from the natural science–based ego psychology embedded in what has come to be called a "one-person psychology," to the object-relational, social—and then dialectical—constructivist, and intersubjective approaches (called in ensemble the "relational turn"), all expressions of what has come to be called a "two-person psychology."

This relational turn traces its roots partly to object-relational imports from Britain, but even more solidly to its indigenous American progenitors rallying around Harry Stack Sullivan's "interpersonal psychiatry" (like Clara Thompson, Karen Horney, Erich Fromm, etc.), who, at the time, in the 1940s, were either extruded from the ranks of organized American psychoanalysis (the APsaA), or completely marginalized within it, in what was then the heyday of ego psychology, but now being revived with all due credit, including as its first forebear, the current great revival of interest in the contributions of Sandor Ferenczi, called now, in some quarters, the very mother of psychoanalysis, in an almost equal place of honor with Freud, the acknowledged father (Ferenczi, once Freud's most cherished collaborator, himself came close to being extruded in his final days).

It is this issue of the collapse of Freud's original unitary vision for psychoanalysis and the rise in its place of a burgeoning and, in ways, bewildering theoretical diversity, or pluralism as we now call it, that I undertook to present in my presidential address to the Thirty-fifth International Psychoanalytical Congress in Montreal in 1987, entitled, "One Psychoanalysis or Many?" (Wallerstein 1988), as a topic of sufficient importance and concern to the worldwide psychoanalytic community, in the hope that a dialogue about it could enhance our shared psychoanalytic understanding and commitment. In that Montreal address, I proposed that this growth in our theoretical diversity, by then widely acknowledged and accepted as reflecting our discipline's state of affairs worldwide, even in America, raised two fundamental questions: (1) What, in view of this ever growing pluralism, still holds us together as common adherents of a shared psychoanalytic science and profession? and (2) the corollary: What do we have in common, that marks us off from other, nonpsychoanalytic psychologies, for surely not every kind of psychological understanding is psychoanalytic?

My own response at the time, which subsequent analytic debate has revealed to be far from widely shared, is that our common ground is to be found in our experience-near clinical theory, and in our concern with anxiety and defense, with conflict and compromise, with self and object representation, with transference and countertransference, and with the like clinical concepts that I feel guide our understandings and our interventions across the entire array of theoretical perspectives. Whereas our diversity, I felt, is to be found in our experience-distant general theories or metapsychologies, which we invoke to try to explain the structure and functioning of our minds, and how we think our technical interventions that are guided by our clinical theory alter that mental functioning toward desired changes or psychic maturity or mental health—however we conceptualize those.

Toward that end, I dubbed our diverse general theories, our metapsychologies, as nothing but our scientific metaphors, quite loosely coupled to our clinical theories and observations, and not at all amenable, at this stage of our development as a science, to empirical testing. Since each of our metapsychologies purports to explain the whole spectrum of psychopathology and the proper roads to its amelioration, I feel that we are without warrant, again at least at this stage of our development as a science, to claim the greater heuristic usefulness or validity of any one of our general theories over the others, other than by the indoctrinations and allegiances built into us by the happenstance of our individual trainings, our differing personality dispositions, and the explanatory predilections then carried over into our consulting rooms.

The following IPA congress, the thirty-sixth, in Rome in 1989, inspired by my Montreal address, was devoted to this topic of the common ground, with three major plenary addresses given by analysts representing the three major regions of worldwide psychoanalytic activity, and trained and practicing within three different theoretical frameworks, in order to explore in the following formal and informal discussions, through the case material they were asked to present, the areas of convergence (reflecting common ground or common understanding) and of divergence, in the way they actually conducted their clinical work. In my presidential address to that congress, entitled "Psychoanalysis: The Common Ground" (Wallerstein 1990), I first reviewed the rising chorus of argument that had arisen in the intervening two years over my thesis of where both our diversity, and within that, our unity (our common ground) resided, and then tried to demonstrate where I felt that the presented clinical material of the three major plenary addresses sustained my thesis.

Needless to say, the chorus of argument at that congress over this issue both widened and intensified. An edited book (Wallerstein 1992) brought together a full spectrum of the diverse views on this controversy over common ground at that time, plus my efforts to then respond to them. The only thing that seemed then indubitably agreed upon by all was that in a field where a central argument had long been over whether in fact it was (or could be) a unified and internally coherent body of theory, with an equally reasonably unified and internally coherent body of technical precepts flowing from the theory, we had now come, over the just prior decades, to a full realization that, in this regard, Freud's dream was not sustained, that we were at that juncture, and had been for, indeed, quite some time, a field marked by a clear and seemingly ever-growing pluralism of theoretical perspectives. Whether this was for better or for worse, whether it signified progress and should be celebrated or was just the fashions of change—maybe inherent in the very nature of what some (Harrison 1970) have called "our unique science"—was itself a hotly debated issue. Of course, by this time the rubric of psychoanalytic dissident had all but disappeared from our discourse.

What then have been the subsequent responses within psychoanalysis to that discourse initiated on this issue of the acknowledged diversity of our theoretical structures? In a long review essay on Stephen Mitchell's 1988 book, *Relational Concepts in Psychoanalysis*, in the section of their review devoted to psychoanalytic model-making, Janet Bachant and Arnold Richards (1993) divide the constituents of what they call "psychoanalytic metatheories" (p. 455) into five major groupings. The first they call the "common-grounders," which they identify with me, a group that they say, rightly, espouses the concept of clinical common ground within the diversity of theoretical approaches in psychoanalysis.

The second group they call the advocates of a multimodal approach to the phenomena of psychoanalysis. This group, exemplified by Fred Pine, is stated to believe that the clinical phenomena discerned in our consulting rooms must forever be approached from within a range of four differing psychologies—of drive, of ego, of object, and of self—with the psychoanalytic clinician always working within the frame of whichever set of theoretical constructs (drive, ego, object, or self) would fit most appropriately with, or illuminate most usefully, the exigent state of the patient in each shifting moment of the therapeutic interaction. As a personal digression, one could, as an exercise, try to make our current range of distinct theoretical perspectives (our variety of metapsychologies) fit into the four psychologies propounded by Pine as encompassing the total spectrum of required or necessary psychoanalytic theories. I would venture that almost none could fit neatly, and that some, the Lacanian comes quickly to mind, would not fit at all, based as it is, as a psychology, on fundamentally different philosophical and linguistic assumptions than hold in any of Pine's categories.

The third group is identified with Leo Rangell and his advocacy of what he calls "total composite psychoanalytic theory," which he states has grown by progressive accretion upon the work of Freud and then the creators of ego psychology—Anna Freud, Heinz Hartmann, Otto Fenichel, and all the others—and that that has always encompassed within its frame what the advocates of other theoretical positions, like the object-relational or the self-psychological, have chosen to split off from the main body, and then have tried to elevate into total systems, efforts, in effect, to split off parts of an organic whole, designated by Rangell as "mainstream" or "classical" psychoanalysis. This can, of course, be seen by the proponents of all other theoretical perspectives as an effort to maintain the one-time American imperialism that saw its own ego psychology as the only comprehensively whole psychoanalysis, with all the other theoretical schools as deviant or split-off partial positions.

The fourth group Bachant and Richards dub the anti-metapsychologists, those represented in America by disenchanted former adherents of David Rapaport, like George Klein, Merton Gill, and Roy Schafer, who would eschew all general psychologies (metapsychologies) in psychoanalysis, casting them out by what Klein called a "theorectomy" and concentrating only on the systematic study and the empirical testing of the clinical theory, the arena within which I have tried to establish our common ground.

The fifth group Bachant and Richards call the "dichotomizers," those, among whom they count Stephen Mitchell as one of the most vigorous and persuasive spokesmen, who see all our variant metapsychologies as falling into one of just two fundamentally different and irreconcilable camps, those based on what is called, on the one hand, drive-structural theory, built on Freud's original structural concepts, which sees the ego as a *pleasure*-seeking organ, trying to satisfy drive pressures in ways compatible with superego demands and the constraints of external reality, and on the other hand, object-relational theory, derived originally from the work of Fairbairn, and with antecedents back to Ferenczi, which sees the ego as an *object*-seeking organ, pursuing human relatedness. Whatever stand we individually take toward each of the five groupings in this categorization of the variety of theoretical perspectives within our psychoanalytic universe, I am reasonably sure that we can all agree that it reflects well the confusing flux, as well as the intellectual ferment, in our collective orientation to the theoretical diversity that has pervaded, and has quite clearly expressed, much of the state of psychoanalytic theorizing of the most recent decades.

But pendulums do swing in ongoing developments in the world of ideas, and, I think, no less so in the system of ideas introduced to the world by Sigmund Freud. Just as a world of theoretical unity was the dominant influence in our field throughout most of Freud's working lifetime, until the rise of the Kleinian movement in the 1920s, that is, and just as it was followed by a world of ever-increasing theoretical diversity that seems so dominant today, perhaps there are now tell-tale signs of significant convergences, at least on the clinical and technical levels, between once seemingly quite polarized perspectives, convergences that may be the harbingers of a not too far off coming together at ever higher levels of theoretic conceptualization, perhaps ultimately at the level of an encompassing and transcending once-again unified general theory or metapsychology. These signs seem quite unobtrusive and are not often remarked as such within the cacophony of our contemporary psychoanalytic world, but I would like to submit that they express our next coming development as a field, and it is at this point that I want to set my attempt at prophesying the future, or at least the coming near future, of psychoanalysis as I see it. This is the question in the title of this presentation. We have come from a once unitary psychoanalytic world, marked by its periodic dissidents, to a world now of accepted pluralism, but where do we go from here?

It seems unsurprising to me that Otto Kernberg is one of those who I feel heralds the new trend that I see developing and wish to present. After all, Kernberg's central lifetime theorizing has consisted of the effort, within American psychoanalysis, to forge links—contra the dichotomizers—between the drive-structural and the object-relational perspectives, through advancing his views of internalized object relationships, consisting of self representations, object representations, and the affective valences that link them, as the fundamental building blocks out of which the structured psychic apparatus of id, ego, and superego is constituted. It is within the framework of this predilection that Kernberg (1993) published "Convergences and Divergences in Contemporary Psychoanalytic Technique," an article that I think has been much less remarked upon than is usual with his writings.

Taking as his starting point, not the general theories of psychoanalysis (our widely divergent metapsychologies), nor even the clinical theories, the more experience-near level at which I have pitched my concerns, but rather the principles of technique that actually flow from our conceptual positions, Kernberg identified and elaborated eleven major areas where he could point to actual growing convergences in technical interventions coming from clearly distinct, and even seemingly opposite, theoretical positions. He also identified seven areas of persisting divergences, but this shorter list seems much less weighty, and concerning some of them, he even could see signs of the coming resolution of the distinctions, or their relegation to a historical past, but no longer a current salient issue. In each instance of convergence or continuing divergence, Kernberg clearly indicated which theoretical perspectives are involved, and in what way their technical implementations and even in places their higher-level explanatory frameworks are moving closer together. Parenthetically, only the Lacanian position seems largely outside of these mostly converging trends.

To give the flavor of Kernberg's exposition, I quote from his highly condensed summary paragraphs:

> A broad survey of the psychoanalytic field reveals both convergences and divergences in technique. The major convergences include earlier interpretation of the transference, increased focus on transference analysis, as well as growing attention to countertransference analysis and increasing concern with the risks of "indoctrinating" patients. Greater emphasis is found on character defences and the unconscious meanings of the "here-and-now." Also noted are trends towards translating unconscious conflicts into object relations terminology, as well as toward considering a multiplicity of royal roads to the unconscious. Regarding divergences, significant controversies continue regarding reconstruction and the recovery of preverbal experience, drawing the lines between psychoanalytic psychotherapy and psychoanalysis, the role of empathy, and the relation of historical to narrative truth. [p. 670]

It is this overview by Kernberg that I feel reflects the still not so widely noticed, or acknowledged, current swing of the pendulum back toward increasing commonality, certainly at the level of our technical interventions in our consulting rooms, and more commonality than I feel many in our field are ready to admit, at the level of experience-near clinical theories, linked closely enough by canons of inference to the technical activities that flow from them. Perhaps, incrementally and ultimately, if this trend prevails, we will be able to build from an increasingly firm base of clinical theory, to painstakingly fashion a more truly unified and scientific broader theoretical structure that could then take its proper place as a full partner within the whole array of human sciences.

At least that is the vision, but it is a vision far from widely shared at this point. The widely influential 1983 book by Jay Greenberg and Stephen Mitchell, *Object Relations in Psychoanalytic Theory*, traced the historical development of what they call the "relational/structure model" within and out of Freud's "drive/structure model," and culminated in their declaration, on philosophical as well as psychological grounds, of the fundamental incompatibility of the two models—very much contra the converging directions just quoted from Kernberg, and contra as well Kernberg's own efforts to create an amalgam, consisting of relational approaches centered on internalized object-relations as providing the building blocks for the creation of the traditional psychic structures.

Greenberg and Mitchell in their book trace the historical unfolding of metapsychology theory, beginning of course with Freud, and then contrapuntally, the development of the differing "interpersonal psychoanalysis" of Harry Stack Sullivan[3] and his followers, followed by the "alternative theorists" (Melanie Klein, W. R. D. Fairbairn, Michael Balint, John Bowlby, D. W. Winnicott, and Harry Guntrip), and then what they call the "accommodationist theorists" (Heinz Hartmann, Margaret Mahler, Edith Jacobson, and Otto Kernberg), and then the "mixed model" theorists (where they place Heinz Kohut and Joseph Sandler, but where I feel they should also have more properly placed Kernberg, based on their very own assessment of him), all this then culminating in a final chapter called "a deeper divergence." Here they unequivocally declare their position: "Placing the divergence of psychoanalytic models which we have traced throughout this volume within the larger context of the divergence of theories about human nature throughout the Western philosophical tradition sheds light both on the durability of the models within psychoanalysis and on the difficulties encountered by those who have tried to combine them" (p. 403). This derives from the fact that "they draw on two of the most fundamental and compelling approaches to human experience," that we are "inescapably individual creatures" and at the same time "inescapably social creatures" (p. 403).

This is the paradox that they say some have attempted to encompass by a "mixed model" approach. But "model mixing is unstable because the underlying premises upon which the two models are based are *fundamentally incompatible*. . . . The drive model and the relational model rest on different visions, and each is a complete account" (p. 403, italics added). This declaration is made even more flatfootedly a little further on:

> The drive model and the relational model are [each] complete and comprehensive accounts of the human experience. The premises upon which they rest constitute two incompatible visions of life, of the basic nature of human experience. . . . These premises are not subject to

---

3. Sullivan always called it "interpersonal psychiatry."

empirical verification. . . . [The criteria on which such theories can be judged] like scope, simplicity, and fruitfulness cannot be determined in any science universally or with pure objectivity. . . . [It depends] on the evaluator's own values and presuppositions. . . . [Ultimately] the evaluation of psychoanalytic theories is a matter of personal choice. . . . Does the theory speak to you? [pp. 406–407]

Though both Greenberg and Mitchell have subsequently retreated somewhat from the absoluteness of this total dichotomization of the psychoanalytic landscape (Greenberg much more so than Mitchell; see Greenberg 2001), their volume had a profound impact in defining and crystallizing the relational turn that has played so major a role in what has been widely declared a paradigm shift in American psychoanalysis, a growing acknowledgment of the major evolution of the now very prominent two-person psychology tracing its origins to Harry Stack Sullivan and his collaborators, and its precursors beyond that to Ferenczi, alongside the traditional ego psychology, dubbed now a one-person psychology with many of those trained classically within it now shifting emphasis in two-person directions—Gill, McLaughlin, Renik, Jacobs, Poland, Boesky, and Chused prominently among them. I have elsewhere labeled these shifting new alliances "The New American Psychoanalysis" (Wallerstein 1998).

Nonetheless, the defining impact of the Greenberg and Mitchell book in counterposing two main emphases in psychoanalysis in America, the one tracing its descent from Freud and the other more from Ferenczi—if not necessarily two fundamentally irreconcilable camps—has been to offer an alternative direction to current psychoanalytic theorizing than that I proffered in drawing upon Kernberg's 1993 paper on convergences (and divergences). This seems to have affected Kernberg's overview as well, since in a later article (Kernberg 2001) his emphasis is on two major and differing crystallizations of psychoanalytic theorizing very much in accord with the original Greenberg and Mitchell distinctions (and even, alongside the two, placing a third way).

In Kernberg's (2001) article, dealing with recent developments, he describes modern psychoanalysis as coalescing into two major contemporary currents. One, he calls the "contemporary psychoanalytic mainstream," and this mainstream he sees as a coming together of the modern Kleinians, the contemporary Freudians (i.e., the ego psychologists in their own modern transformation[4]), and the British independents (or British object-relational grouping), all sparkplugged by the growing mutual influencing, and even amalgamations in technical implementation, of converging understandings within the British Society; the second current Kernberg calls the "intersubjectivist-interpersonal–self psychology" movement.

Kernberg then presents ten shared characteristics of what he calls the "contemporary psychoanalytic mainstream." These are (1) an early systematic interpretation of the transference; (2) a totalistic concept of the countertransference, with an emphasis on countertransference analysis; (3) systematic character analysis; (4) a sharp focus on unconscious enactments; (5) an emphasis on affective dominance; (6) a predominance of models of internalized object relationships; (7) technical neutrality (with the elaboration of what he calls a "three-person model"[5]); (8) a multiplicity of royal roads to the unconscious; (9) a concerned avoidance of the indoctrination of patients; and (10) an increased questioning of linear models of human development.

Kernberg next defines five shared characteristics of what he calls the "intersubjectivist-interpersonal–self psychology" current: (1) a constructivist approach to the transference as opposed to the traditional objectivist approach, (2) a rejection of technical neutrality as both illusory and predicated on hidden authoritarianism, (3) a deficit model of early development, (4) a de-emphasis of the drives, and (5) the conception of the therapy as a new object relationship (implicitly linked to the once discredited Alexandrian notion of the "corrective emotional experience"). For many of these listings, Kernberg indicates the basis for his categorization. For example, in the statement of the first described characteristic of the "contemporary psychoanalytic mainstream," the early systematic interpretation of the transference, he offers, as evidence of the confluence of Freudian ego psychology, modern Kleinianism, and

---

4. See Wallerstein (2002a) for a full description of the evolution and the transformations of modern ego psychology.

5. By a "three-person model," Kernberg means a consideration of (1) the intrapsychic state of the patient; (2) the interactional, or interpersonal, relationship between patient and analyst; and (3) the analyst, in his stance of technical neutrality reflecting back to the patient his overview of the relationship between 1 and 2.

the British independent group, citations from Betty Joseph, Joseph and Anne-Marie Sandler, and Merton Gill.

Then Kernberg puts in a third way, the French psychoanalytic approach—on a par with the other two?—and this is actually elaborated into fourteen characteristics as follows: (1) a focus on the analytic method rather than analytic technique; (2) a strong focus on the linguistic aspects of analytic communication; (3) a sparing use of explicit transference interpretation; (4) bypassing the ego resistances; (5) direct interpretation of deep, symbolized, unconscious conflict; (6) simultaneous consideration of somatizations and enactments; (7) avoidance of the realities of daily life; (8) interpretation of presymbolic psychosomatic expressions; (9) analysis of the symbolic function of the father/analyst as the carrier of presumed knowledge; (10) a focus on archaic sexuality; (11) a strong emphasis on the function of *après coup*; (12) a "progressive" vector of future-directed interpretation; (13) acceptance of the irreducible earliest transference, derived from mother's enigmatic and eroticized messages; and (14) emphasis on analysis of preconscious fantasy.

Implicit in all this is the French opposition to ego psychology, in its imputed emphasis on the conscious and on adaptation to external reality, and its opposition to the relational perspective as well, as a seduction into a superficial interpersonal relationship; the French feel that both those perspectives fundamentally neglect Freud's basic theory of drives and of archaic sexuality. Basically, the French position, as portrayed here, is of an unswerving adherence to the earlier Freud, of drive and libido psychology, before the later (and to the French, misguided) development of the ego-centered or the relational-centered perspectives, each condemned as a retreat from Freud's unconscious. With Lacan, who so influenced all of French psychoanalysis, the rallying cry was always "Back to Freud."

At first blush this most recent overview by Kernberg, with its threefold division, seems a clear retreat from his earlier 1993 article that I quoted as an example of the beginning swing of the pendulum toward documenting the convergences in technical activities of adherents of disparate theoretical perspectives in psychoanalysis. There are indeed some serious and contentious conceptual and technical differences between what Kernberg calls the "contemporary psychoanalytic mainstream" and the "intersubjectivist-interpersonal–self psychology" schools, to leave the so-called French position aside for a moment, as, for example, over the place and continued use of concepts of neutrality, abstinence, and objectivity as psychoanalytic desiderata in the mainstream—as at least goals, if never as fully achieved realities—as against their abandonment in favor of declared authenticity (and often spontaneity) of interaction, including appropriately judicious self-disclosure, in the relational grouping. On the other hand, I feel that all those who would be grouped as intersubjectivist, interpersonalist, and so on, would strongly subscribe—perhaps even more so—to a goodly number of the characteristics Kernberg ascribes to the mainstream (e.g., countertransference analysis, and focus on enactments, on centrality of affects, on internalized object relationships, on questioning linear developmental models, etc.).

What I am suggesting is that hidden within the two major contemporary psychoanalytic currents (or groupings) into which Kernberg now separates (at least) the English-speaking psychoanalytic worlds are many of exactly the same kinds of convergences from seemingly very different theoretical perspectives that I feel he started to adumbrate in the earlier 1993 paper. As for the inclusion of a third, French, way, that could also be read as Kernberg's effort to juxtapose francophone to anglophone analytic thinking in order to lay the basis for the consideration of discernible convergences between these major analytic traditions that have been so significantly isolated from one another, in part because of the language barrier, and in part because of the different philosophical traditions from which they take root. Parenthetically, just as the Kleinians were the first of the departures from the ego psychological development (in which Freud's Viennese followers were taking analytic work in Britain and America), who refused to be extruded from organized psychoanalysis and even claimed a truer descent from Freud's own work, in embracing his death instinct theory as central to their theorizing, so have the Lacanians and those influenced by them been a later deviation from many of Freud's propositions, yet also claiming a truer adherence to Freud's original drive theory and to the continuing centrality of infantile/archaic sexuality.

Simultaneously with Kernberg's 2001 article in the *Psychoanalytic Quarterly*, Robert White published an article in the *Journal of the American Psychoanalytic Association* (2001), "The Interpersonal and Freudian Traditions," which has the subtitle, "Convergences and Divergences," a phrase that Kernberg used in his 1993 article. The thrust of White's article is very much in the same direction as Kernberg's, which I have called the beginning swing of the pendulum away from the previous ever-growing pluralism. White sets an illuminating historical context and offers a provocative analogy. He properly places the original splitting of the two traditions in America (the interpersonal and the Freudian) within "the psychoanalytic wars in New York City in the early 1940s" (p. 427). It was in 1941 that Karen Horney and her followers (Clara Thompson, Erich Fromm, etc.) felt that they had to leave the New York Institute and, in the confusing flux of the ensuing decade, they established their own dissident institute, entered into alliance with Harry Stack Sullivan's simultaneous creation of an indigenous "interpersonal psychiatry," and then themselves split into several separate institute groupings, with some distinct differences, but an overall living within an interpersonal relational framework, some (Horney) with a more sociocultural content, and some (Fromm) with a Marxian-economic content.

What is germane in the context of this article is that for several decades the two traditions, the Freudian and the interpersonal, ignored each other quite thoroughly, and were to a significant degree even ignorant of each other; the one (the mainstream Freudian) was organized within the American Psychoanalytic Association as the official representative within the United States of the international association, and the other grew in a group of independent institutes, mostly in New York and Washington, with some of its adherents sitting uneasily, but in a marginalized way, within the American association.

Here, White analogizes to the British experience: "Modern interpersonal thinking is a fusion of Sullivanian thought and European psychoanalysis [only one stream of it] as mediated by Ferenczi and Thompson. What the Kleinians did in England in the 1940s and 1950s, the interpersonalists did simultaneously and independently in the United States" (pp. 428–429). But here, the analogy breaks down in part, for while the British, after getting past the contention and the rancor of the controversial discussions in the early 1940s, were able to fashion the famous gentlemen's agreement (see King and Steiner 1991) and create an institutional framework within which they could live together and influence each other in ways that have led over the decades to major comings together—in ways that I will discuss further on—the two American traditions lived independently, side by side, with the dominant American Freudian mainstream thoroughly ignoring the other; the recently growing mutual acknowledgment and discourse has come decades later. This difference, to me, has been a consequence of the existence from the beginning within Britain of a large middle group (now called the independent group), which declared itself neither Kleinian nor Freudian, though willing to borrow from each, and offering itself always as a meeting ground and a potential mediating group. There was never an American counterpart.

But the theme of my story, in accord with White's account, is that now there are convergences in America of these two major traditions, and I feel, again in accord with White, that these may well be more significant than the distinctions that Kernberg points to in his article appearing simultaneously with White's. White stated, "I hope to show here that within each tradition there is at least as much difference and dissent as there is between traditions and that moreover, there is now considerable overlap between the traditions. . . . We are now seeing the beginning of a real exchange of ideas. There are journals now that solicit articles from both traditions, a CD-ROM that includes journals from both, and speakers who regularly cross the divide at national meetings" (p. 429).

I would state this same idea in less organizational terms, that so many of the tenets of what is now called two-person psychology, the focus on the interactional and intersubjective quality of the analytic encounter, with its emphasis on the subjectivity (countertransference in the broadest sense) of the analyst as a major contributor to the cocreation of the transference–countertransference matrix, and with the serious modification (if not the abandonment) of the analyst's posture as objective outside observer and epistemic arbiter of reality, etc., have all infiltrated widely into the classical or traditional Freudian perspective. Witness in this context the contributions of Gill, McLaughlin, Renik, Jacobs, Poland, Boesky, and Chused, all trained within that classical tradition.

Witness on the other side the retreat by both Greenberg and Mitchell from the categorical posture of their 1983 joint volume declaring the fundamental irreconcilability of Freud's original drive-structural paradigm and the newer relational paradigm, which they then represented and espoused. For their more current positions on these issues, Greenberg's (2001) article, "The Analyst's Participation: A New Look," speaks to the excesses of relational psychoanalysis when taken to its logical extremes—which historically Greenberg sees as a corrective, or rather overcorrective, response to the prior extremes of ego psychological psychoanalysis when pursued to its extremes—and to Mitchell and Black's (1995) history of psychoanalytic thought in which the final two chapters on current controversies in theory and technique offer a balanced portrayal of the many interpenetrations and imbrications of the two perspectives coming from opposite directions, the classical Freudian and the relational, in their nuanced consideration of each of the listed controversies, on the role of actual trauma versus fantasy elaboration in the creation of psychopathology, or of consideration of past versus present, or interpretation versus relationship factors in the amelioration of psychopathology.

There are still other significant markers of these converging trends. Glen Gabbard (1995) focused on the constantly enlarging place of the countertransference in the center of analytic theorizing and clinical scrutiny as what he called "the emerging common ground." There he took the central Kleinian conception of projective identification, as articulated originally by Melanie Klein as an intrapsychic fantasy, and then enlarged interpersonally by Wilfred Bion (and others), and now more fully and subtly evolved by Betty Joseph (and many others), and brought it into conjunction with the conception of countertransference enactments as articulated by those ego psychology–trained American analysts moving in the interpersonal and interactional direction (Ted Jacobs and James McLaughlin, and again many others), and along the way bringing in Joseph Sandler's (1976) role responsiveness conception as a close enough version of Kleinian projective identification in Freudian clothing. All this Gabbard sees as a growing Kleinian–Freudian consensus on the interactions within the transference–countertransference matrix as a "joint creation," with shifting emphases oscillating between the major emphasis on the contribution of the patient (the original Kleinian position) and on the contribution of the analyst (the recent Freudian position). To me, it is another documentation and example of arenas of convergence between once seemingly antipodal (meta)psychological perspectives, and it is only one among an array of such indicators, albeit a most important one. Further on I will indicate other emerging Kleinian–Freudian rapprochements ramifying within the British Psychoanalytical Society—the long-time uneasy container of three disparate analytic metapsychologies—itself.

As a last citation across this narrowing gap that I am describing, witness the final book by Merton Gill (1994), once one of the major systematizers of ego psychological metapsychology (Gill 1963, Rapaport and Gill 1959), who subsequently renounced it completely in a 1976 benchmark article, "Metapsychology Is Not Psychology," becoming then one of the staunchest advocates of the two-person relational turn in analysis, turning increasingly to the major relational journal, *Contemporary Psychoanalysis*, for the placement of his contributions to theory and practice. In his 1994 book summing up of his finally crystallized views on these issues on which he had done such a thorough about-face, Gill has a chapter, "One-Person and Two-Person Psychology," in which he makes the following sequential assertions: "As criticism of mainstream psychoanalysis has grown with more and more emphasis on object relations, there has been what many would regard as an overshooting of the mark, with a replacement of a one-person view of the analytic situation by a two-person view. As balance is being restored, the question becomes, are both one- and two-person psychologies necessary, and if so, how are they related?" (p. 33).

This is followed after several pages of consideration of this question with:

> If we ask whether human psychology involves more than a relationship with other people, the answer seems obvious. Important though relationships with other people are, there is much more to life than that. That the analytic situation involves two people may be a factor in overvaluing the role of relations with people as the alleged core of psychic life. That relationships with people are intrapsychically represented may also be a factor in undervaluing other aspects of the human psyche. Intertwining issues of relationships with persons with all other aspects of psychological functioning may be yet another factor in the failure to recognize these other aspects. And yet another possibility: because psychopathology is so often a matter of relationships, other aspects of human functioning may be overlooked. [pp. 39–40]

In summation of this section of that chapter, Gill concludes: "For the time being, I assert only that psychoanalysis needs both one-person and two-person psychologies. . . . It is important to note that this discussion of one-person and two-person psychologies has been with regard to the *theories* of the analytic situation. In actual practice, analysts have always, to varying degrees, pragmatically worked in both one-person and two-person contexts" (p. 40). Throughout the book, Gill describes the many kinds of situations in which analysts, alternately or concomitantly, intervene within a one-person and a two-person conceptualization. It is this final embracing of a both/and instead of an either/or position that has been far less remarked about Gill than the quoting of his more familiarly noted prior positions at the seeming extremes of the two poles, the earlier allegiance to one-person, intrapsychic conceptions and the later espousal of two-person, interpersonal (interpsychic) conceptions. This espousal of a both/and, integrative and transcending, posture in relation to many issues in psychoanalytic theorizing is certainly in keeping with my own long-expressed propensities in this regard.

Nor have these crisscrossing trends been played out on only one side of the Atlantic. I mentioned earlier a statement analogizing the events in America to those taking place over a longer time span within the British Society. The deep shift over several decades of Kleinian writing from a focus on early deep interpretation of underlying archaic fantasies with little attention to defenses and resistances, from body-part and part-object centered interpretations, and with an avoidance of attention to inherent countertransference involvement, to what is now called modern Kleinian conceptualizing in terms of the immediate here and now of the analytic interaction with focus on what the analysand is trying to evoke in the analyst and how this impacts upon and influences the countertransferential responses of the analyst, with a dropping away of the old language of part objects and whole objects, of body parts and cannibalistic imagery, has been extensively documented. It brings a whole contemporary generation of British Kleinians (Brenman, Britton, Feldman, O'Shaughnessy, Steiner, and of course Joseph and Bott Spillius, and many others) into far greater accord in clinical behavior and technical implementation with the converging clinical and technical trends from both the American contemporary ego psychological position (now renamed in many quarters conflict and compromise formation theory) and the now ascendant relational (interpersonal, dialectical constructivist, etc.) theorizing, than would have been at all conceivable just two or three decades back (see Spillius 1988, vols. 1 and 2, and Schafer 1997).

All this has in fact led Kernberg (2001) to opine: "All of these developments moved Kleinian analysis in the direction of ego psychology, without explicit acknowledgment of this shift" (p. 523). Further on, after discussing recent modifying trends arising out of their ongoing mutually interactive discourse in each of the three British Society theoretical groupings, he states: "The general consolidation of what I have described as the psychoanalytic mainstream has gradually brought the three traditional currents of the British Psychoanalytic Society closer, to the extent that, in my experience, when hearing clinical presentations by British analysts, it is no longer easy to differentiate those with a contemporary Kleinian background, an independent background, or a contemporary Freudian background" (p. 532). Kernberg credits Schafer's (1997) book, *The Contemporary Kleinians of London*, with conveying to a North American audience a careful, critical, yet obviously sympathetic, exploration of key contributions from modern British Kleinians, and says of this: "A new mainstream of analytic technique within the English-language analytic community seems to be evolving" (p. 525).

From the other side, to trace the concomitant developments within the British contemporary Freudian camp, I have selected the recently completed life work of Joseph Sandler, who stood all his career at the intersect of the three major theoretical perspectives, living in, perhaps often uneasy, harmony within the British Society, the Freudian, the Kleinian, and between them, the predominantly object-relational grouping, first articulated by Fairbairn, Balint, and Winnicott, known originally as the middle group, but now renamed the independent group, because presumably of its lack of an avowed coherent unifying perspective such as they feel marks their Freudian and Kleinian confreres.

Within this diversity—and often contention—in this British array, Sandler, almost single-handedly, over his lifetime represented a harmonizing role, pressing toward an ecumenical synchronization that led Peter Fonagy to characterize him in a *New York Times* obituary as the leader of "a quiet revolution in psychoanalytic thought." An instance familiar to us all is Sandler's (1976) role responsiveness paper that did so much to bring the Kleinian concept of projective identification—though not by that name—into general acceptance and its current widespread employment, now by that name, in the rest of the psychoanalytic world. Let me in this context briefly outline the overall thrust of Sandler's life work to demonstrate why I consider him such an outstanding exemplar of what I feel is the still embryonic, but, I predict, cumulatively growing, trend toward the new convergences that I see as the successor to our present era of psychoanalytic pluralism.

Sandler began this labor early in his career, and at a time of ever-increasing proliferation of psychoanalytic theoretical perspectives, in his capacity for more than two decades (1958–79) as director of the Index Project at the Hampstead Child Therapy Clinic (now renamed the Anna Freud Centre). This was the launching pad for his systematic and truly groundbreaking studies into the logical structure of our bodies of psychoanalytic concepts, and the goodness of fit of these concepts to the data of the psychoanalytic treatments at the Anna Freud Centre, data that were highlighted by the empirical application of the concepts to the indexing of the data. By constantly exploring the degree of congruence, or conversely, of discrepancy, between the index categories that embody the working concepts of our psychoanalytic theories and the clinical data from the ongoing cases at the Anna Freud Centre that were to be indexed in accord with those categories, Sandler and his several collaborators again and again exposed the full range of semantic, definitional, and conceptual problems of our science—and clarified, in often fundamental ways, such concepts as superego, ego ideal, ideal self, pain, trauma, strain, sublimation, affect, motivation, adaptation, internalization, projective identification, object relationships, and transference; the list is seemingly endless [see the volume of his selected papers (Sandler 1987) for numerous examples].

Through this prodigious array of conceptual clarifications, a guiding intellectual thread clearly emerged, the incremental transformation of the traditional drive-structural psychoanalytic paradigm, based on the economics and dynamics of drives and energies, into a more object-relational model, the economics and dynamics of fluctuating feeling states embedded in internalized object relationships, and reflecting the full human feeling range from anxiety, depression, and pain to well-being and safety. And yet, quite oppositely from the dichotomizers cited by Bachant and Richards, who posit fundamentally irreconcilable drive-structural and object-relational metapsychologies, Sandler's evolving transformation of the so-called classical Freudian psychoanalysis into a depth psychology that adapts to changes in feeling states was stepwise accomplished without ever losing the vital linkages to issues of instinctual gratification and frustration, which are after all so centrally important, as the ego balances its conditions of danger and safety, and adaptively regulates its shifting feeling states. In this sense it has been a profound effort at theoretical amalgamation or integration.

Clearly, Sandler's transformative theory building was, as I have indicated, strongly influenced by his professional placement within the British Psychoanalytical Society, where, ever since the famous controversial discussions of the early 1940s (King and Steiner 1991), the three distinct theoretical schools (the Kleinian, the Freudian, and the object-relational or independent group) have existed and taught side by side, with constant interacting scientific discourse, and, inevitably, mutual clarification and influence. But Sandler's was also individually a distinct and major bridging voice in the convergences and growing areas of rapprochement that currently mark the once polemically separate theoretical perspectives that characterized the psychoanalytic landscape in Great Britain, and all over, not so long ago—a shining exemplar, as I have called him, of exactly the growing trend or pendulum return that Kernberg (1993) so comprehensively presaged, and that others have since added to, though Kernberg himself most recently seems to have waffled somewhat on the thoroughness of his own commitment in this direction.

Thus, Sandler, who never tried to develop a distinctive school or movement of his own within psychoanalysis, has indeed emerged (quite unobtrusively) rather as one of the architects of the new integrations that I feel are beginning to mark the vibrant psychoanalysis of today, and that point hopefully to its future, its next positioning of the pendulum. This, of course, is exactly what I think Fonagy had in mind in offering the phrase defining Sandler as a prime leader in a "quiet revolution" in psychoanalytic thought. I should add here that Otto Kernberg, in his own lifelong efforts within American psychoanalysis to forge links between the drive-structural and the object-relational perspectives, by advancing his views of internalized object relationships, consisting of self representations, object representations, and the affective valences that link them as the fundamental building blocks out of which the structured psychic apparatus of id, ego, and superego is constituted, has indeed been a partner in arms with Sandler in these endeavors.

All of this is basically my crystallized overview, and my vision for the future, or at least the near future, of psychoanalysis. It is an amplification and an extension of my own long-time integrative focus on "both-and" rather than "either-or," as typified by my own 1983 consideration of ego-psychological conflict theory vis-à-vis self-psychological deficit theory.[6] I am sure that it is a vision far from agreed to by all, and that, of course, is precisely my subtext in this presentation. It may be that our collective future as a profession, and a clinical practice, will be an economically more modest one, in terms of the size and the material rewards of strictly psychoanalytic work, as many are postulating—certainly as compared with what I have called the halcyon days of the 1950s and 1960s—but in terms of the lure of psychoanalysis as an intellectual calling and commitment, I feel that most of us agree that this is indeed a time of unparalleled intellectual excitement in terms of our current preoccupations and debates.

Central to that excitement is what I view as the still incipient, but, I feel, growing trend toward convergence or common ground, or however we designate it, and that that indeed will be the most exciting near future as the contention of viewpoints plays itself out, whether in a maintained or even an increasing theoretical separateness and divergence, or whether in the direction I predict, and have been over many years committed to, of a growing together of an overarching theoretical and clinical framework for psychoanalysis, a coherently unified theoretical structure that, like cognate scientific structures, can lend itself to the systematic theory testing that constantly refines and amplifies the theory, and gives ever-increasing precision to the clinical applications of the theory in our consulting rooms. I am sure that embedded in each of our individual takes on these present and coming trends, as I have envisioned them, will be our own personal commitments to whether or not we individually feel this to be a good thing for our discipline or not.

---

6. Still other concurring voices can be cited, some from quarters that would not expectedly be grouped among the proponents of a converging "both-and" perspective. For example, Nancy Chodorow, a strong psychoanalytic feminist theorist, argues for the continuing place of a one-person psychology in conjunction with the relational two-person psychology in her 1999 book, *The Power of Feelings*.

References

Bachant, J. L., and Richards, A. D. (1993). Review essay on *Relational Concepts in Psychoanalysis: An Integration*, by S. A. Mitchell. *Psychoanalytic Dialogue* 3:431–460.

Chodorow, N. J. (1999). *The Power of Feelings: Personal Meaning in Psychoanalysis, Gender, and Culture.* New Haven, CT, and London: Yale University Press.

Freud, A. (1936). *The Ego and the Mechanisms of Defense.* New York: International Universities Press, 1946.

Freud, S. (1914). On the history of the psycho-analytic movement. *Standard Edition* 14:1–66.

——— (1923). The ego and the id. *Standard Edition* 19:1–66.

——— (1926). Inhibitions, symptoms and anxiety. *Standard Edition* 20:75–174.

Gabbard, G. O. (1995). Countertransference: the emerging common ground. *International Journal of Psycho-Analysis* 76:475–485.

Gill, M. M. (1963). *Topography and Systems in Psychoanalytic Theory.* Psychological Issues Monograph 10. New York: International Universities Press.

——— (1976). Metapsychology is not psychology. In *Psychology Versus Metapsychology: Psychoanalytic Essays in Memory of George S. Klein*, ed. M. M. Gill and P. S. Holzman, pp. 71–105. Psychological Issues Monograph 36. New York: International Universities Press.

——— (1994). *Psychoanalysis in Transition: A Personal View.* Hillsdale, NJ, and London: Analytic Press.

Greenberg, J. (2001). The analyst's participation: a new look. *Journal of the American Psychoanalytic Association* 49:359–381.

Greenberg, J., and Mitchell, S. A. (1983). *Object Relations in Psychoanalytic Theory.* Cambridge, MA, and London: Harvard University Press.

Harrison, S. I. (1970). Is psychoanalysis "our" science? Reflections on the scientific status of psychoanalysis. *Journal of the American Psychoanalytic Association* 18:125–149.

Hartmann, H. (1939). *Ego Psychology and the Problem of Adaptation.* New York: International Universities Press, 1958.

Kernberg, O. F. (1993). Convergences and divergences in contemporary psychoanalytic technique. *International Journal of Psycho-Analysis* 74:659–673.

——— (2001). Recent developments in the technical approaches of English language psychoanalytic schools. *Psychoanalytic Quarterly* 70:519–547.

King, P., and Steiner, R., eds. (1991). *The Freud-Klein Controversies, 1941–45.* London and New York: Tavistock/Routledge.

Mitchell, S. A. (1988). *Relational Concepts in Psychoanalysis: An Integration.* Cambridge, MA and London: Harvard University Press.

Mitchell, S. A., and Black, M. J. (1995). *Freud and Beyond: A History of Modern Psychoanalytic Thought*. New York: Basic Books.

Rapaport, D., and Gill, M. M. (1959). The points of view and assumptions of metapsychology. *International Journal of Psycho-Analysis* 40:153–162.

Sandler, J. (1976). Countertransference and Role-Responsiveness. *International Review of Psycho-Analysis* 3:43–47.

———— (1987). *From Safety to Superego: Selected Papers of Joseph Sandler*. New York and London: Guilford.

Schafer, R. (1997). *The Contemporary Kleinians of London*. Madison, CT: International Universities Press.

Spillius, E. B., ed. (1988). *Melanie Klein Today: Developments in Theory and Practice*, vol. 1, *Mainly Theory*, vol. 2, *Mainly Practice*. London and New York: Routledge.

Wallerstein, R. S. (1983). Self psychology and "classical" psychoanalytic psychology: the nature of their relationship. *Psychoanalysis and Contemporary Thought* 6:553–595.

———— (1988). One psychoanalysis or many? *International Journal of Psycho-Analysis* 69:5–21.

———— (1990). Psychoanalysis: the common ground. *International Journal of Psycho-Analysis* 71:3–20.

———— (1998). The new American psychoanalysis: a commentary. *Journal of the American Psychoanalytic Association* 46:1021–1043.

———— (2002a). The growth and the modern transformation of (American) ego psychology. *Journal of the American Psychoanalytic Association* 50:135–169.

———— (2002b). The trajectory of psychoanalysis: a prognostication. *International Journal of Psychoanalysis* 83:1247–1267.

Wallerstein, R. S., ed. (1992). *The Common Ground of Psychoanalysis*. Northvale, NJ: Jason Aronson.

White, R. S. (2001). The interpersonal and freudian traditions: convergences and divergences. *Journal of the American Psychoanalytic Association* 49:427–455.

8
The "Taboo on Tenderness" in the History of Psychoanalysis

ELISABETH YOUNG-BRUEHL

As my contribution to this symposium, I offer, first, a general reflection on dissidence in the history of psychoanalysis—with acknowledgment of the essay Martin Bergmann (Part I of this volume) has written for the occasion. Second, I consider the work of an English dissident, Ian Suttie, who, in the 1920s, formulated a critique of Freud and an alternative path for psychoanalysis that has recently begun to be appreciated (although I do not think its true significance has been grasped). I will explore both Suttie's biographical approach to and critique of Freud and his vision for psychoanalytic theory and practice, arguing that his concept of a "taboo on tenderness" offers a way of interpreting the history of dissidence in psychoanalysis.

Until the last ten or fifteen years, psychoanalysis had accumulated during its one hundred years of existence a history made up almost entirely of biographies. Unlike most scientific fields and humanistic disciplines, psychoanalysis did not acquire histories at the time that basic textbooks began to be written, which was in the 1930s, before World War II, starting with Hermann Nunberg's *Principles of Psychoanalysis* (1932) and continuing to Freud's own unfinished *"Outline of Psycho-Analysis"* (1940) and Edward Glover's *Psychoanalysis* (1939). No one would write a *Principles of Psycho-Analysis* now, or a *Psychoanalytic*

Theory of Neuroses (Fenichel 1945), or a *Basic Theory of Psychoanalysis* (Waelder 1966), or *The Technique and Practice of Psychoanalysis* (Greenson 1967). Histories and compendia that survey the various schools of psychoanalysis are now being written because the sense is widely shared in the field that psychoanalysis is no longer a coherent Freudian field in the way that it was through the first three generational cohorts: that of Freud and his original circle, that of those trained by these founding fathers, and a third group trained by the trainees. Now, histories are being written by the fourth generational cohort—the products of the suffusion of psychoanalysis with dissidence that took place in the reign of the third generational cohort. It was up until that ramification of dissidence that psychoanalytic history was written almost entirely in the medium of biography, chiefly because psychoanalysis itself had forced the recognition that theories of all sorts—not just psychoanalytic ones—are the product of their authors' conscious and unconscious minds in ways that psychoanalysis is meant to be able to illuminate. The biographical history of psychoanalysis is psychobiographical. But, further, psychoanalysis lends itself to biography because it is quite uniquely the product of one man's conscious and unconscious mind. Until the 1970s, the history of psychoanalysis was almost exclusively a biographical history focused on Sigmund Freud. After 1953, the Freud literature was indebted to Ernest Jones's three-volume biography, which was the first to be written with access to large portions of Freud's unpublished correspondences. But the Freud literature did eventually begin to include published volumes of his correspondences: first a selected letters and a (heavily edited) edition of the Fliess correspondence appeared, then, one by one, the correspondences with Abraham, Pfister, Andreas-Salome, Zweig, Jung, and more recently, Jones and Ferenczi. So Jones has long since been superseded, although there is no obvious stand-out in the post-Jones crowd.

In the 1960s and 1970s, as their correspondence became available, there were biographical studies of all of the important figures who surrounded Freud, including the first-generation dissidents or schismatics and critics. The exception—and it is a crucially important exception—was Ferenczi, who had been pushed to the margins of the psychoanalytic movement in his last years, while his home base, Budapest, became less and less influential because of the immigration of his younger colleagues. The Freud–Ferenczi correspondence and Ferenczi's late clinical diary remained unpublished until the 1990s, and there is still no biography of him (although his English translator, Peter Hoffer, is writing one currently). What this means is that Ferenczi has made a return to the psychoanalytic scene in the medium of his influence on members of the third and fourth generations—as though he had skipped forward in time to be assimilated into the critique of Freud conducted by the third generation. He has returned more in the medium of his ideas, however, than of his biography, partly for lack of a biography. The slow return of Ferenczi has meant that Ferenczi's ideas, particularly his ideas about instinct theory in *Thalassa* (1923), are not very well understood. He is being selectively assimilated, his instinct theory being left out and his emphasis in his late technical papers on object relations making him the Ur-relationalist.

In the 1980s a biographical literature that focused on the second generation of Freudians began to appear. The two most important figures of that generation for the general history of psychoanalysis, Melanie Klein and Anna Freud, were each the subject of a full biography and several partial studies. Eventually, Wilhelm Reich, Erik Erikson, Margaret Mahler, and others were written about, but, interestingly not the troika of Heinz Hartmann, Ernst Kris, and Rudolf Lowenstein, and not the non-émigré English theorists who were Melanie Klein's younger contemporaries and influenced by her, notably Harry Guntrip and Ronald Fairbairn, and not John Bowlby, whose work has recently become so much more influential, although articles with biographical data about each of these men have been written. Ego psychology and British object relations after the Second World War have not been compassed historically in the medium of biography. But the same cannot be said of the dissident figures who were outside of the Freudian mainstream in its American emigration settings, like Karen Horney and Erich Fromm, whose work was so important for social psychology, and Harry Stack Sullivan, whose work was so important for those in America who worked (as he did) with psychotics in institutional settings. (Recently, after a long delay, Freida Fromm-Reichmann has been the subject of a biography that traces her relations with Sullivan.) There are biographies of all of these figures, because their biographical stories have been understood to be so important for understanding their dissidence.

Absent from biographical study of this second generational group is even a mention of Ian Suttie, who, like Ferenczi, has recently begun to undergo a revival, although a much smaller one (particularly fostered by Howard Bacal, a follower of Heinz Kohut). In 1935, after nearly a decade of exclusion—effectively, censorship—from the *International Journal of Psycho-Analysis* by its editor, Ernest Jones, Suttie completed *The Origins of Love and Hate* (1935), which was influential in England before World War II, but had little impact when it was published in the United States in 1952 (by the small Julian Press, which did the English-language versions of Otto Rank's books). John Bowlby wrote a preface for the original edition, Fairbairn and Winnicott later acknowledged it in their writings. But Suttie died at age 46, in the year that he finished his book, leaving another larger and more thorough project incomplete. No obituary appeared in the psychoanalytic journals, and little documentation is now available for biographical study.[1] So Suttie is a very unusual dissident: a person without followers who, in effect, fell out of the unfolding history of psychoanalysis for sixty years, only to return (like Ferenczi) in the medium of his ideas, not because of or in the medium of his biography. Like Ferenczi, however, he is being ushered back into psychoanalysis without his instinct theory (which I outline below).

A biographical literature began being produced in the 1990s on the third generational cohort of psychoanalysts, which could be defined as the group that was trained not in Vienna, Berlin, or Budapest, but elsewhere by émigrés from those centers who had become training analysts in their new homes before, during, or after the Second World War, from about 1935 to 1955. In this third generation, D. W. Winnicott, influenced by both the Anna Freudians and the Melanie Kleinians in London, has been the subject of several brief biographies and a full one is being prepared by Brett Kahr, while a number of volumes of Winnicott's talks and lectures have been published posthumously by his widow, Claire Winnicott. There is a huge biography by Elizabeth Rodinesco (1944) of Jacques Lacan, who was analyzed by Rudolf Lowenstein in Paris, and an extensive literature about Lacan and his theories has grown up in addition to many volumes of his semi-

---

1. There were reviews of *The Origins of Love and Hate* in England, including a brief one by Roger Money-Kyrle (1936), which concludes, "Dr. Suttie's book will be well received by all who wish to underestimate the extent of infantile sexuality and aggression." Suttie was being portrayed, like Jung, as resistant to the obvious "sexual nature of the infant's relation to his mother" (p. 138).

nar notes and many contributions from those known as *l'ecole Lacanian*. And there is a recent biography of Heinz Kohut by Charles Strozier (2001), which comes after the publication in 1987 of *The Kohut Seminars* and in 1994 of a volume of Kohut's correspondences, including correspondences with those analysts known as the Chicago school. Winnicott, Lacan, and Kohut are the three third-generation figures who are the most biographied, studied, and commented upon, and they are arguably the three who have had the greatest influence on psychoanalytic theory and, to varying extents, clinical practice in the last quarter of the twentieth century. Their influence varies geographically, with the British, French, and American spheres being differently structured.

The biographical literature on the second-generation Freudians, chiefly Anna Freud and Melanie Klein, makes very clear their stances in relation to Freud. They were locked in controversies over who were the true inheritors of Freud and the true continuers. Klein asserted stridently her claim to being the true psychoanalytic daughter, the one who had taken up Freud's (1926) "*Symptoms, Inhibitions, and Anxiety*," plumbed its implications, grasped how the proposed death instinct and theory of aggression ran into that book from Freud's (1920) *Beyond the Pleasure Principle*, and pointed straight to the newborn infant's murderous "schizoid position." Anna Freud, on the other hand, did not assert her claim; she just lived it out in the way she thought best: she dedicated herself to making a clinical science and a general theory of development out of her father's psychoanalysis, extending it to the hundreds upon hundreds of children she and her colleagues saw at her various nurseries and at the Hampstead Clinic, where indexing and comparing cases was the main scientific mode. Klein, by contrast, worked more in the medium of the individual case study and case vignette, having analyzed a much smaller number of patients, particularly before she wrote *Psychoanalysis of Children* (1932).

Klein did not view herself as a dissident, although Anna Freud certainly viewed her thus, and it is in the context of their debates and discussions that Anna Freud got the reputation for closed-mindedness that Bergmann perpetuates in his essay in this volume. It certainly is true that Anna Freud and her group took a strong stance theoretically and institutionally against Klein in the wartime controversial discussion years, but it is also the case that, over the years, Anna Freud herself and the Anna Freudians—especially Joseph Sandler—brought into their own theory and practice many of Klein's ideas. Similarly, Anna Freud was a respectful critic of John Bowlby, and always maintained a very encouraging and collaborative relationship with James and Joyce Robertson, whose films were so important for documenting and extending Bowlby's ideas. At the Hampstead Clinic, Anna Freud's more recent followers—currently, Peter Fonagy—have paid careful attention to the scientific development of attachment theory, incorporating it into their work and research. On the other side, the contemporary Kleinians have been less explicitly attuned to the Hampstead Clinic work, but, nonetheless, have recently fostered the slow rapprochement that has come about since the controversial discussions.

The second generational cohort is the one in which dissidence came to be contained within Freudian psychoanalysis, in the short run by institutional negotiations and in the longer run by theoretical modifications and softening of positions first taken in the heat of controversy and competition. The first-generation dissidents—Adler, Stekel, Jung, Rank (but I doubt whether Ferenczi would have been in their number had he lived longer)—had been schismatics, as Bergmann emphasizes. They were not tied to Freud or his loyal circle by training analyses. When their differences with Freud came to full light, and, particularly when their theoretical differences began to have technical implications or implications for how psychoanalysis was to be practiced in broader, more ethical terms, they left Freud's movement.

In the second generation, groups formed and institutions split within Freudian psychoanalysis, and arrangements were made for the dissenting views to be given institutional space within larger (usually national) institutions. The model of how the British Psychoanalytic Society housed the Anna Freudians, the Melanie Kleinians, and the middle groupers or independents was important in all of the cities where the continental European émigrés ended up. Most American cities that had a psychoanalytic training institute had, in the period of the emigration and after World War II, two antagonistic training institutions—or more. New York, however, was a more complicated case. There was a contained split, which resulted in two American Psychoanalytic Association institutes, one eventually housed within Columbia University's Department of Psychiatry, and the other being the older, free-standing New York Psychoanalytic. Unlike the three British Society training programs, however, these were medical institutes, hostile to lay psychoanalysis—so that both the lay Anna Freudians and the lay Kleinians who emigrated to America were dissidents in this institutional sense. (Anna Freud herself, did not qualify for membership in the American Psychoanalytic.) But there was also in New York a more uncontained split, which had the result, after many complicated reverberations, of isolating from the American Psychoanalytic Association both Karen Horney and the so-called interpersonalist group around Sullivan in Washington and many smaller independent institutes, most of them in New York, some with ties to the interpersonalists. The British model of containment did not apply.

The fissioning of institutes contained within larger organizations had not stopped by the time the third generational cohort came to be the dominating group on the international psychoanalytic scene, but it had lessened. More debate took place in print, and there was less what might be called "argument by pathology"—that is, argument by using biographical techniques to attribute theories to the theorist's pathology or pathological resistance. So it is not surprising that the biographical literature on the third generation is—as one would expect from an accumulating and contentious literature—more complex. However, this literature insofar as it is polemical is not about who is the true heir of Freud; it is about who has surpassed Freud and who is the major contributor to psychoanalysis of a generation that was striving to be *neo*-Freudian or *post*-Freudian, some radically and some not so radically. All the figures in this generation still oriented themselves toward Freud, but they did so while arguing against the second generation's interpretations and expropriations and while searching for new pathways.

This was the situation in psychoanalysis in the 1960s, when psychoanalysis began to face its greatest intellectual challenge from without—a challenge of far greater significance than the resistance from without to Freud's early work and specifically to his libido theory. This was the critique of Freudianism from American, British, and French feminists. The feminist critics were indebted to the work of prewar dissidents within psychoanalysis, to Karen Horney, Clara Thompson, and others who became associated with the interpersonalists and to various postwar individual psychoanalysts and groups that emphasized the cultural determinants in psychic life. But in the history of psychoanalysis, for the first time, a critique from without was assimilated into psychoanalysis, spurring a large portion of the fourth generational cohort—especially the women—to weigh against the patriarchal bias in psychoanalytic theory, practice, and institutional life. There are many important psychoanalytic feminists in this generation, but the career of Juliet Mitchell can be considered paradigmatic for how feminism came into psychoanalysis. She began as a feminist with practical political experience on the British left, then wrote one of the first histories (quite psychobiographical) of psychoanalysis—*Psychoanalysis and Feminism* (1973)—and then went on to train as a psychoanalyst and join the British middle group.

At first, the focus of the feminist critique was specifically on Freud's ideas about female development and feminine character, and the main method was psychobiographical. The method had been urged, for example, by Germaine Greer in her enormously influential *The Female Eunuch* (1970): "Freud is the father of psychoanalysis. It had no mother. . . . Freud himself lamented his inability to understand women, and became progressively humbler in his pronouncements about them. The best approach to Freud's assumptions about women is probably the one adopted by Dr. Ian Suttie, that of psychoanalyzing Freud himself." By reading Suttie and other dissidents who expanded the charge that Freud was "antifeminist" into a consideration of the whole Freudian domain, including Freud's "metapsychology" and his ideas about "civilization and its discontents," feminist psychoanalysts were the first group in the history of psychoanalysis that was international and not dependent on charismatic leadership and that was able to transform psychoanalysis fundamentally, although not quite to the point where they have won a mention in Bergmann's history![2]

Now that histories of psychoanalysis are beginning to be written—mostly from within the field, by psychoanalysts, the younger ones being part of the fourth generation[3]—historiographical questions arise.

---

2. There are now quite a number of histories, among them a very thorough and well-researched one from Mari Jo Buhle, *Feminism and Its Discontents: A Century of Struggle with Psychoanalysis* (1998). But this volume does not mention Suttie or his "taboo on tenderness" concept that I present below.

3. In Great Britain, more historical writing about psychoanalysis is being done by academics who are not psychoanalysts because there is a lively network of psychoanalytic studies programs in British universities and because British academic feminists have been more coordinated to psychoanalysis than was the case in America until recently.

The theory and method of history need to be considered by the historians, and any assessment of the histories also involves questions of theory and method. There is also now a move toward finding frameworks and cataloging not just different schools but general patterns. As can be seen in Bergmann's essay and Robert Wallerstein's chapter, the key words that mark the search for general patterns for them are *convergence* and *divergence*.

The contemporary histories of psychoanalytic schools incorporate the biographical tradition; they are psychobiographical, seeking to show how dissident theories arose from the conscious and unconscious minds of the dissidents. This implies that these histories are also informed by a theory—explicit or implicit—of the psychology of dissidence itself. As Bergmann points out, the first psychoanalytic theory of dissidence within psychoanalysis came from Freud, and it was that dissidence is a form of resistance. Freud felt that his libido theory, in particular, roused resistance in those who were interested in psychoanalysis but not yet adherents, like Bleuler, and even in those who did become adherents, like his colleagues Adler and Jung. But this simple theory of dissidence was, I think, given up after Ernest Jones brought it to its acme in his biography of Freud. Although he thought of himself as a cataloger of resistances, Jones was also telling a story of dissidence that focused on battles for succession, power struggles, and rivalries among the sons (even when the sons were daughters), or what is generally known in literary circles as "the anxiety of influence." Both Jones's biography and his institutional role—for instance, as the rivalrous critic of Ferenczi and diagnostician of Ferenczi's alleged mental decline—revealed him as an exemplar of the psychoanalytic power broker, relishing conflict. Some current historians continue to do battle chronicles in this Jonesian mode, but many are also showing more appreciation for the diversity of motives for dissidence (if not any more complex theory of dissidence) because there is no clear way of the sort Jones felt he possessed to distinguish Freudian from non-Freudian.

To my mind, the first step in the direction of a more complex theory should be acknowledgment of how consistently dissidents of the most diverse types (biographically speaking)—that is, not just resistants and not just power-seekers—have aimed at the same pillar of the Freudian edifice. As had been the case with the first dissidents within psychoanalysis, men who had come into Freud's orbit between 1908 and World

War I, and as had been the case with the second generation as it struggled over how to inherit Freud, the third generation was focused in its criticism, as in its effort at renewal, on Freud's libido theory or, more broadly, on his theory of instinctual drives. This is the theory that, in no matter which of its forms, has always been the magnet of criticism. The first-generation dissidents wanted either to reform it, as Adler had, or to transcend it, as Jung had. Freud himself, of course, had forseen in his "History of the Psychoanalytic Movement" (1914), that the Adlerian path of reformation and the Jungian path of transcendence would be sources of great challenge to psychoanalysis, and he was certainly right, although he thought the more powerful challenge would come from the Adlerian direction, when, in fact, it was Jung who became the founder of a new charismatically organized school and, eventually, a worldwide organization.

I question why the instinct theory is the magnet of criticism. After the earliest generation of dissidents, the instinctual drive theory that has been the magnet of critique was Freud's second one, the so-called dual instinct theory of Eros and Thanatos, not his first one, the more Darwinian version featuring sexual instincts and ego instincts—sex and hunger, as Freud summarized it. The Darwinian first theory has practically disappeared from psychoanalytic history except insofar as that history talks about resistance to the sexual theory (without mentioning the ego instincts). Similarly, the Darwinian version has disappeared from all the contemporary histories (including Bergmann's), particularly when they are framing psychoanalytic history as a battle over drive theory. Ironically enough, this history writing is making the Freud of the first instinct theory into a kind of dissident voice in psychoanalysis, pushed completely to the margins.

Each fourth generational school of psychoanalysis now has a historiographical tradition that features a narrative of the battle over drive theory, but the most rigidly dualistic "us vs. them" narrative is coming from relational psychoanalysis, where drive theory has become a shibboleth. Greenberg and Mitchell's 1983 compendium, *Object Relations in Psychoanalytic Theory*, which, by the way, has no mention of Suttie in its extensive tours of object relations theorists, launched this mode, but it has now been translated into history in, for example, Joseph Schwartz's *Cassandra's Daughter: A History of Psychoanalysis* (1999). In sweeping strokes, with the tone of a melodramatist, Schwartz shows psychoanalysis heading inexorably toward his own camp, the relational point of view:

> From its very beginning, psychoanalysis has been undergoing a paradigm shift involving one great generalization about human psychology: the fundamental conflicts in the human inner world lie not in our seeking a reduction in tensions caused by unsatisfied drives but are associated with difficulties in satisfying a fundamental human need for relationship. The historical circumstances informing the playing out of the paradigmatic tensions between a drive-instinctual versus a relational point of view were the highly traumatic social events of war and revolution in Europe—the introduction of the mechanized killing during the First World War, the failure of the German revolution of 1918, the failure of the Hungarian revolution of 1919 and the catastrophic counterrevolution associated with the name of Adolf Hitler. In the inter-war years, psychoanalysis's center of gravity shifted from Vienna and Berlin to New York and London. The tension between the instinctual and relational points of view of human inner conflict then developed in two distinct strands, American and British. In America, an interpersonalist approach to the most extreme forms of mental distress by a group of workers in Washington, D.C., amongst whom the name of Harry Stack Sullivan stands out, located the source of psychic pain in ruptured, non-existent or abusive relationships. In Britain, the powerful theory of object relations, associated originally with the name of Melanie Klein, who took psychoanalysis in to the nursery to treat childhood terrors and anxieties, led to relationship failure being identified as the source of mental disturbance, as was later articulated by the Scottish psychoanalyst Ronald Fairbairn. [pp. 12–13]

Ian Suttie, writing from 1923 to 1935, was almost alone among the British in his interest in Freud's first instinct theory, the Darwinian one featuring sexual instincts and ego instincts. He put the ego instincts at the center of his own theoretical and clinical contribution, and wrote a sustained psychobiographical critique (before any biography of Freud existed) of Freud's emphasis on the sexual instincts at the expense of the ego instincts. The completely unjustified and deleterious turn Freud made to the idea of a death instinct was, in Suttie's judgment, a turn away from the ego instincts and their manifestation, affectionate love or tenderness. Suttie, in effect, represented the road not taken by Freud, the dissident inside Freud himself.

While Freud was still in his Darwinian phase as an instinct theorist, he had vacillated over the question of which of these instinct groups—the self-preservative or the species-reproductive—had priority in human development (meaning which were first manifest and also which were most influential or determinative). *Three Essays on the Theory of Sexuality* (1905) contains both the idea that libido is prior and all other instincts manifest themselves in the context of its repression or aim-inhibition into tenderness or affection and the alternative view that the species-preservative affectional or tender instincts lay down the channels in which libido flows—as suckling at the breast lays down the channel for oral sexual gratification.[4] This matter was never really resolved before Freud, defending himself against Jung's effort to turn libido into a generalized psychic energy, first reemphasized the importance of libido and then de-emphasized the importance of the self-preservative instincts by subsuming them into the life instincts, Eros, and then opposing Eros to the death instinct. The self-preservative instincts never entirely disappeared from Freud's theorizing, but they definitely receded; in Freud's theory of technique, and in the practice of Freudians, affection or tenderness remained, but seldom called by those names.

As I noted, almost everyone in the second generation who criticized Freud's instinctual drive theory was reacting to his theory as formulated after *Beyond the Pleasure Principle*, that is, they were reacting to the Eros and Thanatos theory. And they went in basically two directions of critique: either they followed Melanie Klein in thinking that the death instinct needed to be given priority in development, with the sexual or libidinal coming forth to make "depressive position" reparations for aggression in the "paranoid-schizoid position," the infant's first phase; or they went in the direction indicated

---

4. The conflict in Freud's thought was apparent in *Three Essays on the Theory of Sexuality*, but also again in Group *Psychology and the Analysis of the Ego* (1921); as Suttie (1935) pointed out, p. 195: "We find Freud talking of an 'easy transition' from a nurtural tie to a sexual tenderness, and, further down the paragraph, of a 'complete fusion of tender and jealous feelings and of sexual intentions.' This seems to imply the original independence of sexual and nurtural impulses. On the next page, however, he says that the child's first love is 'typically coordinated with the Oedipus complex.'"

by Fairbairn and others of prioritizing object relations and viewing libido and aggression as derivatives of object relations. These could be called the neo-Adlerian and the neo-Jungian directions: a direction prioritizing aggression, and a direction de-emphasizing the instinctual domain altogether. (I am going to leave out of the account here Lacan's complicated emphasis on the sexual instinct, his effort to be more Freudian than Freud, because he really redefined in an idiosyncratic way the notion of instinct.)

Except for Suttie in England, it was only in Budapest that the ego instincts remained a crucial ingredient of theorizing.[5] Ferenczi himself embraced Freud's death instinct formulation, but when he came to write his last papers on technique, Thanatos was nowhere to be found, and his attention was all on "primary love." For others in the Budapest school, primary love was an ego instinct, as can be seen in Michael Balint's essays of the 1930s, particularly in the 1933 essay "Two Notes on the Erotic Components of the Ego Instincts." It was this focus on love, as an ego instinct, that was also adopted and elaborated by Ian Suttie, whose wife and sometime coauthor Jane was one of the first translators into English (via German) of Ferenczi.

In a letter accompanying his unsuccessful 1923 submission to Ernest Jones, editor of the *International Journal*, Ian Suttie summarized the way in which he imagined the relation between the sexual instincts and the ego instincts:

> I thus regard love as social rather than sexual in its biological function as derived from the self-preservative [ego] instincts not the genital appetite and as seeking any state of responsiveness with others as its goal. Sociability I consider as a need for love rather than as aim inhibited sexuality, while culture interest is derived from love as a supplementary mode of companionship (to love) and not as a cryptic form of sexual gratification. [Brome 1984, p. 144, citing Suttie to Jones, April 15, 1923]

---

5. In America, the ego instincts were explored by Thomas French, Robert White, and other ego psychologists, but they spoke of the "instinct of mastery" or of "effectance," not the ego instincts as nurtural and object-seeking in the Budapest school manner. Elsewhere (Young-Bruehl 1999) I mentioned this American strand and considered the Budapest school contribution, but I did not present Suttie's work, which I did not know at that time.

In this formulation, it is clear that Suttie had not yet begun to mount a criticism of the death instinct theory; he was only dealing with the way in which he felt that Freud in his first instinct theory had emphasized sexuality at the expense of love or what he would come to call tenderness (adopting this word from Ferenczi, whose last essay was entitled "Confusion of Tongues: The Language of Tenderness and of Passion").

When Suttie had made a study of Freud's death instinct formulation—it was this study that, as he said "terminated my own rather blind devotion to Freud" (Suttie 1924, p. 194)—he criticized it on biological, ethological and psychological grounds, but he also approached it psychobiographically. He pointed to the places in Freud's writings where Freud marked a limitation in his own experience: his admission in "*Civilization and Its Discontents*" that he had never experienced the "oceanic feeling," his realization in "Female Sexuality" (1931) that " the first mother attachment has in analysis seemed to me so elusive, lost in a past dim and shadowy, so hard to resuscitate, that it seemed as if it had undergone some specially inexorable repression." Then Suttie indicated how these passages revealed a bias in Freud toward seeing the father looming in all infants' lives as the determinative figure and against recognizing the mother–infant "love reciprocity." This bias put Freud in harmony with the sexist "law of the father" bias of patriarchal culture generally. As Suttie put it, "Freud has, as a result of the 'specially inexorable repression,' a grudge against mothers and a mind-blindness for love, equal and opposite to the mind-blindness and repugnance that many of his opponents had for sex" (p. 189). One of the key manifestations of this antifeminist bias, Suttie held, is Freud's antipathy (expressed in a few dismissive lines in *Group Psychology* [1921]) to the great mother cults of antiquity and his insistence on reading the history of human sacrifice as a matter of filial rivalry against the father and paternal animosity against incestuously inclined sons. Suttie thought that Freud had, as a student of jealousies, emphasized penis envy in women, "Ethnology teaches us that this is an artifact of a particular type of culture," and missed the most fundamental of jealousies, "that of the man for the woman's reproductive and lactational powers" (p. 190).[6]

---

6. Suttie came to these assessments at about the same time that Karen Horney (1926) did. The work of Bachofen (1861) on "mother right" continued in England by Briffault (1927, 1931) and other anthropologists, probably influenced Suttie (see Burston 1986).

Freud's father worship shows itself again in his overlooking the primal fact in the Oedipus legend itself, namely, that the initial aggression came from Laius, the jealous father, himself (the oracle was Laius's baby self).[7] Yet an impartial study of the mythology would have shown the preponderance of the regressive jealousy of the father for the baby as such, girls and boys alike, over the precocious jealousy in the son for his father's sexual privileges. But it would have shown him that the greatest jealousy of all is that of the older for the younger child (Cain, Cinderella), a point upon which Freud touches very lightly, perhaps because it shows the mother as esteemed otherwise than sexually, perhaps because it shows her as the prime mover in the moralization of mankind. She first created "the band of brothers," she armed Cronus with the sickle that was to protect her children against their father's jealousy. Freud can see none of these things. [p. 190]

Generally, Suttie thought that Freud's inattention to mothers and to love, and his concentration on fathers and sex, led him to a social theory that "makes the overcoming of the aggressiveness and selfishness of the individual the key to socialization in individual development. Society is always regarded as the product of compulsion, never of mutual attraction" (p. 192).

In Suttie's view, Freud's work had, from the start, showed his bias, but the postulation of the death instinct theory indicated the bias operating at a new level of intensity. The theory arose not from empirical work but from a speculation that, as Freud himself said, won such a hold over him that he came to be unable to think otherwise. For individuals, the Freudian theory meant that "hate is a spontaneous, ineradicable appetite and all motive is egoistic," while for societies it meant that "all cultural interest is a substitute for sex gratification and all else is materialistic, utilitarian interest." By contrast, Suttie (1935) argued for looking to the child's relation with its mother for the origins of love and hate:

> I see in the infant's longing for the mother an expression of what in free-living animals we call the "self-preservative" instinct. Consistently with this, I see in anxiety and hate an expression of apprehension or

---

7. The Hungarian-trained Georges Devereux, an anthropologist as well as an analyst, advanced this interpretation (Devereux 1953 and other papers).

discomfort at the frustration, or threatened frustration, of this all-important motive. . . .

In animals born or hatched in a state of nurtural dependence, the whole instinct of self-preservation, including the potential dispositions to react with anger and fear, is at first directed toward the mother. Anger is then aimed not at the direct removal of frustration or attainment of the goal of the moment, still less at her destruction, but at inducing the mother to accomplish these wishes for the child. Instead of being the most desperate effort at self-help, [anger] has become the most insistent demand upon the help of others—the most emphatic plea which cannot be overlooked. It is now the maximal effort to attract attention, and as such must be regarded as a protest against unloving conduct rather than at aiming at destruction of the mother, which would have fatal repercussions upon the self.

Hatred, I consider, is just a standing reproach to the hated person, and owes all its meaning to a demand for love. If it were a desire (or appetite for destruction for its own sake), I cannot see how it could be focused so definitely upon one individual and as a rule upon a person who is significant in the person's life I would say, "Earth hath no hate but love to hatred turned, and hell no fury but a baby scorned," for hatred, except for a preferred rival or a rejecting lover, does not seem to exist. [pp. 13–14]

I am not going to go further into Suttie's biological and philosophical arguments against the death instinct theory here, but only note that he was making a case for a "taboo on tenderness" in Freud's life and work, and thus in psychoanalysis—and, I think one could argue following his line of thought, a taboo in writing the history of psychoanalysis as well. This taboo, Suttie thought, was in the realm of theory—and especially speculative theory, without empirical base—and not in the realm of practice. Suttie (1924) felt that the "metapsychological" domain and the domain of clinical work had so diverged after Freud's death instinct theory was proposed that "an intermediate body of theory has arisen to meet the needs of clinicians" (p. 205), even though some techniques ("the ultrapassive technique") and some rationales for cure still reflected strongly the "taboo on tenderness." In Freud's own mind, Suttie claimed, a conflict between the "absolutely asocial egoistic pessimism" underwriting the death instinct theory and the optimistic residuum nurturing primary ego instincts simmered on in two underdeveloped areas: the notion of the ego ideal, which shows people conditioned by the approval or dislike of others in their social world; and the notion of the superego as made up of introjected others. Similarly, a conflict in Freud between his theorizing self and his clinical self continued (although the clinical self would never have gone so far as to split with the theoretical self). This is Suttie's no-holds-barred psychobiographical summary:

> Contact with concrete people—particularly in the child-like role of dependent helpless sufferers who trust the physician with their inmost secrets and display emotion without reserve—overcomes Freud's own bitterness and evokes parental love. In the free fantasy of the metapsychology, however, his own childish rage and despair find expression in extreme antifeminism, the subjection of love to sex, the acclamation of aggression and hate as universal—a complete social pessimism. The thwarted purpose is (covertly) revealed in the theory of the death wish, for the dissolution desired is psychic—in fact, nothing but a loss of the boundaries which delimit the self from the mother (his personal horror of death is manifestly related to this). Freud's theory is the work of a thwarted infant revenging itself on mother. His practice is that of the ambitious parent who would teach the whole world to grow up—his way. [p. 211]

From Suttie's point of view, an answer to the question I posed above about why the magnet of criticism in Freud's psychoanalysis has been the sexual theory (for the first-generation dissidents) and then his dual instinct theory (for all subsequent generations) would be that the magnet is the site of the taboo on tenderness in Freud's theory. Critics have emerged within Freudian psychoanalysis as wanting to break the taboo—as Ferenczi did, as Suttie himself did—or, far more frequently, to perpetuate the taboo in some different way, each of which involved occluding the Darwinian version of Freud's instinct theory and its notion of the object-related ego instincts. Melanie Klein perpetuated it by embracing the death instinct theory; Jacques Lacan perpetuated it by embracing the sexual theory and "the law of the father"; various object relations theorists from Fairbairn to the contemporary relationalists have perpetuated it by contrasting a monolithic drive theory to object relations without any sense that there might be a motivation for love, an innate drive for creating object relations.

There are many ways to write the history of psychoanalysis and to point to general patterns within it. Bergmann has given us one, and a very interesting and wide-ranging one. I am suggesting in this reflection another: a history that identifies a taboo—the antifeminist taboo on tenderness—in the heart of psychoanalysis and sees psychoanalysis's history as a struggle over that taboo, a struggle that has taken myriad forms and has, now, brought forth myriad theoretical and clinical and institution questions. Ian Suttie, who identified the taboo after the First World War, at just the moment when psychoanalysis was organizing and institutionalizing (and at just the moment of the "first wave" women's movement and the first feminist critique within psychoanalysis), fell under the operation of the taboo himself. But times have changed, and the current condition of psychoanalysis may be one in which his voice can be heard again.

References

Bachofen, J. (1861). *Mutterrecht* [Mother right], trans. and abridged by D. Partenheimer. Lewiston, NY: Edwin Mellen, 2003.

Balint, M. (1933). *Two Notes on the Erotic Components of the Ego Instinct, Primary Love and Psychoanalytic Technique.* New York: Liveright, 1953.

Briffault, R. (1927). *The Mothers: A Study of the Origins of Sentiments and Institutions.* New York: Macmillan.

———— (1931). *The Mothers: The Matriarchal Theory of Social Origins.* New York: Macmillan.

Brome, V. (1984). *Ernest Jones: Freud's Alter Ego.* Caliban.

Buhle, M. J. (1998). *Feminism and Its Discontents: A Century of Struggle with Psychoanalysis.* Cambridge, MA: Harvard University Press.

Burston, D. (1986). Myth religion and mother right: Bachofen's influence on psychoanalytic theory. *Contemporary Psychoanalysis* 22:666–687.

Devereux, G. (1953). Why Oedipus killed Laius. *International Journal of Psycho-Analysis* 34:132–141.

Fenichel, O. (1934). *Outline of Clinical Psychoanalysis.* New York: W.W. Norton.

———— (1945). *The Psychoanalytic Theory of Neuroses.* New York: W.W. Norton.

Ferenczi, S. (1923). *Thalassa: A Theory of Genitality.* New York: *Psychoanalytic Quarterly*, 1938.

Freud, S. (1905). Three essays on the theory of sexuality. *Standard Edition* 7:125–245.

———— (1914). On the history of the psycho-analytic movement. *Standard Edition* 14:3–102.

———— (1920). Beyond the pleasure principle. *Standard Edition* 18:3–64.

———— (1921). Group psychology and the analysis of the ego. *Standard Edition* 18:67–143.

———— (1926). Inhibitions, symptoms and anxiety. *Standard Edition* 20:77–175.

———— (1931). Female sexuality. *Standard Edition* 21:223–243.

———— (1940). An outline of psycho-analysis. *Standard Edition* 23:141–207.

Glover, E. (1939). *Psychoanalysis: A Handbook for Medical Practitioners and Students of Comparative Psychology*. London: Staples.

Greenberg, J., and Mitchell, S. (1983). *Object Relations in Psychoanalytic Theory*. Cambridge, MA: Harvard University Press.

Greenson, R. (1967). *The Technique and Practice of Psycho-Analysis*, vol. 1. New York: International Universities Press.

Greer, G. (1970). *The Female Eunuch*. New York: Bantam.

Horney, K. (1926). The flight from womanhood. *International Journal of Psycho-Analysis* 7:324.

Klein, M. *(1932)*. *The Psychoanalysis of Children*. New York: Dell, 1976.

Money-Kyrle, R. (1936). Review of Ian Suttie's *The Origins of Love and Hate*. *International Journal of Psycho-Analysis* 17:137–138.

Nunberg, H. (1932). *Principles of Psychoanalysis: Their Application to the Neuroses*. English trans. New York: International Universities Press, 1956.

Roudinesco, E. (1944). *Jacques Lacan & Co.: A History of Psychoanalysis in France, 1925–1985*. Chicago: University of Chicago Press.

Schwartz, J. (1999). *Cassandra's Daughter: A History of Psychoanalysis*. London: Penguin.

Strozier, C. (2001). *Heinz Kohut: The Making of a Psychoanalyst*. New York: Farrar, Straus, & Giroux.

Suttie, I. (1924). Metapsychology and biology: some criticism of Freud's "Beyond the Pleasure Principle." *Journal of Psychopathology* 5:61–70.

———— (1935). *The Origins of Love and Hate*. New York: Matrix House; Agora, 1966.

Waelder, R. (1966). *Basic Theory of Psychoanalysis*. New York: International Universities Press.

Young-Bruehl, E. (1999). The hidden history of the ego instincts. *Psychoanalytic Review* 86:823–851.

9
Charles Rycroft: A Study in Dissidence and a Psychoanalytic Cautionary Tale

Martin S. Bergmann

I came across Rycroft's (1985) book *Psychoanalysis and Beyond* after I had already finished my monograph, but the word *beyond* attracted my attention. The book is a collection of essays, the most important being "On Ablation of the Parental Images" (Rycroft 1965/1973). This piece was rejected by the International Institute of Psychoanalysis, and the collection of his essays was published by the British Institute of Psychoanalysis because it was critical of psychoanalysis. I decided to add this chapter because Rycroft is a type of dissident we should include in our coming discussion.

The Freud Museum Web site provides the following information on Charles Rycroft, who died in June 1998:

> Charles Rycroft was a significant figure in the modern history of psychoanalysis. Best known for his "Critical Dictionary of Psychoanalysis," his ideas and interests ranged widely between philosophy, biology, history and art. He criticised the rigidity of psychoanalytic formulations and the institutionalisation of psychoanalysis, resigning from the British Psychoanalytical Society in 1968.
>
> In the early 60s Rycroft passionately argued that the theoretical ideal of "rationality" proposed by ego psychology alienates human adults from the creative springs of inner communication and emotion.

His work on dreams and symbolism stressed the essentially positive function of these "flights of the imagination," and in doing so he posited new ways of thinking about psychic development. As a humane and perceptive clinician Rycroft focused on the nature of language and preconscious communication in the analytic encounter. His books include *Imagination and Reality* (1968), *The Innocence of Dreams* (1979), *Psychoanalysis and Beyond* (1985), and *Viewpoints* (1991). . . .

Rycroft argued against the "tyranny of psychic determinism," as he called it. He did not regard psychoanalysis as a causal theory but as a theory of meaning, and he offered interpretations and ideas in a questioning, tentative way—non-dogmatic yet carrying authority and authenticity. Indeed he devalued interpretations as the curative factor in therapy.

I am going to follow psychoanalytic precedence by including a case presentation. It is by now well known that a case can neither prove nor disprove a theory; however, what it can do is throw a sharper light on the issue discussed.

Unlike the other dissidents discussed earlier, Rycroft did not create a dissident school of his own; he became a private dissident as it were.

I therefore decided to withdraw from the society, and over the years I have continued a long term strategic withdrawal such as by now, in 1984, I am not a member of any psychoanalytical organization. [Rycroft 1984, p. 206]

Charles Rycroft was born on September 9, 1914, just as World War I was breaking out. He was the youngest son of Sir Richard Nelson Rycroft and his second wife. Sir Richard was the fifth baronet and a famous fox hunter. He died when Charles was 11. Following the rules of primogeniture, the manor passed to the oldest son, Charles's half-brother. The mother, demoted to the position of poor relative, became clinically depressed.

Rycroft does not say so, but our psychoanalytic knowledge permits the hypothesis that a depressed parent often turns to the child, reversing roles. The failure of the child to cure the parent is a common reason for becoming a psychoanalyst or therapist. Rycroft went to Cambridge and became a reader in history there. Under the influence of the Bloomsbury group he tried, like Strachey and Karin Stephen, to become a lay analyst. This was at that time the aristocratic road to psychoanalysis in Britain; it entailed a visit to the continent and an analysis by Freud or Abraham. But Jones would accept him only if he would become a physician. He qualified in medicine in 1945 and in psychoanalysis in 1947, having been analyzed by Ella Sharpe and Sylvia Payne.

I suspect that his failure to be accepted as a lay analyst and accepted only as a physician repeated the trauma of his loss of status after his father's death. I find confirmation of this in the following statement:

> Although it had vaguely occurred to me that psychoanalysis was an activity for which I might have aptitude I tacitly avowed that it was a profession reserved for Central Europeans who at the time I believed to be intrinsically more intelligent and cultured than the English. However during my third year at Cambridge I become friendly with members of the Bloomsbury family who all talked about psychoanalysis a lot and believed it to be the science of the future. [Rycroft 1984, p. 204]

Behind the idealization of Central Europeans one can read the statement as an ambivalent attitude toward psychoanalysis. Rycroft does not state that he shared the enthusiasm of Bloomsbury.

In a paper titled "Where I Came From" (1984), Rycroft stated, "If I had known about the psychoanalytical movement's sectarianism and its tendency to engage in unedifying infighting I would, I suspect, not have applied for training." The statement confirms what we would otherwise only suspect, that the dissidence effects the idealization of psychoanalysis that many need to continue in the profession. In 1968 the International Institute of Psychoanalysis published Rycroft's *Imagination and Reality: Psychoanalytical Essays 1951–1961* but refused to publish "On Ablation of the Parental Images or the Creation of the Illusion of Having Created Oneself." This essay, written in 1965, was only published in 1985. By that time Rycroft no longer considered himself to be an analyst.

For the purposes of this monograph the essay is of particular interest. In the first part of this paper Rycroft described a clinical entity not significantly different from Helene Deutsch's (1942) description of the "as if" personality.

The ablators have destroyed the parental introjects. They neither follow their parents' footsteps nor rebel against them; they do not use the parental images as internal points of reference. They find the parents' physical proximity meaningless and do not care whether their parents are dead or alive. All remembered events seem unreal, strange, trivial, and alien. As a result the process of self–re-creation can be imaginative and creative but it is also false. Images in dreams may be iconic representation of ideas but they are not symbols of object.

One may agree or disagree with this description but there is nothing heretic about it. What made the paper unacceptable to the International and unprintable in a psychoanalytic library book was the idea that ablators are drawn to psychoanalysis by choosing an analyst they are acquiring a parent they themselves discovered: "They become proselytizer of their own analyst's theories as much out of personal vanity as out of genuine appreciation and gratitude for his understanding and skill. . . . The analysand patronizes his analyst, while he shines in the reflected glory of someone whom he himself elected to idealize" (p. 227).

Ablation is responsible for the idea "that nothing was known about human nature before Freud. Psychoanalysts prefer to believe that psychoanalysis arose as an autonomous idea in the mind of a genius." Because ablation was at the core of psychoanalysis itself, "psychoanalysts were eager to hive off psychoanalysis from medical and scientific groups while it could arguably have remained attached" (p. 228). As a result a group fantasy emerged that the psychoanalyst movement is an elite, a calling rather than a profession. In Rycroft's view it was not the outside world that rejected Freud's work but the unconscious need of early psychoanalysts to remain an elite group. It is not difficult to see in the reproaches of Rycroft a repetition of the reproaches of Christians against Jews.

Because Rycroft's paper was both a contribution to psychoanalytic diagnosis as well as a critique of the history of psychoanalysis, this paper was unprecedented and unacceptable. Rycroft's paper can with profit be compared with Ernst Kris' paper, "The Personal Myth" (1956) that had no difficulty in being published; the difference is that Kris didn't attack organized psychoanalysis. Increasingly Rycroft found that psychoanalysis bears a disconcerting resemblance to religious and political movements.

Another reason for divergence from Freud took place when Rycroft read Suzanne Langer's (1942) book, *Philosophy in a New Key*. I have already discussed a similar encounter between Lacan and De Saussure and Heidegger. The need to incorporate other thinkers into the mainstream of psychoanalysis is a difficult task and one of the reasons for dissidence. Langer differentiated between discursive and nondiscursive symbolism. In discursive symbolism words have fixed meanings arranged according to agreed-upon rules; in nondiscursive symbolism the meaning of images has to be derived from their context (1942). "The battle of Waterloo took place on June 18, 1815" is a discursive statement and has only one meaning, it is either true or false. But a dream or a poem is nondiscursive and may have no meaning or many meanings. This encounter led Rycroft to question Jones's 1916 paper on symbolism and Freud's *The Interpretation of Dreams.*

Rycroft found the distinction between discursive and nondiscursive richer in meaning than Freud's differentiation between primary and secondary processes. Along similar lines Rycroft found T. S. Eliot's "disassociation of sensibility" indispensable. The scientific and objective point of view is in this new outlook incompatible with the imaginative and subjective. In the paper "The God I Want" Rycroft stressed this incompatibility: "Those who adhere to the scientific stance can find no place in their philosophy for art or intuition, while those who adopt Eliot's solution can make nothing of technology. Finally those who adopt the psychotic solution of jumbling the two stances together becomes confused, bewildered and incomprehensible to others" (p. 284). This despair over the overcoming of the "disassociation of sensibility" may be the rock bottom that drove Rycroft out of psychoanalysis. Because the metaphorical language, the only language in which the self can be understood, is untranslatable into discursive language Rycroft came to a pessimistic conclusion: "The only person who is really in the position to know one's own nature is oneself. The only person who both was there at the beginning and will be there at the end is oneself" (p. 290). This statement not only negates the very possibility of the psychoanalytic encounter, but also leads to a sad conclusion for a psychoanalyst to reach. Only a lonely man could have written these lines. It also says a great deal about how Rycroft felt about how well he was not understood by his own analysts. The two analysts that Rycroft had were highly competent and yet as time went on Rycroft reached the pessimistic conclusion that no one understood him. Elsewhere Rycroft acknowledged that to his own surprise he came close to Jung's position.

Another cornerstone of psychoanalysis that Rycroft struggled with was that of inner conflict. In "The Innocence of Dreams," published in 1979, Rycroft saw dreams as the way we think while we sleep. Had Freud read this book he may have been tempted to exclaim as he did to Adler, "This is not psychoanalysis!" Reading *Psychoanalysis and Beyond* leaves me in no doubt that Rycroft was a well-trained psychoanalyst. A paper titled "Miss Y: The Analysis of a Paranoid Personality" (Rycroft 1959) shows that he was a gifted clinician. What went wrong? The orthodoxy of the British Psychoanalytical Society was a factor. Many of the criticisms of Freud were well justified, but in my opinion these can only lead to dissidence if a lingering wish for idealization has not been met. Could Rycroft have had a better and more complete analysis? In theory yes, but given the sociology of psychoanalysis, probably not. Can we prevent well-trained psychoanalysts from becoming disappointed in psychoanalysis of some point in their career? Probably not.

In dealing with the phenomenon of Rycroft, classical analysis would dismiss him in the name of resistance to the burdensome truth that Freud discovered. If my presentation is to be believed, the emphasis on resistance to Freud's discovered truth was not productive and contributed to the creation of an orthodoxy that is not in the best interests of psychoanalysis. Precisely because Rycroft did not start a school of his own and therefore avoided controversy, his case is instructive. Can we understand dissidence better? Can we help create a climate of opinion in which future Rycrofts will not try to go beyond psychoanalysis? It is in this spirit that I am adding him as a specimen for our consideration.

References

Deutsch, H. (1942). Some forms of emotional disturbance and their relationship to schizophrenia. *Psychoanalytic Quarterly* 11:301–321.

Kris, E. (1956). The personal myth: a problem in psychoanalytic technique. In *Selected Papers*. New Haven, CT: Yale University Press, 1975.

Langer, S. K. (1942). *Philosophy in a New Key: A Study in the Symbolism of Reason, Rite, and Art*. Cambridge, MA: Harvard University Press, 1985.

Rycroft, C. (1959). Miss Y: the analysis of a paranoid personality. In *Psychoanalysis and Beyond*. Chicago, IL: University of Chicago Press, 1985.

———— (1965/1973). On ablation of the parental images *or* the creation of the illusion of having created oneself. In *Psychoanalysis and Beyond*. Chicago: University of Chicago Press, 1985.

——— (1968). *Imagination and Reality: Psychoanalytical Essay 1951–1961*. New York: International Institute of Psychoanalysis.

——— (1979). *The Innocence of Dreams*. Random House.

——— (1984). Where I came from. In *Psychoanalysis and Beyond*. Chicago: University of Chicago Press, 1985.

III

CONFERENCE PROCEEDINGS

OPENING SESSION, FEBRUARY 14, 2003

Bergmann: I wish to thank the Fund for Psychoanalytic Research and Development for sponsoring and financing this symposium and for their trust in me to navigate this conference through rough waters, for there probably is no other subject in psychoanalysis that creates as much heat as the subject of this conference.

I also want to thank all the participants for their cooperation and for their contributions. I want to thank particularly André Green for crossing the ocean and Tony Kris for suggesting that this conference be held on my ninetieth birthday. I cannot imagine a more magnificent way of celebrating such a birthday as leading this conference. Indeed, I cannot think of a psychoanalyst as fortunate as I am today.

The meetings of the International have accustomed us to debates where participants pass each other by, learning little from each other. I have another ideal in mind: a group of analysts probing together a difficult problem and coming up, by mutual stimulation, with ideas each one of them alone could not have reached. I am not unaware of the difficulties of such a conference but I very much wish to bring this conference to a productive conclusion. If we succeed, we will make a contribution to our field.

One difference in opinion struck me as particularly profound. André Green believes that the answer to our problems is a clearer understanding as to what

259

constitutes a psychoanalytic core, while Kernberg, Wallerstein, and Scharff put their trust in a growing consensus between the major trends. These two approaches highlight the scope and depth of the problems we face. A symposium requires tension that, it is hoped, can lead to a broader synthesis; I believe we have it if we see my essay criticized from one side by André Green as irrelevant and by Elisabeth Young-Bruehl on the other as inadequate to the task. I welcome both.

I very much hope that our discussion will be a productive one. I think of André's idea that history cannot teach us very much and we have no time for regrets, and on the other hand Elisabeth's criticism that dissidents during Freud's life were of a personal nature too close to Freud and needed to find their own voice, while the core of dissent of the generation after Freud was the battle over who was Freud's legitimate heir. We can no longer speak of dissidence but of interpretation of Freud's legacy. The differences between André and Elisabeth alone should be enough to get us started.

The title of our conference is "Understanding Diversity and Controversy in the History of Psychoanalysis." I would like to emphasize the word *understanding*. We will not try to agree or form a consensus but we wish to be united in our efforts to understand this aspect in the history of psychoanalysis. We have modeled this conference after the model of a previous conference, "The Hartmann Era," in 2000.[1] Then as now I have written an introductory essay to serve as the springboard. Invited participants contributed essays of their own responding in part to my presentation and now we are about to start the third part of the conference, the general discussion.

With your permission I would like to begin the conference by an attempt at formulating a psychoanalytical hypothesis (it may become a psychoanalytic theory) as to why there is so much passion and vehemence in the discussion of the differences in point of view among analysts. Why have we failed in the effort to conduct our disagreements as the Latin proverb demands, *"Sine ira et studiorum,"* that is, without anger and in an attitude of study? I wish to do this for two reasons: first because of the intrinsic importance of the subject, and second because I hope to prevent our conference from suffering the same fate. I recall that after the controversial discussions of the British Psychoanalytic Society were published by King and Steiner a group of analysts asked me to organize a study group to read this book. To my amazement I noticed that instead of studying the problem the group was in danger of refighting the Anna Freud–Melanie Klein battle. I want us to study the problem of dissidence and controversy, not to repeat it.

---

1. Bergmann, M. S., ed. (2000). *The Hartmann Era*. New York: Other Press.

My own survey has led me to certain insights that I would like to enumerate as an introduction to the discussion.

Freud not only created psychoanalysis, but during his lifetime no psychoanalyst beside Freud wrote papers that have survived as milestones in the history of psychoanalysis. Tausk's 1912[2] paper on masturbation stands out, as does his 1919 paper[3] on the influency machine. Abraham's papers on the pregenital phases and his 1924 "A Short Study of Development of Libido Viewed in the Light of the Mental Disorders"[4] were important amplifications of Freud but didn't break new ground. By contrast the papers by Karen Horney and the two last papers by Ferenczi—"The Unwelcome Child and His Death Instinct" in 1929,[5] and "The Confusion of Tongues between Adults and the Child" 1933[6]—did break new ground. In 1976 I published a book titled *The Evolution of Psychoanalytic Technique*[7] in which I cited many papers written by psychoanalysts that seemed to me significant. Looking over these papers a quarter of a century later, I was struck by the fact that they appear dated in a way that Freud's work does not appear dated. I therefore concluded that during Freud's lifetime he was psychoanalysis. He was the father but also almost the only creator of psychoanalysis. To disagree with Freud was for psychoanalysts as well as for dissidents an act of patricide. It was equated with patricide along with Hanna Segal's paper,[8] symbolic equation, and not a symbolic act of patricide. What Freud said about the original crime in "Totem and Taboo" (1913)[9] may or may not have happened in history but it certainly was

2. Tausk, V. (1912). On masturbation. English trans. *Psychoanalytic Study of the Child* 5:61–70. New York: International Universities Press, 1951.

3. ——— (1919). The influencing machine. In *The Psychoanalytic Reader*, ed. R. Fleiss, pp. 852–885. New York: International Universities Press, 1948.

4. Abraham, K. (1924). A short study of the development of the libido, viewed in the light of mental disorders. In *Selected Papers of Karl Abraham*. London: Hogarth and the Institute of Psycho-Analysis.

5. Ferenczi, S. (1929). The unwelcome child and his death instinct. In *Final Contributions to the Problems and Methods of Psycho-Analysis*, pp. 102–107. London: Hogarth and the Institute of Psycho-Analysis.

6. ——— (1933). The confusion of tongues between adults and the child. In *Final Contributions to the Problems and Methods of Psycho-Analysis*, pp. 156–167. London: Hogarth and the Institute of Psycho-Analysis.

7. Bergmann, M. S., and Hartmann, F. R., eds. (1976). *The Evolution of Psychoanalytic Technique*. New York: Basic Books.

8. Segal, H. (1957). Notes on symbol formation. *International Journal of Psycho-Analysis* 35:258–341.

9. Freud, S. (1913). Totem and taboo. *Standard Edition* 13, pp. ix–162.

enacted in the history of psychoanalysis but with a different result: both father and rebellious sons surviving. Freud discovered the centrality of the
Oedipus complex, and the history of psychoanalysis reenacted it. Because the
murder of the father is reenacted in the history of psychoanalysis the disagreements have the vehemence, and the impact of the oedipal discovery haunts
the history of psychoanalysis.

Psychoanalysis by its very nature promises more than it can deliver. Hopes
are aroused that can only to a limited degree be realized. The limitation of one's
personal analysis and particularly the self-analysis that is undertaken as a result of the limits of the personal analysis is an important source of controversy.

The very structure of psychoanalysis is conducive to dissidence. The
analysts of all schools listen to their patients, but in order to keep the communication alive, in order to prevent most analysands from going in circles, they
organize the data in a way that provides structure. All schools organize, but
not all organize along the same lines. The superiority of one organization over
the other in terms of deeper understanding of oneself, resumption of growth,
the realization of one's potential capacities, and a better relationship to the
reality principle is difficult to evaluate. Furthermore, the very process of organization itself becomes cathected because it has unconscious meaning, as
stressed by Grossman. It probably contains elements of reaction formation that
in turn gives it a defensive hue.

Every psychoanalysis leads to questions that cannot be answered by the
psychoanalytic interview. We hypothesize about what goes on in the first
months of life without being able to reach a conclusion. Hypotheses that cannot be verified are the breeding ground of controversy. This was best illustrated in the controversial Freud–Klein discussions.

Just a few days before our conference Leo Rangell published in a paper
titled "The Theory of Psychoanalysis: Vicissitudes of Its Evolution,"[10] which
deals with the very same topic as our symposium. Rangell advocates "a total
composite psychoanalytic theory" (p. 1126) that is both cumulative and unified. It features a blend of the valid old concept and the valid new ones. In
this theory every viable contribution made by alternative theories finds a home.
Rangell visualizes an embracing umbrella that includes drive and defense, ego
and superego, self and object, intrapsychic and interpersonal, internal and
external world. When reading the paper I was reminded of Isaiah, Chapter 11,
"The wolf also shall dwell with the lamb and the leopard shall lie down with

---

10. Rangell, L. (1999). The theory of psychoanalysis: vicissitudes of its evolution. *Journal of the American Psychoanalytic Association* 50(4).

the kid; and the calf and the young lion will lie together. . . . And the lion shall eat straw like the ox. . . . And the earth shall be full of knowledge of the Lord."

Like Wallerstein and Kernberg, Rangell believes that after a long period of revisionism, the pendulum is beginning to swing back again. Rangell quotes with approval Goldberg's 1999 plenary address, "The Two Heinzes—Kohut and Hartmann—Must Be Joined in This Reconciliation of Empathy and Judgment."[11] As if to emphasize that all may not be well, Rangell also quotes Fonagy (2002),[12] "I came to bury free association, not to praise it" and in its place would put "free conversation." At the end of his paper Rangell argues against Charles Brenner, who can be seen as our most recent dissident. In my opinion it is less interesting to argue against Brenner than to think about the puzzle of how a man who for many years was in the forefront of psychoanalysis eventually is led to question its basic assumptions. It is the denial of the ferocity of the emotions involved in the controversies that ultimately leads me to believe that Rangell's solution is utopian. Unlike myself Rangell would not be interested in the kind of symposium we are planning. His only difficulty would be that not everyone will be persuaded to accept his vision of what is included and what is left and of his total composite psychoanalytic theory. It is because I do not believe that any one of us has the answer to why there is such vehemence in psychoanalytic discourse that I hope that our deliberation will be productive.

If we succeed in this conference to develop a reasonably satisfactory theory of the underlying reasons for the vehemence in psychoanalytic controversies, we may not have to repeat it. I now look forward to the discussion of this subject.

The second question for our symposium to address is, How is dissidence during Freud's life, and the fact that after his death different schools of thought on psychoanalysis created a controversial diversity, to be taught in the psychoanalytic curriculum? This question may at first seem like a narrow, pedagogical one, but some reflection will show that it goes to the very core of what psychoanalysis faces today.

There is a problem here with which I have some experience. If you discuss these issues early in the psychoanalytic curriculum, the chances are that you will only bewilder the students. On the other hand, if you wait too long, a kind of rigidity has already set in. I would like to begin by reminding you of Otto Kernberg's (2000) paper, "A Concerned Critique of Psychoanalytic

---

11. Goldberg, A. (1999). Between empathy and judgment. *Journal of the American Psychoanalytic Association* 50:1109–1136.

12. Fonagy, P. (1999). Memory and therapeutic action. *International Journal of Psycho-Analysis* 80:215–225.

Education,"[13] and even further back to Bernfeld's 1962 paper, "On Psychoanalytic Training."[14] Kernberg's paper ends with fifteen questions addressed to the training institutes. The second question is the following: Are multiple psychoanalytic theories and clinical approaches respectfully taught? It seems to me that the very structure of the current psychoanalytic societies makes it unlikely that this test can be met.

In an earlier paper (1986), Kernberg[15] differentiated four models of education:

1. An art academy that aims to train expert craftsmen with emphasis on ideal technique.
2. The model of a trade school that aims to teach a clearly defined skill.
3. The model of a monastery teaching religious beliefs. In this model Freud will be idealized as religious figures are idealized.
4. The university model. It is in this model that the candidate "would have to absorb not only Freud's writings but also those of psychoanalysts who reached theoretical and technical conclusions that differ from Freud."

The last model is the one preferred by Kernberg and I feel reasonably sure that it will be followed by all or most participants in this symposium.

It is not difficult to visualize in cities like New York, Chicago, Los Angeles, London, Paris, and Buenos Aires psychoanalytic universities with the best teachers drawn from various institutes teaching their courses, and candidates graduating and joining the institutes of their choice. But what stands in the way is the structure of the analytic societies, each built around a particular school.

I asked myself in connection with this question if you are trying to introduce a student to the history of psychoanalysis, and you are discussing the period until 1939, are there any papers written by others than Freud that you would consider of the same fundamentality that Freud's papers are? While I could think of a number of very good papers—like the papers by Tausk on

---

13. Kernberg, O. (2000). A concerned critique of psychoanalytic evaluation.

14. Bernfeld, S. (1962). On psychoanalytic training. *Psychoanalytic Quarterly* 31:453–482.

15. Kernberg, O. (1986). Institutional problems of psychoanalytic education. *Journal of the American Psychoanalytic Association* 34:801–834.

the influencing machine and on masturbation (see fns 2, 3) and the paper by Abraham on the psychosexual phases and his 1924 study (see fn 4)—I slowly came to the conclusion I didn't find a single paper by anybody besides Freud about which you could say: If that paper had not been written, psychoanalysis would have suffered or developed along a different line. There is something truly astonishing about the creation of psychoanalysis—the extent to which it was not only created by one man, but actually maintained by him until his death. There isn't a single paper by somebody besides Freud about which we can say: this paper is absolutely necessary in teaching. It's a sobering experience.

Green: My idea was that the psychoanalytic theories that are always produced by a single person—an author—are not quite the same as any other discussion in any other field—whether you discuss physiology, history, or any other discipline, because most of the authors not only made the theories themselves but also gave what they thought was their conception of the mind, in general. And in this conception of the mind, they put not only their internal conflicts and their problems, but also their view, their concept of what is man, how man is, of what man is made of, how it comes out that man becomes this and that and the other thing. Now we have to be aware that not only in the case of Freud but also in the case of others like Melanie Klein, like Lacan, like all the great thinkers of psychoanalysis, theories are painful to accept because they go directly to the beliefs and the convictions of what men are, what they think of themselves. Let's get out of generalities; it would be my idea that the drive concept is not a question of disagreement of dissidence. It's really a crucial question about agreeing or not agreeing with Freud. Not because it is Freud but because of the conception of man that derives from it. As we say in French: "*On n'est pas des bêtes.*" We are not beasts. It is about sex that these things are said. So I believe that as time went by, each one, in his own way, proposed something else. I can understand both the history of dissidence and it is still going on now as a critic around the drive concepts in Freud. There was an attempt to try to replace it by something more acceptable. In object relations theory, there is the idea that what happens between you and me is more important than what happens inside myself, my inner struggle and what dreams are about and what my behavior is about. In French, "*Qu'est ce qui fait courir les gens?*" After what are people running? This idea, which was in Freud's mind and never left him, is today questioned. And it was questioned earlier. There is Freud—what he called the pleasure principle; and Fairbairn openly criticized Freud because he found him too hedonistic (and I'm rather surprised that Jill Scharff's paper about the object relationship doesn't mention it). Freud was criticized as sexually obsessed, too much of a hedonist. He was criticized as too much attached to pleasure. And as we say in French: "*Il y a autre choses dans la vie que.*" There's something else in life than pleasure.

Another movement came after Fairbairn, who was mainly concerned with a change of paradigm: what people are looking for is to have relationships first. This is very important because it brings the theory of attachment, and we see that if the libido is not pleasure seeking but object seeking. There is no longer pleasure seeking but there is object seeking for the sake of security. The attachment theory is a theory about security. Now I question—Are people really moved and oriented and motivated by security or by pleasure? I am on the side of Freud. So if we have to consider dissidence, I suppose this would be a good criterion to discuss the links between the drive concepts, the pleasure seeking, and what is the nucleus of psychoanalysis. Bion describes what he calls the alpha function. Let's not expand on this; let's just say that for him, the alpha function is what makes the fact become psychical. By contrast, beta functions are those that cannot be integrated and have to be expelled. But what does he give as an example of the alpha function? It is the stuff of which myth, passion, and dream are made. So we see that even Bion is a dissident. The fact that he thinks that the important link is among myth, passion, and dream indirectly gives us the idea of the goal of the psychic. We have now, in analysis, two tendencies. The one—the modern one—is the intrasubjective view. The other is the older intrapsychic view. In the intrapsychic model all events that are psychologically significant take place within the person; in the intersubjective they take place between the two participants. If you take the dream and you try to analyze it, you are dealing with the intrapsychic point of view. Only with that view can you make any progress in the understanding of the dream. For the intersubjective, the model is transference. You cannot understand transference except with the interpsychic point of view, unless of course you consider that the interpsychic is projected on the outside. But really what happens between these two people—countertransference, transference—is of capital importance. Now these two points of view have been opposed. In my idea, we have to bring them together, the intrapsychic and the intersubjective. And each one coexists with the other and this is the originality of psychoanalysis.

Kernberg: A brief quote from Max Gitelson, that I mention in my paper, you will all remember it. Max Gitelson said, many years ago, "There are many people who believe in psychoanalysis except sex, aggression, and transference."

Blum: I was reminded, as you were speaking, André, of Freud's comment about having disturbed the sleep of the world. He mentioned Copernicus, Darwin, and then himself. Because the human being is really, to some extent, moved by irrational, unconscious forces. And Freud felt that was a major source of the resistance to psychoanalysis. The drive aspect that you bring up is very important; it falls under the rubric of the dynamic unconscious and the world was, in some respect, just as unhappy and disturbed to hear about other aspects of the unconscious, including the punitive superego, that people were ruled by archaic forces within them. The unconscious motive toward destruction and self-destruction and so forth. To my mind, that is one of the reasons that we are confronted with what Martin Bergmann brought up at first, namely the vehemence. While the vehemence can be a reaction to orthodoxy and rigidity, it usually has powerful clinical components. I think one aspect of the vehemence is that forever people are very concerned about the eruption of their own unconscious conflicts. And these conflicts require intense defense. The more insecure the persons are, the more likely they are to be vehement about their opposition to psychoanalysis, or, conversely, they become a proselytizer or a defender of the faith. I believe that Freud was correct when he spoke of the analyst's unconscious resistance, a latent content behind the manifest vehemence, and of the need on the part of some analysts—a minority, it is hoped—to be defenders of the faith, to vehemently protect and defend certain viewpoints with anger and even with expulsion of those who disagree if they were in a position to do so. This rejection of any differing formulation is probably because of their own unanalyzed, or insufficiently analyzed, conflicts, or group identification and loyalty or narcissistic investment in their own position.

This problem also involves the way in which people were trained and to some degree may continue to be trained in isolated institutes. The candidate could be subjected to the kind of training in which any challenge, any sign of being a dissident was met with opposition in an ambience of being threatened, and even being looked at as a possible heretic. That kind of atmosphere had its own ramifications in terms of stifling creativity. One analyst asserted, "It's amazing how creative some candidates were at the beginning of their training and how dull they seemed after they graduated." Sometimes candidates emerged from their training very inhibited, very much needing to show that they were loyal to what they had been taught, that they were positive adherents and in no way had any heretical tendencies. Of course the creativity and independent judgment of many candidates improved with training.

There are several more things I want to mention. Martin brought up the question, Is there any other paper, other than Freud's papers prior to his death, that we would regard as absolutely essential? I think that was a fascinating idea. And I think that probably there isn't, though there are many other superb contributions. One factor is that Freud was such a towering genius that there was no one else who could contribute and formulate psychoanalysis as he did. There was a second factor, which was that the early analysts tended very much to identify with Freud and to seek his instruction, his approval. They vied with each other for his love and approval. This was true of the pioneer analysts. It was in many ways a small coterie of disciples in the beginning. A third factor was that in the early period, when there was so much external opposition to psychoanalysis (they didn't quite foresee that this would continue over the whole course of the century except for a short ten- or twenty-year period), that it was necessary, in terms of the group process, to really feel that they could protect, defend, and advance psychoanalysis with minimal internal and external threat. They were an avant-garde, little-analyzed group that had to protect themselves in order to be able to create the kind of discourse that promoted and enriched understanding without interferences of opposition. In the process, something was gained and something was lost. They lost the opportunity to further explore their own internal divergences and alternate interpretations, but they also formed a more cohesive group. This group process also fostered their ability to formulate and build upon the core of psychoanalysis, as well as group regressive phenomenon. There's another point that Martin made in the paper on psychoanalytic orthodoxy in the *International Journal*. And it had to do, among other things, with Freud himself, with Freud's attitude toward change and toward other ideas. Freud can be cited both ways. Freud can be cited as receptive to new ideas, open to new ideas, encouraging those who were different. And Freud can also be cited as opposed to divergence, stating that, in effect, I determine who is an analyst and who isn't. In effect, he actually fostered both orthodoxy and unorthodox independence. On balance I believe that Freud was receptive to innovative ideas, or not antagonistic, while retaining his own skepticism and caution. Freud was more ready to acknowledge mystery and perplexity than dogmatic followers.

Ostow: Sounds like Goering: "I determine who's a Jew."

Blum: That was said by the mayor of Vienna during Freud's time.

Bergmann: "Who is a Jew, I determine," was said by Karl Lueger, the anti-Semitic mayor of Vienna. In 1995, Bill Grossman wrote a paper on what makes for ideology and I hope that he will help us get further on this point. If we focus on understanding, we can do something that is not as yet found in the analytic literature. Out of Socrates's philosophy grew four or five different philosophical schools; I would like to focus on how it happened that we have different psychoanalytic schools. If there is a psychoanalytic concept that can help us understand dissidence, it is reaction formation. That may also be essential in helping to understand the vehemence in the discussions. Apparently, no ideological commitment is possible without a residue of reaction formation.

And the residue of reaction formation is also responsible for the vehemence in psychoanalytic discussion. If we can conduct this conference without refighting the battle and try to understand it, there will be something to be gained.

Green: I would like to raise a point of order. I think we have here a very complex situation. We have to sort out the points of view, which would lead us in the discussion. I think that first, personal matters should not come into play. The fact that Mr. So-and-so had not been fully analyzed is not a valid argument. And sociological matters shouldn't come into play either, such as who were the analysts. We have to focus on the internal content of the ideas, why an idea was at a certain moment defended and why it has been successful or rejected. If we take this basis to discuss ideas and not personal matters or sociological factors, we shall be able to avoid mixing up everything because we are not able to give a total picture of it and we have to select. If, for instance, we consider a theory, let us consider this a hypothesis. Let us consider a theory as a kind of organism—a kind of body—not only a body of knowledge but a kind of body. And this body produces other ideas contrary to it or in agreement with it and there is a permanent struggle—a permanent struggle with what are the new points of view and how the points of view seem to apply. The French mathematician Rene Thom, who is now dead, said, "Ideas defend themselves like living organisms." I think we should pick up this idea.

Grossman: I'd like to make a small amendment to that. I think it's true that it's very important to think of a theory as a system of thought that has its own internal logic and that has its own consequences and so on. But I think for a discussion like this, we really have to consider something that as analysts we all know: how something is read depends on the thinker and the reader. Theories don't move by themselves. They move by people thinking about them. If we take only the twenty-three volumes of the *Standard Edition*, then we have a circumscribed body of thought. But what we see is that it doesn't speak for itself because the readers read it differently. And it seems to me this is the motor of this controversy. We shouldn't talk about it only in terms of resistance and adequate analysis because it's in the nature of a text that it allows itself to be interpreted differently by different readers. And the history as André's friend Jorge Luis Borges said, you know, that history determines how the texts are read. We don't have to go to history, as you said in your paper too. In this group everybody reads the history differently. They read the papers differently. One of the consequences of that is—what André said is correct—the basic ostensible conflict between paradigms: the intrapsychic and the intersubjective. But I think that the point is that these are frameworks. There are many other dichotomies that people establish. What is more important, security or drives? To me these are not in conflict as explanations. The two do not attempt to explain the same things and they may be interconvertible. And I think that's a similar problem in some aphoristic kinds of statements, like Fairbairn's comment that libido is not pleasure seeking but object seeking. To me, it's not a matter of a choice. It's a matter of what you want to focus on. They are not alternatives, in my way of thinking. If we went through a lot of the dichotomies that people propose, we would find a similar thing to be true—we will discover a complex hierarchical organization of thinking. The question is, How are they related? The relationship between drive and security is interesting in another way. You recall Sullivan's position was that what people look for is satisfactions and security. And you could say crudely—very crudely—that is a kind of parallel to Freud's idea of libidinal instincts and ego instincts. One of the jobs ahead of us is to decide when are we dealing with real dichotomies and when are we dealing with nondichotomies. When are they at different places in the theoretical structure?

Kernberg: I would like to go back to the question of vehemence. The one thing that can be said is vehemence indicates there is a hidden agenda. In other words, we're not discussing only what's on the surface but there are other things that are coming out around this. You're absolutely right, the intensity of the vehemence is worthwhile to be examined because there are other agendas and as long as they remain hidden, they can't be resolved and the vehemence is an indirect way of resolving something that hasn't been put on the table.

Ostow: The hidden agenda may be personal as well as scientific.

Kernberg: What may make the discussion of the hidden agenda complicated is that there may not be one but several and that there may be disagreements around this table about what is the nature of the hidden agendas. It would be useful for us to spell out what we think are the hidden agendas. And as we go from issues about the content of Freud's basic thinking and the nature of personal psychopathology and institutional dynamics of psychoanalysis, such as Harold Blum mentioned, there may be philosophical influences regarding the conception of man and society that are infiltrating psychoanalysis without anybody being aware of it, until there is a shift in the external culture or in a changed culture in relation to a dominant form of thinking in psychoanalysis. These are different ways of looking at the problem. André stresses the basic philosophical concept. I agree with that as a major issue.

There are also other issues—political ideologies. For example, if you look at Adler, you can see the political agendas—the influence of Marxism—become important in psychoanalysis to the extent that there have been splits in the psychoanalytic movement, such as in Argentina. The issue of religion as a philosophical issue also emerges in the Freud–Jung relationship. There are several issues that have different importance in the relationship of different dissidents. One is the problem in the development of psychoanalytic understanding; our main instrument is the psychoanalytic situation, which doesn't lend itself to a kind of objective, empirical resolution. How do you decide between Kohut's views of narcissism and Rosenfeld's views of narcissism? One source of fear is over new ideas, the fear of uncertainty. So here we have a problem of scientific methodology. Partial currents, political currents, ideology, philosophical issues, institutional ones, and of course personal regression. And personal regression doesn't mean necessarily that someone was insufficiently analyzed. It may have to do with a regressive pull of nonfunctional organizations. And the psychoanalytic institutions, organizationally, I think, have been nonfunctional for a long time; they foster regression, and they bring out the worst in well-analyzed people. When you say they have not been well analyzed, I think any of us, if you put us long enough into an impossible situation, we all would behave neurotically. So I'm suggesting that each of us try to spell out some of the important influences that explain the vehemence and the paradox that Martin Bergmann points out so beautifully—that sometimes there's lots of vehemence about something that a generation later is accepted by everybody. And the politics of the moment influence things. I remember the atmosphere in South America in the 1960s: Freud and Marx—could they relate or not? That was the issue.

Green: That was in 1924.

Kernberg: In 1924, but then came the second wave, which culminated in the pathetic figure of Marie Langer. All very well intentioned people.

Kris: I thought also as Otto Kernberg did that uncertainty is a very important part of the story of vehemence. Remember Hilaire Belloc's statement: "Let us never, never doubt what nobody is sure about." And in psychoanalysis you have to deal with uncertainty. But Otto also talked about objectivity and the fact that it's very hard even to approximate it. In other sciences, theory and perspective are very important in generating one's research. It's like a rocket that eventually jettisons its original boosters and goes off into space; in other sciences the findings can be eventually evaluated on their own. That is never true in psychoanalysis. The psychoanalytic observation is always subject to the perspective with which you view it. There's no getting away from that in psychoanalysis. In fact, it seems to me astonishing that so much was accomplished in spite of that fact.

The other thing Otto referred to, I have to put in slightly different terms: learning psychoanalysis is always personal, in two ways. We always learn psychoanalysis from someone or from a group of people. And it always involves our selves. It is impossible for it not to. You can't be an analyst if you are not constantly able to learn, but as André Green has pointed out from time to time, one can overdo that. So there's a balance. Invariably, psychoanalysis is personal. It's personal and that too contributes to vehemence. You have people who are part of a tradition, and one is identified with one's teachers and one is identified with one's own work on oneself done in a particular way—one's way of learning. Then somebody comes along and challenges it. They're not just saying, "You know, there are some new facts." They're saying, "Your whole being as an analyst is in doubt." The first thing you want to do is wipe them out—that's a source of vehemence.

Bergmann: When I wrote my essay, I did not arrive at a comprehensive theory of vehemence and that's why I wanted it to be discussed here. But a few ideas did emerge, which I didn't know before I started—a good sign because something occurs to you as you work that you were not aware of before. Dissidence is fueled for a number of people by failures of their personal analysis. We tended to minimize, in the history of psychoanalysis, the role of unsuccessful analysis, which results in new problems, which a person has to face. We had the illusion that if you analyze a patient unsuccessfully, it means that he was not changed. No! The unsuccessfully analyzed person was damaged or was in some way thrown out of the balance they had before and didn't find another balance. So at least one source of dissidence was the revenge of the self-analyst on his previous analysis. And that I could find in a number of cases—in Karen Horney's case, in the case of Jung, and, overtly stated, in the case of Kohut. Dissidence is the hubris of self-analysis over the analysis that was not satisfactory.

If you follow the controversial discussion between Anna Freud and Melanie Klein, another problem emerges. Analysts have a tendency to get agitated over issues, for which the psychoanalytic interview can offer no answers. Certain basic data that we need for our work's philosophy are not answered by our current—or any future—technique. Much of the discussion between Anna Freud and Melanie Klein takes place about what happens in the first months of life where we really have no way of knowing in terms of our experience. We make certain deductions about it and then for some reason—which I don't understand fully—these deductions become particularly dear to us. In other words, we do not differentiate between what we know from solid clinical evidence and what Freud or Klein or Kohut assume to be so. Open admission of what we do not know is difficult to achieve. We fear to appear to our patients and audience as the emperor without clothes from the fairy tale. Vehemence enters into our discussions because so many irrational reasons converge from various sources and make the discussion unproductive. And that's why I would like to have this symposium not necessarily ending in agreement but in an advance of our ignorance beyond the limits of where it is now.

Ostow: In 1957, the Israel Psychoanalytic Society had a meeting called "Why War?" in which some of us . . . Do you remember that?

Bergmann: I was there, yes.

Ostow: And the introductory speech was given by Shimon Peres. I remember this was fifty years ago. Peres was a young man. He made an interesting observation. Throughout history there are societies that are prebelligerent. There are societies that are belligerent. There are societies that are postbelligerent. Postbelligerent, for example, is the United States and Canada. I think the history of dissidence goes along the same way. The issues that excited people over two generations ago in analysis we can talk about now easily. Whereas there are other issues that excite us. Let me give you an example from my own experience. In the 1950s and the early 1960s, I suggested introducing drug therapy into psychoanalysis. At that time, that was met by tremendous vehemence—great antagonism and fury. I was never appointed a training analyst for that reason. Now, it's postbelligerent. We don't talk about it. It's assumed. As a matter of fact, Steve Roose said a while ago that, in his opinion, the introduction of psychopharmacology into psychoanalysis is the most important advance in analytic treatment in the past ten years. But that's an example of dissidence, which had to do with what Tony Kris said: if you challenge people in the very essence of their being as analysts—to say nothing of the economic situation—people get angry. You get the anger and that's the dissidence until it becomes clear to everybody that that's the way to go. Then you start fighting about something else.

Green: I'd like to come back to the problem of people who are supposed to not have been well analyzed. I think that in Martin's view, there is an implicit question: What distinguishes a full analysis, a successful analysis? We know by experience that sometimes we can't go beyond certain limits because if we do go beyond them, the equilibrium of the patient will be disturbed and he will get worse, as you say. So the people who are not well analyzed were not only incompletely analyzed, they were analyzed in such a way that they provoked a breakdown in them and a reorganization after the breakdown. Technically, do we have to fix certain limits to analysis considering the person that we are analyzing? Which means that we give up full analysis for the sake of the patient.

As to Kohut being not satisfied with his analyst and making the rest of the work through self-analysis, self-analysis is really what you can only be in agreement with, because you're the patient as well as the analyst. And the supposed analyst, which is in the mind, tells the patient what the patient wants to listen to and wants to hear. So I do not believe in such an example as Kohut's two analyses in which everyone knows that the second analysis is a self-analysis. I'm just informed that Kohut was happy to find good answers to his problems and probably got better.

About vehemence—and it's a really important point that Martin raised. Taking the example of the Anna Freud and Melanie Klein controversies, each of them referring to events in the first year of life, about which nobody knows anything. But people are not content with admitting that they do not know anything. They create the evidence. For instance, they say, "OK, we disagree. Let's go to observational methods." So they look at the baby and say, "See, he's exactly doing what I'm writing!" There is an implicit idea that the earlier the facts, the more evidential they are. If you can find facts instead of the Oedipus complex at the first year, what you find in the first year of life will explain what the Oedipus complex would not be able to explain. This idea of going always backward brings the idea that the newborn gives you all the answers. It's easier to project on the poor baby whatever you think. And the baby will not say, "No, you're wrong." There's no resistance in the baby. The resistance is only in the observer, and the observer is not aware of his resistance.

Blum: Martin, I think that regarding the question of insufficient analysis, what I was trying to bring up in the beginning was not a statement about a particular person—except historically—because the pioneers really didn't have analysis. They either had no analysis or insufficient analysis. Ferenczi had seven weeks of analysis, total, divided between three occasions: two weeks, three weeks, and two weeks.

Green: On a horse!

Blum: That was Ferenczi's treatment of his commanding officer. He told Freud that was the first treatment on a horse! But the same thing may be said of Jung who really had no analysis to speak of except some self-analysis. Rank wasn't analyzed, though he absorbed something by osmosis, by being Freud's secretary. When we get to Anna Freud and Melanie Klein, that's a whole other situation. I was reminded in this discussion of the exchange of letters between Jones and Freud—Jones complaining to Freud that he thought his daughter was insufficiently analyzed. Freud wrote back and said, "I can assure you she had a better analysis than you did," knowing that Jones had been analyzed by Ferenczi. It was a very short analysis and complicated by all kinds of breaches of confidentiality, distortions of communication, and other group problems among the pioneers of analysis.

So when we talk about the dissidence, we have to take into account the fact that many of the early analysts had very little or no analysis. The theory changed. The technique changed. Many of the pioneers who did have some analysis were analyzed with a very early theory, for example, with early Freud rather than with Freud's more developed views. Freud commented, in a letter concerning one of the cases in *Studies on Hysteria* to the daughter of one of those ladies: "I really didn't understand at that time what your mother's problems were. I took what she said at face value. I had no idea about the nature of the unconscious, the way I understood it later. And had I had the kind of experience I now have, I would have seen things very differently." He indicated the treatment, of course, would have been very different. Insufficient analysis does not mean the analysis really wasn't successful. Consideration of the kind of analysis that we're talking about, involving these so-called dissidents, would have to take into account the fact that psychoanalysis itself was in its infancy.

Young-Bruehl: I'd like to return again, from another angle, to your question about vehemence and what influences it. I would like to approach from the field of sociology of knowledge—but with a psychoanalytic spin. The great theorist of controversy within the sociology of knowledge was Karl Mannheim and particularly in the book *Ideology and Utopia*,[16] his masterwork. He was married to Julie Mannheim who was a psychoanalyst and a big influence on his thinking. One of the things that Mannheim always pointed out about the history of sciences is that two factors are in place. There's very little controversy and very little vehemence within the science as it develops. Typically there is a core of beliefs that is accepted and handed down through generations, which holds together even though peripheral contexts around the core may evolve and change. The other factor is that the science is—to use a phrase of Nietzsche—"blown up to the macrocosm"; it becomes a science that is totally encompassing, has a totalistic bent to it, and can explain or relate to factors across the universe, as it were. But every science that maintains a kind of continuity is ultimately a cosmology that finds analogies between the microcosm of human beings and the macrocosm.

---

16. Mannheim, K. (n.d.). *Ideology and Utopia*. New York: Harcourt, Brace.

Those factors are interesting to take into account. A science like medicine, in the Western tradition, had in Greece a founding school—the Hippocratic school—focused on a core belief that maintains itself through the Renaissance. Galen was a great revisionist but even he retained the core belief in four humors, which were reflected in the macrocosm, in the form of four elements that organized the entire human world—a totalistic system.

I'm going to talk about dissidence against the background of these remarks. Dissidence is equivalent to sectarianism. Within an unfolding science, a science with a history, when there begin to be sects, which narrow the vision of the science and take it away from its concern with politics, from its concern with cosmology, its embeddedness in a total vision so that it becomes focused in on just one thing that it's attempting to explain or that it's attempting to do or one activity that it's attempting to theorize aloud, then tremendous vehemence surrounds this on the general principle that the less that is at stake, the greater the argument. Physics, for example, is a science that even though it has many controversies within it, doesn't have this vehemence because the view is so large and so encompassing and it never comes down to a small part of the world that it tries to explain. Sectarianism, and dissidence associated with it, is equivalent to reduction of something. So what happens when sectarianism takes over a field, and everybody is looking for the one key that unlocks all the mysteries? All other keys must be rejected, and those who advocate other keys must be rejected with them. But it's a smallness of view that allows people to think that there might be one key to all the mysteries. In the totalizing visions, there is never one key. There are always basic elements like the "humors" or something like that, but you look at them through different angles, when you're looking into the psyche or when you're looking in the political domain or when you're looking at cosmology.

There are many ways to look at the history of psychoanalysis, and one is to see it as a science, which Freud, with extraordinary quickness, took from a therapeutic vision right up to a cosmological view, to *Totem and Taboo* and then *Civilization and Its Discontent*. After Freud, a progressive sectarianism developed in which the view becomes narrower and narrower and what is to be explained becomes smaller and smaller. Psychoanalysis as a movement becomes more and more isolated from political affairs. Part of the controversy between psychoanalysis and Marxism really had to do with whether psychoanalysis was going to be in any way political—whether it was going to have a political vision or not, whether Marxism would have to save psychoanalysis from its attackers. As it became more institutionalized, it became more detached from political affairs, more detached from the other sciences, it became an isolated discipline. It moved itself away from biology. It moved itself away from physiology. It moved itself away from physics. We are at an interesting moment now—and that's one reason why we're having this discussion—in which that isolation of psychoanalysis became so profound that psychoanalysis was ridden with sectarianism, and people have realized that this is a death knell upon psychoanalysis. So now the impulse is to resurrect neuroscience. But we should also have a conference with the physicists! Let us please get back in touch with the lost literary critics—an effort to connect or reconnect because this vehemence that has been so destructive within the science itself is connected to sectarianism of the whole field, to detachment from those around.

From another angle, this narrowing of psychoanalysis and that detachment of it from other disciplines, the detachment of it from a macrocosmic view, an effort to explain human nature as part of nature, which was always the impulse of science, this narrowing could be described as making the psychoanalytic family into a more and more nuclear family—tighter and tighter inside itself. All of the dissidence of families in which infanticide and patricide and all the other "-cides" that are aggression within the family are definitely functions historically and culturally of the narrowing of the family into units detached from larger tribal units, if you will, so that the relationships between parents and children become more vehement, more and more conflicted both in the domain of action and in the intrapsychic domain. Psychoanalysis became—even though it grew as a movement, in terms of the actual numbers of people who became involved in—reduced in terms of the attention that was given to the training analysis as affiliation within the field. All kinds of things made it a more and more nuclear experience, even though it involved larger and larger numbers of people.

Bergmann: I do not think that we became more narrow, because if I think about the disagreement between Kohut and Freud, Freud's basic philosophical idea still was the idea of the enlightenment expressed by Goethe: "The greatest source of happiness for mankind is the personality." Kohut broke with this tradition of the Enlightenment and substituted the capacity to have a selfobject as our deepest happiness. One thinks about Margaret Mahler's separation, individuation, and the emphasis on individuation as the aim, and then comes Kohut and says, "The aim is not individuation. The aim is not development of the personality. Happiness consists in finding a selfobject. That's what we all need for happiness." There is a fundamental philosophical change of focus—I would say it's almost the contrary—that psychoanalysis is open to such fundamental disagreements, like what is the aim of human development. The greater the basic philosophical differences, the greater the vulnerability.

Another example, it seems to me, is the idea of Melanie Klein of the development from the paranoid position to the depressive position. You discover that although she didn't know it, this was a major item within Kabalistic thinking. The purpose of man is to make *tikkun*, meaning to correct, to improve the world in some way. The world suffered a catastrophic breakup and the pious man's function is *tikkun*, Hebrew for repair.

The idea of Melanie Klein's depressive position and the idea of the Kabalistic repair have a great deal in common. I see psychoanalysis as reflecting larger ideas. I don't see that we are getting to a more narrow point of view. Yes, maybe the contact with the rest of the sciences is lost, but the contact wasn't that great to begin with. If anything, we are tackling ideas that are beyond our capacity to handle and we do not clearly state, "The answer to this question is beyond psychoanalysis' capacity to solve." If anything, I tend to see our debates as extending our range beyond our old limits.

Young-Bruehl: This may be your point of view, Martin, but I don't think it's true of the field. It seems very obvious that since the Second World War, nobody outside of the field of psychoanalysis could read its journals or cared to. Psychoanalysis began to communicate in an internal language, even an internal language for debating, but this was a language that became unreadable to anybody outside of its field—a highly technical language that had lost its philosophical foundations. Certainly there are people within the field who were always broad thinkers, but the field itself grew ever narrower.

Kernberg: We are tackling simultaneously different hidden agendas. We should put on the table issues around which the vehemence of disagreement centers and discuss them one after another. One issue has to do with the psychology of psychoanalytic institutions and the development of dissidence as a rebellion against authoritarian aspects in psychoanalytic institutions, and the power of training analysts and educational committees. The second controversial issue is to what extent personal psychoanalysis is a radioactive process that creates dangers when it doesn't go well or let's say when it doesn't go well in the context of an institution that may already be dysfunctional. Third is to what extent some basic contributions of Freud are contrary to mass psychology. When we say that humankind can't accept certain ideas, we know that many individuals can accept them. But mass culture—conventional culture—undoubtedly has enormous difficulties with certain concepts relating to the drives, particularly the sexual drive. It is opposed particularly to infantile sexuality. This is a major issue for cultures throughout history. There's no doubt that Freud touched on something when he proclaimed the existence of infantile sexuality against the cultural attitude of the innocence of childhood. Similarly the discovery of the pervasiveness of unconscious aggression ran counter to all the utopian ideologies from Marxism to religious fundamentalism. Certain basic concepts of psychoanalysis, by their very nature, had to be rejected by mass culture or conventional culture; the opposition to Freud dressed itself up in particular ideologies.

We also have to address the temptation within psychoanalysis to expand the nature of its understanding of the human being into an ideology—to make psychoanalysis itself an ideology. Psychoanalysis as an ideology has crept into the psychoanalytic movement. Psychoanalysis has a way of claiming to know what is the right way of living, thus challenging religion and challenging political ideologies. I think that that may be a problem within psychoanalysis more than of the surrounding culture; psychoanalysis as an ideology in turn creates conflict and brings about dissidence.

There's a dissidence that we haven't mentioned so far—analysts who create societies of psychoanalytic psychotherapy, being faithful to Freud's basic concepts but carrying out the treatments with other techniques. Until very recently, we have seen psychotherapy as a kind of a heresy, as something to be rejected as threatening psychoanalysis; psychotherapy may be one of our illegitimate children creating problems. Yet, psychoanalysis is an understanding of the nature of man that can be expressed in various technical approaches. There has been a fear that the destruction, or the questioning, or the exclusive nature of one instrument, psychoanalytic technique, could mean the destruction of psychoanalysis itself. It's a list of issues.

The main reasons for dissidence are:

1. The pathology of psychoanalytic institutions
2. The opposition to some of Freud's basic discoveries
3. Psychoanalysis itself becoming an ideology
4. Conflict between psychoanalysis as a science of man and psychoanalysis as a specific technique

Green: I'd like to come back to the difference between the comments of Martin Bergmann and Elisabeth Young-Bruehl. I think Elisabeth is right when she says that we got into a more narrow field, but I'd like to give a specific meaning to that. The first stage of analysis stopped in 1913 with *Totem and Taboo* because Freud covered all that he wanted to cover. In retrospect, of course, going into fields that were not Freud's expertise was a mistake. The Leonardo mistake is the biggest one. But as you know the mistake was not acknowledged and it is still taught in the schools of art. I think that the reaction within psychoanalysis was, "We don't want to have fights around fields that we don't know well, so we will concentrate on the field of clinical psychoanalysis." Thus the scope of psychoanalysis was narrowed. But it didn't change anything because Martin is right. Within clinical psychoanalysis, the vehemence became stronger: "I have the truth and here is the truth." So we can have the formation of a sect and that is within a field that we are supposed to know because we have been trained for it—the field of clinical psychoanalysis. As a result applied psychoanalysis has been quite paralyzed. If you submit to a publisher a book of applied psychoanalysis written by a psychoanalyst, the publisher will reject it.

Concentrating our work around clinical psychoanalysis didn't solve any problems. This I want to emphasize strongly: one of the problems of the dissidence we are speaking of—I mean contemporary dissidence; I'm not going back to Jung but to contemporaries—is that people do not realize that they do not talk about the same type of patients. The patients they're writing about are not Freud's patients. Melanie Klein's are not Freud's patients. Lacan's patients are not Melanie Klein's and so on. Everybody seems to think that there's no problem because we're all speaking of the same type of patients. I think the differences between the patients is very important.

Now one last point about the comments of Elisabeth and Tony Kris: I think that Elisabeth said—and this is something that we hear all the time—psychoanalysts are isolated from the other disciplines. Psychoanalysis has lost contact with the other sciences. Tony said this could not be avoided because of the reference to subjectivity. For instance, there's a paper by Fonagy who writes about a paper of Paul Wachtel separating experimental psychology and physiology on one side and insulating poor psychoanalysis on the other side and making links difficult. But links are not possible to make because of subjectivity. Now we live in a world in which intersubjective and relational are common expressions. But I'm sorry to say that we have no theory of a subject. We have no theory of what is a subject. All we have theory of is what is an ego. We have a theory of what is a person. But we have no theory of what is the subject. Even in the intersubjectivist movement, there is no theory of what a subject is. And unless we pay attention to that, I do not see how we will able to clarify why there is such a discrepancy between the so-called scientific method and the psychoanalytic method, which is scientific in its own way, not in a way that has to fit with the models of the other sciences.

To summarize, a narrowing took place. The fact that there is a narrowing doesn't diminish conflicts and vehemence. We are separated from science because of the theory of subjectivity. One last thought: there are signs in science that things are beginning to change. Gerald Edelman's book, *Bright Air, Brilliant Fire*,[17] is dedicated to Freud and Darwin. He writes that from his point of view as a man of science, Freud was right. There is a new trend in science, which is called hypercomplexity, and that psychoanalysis meets some of the

---

17. Edelman, G. (1992). *Bright Air, Brilliant Fire*. New York: Basic Books.

requirements of hypercomplexity. You were speaking of the difference between the macrocosm and the microcosm; one of the three points of view of hyper-complexity is the holographic point of view. We have new ideas in the culture, which could bring a rapprochement between psychoanalysis and contemporary science.

(Dinner Break)

Bergmann: I would like to open this session on a personal note before we go to the discussion. I want to thank all of you for coming to celebrate my ninetieth birthday. I think that no analyst has been as privileged to have a meeting like this one on his ninetieth birthday. I feel very fortunate and I want to thank Tony Kris for this idea.

Ostow: I would like to follow up on André Green's remarks about the fact that there's no objective way of determining which theory is right. What determines the validity of a theory? A theory is useful if it predicts. None of our theories predict anything. A theory is useful if it provides patterns that we can recognize in the universe of phenomena that we're examining. Those are the criteria that we use in examining whether a theory is useful to psychoanalysis. The Oedipus complex is very helpful because we can recognize that pattern in our patients. Resistance can be recognized as a pattern and so can transference; these are patterns that we recognize. One pattern does not exclude another. They can be arranged simultaneously for different purposes. When we analyze a patient—when we do psychoanalytic psychotherapy—we employ Freudian patterns all the time. These are classical psychoanalytic paradigms that we look for in our patients. I'm engaged—Martin is a participant in this too—in an interdisciplinary study of the affective resonance of religious liturgy and religious worship. For that purpose, I find attachment theory extremely helpful—much more helpful than anything else. Martin in his participation is very happy using classical analytic theory, Freudian theory, and he can use it quite well. But we can both use these different paradigms in that work. When I do my work with psychopharmacology, I go back to Freud's energy theory, which has been incidentally abandoned silently by most analysts. We don't talk about the fact that we deviate from Freud's energy and economic point of view. There was a common understanding in the 1940s and 1950s—certainly when I was trained as an analyst—that this is a nineteenth century hydraulic model that we no longer talk about as if the laws of hydraulics have been repealed. I hadn't heard that they'd been repealed nor had the people who can't deal with quantitative concepts substitute any other quantitative concepts. But to return to psychopharmacology, I find that an extremely useful paradigm and I've extended Freud in the field of mood regulation, which depends on these quantitative concepts and for that purpose can be used for prediction. Theory can be tested by its predictive value—which medication will be effective and which will not be effective. These are predictions that can easily be confirmed. But the question is, What other criteria for establishing the validity of a theory can we formulate?

Kernberg: There are really several issues here. Regarding the comparison of theories: within the clinical realm, we have the possibility of comparing theories even without establishing strict protocols of empirical research because the cumulative experience of a generation of analysts eventually leads to inclination versus one or the other model. To give an illustration, the Kleinians started out with a technique interpreting whatever was going on in the transference in terms of assumptions in the first three months of life and were impervious to any outside criticism of that. This went on for twenty years and then they gradually realized that they were simply not curing their patients, who were expressing daily experiences in baby language, and gradually shifted under the cumulative experience. This led to a radical shift in technique, without acknowledging the influence of anybody outside nor that they had changed and without touching in any way Melanie Klein herself. The saints were left in their place. But they changed radically. The contemporary Kleinian theory has absorbed things from ego psychology. So there are ways in psychoanalysis for different models to come closer to each other.

You may use the psychoanalytic approach influenced, say, by Kleinian ideas and ego-psychological ideas—what I would call the analytic mainstream. On the other hand, you may use a self-psychology approach; the effects on treatment are different and that is being recognized. With self psychology, usually, you don't touch the object relations in patients' sexual life, you assume that they had no oedipal problems. If you use a standard psychoanalytic technique, it turns out they have deeply repressed oedipal problems. Their sexual lives change as do their relationship to people, so it seems to me that in practice, in spite of the blending of self psychology with intersubjectivity and relational theories, the radical approach to the analytic treatment of narcissistic patients that Kohut proposed is disappearing, at least while the standard psychoanalytic approach to narcissistic patients continues to show up in the literature. Because we don't have methods by which we can accelerate the study of differences between techniques in empirically designed studies, we have to depend on the cumulative experience of many years. This technique for waiting for results activates the insecurity around the field, around the profession, and it creates vehemence because the insecure institution is perceived to be under attack. Some of the controversy really reflects submission and rebellion against the institution. If you look at the sociology of psychoanalysis, you will discover that quasi-dissidents come particularly in the middle of the most rigid, traditional, monolithic institutions. For example, within the rigid Kleinian atmosphere of Argentina, you have the popping-up of Lacanism all over the place. They don't read Melanie Klein anymore! I talked with an Argentinean training analyst from the *Journal of the American Psychoanalytic Association*. I was astonished! I saw in a miniculture the same thing in Chile—rigidly Kleinian. All of a sudden, there is an intersubjectivity group going in the opposite direction. In Los Angeles, the most traditional ego-psychological society, the Kleinians popped up. And just to make the point, the same Kleinians became intersubjectivists. On the other side, of course, we have the defenders of the law and of the true religion who are equally vehement. There are other dynamics, but that's certainly an important one, and the fact that our science progresses so slowly contributes to the uncertainty, because, as you see, I'm in disagreement with your statement, Martin, that we can't compare theories. We can expect concrete patterns and tangible results from any theoretical approach that has clinical applications.

Grossman: What you are all describing is like political movements. Institutional changes, sociological changes, group psychology—all of these things, I agree, are important. But I think the question of comparing theories is a very different question. We could compare theories but it's very different from the question of why do theories change. Since we all agree that there is no systematic constraint on method and criteria for demonstration, you're talking about a movement in the history of ideas. It's true, it's based on experience, but movements in the history of ideas are always based on experience. It's not limited to psychoanalysis. I'm not saying we should dismiss it for that reason. Yes, you can compare theories, but what is hard to measure is their effect. The reason people use them has to do with a lot of variables. We should be talking about what having a theory means to people—what it does for people. The fact is that even in hard science, if you look at the literature on science as process, it's the same kind of issues. Yes, there are constraints in scientific method and research but even so funny things happen. Things pop up in the way of information and evidence that are totally ignored. Ideas in psychoanalysis appeared in the 1930s that had to be rediscovered later. And that's because of something that's going on in the institutions, and we can also ask why the psychology of the individual requires theories and for what purpose. On one extreme, we could compare them as systems and analyze their paradigms. This is an important thing to do because maybe we'll find out that at certain periods of time, certain paradigms are more appealing for reasons that we would have to discover, if we can.

One of the issues—and this is why Martin wanted me to talk about it—is why people need theories. If you look at the data from that point of view, you have a whole set of intrapsychic forces for which theories are very important, and this comes right out of Freud. In *Totem and Taboo*—regardless of whether Freud was a good or bad anthropologist, the book is an important document on psychoanalytic thinking—one of the points Freud made was that as soon as a system is consciously considered, you have two streams of thought: one conscious, with ideas that belong to the system, and the other unconscious. The meaning of that system for the people who hold it is one key to what goes on in analysis. And then, of course, the issue is the relationship of the analyst's education in relation to particular theories and particular authorities. For Freud, again, there really is—from a psychological point of view—no difference between a scientific theory, an ideology, a religion, and a delusion, and he was willing to compare his own thinking to delusions. As to conviction, he describes it beautifully—how the conviction in believing in particular ideas, theories, delusions, religion, has to do with an unconscious truth of a personal nature that makes it real for the person with whatever other value it may or may not have.

Kris: Bill, are you adding that to the list of sources for vehemence?

Grossman: In fact, no, though it's relevant. What I'm offering is what I view as a kind of psychoanalytic view of where vehemence resides in the individual. One of the things of interest to me is that I have seen and heard about patients who are in various degrees and in various ways, very much involved with theory. One can see in the course of the analysis—or the psychotherapy—how theory enters their minds in some circumstances as a factor in dealing with threatening objects, including the therapist. At certain points, the patients turn to theory in order to protect themselves. I've known of patients who were similar to those people who write up their own analysis as a case of a patient they had treated.

I'm sure everybody has had this experience because you don't even have to be treating theoreticians to get it. Many patients have a point of view about psychology and about their own pathology and about the analyst's pathology and they're happy to offer it at crucial moments where it serves a useful purpose. So I think in fact we know a lot about vehement protection of ideological, theoretical, religious ideas. That is also how delusional ideas are maintained.

Ostow: Martin, what's the source of vehemence in religious conflict? There's nothing more vehement than religious conflict.

Blum: I would not want to see us get hung up on vehemence in a very digni-fied, nonvehement discussion. Because I think we really need to do what we started to do, which is to look at the way theories are formed, the way theo-ries are developed, to be able to compare the different theories, to look at the dissidents as we called them and to see in what way, from a theoretical view-point, their ideas differed. One of the main points of the conference is to con-sider in what way they contributed to analytic theory even in the process of diverging. These are complicated questions. So one of the purposes of the conference is to not only to look at the various individuals as dissidents but also in a subtle way as contributors. Some of the aspects they brought up were in one way or another incorporated from the periphery into the core of psy-choanalysis. I do not want us to overly focus on only vehemence and not have the central issue of the ideas themselves, the theories themselves, be sub-sumed under the issue of vehemence.

Having said that, I think there's another source that I'd like to mention about the problem: Are there any transferences to theory? Theory can take on various meanings. It can represent a love object; an idealized object; a dispar-aged or demeaned, degraded object; a hated aspect of the self; a selfobject, etc. Look at Thomas Kuhn and his discussion of paradigms in *The Structure of Sci-entific Revolutions* (1962)[18]—how they evolve and how they finally break down. We could add from an analytic viewpoint about theories in general—it's not just true of analysts; Kuhn was addressing all of science—that there's a nar-cissistic investment that inevitably develops to a particular theory. The theory you were brought up on; the theory you grow up on; the theory that you identify with your teachers and their teachings; the theory with which you feel comfortable because it becomes part of your psychoanalytic identity; and I think that's what Tony Kris was saying—it becomes part of the core of your analytic self, your very identity as an analyst. But that narcissistic investment can be problematic. It can be supportive in some ways—we do very lonely work. But in other ways, it prevents being open minded and being receptive to challenges to the theory and a readiness to change. One of the wonderful things about Freud was his capacity to analyze his own narcissistic investment, and to be critical about his own theories and to be ready to change if he thought a change in theory was justified. Bill Grossman brought up—and I was so glad to hear the words—"soft science." For those of us who view analysis at all as a science—because there are those who say it is not a science anymore—but for those who view it as a science, it is certainly a soft science. It cannot be

---

18. Kuhn, T. (1962). *The Structure of Scientific Revolutions.* Chicago: University of Chicago Press.

replicated as can an experiment in chemistry or physics; the predictive power of clinical psychoanalysis is very limited.

Ostow: If at all.

Blum: If at all, and it's a very private kind of work. It's hard to compare data because everyone works and organizes data differently. Regarding what Otto Kernberg and I were both talking about—the problems of group attachments, loyalties, identifications—although the groups have changed—the Freudians, the Kleinians and so forth—my own experience in going to international meetings is that conversions are very rare. The Kleinians go to the meetings. They come back Kleinians. The Freudians go to the meetings. They come back Freudians. The Lacanians come back Lacanians.

Ostow: Conversion occurs after the meeting—not during.

Blum: But then you see the people come to the next meeting, so often under the sway of repetition. The conversion phenomenon is rare and analysts tend to remain within their group's theoretical and ideological commitments. Each theoretical school claims an advance in explanatory reach and therapeutic efficacy.

Kris: Hal, I remember a wonderful comment I heard in the late 1970s. Somebody I met at one of the national meetings said, "Winnicott has arrived in Denver."

Ostow: There's a story about an old woman who won a raffle in the Soviet Union in the 1950s, and the prize was the opportunity to talk to Khrushchev. And so she was brought to Khrushchev and he said to her, "Little old mother, what would you like to talk about?" And she said, "Comrade Khrushchev, I've wondered for a long time, was Communism invented by philosophers or by scientists? What do you think?" He said, "That's a very interesting question. I hadn't thought about it. But thinking about it now, I think it's philosophers." She said, "I agree with you because if it had been scientists, they would have tried it on rats first."

Bergmann: I have a problem with whether that story should or should not go into the record.

Blum: Well, the last point I wanted to make is to answer what Otto said about accumulated experience, accumulated knowledge. It's for that reason, André, that I think history is important because we change and we learn very gradually.

Green: I am not against history.

Blum: It was Freud who said the best way to understand psychoanalysis is to study its history and development. So the historical viewpoint lends an additional dimension by virtue of the fact that we can study the incremental changes over time and get a better view of how theories changed, why they changed, and at what point divergences occur. The study of theoretical change involves individuals and groups, and requires a process of reconstruction. The collection and evaluation of data in psychoanalysis is a slow process, subject to greater subjectivity as soft science.

Green: It depends on how you think of history. I wanted to come back to this topic of Ferenczi because that's what we decided to talk about. Melanie Klein had her first analysis with Ferenczi. She was not satisfied. She went to Abraham. She was very satisfied with Abraham and she created the Kleinian theory. With Ferenczi, as you beautifully showed in your essay, Martin, there is a very important period from 1929 until his death in 1932 in which there is a burst of creativity and in which he writes the papers that are absolutely revolutionary. They raise an enormous resistance, I would say, and the only thing I do not quite agree with in your essay, Martin, is when you say that Ferenczi wrote his clinical diary while he was dying. Of course it was the last year—it was 1932—but I think that his mind was clear in 1932. What he writes in the clinical diary is of enormous importance because he was the first one to really talk of some ego defense mechanism that was specifically ego—beyond Freud. And what happens with that? Everyone says, "Poor man lost his mind." And that's true but what happens? It happens that not only with Balint, who was a direct pupil of Ferenczi, but also with Winnicott, people say, "Ferenczi already described that." So you see, I'm very much in favor of history but of a kind of history with repressions—forgetting, resurrections in modified form. By studying history people become aware that things are rediscovered. What Otto Kernberg was saying about the climate in Latin America is one thing that we seem to be afraid of saying aloud. The reason for these changes—how people change from Kleinians to Lacanians or intersubjectivists—is that our theories do not work. They do not work in our attempt to cure patients. If the theories were good for curing patients, people wouldn't have a need to change and this is why we are in constant progress or in constant change because we find some truth in them and we always hope that the theory of the neighbor will save us from our mistakes with patients. Because one important thing is that we have to compare our theories with how much we are satisfied with the results with our patients. Unless we do that, discussion is useless. I think it is true that we have to consider the results according to the different types of patients. Classical techniques are good enough for ordinary neurotics. But when you consider the patients who are treated by British analysts—whether independents or Kleinians—obviously classical techniques fail with them. I think that when global populations of analysands are considered, we have to consider the theory that fits the type of patients to which it is being applied.

Kris: Well, I'm out of date. We're now on Ferenczi and I think we should stay there.

Bergmann: I was very happy in what you said, Bill, because I drew even a more radical conclusion from your 1995 paper[19]—namely, if I know the full reasons for my ideology, then I am not going to have the need to defend it fanatically because I know why I arrived at it. In other words, fanaticism— and this is true for religious fanaticisms as well—is always based on the fact that some part of my thinking is unknown to me and that part forces me to take on a defensive attitude and to feel attacked. Ultimately, the vehemence has something to do with a paranoid basis that every ideology is ultimately rooted in. I asked myself, What analytic contributions have actually changed the fate of psychoanalysis after Freud? I would give first place to Winnicott because his idea of the holding environment is by far the most radical idea that was introduced into postclassical psychoanalysis.

A similar point can be made about Loewald, too, because along similar lines, he also introduced a significant change. But Winnicott, in a strict sense in which I use the word *dissenter*, did not consider himself a dissenter, nor did Loewald. They did not say, "Let me tell you how wrong Freud was." On the contrary, what Winnicott said was, "Freud started us going and whatever his mistakes were, I'm not that interested in because without him we would not be where we are." I tend to believe that Winnicott was less defensive in his ideology and therefore in my scheme less in need of becoming a dissident in the sense of emphasizing the wrongness of Freud on this or that item.

Kris: Just to put a couple of things together that were said. It was stimulated by Otto Kernberg's reference to the response to rigid technique. I think Kohut made a contribution against the rigid application of technique. He changed technique for many people in this country—I'm not sure about the rest of the world. What I believe he did was to say that analysts claimed they were neutral but were in fact not neutral, were in fact constantly critical and hostile to

---

19. Grossman, W. I. (1995). Psychological vicissitudes of theory in clinical work. *International Journal of Psychology* 76:885–899.

their patients and he said stop it. If a patient tells you she loves you, don't tell her that you're not Catholic like the priest she loved, and so forth. I don't believe that that is strictly dissidence. That part of what he did was a correction of bad technique, and I think that is quite different from the creation of a total theory carefully worked to solve the problem that André Green was talking about—sexuality. A dissident theory is one that excludes. Elisabeth Young-Bruehl was talking about the narrowing; any dissident is someone who focuses on one aspect or another—what Anna Freud referred to "this-only analysis or that-only analysis."

I believe these things can be put together in a rather simple formulation. There is an aspect of dissidence that creates a theoretical system that excludes data. I don't terribly care what version of Freud we adopt. What's to me most important about the way Freud went about his business was that he constantly tried to include more. All the time, he was trying to include. That was also the best in his followers; they tried to include. You're right, Martin, that Winnicott was one of those who added something without trying to say, "But we mustn't talk about such and such or we mustn't think about it or it isn't important." I agree with you—he's not a dissident.

Bergmann: The question really is whether this hypothesis of mine can hold water. Namely, there are two elements necessary for dissidence. One is hostility and the other is paranoia. Some degree of that is really what gives the juice to dissidence. In my opinion the controversy among religions are the need to defend the religion against something within the believer that he is not willing to admit. Conversely, if we have a full understanding of what makes us do what we do, our attitude toward disagreement does not evoke that kind of a defensiveness.

Kris: Martin, when you use the word *paranoia* I think you complicate your argument. Isn't it enough to say that when a theory or religion gets used to avoid knowing something—basically inside—that's going to lead to an aggressive or hostile reaction to anyone else? It isn't necessary to say what it is inside the person that creates dissidence because I think it's too general and I doubt very much that all dissidents are the same vis-à-vis their need to exclude. The striking thing is the need to exclude. That was what Elisabeth was talking about, and that's what André was talking about from the beginning.

Young-Bruehl: To respond to one thing that is implicit in what you were saying, Tony, that has not come out yet. Most of the time when we've been talking about dissidence, it's been in relation to theory—psychoanalytic theory generally or to meta-psychology. But Tony, you are pointing to something different. It was one of the interesting claims that Ian Suttie made, which I tried to explicate. He felt there had grown up within psychoanalysis a kind of subdomain of theory of technique, which was more accommodating to different point of view and points of view different from Freud's. It bears on Ferenczi's role in the history of psychoanalysis because he was acknowledged in his lifetime and even afterward as the great theoretician of clinical technique. Ferenczi's theoretical view, which is embedded in his "Thalassa: A Theory of Genitality,"[20] has been completely occluded from the history of psychoanalysis, as though he never wrote it. And mercifully perhaps, as it is an arch-Freudian libido theory that takes the libido theory further into "bio-analysis" as he called it— biological speculation. This disappeared. Ferenczi is not a dissident in theory. He's a dissident in the theory of technique.

Originally when people were dissidents—Rank is a perfect example—there was a complete correlation between the innovation in theory, such as the birth trauma theory, and a technical innovation to shorten analysis and go directly to the birth trauma without passing through anything else. The technical innovation and the theory of technique were complementary. But in the later history of psychoanalysis, that is sometimes the case and sometimes not. Winnicott is a really important theorist for many reasons. I tend to agree with you, Martin, about his centrality. But all of his innovations are really in the theory of technique; even fundamental notions like the true self and the false self, I think, are for the sake of technique.

Green: The innovations are theoretical too. Who invented transitional phenomena?

Young-Bruehl: Ferenczi, as Winnicott acknowledged. The transitional phenomena first appeared conceptualized in "The Confusion of Tongues," in the context of theory of technique. The importance of making the distinction between dissidence within the realm of general theory and dissidence within the theory of technique was, to address your point, that we have a problem, namely that our technique often does not cure, and many dissidents within the history that we are looking at were centrally moved by the fact that they were not cured by their analyses even if they wouldn't say it in such bold language. Kohut was one of them, and for very narcissistic reasons he did need to proclaim his experience of not being cured—the root of his innovation.

---

20. Ferenczi, S. (1923). *Thalassa: A Theory of Genitality.* English trans. Albany, NY: *Psychoanalytic Quarterly*, 1938.

Green: What you say is more fully true if you think that what Winnicott had in mind was the criticism of Kleinian technique. It was not only the problem of technique in general but about his relationship with his Kleinian colleagues.

Young-Bruehl: Yes, absolutely and he spoke as a pediatrician who had seen hundreds of children and felt that there was something very suspicious about the way the Kleinian technique developed as a generalization of one case.

Green: But there is now a very important movement you may be aware of. I'm sorry Riccardo Steiner cannot be with us because he is much more competent than myself but as I have many friends in the British Society, and I am aware of these issues. In the British Society, until very recently, in spite of the movement of the contemporary Freudians, Freud was not in fact taught in the institutes and in the training program. There were Freudian seminars but not close readings.

Young-Bruehl: Among the Kleinians, you mean?

Green: No, even among the Freudians. They would start the seminars speaking for five minutes and saying, "What Freud said was this and that and the other thing. Today we think . . ." and they gave their own point of view but there was no study of Freud. There are some independents who had corrected the situation—mainly Gregorio Kohon and Rosine Perelberg. Why? Because Kohon is of Argentinean origin and read French literature in Spanish. Perelberg was of Brazilian origin and knew all the literature by the same token. And now there's a renewal of interest in Freud in the British Society. Sandler was the contemporary Freudian but in fact he was Sandler, not Freud.

Bergmann: We already started the discussion of Ferenczi but I'd like now to end this and really to thank everybody because I feel rather happy about what this general discussion yielded. Let's turn now to Hal Blum's paper on Ferenczi, and even though the hour is late, let's see if we can start the discussion. I would like to ask for a volunteer to open the discussion.

Blum: Elisabeth, in a way you opened it because you were saying that you thought that Ferenczi didn't really alter theory but he changed technique, and I think that would be an interesting discussion as well as bringing up the relationship between theory and technique and how close the two are correlated in Freud, but not in Ferenczi. Ferenczi's technical departures and experiments are partly related to his disappointments with clinical psychoanalysis, his therapeutic zeal, and his efforts to analyze highly disturbed refractory patients.

Bergmann: Since there is no volunteer, I will start with my reaction to your paper. Your paper is interesting because it not only recapitulates Ferenczi's contributions but also adds what some of Ferenczi's own personal difficulties may have been, and it's an attempt to reconstruct the relationship between the theory and the person. Now that is one of the most controversial questions: How much are we entitled to go from the theory to the person who created the theory, and even if we say that a theory is based on a personal psychology, does it invalidate the theory? Even though something can have deep personal reasons, it still could have captured an aspect of impersonal truth. The relationship between the personal and the objective is more complicated than we assumed when we said that the only valid discovery is the objective one devoid of personal needs and that the one which is personal is not valid. Psychoanalysis at its best is a theory about an interesting mixture between the personal and the nonpersonal and how out of the personal, the impersonal— or at least the impersonally valid—can emerge.

The first Ferenczi paper, "The Unwelcome Child and The Death Instinct,"[21] was the first clinical application of the death instinct and to me it's one of the great papers because I have time and again come to the conclusion that while the cockroach has a total desire to survive, it has no death instinct; the human being does need persuasion in order to wish to live and has to be welcomed into the world. This has been to me one of the important ideas. I am more ambivalent about "The Confusion of Tongues"[22] for the same reason that you were ambivalent, because implicit in this paper by Ferenczi is the assumption of the innocence of the child. Here we are coming to one of the questions of dissidence. For some people infantile sexuality may be difficult to accept; for other people, the Oedipus complex is difficult; for a third person, the death instinct. But if I compare the two papers, the "Unwelcome Child" and "The Confusion of Tongues," I give Ferenczi very much more credit for the first and much less for the second because this whole idea that the child doesn't know what he's doing and that the adult mistakes the play of the child for the sexuality of the adult, although useful, is in my opinion not quite correct and Freud's idea of infantile sexuality is superior.

21. Ferenczi, S. (1929). The unwelcome child and his death instinct. In *Final Contributions to the Problems and Methods of Psycho-Analysis*, pp. 102–297. London: Hogarth, 1955.

22. ———— (1933). The confusion of tongues between adults and the child. In *Final Contributions to the Problems and Methods of Psycho-Analysis*, pp. 156–167. London: Hogarth, 1955.

What I found particularly interesting historically, Hal, in your paper, was that mutual analysis began in 1909 when Jung, Freud, and Ferenczi exchanged dreams on the ship to America. Your idea of the wise baby as an attempt to be both the wisest and to continue to be a baby was excellent because it follows exactly the law of the unconscious, which refuses to accept contradiction. Ferenczi said to himself, "Why shouldn't I be the wisest analyst and also the baby?"

Kris: There's a very interesting description of an analyst who's on the border of dissidence, and I think that was Hal's point because it's full of Sturm und Drang and you presented Ferenczi very clearly and very well and you leave us with questions. To me Ferenczi was really not much of a dissident. Right at the end, he was probably not functioning. I agree with André Green—if you read the diary of 1932, you do not have the feeling of a man with organic brain disease, and on the contrary one of the things that impresses me most is Ferenczi's saying, "My experiments were failures." That was a triumph of intellect and couldn't possibly be the product of somebody who had an organic brain disease; he said so many things of great value and he didn't create a full alternative theory. To the extent that he insisted on the innocence of childhood, he was shutting out facts. In the rest of it he was working toward an understanding of how children and adults relate, and he had a much better grasp of it. Hal, I think you demonstrate all of that and give us a very human picture of dissidence.

Green: I'd like to come back to some of the points on Ferenczi. First about the innocent baby: of course, there are reasons to believe that Ferenczi wrote something like that, but if you think about the very early Freud, before writing the three essays, the Freud of the drafts and the correspondence with Fliess, he was right in assuming that infantile sexuality was not adult sexuality. He labeled it as presexual, meaning that puberty marked the change. If you read Ferenczi in this view, you understand that it is a confrontation between this presexual, prepubertal sexuality of the child with the parents' full-blown sexuality and the influence of one on the other. Another point would be what Martin Bergmann said about Winnicott. I agree with him. But one of the contributions of Winnicott was to say that because Freud dealt with patients who had reached a certain maturation and development, it was a pathology of, he says, the whole person. And Winnicott says that instincts existed but in order to witness the existence of instincts there must be an ego. An ego can develop only with the aid of the holding environment. Winnicott is saying that Freud is right, but he addresses people who have already made the first steps before coming to treatment. What I'm talking about is these first steps where sexuality may be present but there is no awareness of it. This is an important point between Winnicott and Freud. Winnicott was trying to understand the critical strides before the rise of infantile sexuality. You can also understand Ferenczi in that way.

Kris: That's what he means by innocence?

Green: I don't know what he meant. There's something I would like to say in general. When we refer to these ideas it is impossible for us to make a distinction between the ideas and what we think of these ideas today. For instance, when I refer to the drive concept, I do not refer to what Freud wrote on the drives. I refer to how we see the drives today in order not to eliminate them. We are not doing an archealogical study—trying to find what Freud really thought or what Ferenczi really thought—but we are always dealing with how we understand what they meant in today's experience.

Bergmann: How do you understand the idea of the innocent child in today's experience or the misreading that the adult does of the sexuality of the child?

Young-Bruehl: Well, sometimes concepts have to be set up so that they illuminate each other. I don't think that the real emphasis in Ferenczi is on the innocence of the child. It goes more like this: If you think of the child as innocent, it may allow you to admit into your theory a mother for the first time in the history of psychoanalysis—a mother who does not love her child. If you tone down the contribution of the child to that relationship and see the child more as the victim, then you can entertain the idea that the mother was the abuser. This idea was so impossible before Ferenczi's work—the Oedipus complex doesn't ask whether Jocasta was a nice lady.

Green: I'm not sure that all mothers thought their babies were innocent. The way they address the baby, they say, "Oh you dirty little pig." And they joke but we know that in joking a lot of unconscious fantasies come out. So the idea of an innocent baby is only in certain mothers, and I don't think they are the most normal mothers.

Bergmann: There's also one amazing aspect of Hal's paper that I think needs to be emphasized—the revival of Ferenczi. That it has taken place is really an interesting phenomenon. In another paper on Ferenczi I wrote that part of the reason for the Ferenczi revival was that the William Alanson White Institute and other organizations where looking for a patron saint and they found their patron saint in Ferenczi and thus they gained status in longevity; they could claim a psychoanalytic ancestry, as all religious organizations have to do. Because after World War II the whole trauma idea, including social trauma, returned with so much force, and Ferenczi was the exponent of trauma. Revival is to a certain extent dependent on what twists and turns society takes, so it's not necessarily the ultimate truth of the value of the contribution of an analyst but rather whether or not the world turns toward him or away from him. This was a new emphasis that deserved attention.[23]

Kernberg: It seems to me that this is one of the factors that have already come up several times in talking about various individual dissidents or nondissidents—whatever one wants to call Ferenczi. For a moment, going back to Kohut, Tony Kris pointed out several things. First, Kohut discovered something new that was interesting and probably could be incorporated into the body of psychoanalysis. Second, he linked that up with a frustrating personal experience with his own analysis and his own analyst, and thus added intensity to it. Third, he linked that up with a broader institutional rebellion against ego psychology, rejecting the theory of drives and replacing it with the theory of universal love. Fourth, he corresponded to a cultural atmosphere that derived from the optimistic, adaptational quality of Hartmann that was still experienced by a stable society. Kohut played right into the narcissistic, self-indulgent atmosphere of a highly satisfied, effective, enriched America of the 1970s. "We all love each other. We don't need to think about rigid rules and aggression anymore." We can start with personal psychopathology, go on to institutional dynamics, and end in cultural currents, all these factors combine in dissidence in different proportions—at least these three and probably more. Ferenczi was under the influence of the resurgence of the importance of trauma and the impact of the First World War, and he rediscovered trauma when trauma again became fashionable. He was rediscovered when trauma became an ideological point as opposed to drive derivatives. Ferenczi became popular because his democratization of the mutual analysis fits into the antiauthoritarian attitude of intersubjectivists. We have these various historical trends coming together.

Blum: There are a number of considerations as to why Ferenczi became popular in post–World War II psychoanalysis. One of them was definitely the war itself and the Holocaust stimulating new attention to trauma past and present

---

23. Bergmann, M. S. (1996). The tragic encounter between Freud and Ferenczi and its impact on the history of psychoanalysis. In *Ferenczi's Turn in Psychoanalysis*, ed. P. L. Rudnytsky, pp. 145–159. New York: New York University Press.

and interest in all aspects of trauma. There was a return to the influence of reality on the psyche after intrapsychic fantasy had been overemphasized as if the external world had no relationship to what was going on intrapsychically (although it has to be said that Freud never gave up the idea of the significance of trauma until his dying day). *Moses and Monotheism*[24] is one of the most seminal explications of trauma and its psychological significance and consequences.

But at that time, in the 1950s, there was also new attention, particularly by the British, on countertransference. The whole British group, including Winnicott, turned its attention to the significance of countertransference in a way that advanced the theory beyond Freud's basic concept. Freud's emphasis had been on the blind spot that countertransference creates, not so much on the ubiquity of countertransference itself. The new propositions indicated that countertransference could also be used in a way that facilitated the understanding of the patient. Countertransference was then not just an impediment or an obstruction. One could regard countertransference from contrasting points of view, of impending and facilitating analytic understanding and interpretation.

Kris: Could you add to the list Michael Balint, who made this connection?

Blum: The person that this refers to is Sandor Ferenczi. I can almost use Tony Kris's words and have them come right out of Ferenczi's mouth. Ferenczi said, "If the patient accuses me of being insensitive or critical, I have to ask myself is this not just a transference—an irrational transference—but am I really being insensitive and critical and is the patient responding to this? Is the patient consciously or unconsciously picking up something in me?" It was Ferenczi who really began a new focus on the analyst's mind, the analyst influencing the analytic process with bilateral, unconscious communications that go on in analysis. It was not that Freud had overlooked the mind of the analyst, but Ferenczi gave it new emphasis and advanced exploration of the analyst's personality in the analytic process.

Then in the 1950s, when the British expanded this point of view (speaking of the fate of new ideas), not one of them referred to Ferenczi. He was still the person who had become an "un-person." He had, so to speak, been written out of the literature at that point. He was rediscovered in the context of a new interest in countertransference and in psychic trauma. As so often happens, the pendulum went much too far. In Latin America, the countertransference almost

---

24. Freud, S. (1939). Moses and monotheism. *Standard Edition* 23.

became the carrying vehicle of the treatment more than the transference. It was as if one could carry on the treatment just by analyzing the countertransference. But I think Ferenczi's focus encompassed more than countertransference. He tried to identify the actual, real attitudes of the analyst, the character of the analyst, the values of the analyst, the theoretical commitments of the analyst. He was the first one to open up this discussion, and it is a contribution to the way we understand the complexities of the analytic process.

Kris: You have the interesting situation of the dissident who expands the psychoanalytic horizon.

Blum: Exactly, and that was one of the things I set out to do in "The Wise Baby and the Wild Analyst" (Chapter 5, this volume). Ferenczi could regress, but at the same time he could, like some of our borderline patients, be extraordinarily creative. He was one of the most creative people in the history of psychoanalysis. It's important that we look upon him not reductively as a dissident but as a creative contributor.

Green: He did not have the time to become a dissident, and he would never have accepted parting from Freud.

Blum: He was much too attached to Freud, and Freud loved him. They were very close to each other. Ferenczi displayed a peculiar combination of regression and progression, of confusion and creativity. Ferenczi's illness in some way spurred the creativity while also impairing it in his regressive moments. In some quarters, after the insufficient past attention to Ferenczi, there has been a reactive overcompensation with idealization.

Kernberg: A small additional factor: Ferenczi's mixture of psychoanalysis and sexual involvement with both mother and daughter created an excitement in the psychoanalytic community similar to the excitement created by Masud Kahn, because on the surface we have debates about technique, professional ethics, and underneath all our discussions is the oedipal situation that is acted out in the institution that is studying it. The psychoanalytic encounter creates excitement because the psychoanalytic situation comes closest to the oedipal situation—much more so than any ordinary or neurotic love relationship, because it's an intimacy in which there is a prohibition on sexual expression on top of which there is also a discussion of the sexual aspect of this intimacy while the prohibition is maintained. It is the most intense potential seduction, and we can congratulate ourselves that we have no more than 1 percent of boundary transgressions.

We have denied the excitement because that's one of the problems of doing psychoanalysis. That's the radioactivity of the method, it is the same as the denial of the oedipal conflict between analysands and analysts. Our candidates are supposed to resolve the transference in their personal analysis and to identify with their analyst. It is an essentially contradictory demand that we make, plus we slap them with the distortion of neutrality into anonymity—the typical authoritarian consequence of the 1950s. So the combination of that demand for resolution of the transference on the training analyst with identification with him, plus the supposed anonymity of the analyst creates unanalyzable idealizations, and splitting off of persecution, and the intensity of oedipal rivalry, and submission. This may be one more factor why, once a fight comes up between the symbolically paternal and the filial generation, it acquires this degree of vehemence.

Blum: One more aspect of Ferenczi that deserves emphasis and indeed is emphasized today is the acknowledgment of his contribution to the treatment of the very ill patient. His therapeutic interest surpassed that of Freud. Freud was uncomfortable with psychotics and with very regressed or developmentally arrested patients—Freud had the understanding that he didn't like to work with them. Ferenczi, on the other hand, was very interested in analytic work with the extremely ill patient. Some of his findings are landmarks in the history of the understanding of borderlines and of ego-disturbed patients, of developmental arrests and developmental deviations. In retrospect, as wild as some of his technical experiments were, we can also say that they were an effort on his part, with excessive therapeutic zeal, to help patients who had not been helped by other techniques. As countertransference enactments the technical departures expressed his wish for further dependent help from Freud, as well as his independence of Freud.

RESUMPTION OF MEETING, 10 A.M. FEBRUARY 15, 2003

Bergmann: Yesterday we did not discover anything unbelievably startling about the vehemence in the psychoanalytic discussion; nevertheless, we all felt that it was a very good and productive meeting and that our understanding of the vehemence in the discussion of dissidence had become clearer. We have not solved the problem but we have enlarged it. As to the second problem, when and how to teach the history of dissidence, although we did not speak about it as much, there was agreement that each one of the dissidents contributed something, and that many of the ideas of the dissidents were taken up later. The development of psychoanalysis becomes dramatic and interesting. We can no longer look upon dissidents the way Freud did and say that they were resisting a particular truth. The issue of truth has become much more complicated, not because of inner development within psychoanalysis but because the whole language of science has changed. So one has to look upon the question of controversy from a broader point of view and thereby it also becomes more interesting.

I asked all of you to read Otto Kernberg's paper, and his paper seems to me a wonderful continuation of the discussion. So with your permission, Otto, can we start with your paper?

Kernberg: I feel honored.

Ostow: His paper was a wonderful summary of the discussion.

Bergmann: How Otto anticipated the discussion and summarized it in the paper is a miracle.

Kris: Talking of miracles, Martin, your comment overlooks the fact that he influenced the discussion.

Bergmann: The magic is gone. Otto, I'm going to begin by asking you a question. I was very much interested in the gradual change of your views after you left Chile and came to America. Since we are interested also in some less conscious aspects, do you think that your changing from one school of thought to another was connected with some inner changes within you or was it a purely intellectual change, which had no other reverberation in your general thinking about the world or about yourself? We want to take the rare opportunity where we have a member who actually changed his mind to see if we can learn something. Without asking you for your deepest secrets, I would like you to comment about the impact of changing an analytic school from one group to another on your general outlook.

Kernberg: Martin, you just asked me something contradictory: to state the personal reverberation without personal disclosure.

Bergmann: That's called compromise formation.

Kernberg: I would be glad to say something personal, too. I have no problem with this. I started out in Chile under the influence of Ignacio Matte Blanco. I don't know who among you knows Matte Blanco, who already was half of a dissident in the sense that he challenged the rigidity of the controversial discussions in London—he was there. He emphasized that there was a danger that psychoanalysis would become a religious struggle of subgroups rather than developing scientifically. He was my professor of psychiatry and the director of the Psychoanalytic Institute. He was the charismatic figure, and he influenced me enormously. He said, "You speak German? Okay. You're going to read Bumke." I thought he wanted me to read a book and I went to the library. I had to read the sixteen volumes of Bumke! And I read them, damning the fact that I told him that I spoke German. But it turned out that I learned a lot. I learned descriptive psychiatry, description without any theory—the typical German nineteenth-century psychiatry.

So I came with that baggage into psychoanalytic training with Matte Blanco. We read ego psychologists. We read Kleinians. At first it was mostly ego psychology. Fenichel's book on technique was the technical base, and technique was taught religiously. There were even written tests—who said what and when—which I found very helpful. But then the Argentineans came in. The whole institute became Kleinian, and all of a sudden what we had learned the first year was questioned; it was no longer true that there was a group of fanatic Kleinians. I thought this was very interesting, but at the same time I felt uneasy; the Kleinians said that Matte Blanco was reactionary because of his openness, and I felt identified with him.

My first analyst was very much identified with Matte Blanco. I shifted to my second analyst, who was one of the Kleinians. I was quite rebellious against everybody at that time. My second analyst convinced me through my own experience of some of the Kleinian discoveries about primitive functioning that I could see in myself, but at the same time I resented that this was an all-or-nothing orientation. So when I had a chance to study psychotherapy in the United States—I had a Rockefeller Foundation grant to study research in psychotherapy, which I had started to do in Chile—I decided, while in the United States, to see what the ego psychologists had to say.

I went to the Washington-Baltimore Institute, one of the most traditional institutes that one can imagine. I had already completed my analytic training. I had not yet graduated because I had not yet fulfilled all my requirements. I went as an advanced guest student and stayed for a year. I was studying with Jerry Franks's psychotherapy research group at Johns Hopkins when I met for the first time Harold Searles and Otto Will, and I became very impressed with their work with schizophrenic patients—particularly with Searles'. I wanted to meet Frieda Fromm-Reichmann, but she died a month before I got to the United States. I was very impressed by her writings about the treatment of schizophrenic patients.

So I was simultaneously in the Baltimore Institute and having seminars with Will and Searles. I talked about Will and Searles at the Baltimore Institute, and the others looked at me as if something were wrong with me. So I learned to shut up. That was very clear.

I returned to Chile. But there were interesting worlds in the United States, both in the culturalist school and in ego psychology. On my second trip to the United States I went to Topeka, Kansas, with the wish to study ego psychology in depth, but at the same time to see how ego psychology and object relations theory related to each other. I thought, as long as I'm in the United States, I'll study more of the object relations school. I found that the rigid ego-psychological approach in Topeka and the complete unwillingness of the others to even enter into a discussion with me made me feel somewhat isolated, until I came into contact with Jock Sutherland, who was the director of the Tavistock Clinic and editor of the *International Journal of Psycho-Analysis* and was very close to Fairbairn. So then I learned about Fairbairn and the fundamental importance of affects in object relations. When Edith Jacobson and Margaret Mahler came to Topeka, I had a sense of openness at the possibility of bringing these perspectives together. So that's my professional history in a nutshell.

I became a close friend with Jacobson. She and Fairbairn proposed two syntheses of early development. She was integrating the theory of drives, and I felt this was very convincing. I felt there was a discrepancy between Fairbairn's theoretical rejection of the aggressive drive, which I found questionable, and his clinical utilization of highly sophisticated concepts regarding aggression. I could kick myself for not having asked Edith whether they knew each other. To this day, I don't know, but they wrote simultaneously. I don't know whether Fairbairn read Jacobson or Jacobson read Fairbairn. But if you look at their work in parallel, you can see how they converge.

The real shock of my life was when I came to New York because then I already had a certain reputation. I became a member of the New York Psychoanalytic Association and of the Columbia Psychoanalytic Association and some of you know the rest of the story. I had shocking experiences. Just to give you one example: at the New York Psychoanalytic, I was asked to give a talk about Edith Jacobson on her eightieth birthday because it was clear that I had become her disciple, and if there was anyone whom I felt I was following closely, it was Jacobson, whom I thought permitted me to synthesize many things. I said I would be delighted to give the lecture. As soon as I'd agreed to that—and remember I was only a month in New York and I didn't know anybody yet—I started getting phone calls. Somebody called and said, "You don't know me. I'm so-and-so from the New York Psychoanalytic and I'm just calling because Edith Jacobson is rather old and frail so don't talk too long." I said, "Thank-you. That's very kind of you." The next day I get another call: "I'm so-and-so. You don't know me. Edith Jacobson is rather frail and old so don't talk too long. Make it brief." I got sixteen phone calls in the course of two weeks, and I became as paranoid as I've ever been! I thought that people were looking at me on the street. I asked Paulina, my wife, "What should I do about this? What is this all about?" It became clear to me there was an organized campaign to get me to resign from that talk. It seemed so crazy I didn't know with whom to talk. Finally, after call sixteen, I called the program chairman. I said, "I have had sixteen calls. If I get one more, I won't give that talk and I'll tell the entire world the way the New York Psychoanalytic is treating me."

Bergmann: It's a wonderful example of vehemence.

Kernberg: There were no more phone calls! I gave the talk. I spoke for an hour and 15 minutes and Jacobson was very happy with it. People were happy. That talk was the paper I published about her work.[25] At Columbia, I was treated very well. When I came to New York, I was invited to dinner at the Columbia Club on 43rd Street. I thought: "That's wonderful. How well they treat me!" We met there. They took me to a wonderful Chinese place next door. The leadership of Columbia was there—seven of the most influential people. At the dinner, the director of the institute said, "You know, we really wanted to talk with you. You're well known and you're very enthusiastic and charismatic. We want to tell you that Columbia has had a charismatic leader and we are just barely out of his shadow. And we don't want that. But we're very worried that you are going to bring this to us. We are open. We are interested in your ideas but we are very worried about that. What can you tell us about the possibility that you will form a school and start the same problems that we had?"

I was paralyzed. I just looked at them and I told them I came from Topeka to New York among other reasons because I didn't have much new to learn there. I was in a serious position in Topeka. I was running the hospital and I wanted to be with a broad spectrum of colleagues from whom I could learn new things. To assume that I was interested in becoming a charismatic leader was a total ignorance of my personality, of my person, which they could be forgiven, but also an ignorance of what I'd written, which was an effort to bring things together rather than saying, "This is me; it is unique and new and whatever." So it ended well. Columbia became my home. I went through all the rituals. I had been a training analyst in Topeka but I had to be examined again. The committee examined me as to whether I could be a training analyst. So I went through all the rituals. Alex Beller—I don't know whether

25. Kernberg, O. F. (1980). The contributions of Edith Jacobson. In *Internal World and External Reality*. New York: Jason Aronson.

you remember him—was the chair of the committee that interrogated me. I totally identified with Columbia. And of course the New York Psychoanalytic has changed greatly since then and has become a completely different organization. But from 1973 to 1975, strange things happened to me at the New York Psychoanalytic. There was a spy in my seminar. I did a seminar, which the candidates thought was the best seminar of the year; I was never asked to give it again. Then I could only do a colloquium. One of the analysts came to my seminar with a tape recorder. I thought, Oh my gosh, he is really open-minded. And later I was told that he had been asked to do this to see what kind of things I was going to teach. I attended the faculty meetings at the New York Institute that were dedicated only to reading the minutes from the last meeting and changing them. The "in" group and the "out" group were fighting. During the year that I attended those meetings, not once was there any educational method discussed! Only the minutes of the last meeting and who said what and why. My relationship with and view of the New York Institute and Society has radically changed; or rather, they have radically changed.

The nice side of this is that, as soon as Kohut came on the scene, they forgot about me. Weinshel and Calef wrote a paper on the new revisionism against me, and Calef, in a conference in San Francisco, where I gave a talk, was sitting there and he yelled at me, "Go tell it to the marines!" Harold Blum, who became a good friend, was attacked because he was my friend. I understand some people stopped talking to him. When I gave a talk at a plenary session of the American Psychoanalytic Association about psychoanalytic education, the chairman of the program committee was called by the board of professional standards to explain why I had been asked to give that talk without checking with them. It was my paper "Institutional Problems of Psychoanalytic Education."[26]

Bergmann: The vehemence we talked about came back.

Grossman: What do you mean came back?

Bergmann: Look at the strong feelings Otto has shown this recollection.

Green: But I can tell the same story on a more reduced scale. I won't be long but I applied as a candidate in 1955. I attended the institute and I found that the teaching there was poor. We had a very big event—the Bonneval meeting, where representatives of the two societies met together under the patronage

---

26. Kernberg, O. F. (1986). Institutional problems of psychoanalytic education. *Journal of the American Psychoanalytic Association* 36:799–834.

of Henry Ey, who was a famous psychiatrist. And there the meeting turned to the advantage of the Lacanians. I thought to myself, I have to go and see what's up, because I knew Lacan. I had heard him but I had not followed the public seminar he used to give. So from 1960 to 1967, I attended Lacan's seminar, which was weekly. Lebovici was selected to tell me that I had to choose. I said, "I have already chosen. I am a member of the Paris Society." There was persecution of people who went to listen to Lacan, not to participate in the activities of this group. Lacan tried many times to bring me to his side, to make me resign from the society and I never did it because I knew that that was a disaster. I think I was right.

For twenty years I had been considered a persona non grata. I wanted to have my own opinion. The climate was very bad in the society, and it is so until this generation. The old leaders were put aside so that a new generation could come and speak more freely. At least you could speak of Lacan. You could speak in a seminar. You could go to the seminar of Lacan if you wished but there was strong bureaucratic pressure.

After that I met the people from the British society in 1961 and I started to have regular relationships with some of them. What I found in the British society was precisely what was lacking in Lacan—I found the clinical orientation and the clinical spirit and skills that I needed. So I became a kind of go-between between the French and the English, and the more time went by, the less I was attracted to Lacan. I had taken what I thought was the most important of his teaching and I had closer relations with the British society. The French read a lot of translations. But if the book is not translated, they do not learn English to read it. I tried to do it and I read a lot of literature that was not translated, and this brought a change, I think, with my generation and others. There was also *La Nouvelle Revue de Psychanalyse*—Pontalis, Didier Anzieu, Smirnoff . . . And this brought a new spirit; it opened the windows of the Paris analytical society. There was a kind of interaction between the two societies.

When I started to go to Lacan, I had not the feeling of going to a dissident. I had the feeling that all the others were dissidents and he was the true heir of Freud, it took me some years to see that that was completely false. What Lacan said—when you look at the texts, you see that Freud never said such a thing. I have learned—in a way like Otto, but on a more reduced scale—that there was no one psychoanalysis. Obviously, even in France, the way people thought, the way people worked, the way people wrote, there were expressions of their own interpretations of psychoanalysis and nobody could claim to be an orthodox Freudian.

In general, there was a mistrust in American psychoanalysis in the times of Hartmann and Gittelson. The mistrust was reciprocated. When people came to conferences in Paris and when they saw what the French literature was, they were full of contempt. They didn't want to have anything to do with it. To complete Otto's development, after his meeting with Jacobson and Fairbairn, there's one last phase: his discovery of French analysis, which has influenced him a lot, and as he could read French, we could discuss with him more openly than with the other Americans. When Otto happened to view the French, he didn't mean speaking with the Lacanians. He was speaking with the people of the *Nouvelle Revue*—Pontalis, Laplanche, Anzieu.

We can see a division between two types of dissidents: one type, which I call a singular dissident, is a person who has something to say and tries to create a movement around it; the other type is the bureaucratic dissident, someone who feels mistreated or not recognized, and thinks he has to create dissidence for bureaucratic reasons. What Otto says showed that he could have been on the verge of dissidence at some time because of bureaucratic reasons.

I would like to add one thing before stopping, and this will probably shock many of you. Psychoanalysis is a masochistic profession. It means that you have to integrate and to accept a certain dose of masochism born from your experience with the patients, the patient's masochism, the patient's aggression, the patient's resistance, and so on. You have to bear all that. Some people cannot stand it and they want some kind of gratification coming from outside—being recognized by pupils, by followers. There are so many changes because I believe that many of our theories do not work for certain types of patients. So what to do about it? One person comes and says, "I have the answer!" He pretends to have the answer but he doesn't. In the history of psychoanalysis, as far as the classical neurotic patient is concerned, we can say that the results are not so bad and the theories and the clinical descriptions seem to fit. If you are treating a borderline and you refer to Freud, you won't find one pertinent line in Freud. So this is why we are trying to find something else out of Freud and we go to dissidents who pretend to have the answer. Ferenczi's case is really one of the most conspicuous. Ferenczi tried very hard, but as I said before, psychoanalysis is a masochistic profession. Ferenczi's masochism was much more developed than anyone else's. Because of this masochism, he created mutual analysis, which today seems to us completely mad, because when you think about it, you can do mutual analysis with one patient, but do you realize what it means to do mutual analysis with eight or nine or ten patients a day? That's completely mad! And Ferenczi was mad in the sense that in the end, the masochistic trend took over. It was more than reparation. It was self-sacrifice. If we are classical orthodox analysts, we select a neurotic type with neat delineations, no borderline features—classical neurosis. Okay, we have an analysis—four, five, six years and the patient also gets better. The patient gets better treated by other methods. But when we have the type of patients that we're talking about—either Otto or myself or other persons in this room—then you have to invent something and this is where Winnicott comes in. This is where other British people come in. And it's not a matter of object relations. For instance, people do not know that Winnicott was not an object relationist 100 percent. Madeleine Davis, in her 1981 book,[27] makes the point very clear—he was not an object relationist. He was half object relationist. But as for the type of patients he treated, after Winnicott's death, I treated one of his patients and I can tell you that all he wrote was right. He was totally honest. Maybe you could object that he didn't say this or that or the other thing but he was honest and I think it is much more the type of pathology that we have to discuss in relation to dissidents.

Bergmann: It's not an accident that Otto and André spoke because they stand out among psychoanalysts as an example. The fact that in your development you went through various points of view, looking, trying to understand and then arriving at a synthesis of your own. You both have given contemporary psychoanalysis a new ego ideal—of the creative analyst who reads, who even travels and who after a considerable amount of effort, arrives at a synthesis on his own. You read their work because you want to understand the synthesis they created. Sometimes it's easy and sometimes it is not. I have been teaching André for a good number of years to American students and jokingly I said, "Someday I'm going to write a paper, 'American Citizenship for André Green,'" because in your writings and in the way in which you put things, André— it's not that my students disagree with you. They don't understand you.

Kernberg: Martin, there's another theme here that I think we have been talking about—I just want to underline it. You just said something very important and right but at the same time also funny. It is as if psychoanalysis— imagine a country where the universities are totally separated. In Boston, they study the little toe. In Chicago, the left eye; in Los Angeles, they study the right kidney. Each of them has its own observations and declares that the rest doesn't exist. And there's a student who travels from one place to the other and is able to get a feeling for the human being and put it together. Martin is saying that's what we could do. I'm caricaturizing, but you get my point. The real problem is this monopolizing—dogmatic rigidity of each little place in contrast to a functional atmosphere that tolerates dialogue. I'm sorry that Bob Wallerstein is not here because I disagree with him on this point. Bob Wallerstein thinks that we have to tolerate pluralism because it's all the same. I think

27. Davis, M., and Wallbridge, D. (1981). *Boundary and Space: An Introduction to the Works of D. W. Winnicott.* New York: Brunner/Mazel.

that we have to tolerate dialogue—not to bring it all together but for an education as to what works and what does not work. Pluralism, in contrast, has become a mask for eclecticism. This eclectic tendency brings with it a watering down—if everything goes, nothing means anything anymore. If an institution can tolerate violent different viewpoints, not in order to bring them all together, but to permit people to compare and make decisions among them while at the same time, the science progresses, that would be the ideal of a university of the psychoanalytic schools. Theories would be affected by experiences with different patients, and the theoretical developments and the technical developments related to them—to confront them, to try to develop the field—that's what we have been missing. The question is, To what extent is this historically determined by the authoritarian structure that Freud created? Or to what extent are we blaming Freud unfairly and the training institutions that we created? The training analyst system is the source of many troubles—all of that really was brought about without the awareness of an early generation of analysts. Freud was an innocent regarding organizational psychology, although he was a prophet when it came to mass psychology. It may be that in our educational system we have created a kind of monster—tracing it unfairly back to the early disciples—and that this is what makes any wish to be open, to bring things together, immediately suspect as dissidence. If you add to this personal disappointment and narcissistic problems, then the whole system blows up.

Neubauer: It seems to me that André Green raises an important additional question. He says the dissidences occurred with the disappointment of the clinical experience. They address themselves, very often, to different conditions of pathology. Therefore, we would have to say we cannot expect a synthesis of the various components; rather we have to ask, What is the diversity of approach within psychoanalysis and its correspondence to the pathology of the patient? When you find the patient with preoedipal, major disappointment, do you go along with Ferenczi's ideas or narcissism with Kohut? We select from the variety of propositions those appropriate for a specific pathology. Now if this is so, the question then arises: Where do the pathologies then demand responses beyond the core of psychoanalysis? André's paper starts out with the definition of the core of psychoanalysis. What is included in the core of psychoanalysis in connection with the particular treatment of the patient? It is not so much a synthesis but rather a diversity and selectivity.

Green: One important question is to try to understand while traveling and knowing and reading why do these people—I mean Ferenczi, Hartmann, Melanie Klein—why do they say that? On what ground? About what type of patients? And is it true that what they say is applicable to any kind of patient? I do not believe it is. So we have to consider dissidents under this diversity of pathology.

Kris: The way you spoke about theory, it's as though one sees a patient and one figures out in one's head from the theory how to approach the patient. It's just not how we do it. I think we use our theory to understand what kind of a thing we're doing but then theory becomes an interference. If you have a theory that's more or less oriented to the patient who can talk freely in analysis and you have a patient who is practically silent because of affect block, your theory interferes unless you can give up the theory. Or do you find a new piece that you add in some way—or modify the theory—so that you can continue to work? I think it's the difference between theory as the positive means to understand and theory as the interference that blocks us.

Neubauer: When one speaks about the dissidents as honestly attempting to enlarge, to search for new or different answers to the problems, which they had to confront, the question becomes, To what degree were they more successful in their new approach, treating their patients? What data do we have that says, Can we prove that what this person did was more successful than somebody else? How successful is André Green with what kind of a patient, which may be different than other treatments? Is there a clinical proof that these dissidents have contributed something that we can say has been to a certain degree successful or not successful except for Kohut? Our material has not yet indicated the additional data around which the dissidents could tell us in which way they had been successful.

Nunberg: But then there's also the question of how much is it the theory or the theoretical orientation that is responsible for the success of failure. We lack the data.

Green: When we think of our practice, theory never comes first. You can't see your patients with a theory in your mind. I'll give you a very concrete example, not a patient but an example. Let's take the Oedipus complex. With some patients—and Winnicott wrote about it—I see no signs of any Oedipus complex. And of course you can answer by assuming a preoedipal or pregenital fixation. I think Winnicott is wrong. Because if you take the Oedipus complex at face value, as a particular phase or structure, you can say that you see no signs of it in the patient. But you can also understand the Oedipus complex differently and see how it fits the patients with what is lacking in the clinical picture. The lacks the patient is presenting are part of our conception of the

Oedipus complex. I don't think it would be so interesting to restrict ourselves to a historical point of view by saying on such a day Mr. So-and-so said this and that and the other thing. Even if I say I am strongly in favor of drives, the way I understand drives today is not the way Freud wrote about them. We have to reconsider even the concepts on which we lean heavily and that are supposed to be classical, we have to consider a new approach. This changes the problem of dissidence.

Kernberg: We are using the term *theory* too globally. I'll illustrate with an example. I liked what André just said about the different forms that the oedipal constellation takes under different pathological circumstances. The same is true with narcissism. I had the following experience: I had a patient in analysis when I was a candidate in Chile who was diagnosed as being an obsessive personality type. Now I know he was a typical narcissistic personality. I analyzed him for three years. I had to stop the analysis because I went to the United States. A colleague of mine then took the case, who then told me, shocked, that I had not touched that patient at all. And I agreed with her. It was a patient I never touched. A total failure. I wrote it up when I became a member of the American Psychoanalytic. I thought it would be helpful to describe a failure of analysis. After three years, I went to visit Chile and my colleague said she couldn't touch him either.

I came to the States, I saw a patient exactly like the one whom I hadn't been able to help. I analyzed this patient under the supervision of Hermann Van der Waals.

Green: On narcissism?

Kernberg: I asked Van der Waals if he would supervise that case. I told him what my problem had been with the first patient. He said yes and we started working and I used my Kleinian concepts to analyze the pathological grandiose self. And that patient changed. It was a tremendous success. And Van der Waals told me, "Let's write about narcissism." And he gave me a box with case records he had collected on narcissism just before he died and I left with that box, and then I started to write about narcissism. Then I read Herbert Rosenfeld and I saw that in some ways, we had done exactly the same kind of clinical work. When Rosenfeld came to Topeka, I talked with him and it reinforced my view. Now here you have a different view of treating patients on a clinical level. That influences theory, yes, but it influences it in terms of the difference between this kind of pathological narcissism and the normal narcissism. That change of theory is a partial one. If you reorganize your concept of narcissism, it fits into the general psychoanalytic theory of narcissism. Under ideal circumstances, different patients require different theoretical developments at an intermediate level. They then create the task of relating them to a comprehensive theory. This is a slow and gradual task. This is what ideally should happen. It doesn't happen because when we come to conditions that foster dissidence, people get stuck at that intermediate level and transform it into the whole truth. If there's personal psychopathology in the therapist, then all hell breaks loose; only slowly do we learn that a third step is necessary, a slow, gradual modification of the global theory throughout time. That would be the ideal way to proceed because it would bring together different clinical situations and partial theories. That does not happen, I believe, because of the organizational rigidity of institutions that are afraid that any such development immediately threatens the edifice of local authority.

Blum: What's been said has been wonderful and yet what we heard overstates the case. For example André, to make your point, which I think was a wonderful one, about the fact that we really have reacted over time to patients who are very different and have been forced as it were to reconsider our theories in the light of looking at different forms of psychopathology that the original theory did not adequately address. With respect to Freud—and I don't think I'm just being a Freudian defending Freud—the fact is that Freud did say things that are quite relevant to the understanding and treatment of the borderline.

Green: Examples, please.

Blum: A number of examples—we could really go through the texts of Freud to show that it's there, though scattered and not systematically investigated. For example, in "Analysis Terminable and Interminable"[28] he discusses the fact that everyone's ego is more or less normal and may approximate psychotic elements: "A normal ego of this sort is, like normality in general, an ideal fiction. The abnormal ego, which is unserviceable for our purposes, is unfortunately no fiction. Every normal person, in fact, is only normal on the average. His ego approximates to that of the psychotic in some part or other and to a greater or lesser extent" (p. 235). In the Wolf Man case, at the end of the report, when Freud reviews his own formulations and questions them, he brings up the notion that the Wolf Man, after all, suffered from a severe developmental disturbance. And an analysis as Freud then understood it could not quite set the Wolf Man back on a normative course. Freud raised the whole

---

28. Freud, S. (1937). Analysis terminable and interminable. *Standard Edition* 23, pp. 209–253.

question about the Wolf Man's disorder that went beyond the Wolf Man seduction trauma when he was 18 months of age. The traumatic experience that
Freud stressed and related to castration anxiety and so forth did not divert
Freud from questioning patients with a very severe early developmental dis-
organization. [Editor's note: In "From the History of an Infantile Neurosis,"
Freud writes, "But his seduction gives the impression not merely of having
encouraged his sexual development but of having, to an even greater extent,
disturbed and diverted it. It offered him a passive sexual aim, which was ultimately incompatible with the action of his male genital organ" (p. 108).][29] I
don't want to go on because it would be peripheral to our topic. There are
many other points in Freud where one could show a concern and really a deep
interest in forms of psychopathology that he couldn't explain at the time and
with just hints of later theoretical developments. At the same time we have
gone far beyond Freud, for example in our group of preoedipal transference
manifestations, narcissistic transference, countertransference, etc.

Green: But we agree that people overlooked these observations.

Blum: This demonstrates the point also that Otto Kernberg and I brought up,
which is that over time, these become opportunities for gradual expansion,
alteration, and modification of theory. The point about theory entering treatment in this dichotomous way, facilitating and impeding, is very well taken
but theory is always present. The way the analyst organizes the data inevitably involves preexisting theoretical commitments that may be conscious or
unconscious. But they're there. The uncertainty principle applies in psychoanalysis because of the complexity of the human mind and limitations of theory
and technique. We never have a complete view of what's going on, a complete understanding. We have to live with uncertainties. I think that's related
to the reality ego as well as the narcissistic vulnerability of the analyst. The
analyst also needs theory in order not to be overwhelmed by complexity, but
there are other reasons anyone who has gone through any kind of analytic
training develops a certain degree of theoretical commitment.

This brings me to still another point, which I thought was one of the essential points in Otto's paper, and I too wish Bob Wallerstein was here. I don't
agree at all with his idea of common ground. I think one problem is theoretical
rigidity and an excessive orthodoxy, which can be very stifling and suffocat-
ing. But on the other side there's an equally serious problem with the idea of

---

29. Freud, S. (1918). From the history of an infantile neurosis. *Standard Edition*
17, pp. 3–122.

common ground and the idea that you can accept, integrate, or reconcile radically different theoretical frameworks and systems. To my mind, that becomes a kind of irrational eclecticism, and I would differentiate between pluralism and eclecticism. It's one thing, as Peter Neubauer was saying, to have different points of view, a diversity of opinion, different theoretical approaches, different inferences or hypotheses. It's quite another thing to say that they are equally valid or that they all reconciled and synthesized with each other. You come up with Hungarian goulash!

Neubauer: That's not bad.

Blum: Sometimes it's very tasty. Some people like it. But it's not really truly nutritive. Whereas in the past we were confronted more often with the problem of a complacent orthodoxy, particularly going back to seventy-five years ago, today the problem has shifted more on the other side to a kind of superficial eclecticism. There is a difference between debate about difference and denial of difference.

Green: Anything goes.

Blum: Anything goes and anything can be meshed and mixed up with anything else and used in the same way. Bob Wallerstein in his paper indicated that the theories can be viewed as equally valid. It is really the reverse—it's our obligation to think about the different theories, to test them in our own clinical work, and to see to what degree we think they are or are not valid, that they fit or don't fit. How do they articulate with the core theories of psychoanalysis? How do they fit with each other? How do they fit into the theory of ideas and the evolution of psychoanalytic thought? Does the proposed innovation contribute to therapeutic effect?

Ostow: The problem is that we have no criteria, Harold. Peter Neubauer made the point just ten minutes ago—we have no objective test that says this theory is valid and that is not. Theories are useful because they help us recognize patterns in our patients. For certain patients this theory is useful. For other patients that theory is not useful. We tend to use what's available to help us with the individual patients. We have no way of confirming any theory. No theory helps us to predict. Our theories help us to recognize, not to predict.

Bergmann: We now have some of the vehemence we spoke of among us.

Grossman: I have two comments. It's a question of how to deal with differences. The important issue is not to tolerate differences but to learn something from them, which is what the two case histories that were presented really are about. [Editor's note: The reference is to Kernberg's and Green's description of their educational history.] They're about people who want to learn things from the differences that they find. The other one is a quote on the function of theory that is very interesting because this is from a paper written by Nina Searl in 1936, "Some Queries on Principles of Technique."[30] She is a good example of a certain kind of dissident because she was a Kleinian, and she was hounded out of the Kleinian group because of her ideas. It was in the controversial discussions that Melitta Schmideberg made some comment about this and upbraided her colleagues for driving Searl out of the movement. She gave up being an analyst because of how badly she was treated by the Kleinians. This is one of two papers in the analytic literature from that period that are extraordinarily modern in their conceptualization. The other one is Waelder's paper on multiple function,[31] which is essentially about the construction of complex systems in mental life. Searl wrote, "The function of theory is to help the analyst's weaknesses on extra-analytical occasions and is of use to the patient only in this indirect fashion. Theory is the hypothetical skeleton on which we seek to reassemble the array of facts and their relationships, which our mind cannot otherwise hold in any ordered cohesion. But we never shall know about the human being in this way or even create any gross resemblance to the living interaction of living psychic tissue."

Ostow: The function of theory is to reduce complexity. The human mind is capable of handling, of containing only a certain degree of complexity. Theory helps you to organize and to reduce complexity.

Grossman: And at the same time can mislead you, limits your vision, and focuses you on parts of the whole.

Bergmann: I'd like to move on because we want to start another chapter, so let me just say a few things about the complexity of our subject. Certainly it would be ideal if we could say that a certain type of patient is treatable by this

---

30. Searl, N. (1936). Some queries on principles of technique. *International Journal of Psycho-Analysis* 17:471–493.

31. Waelder, R. (1930). The principle of multiple function. English trans. *Psychoanalytic Quarterly* 5:45–62.

method and another type is treatable by another. If we could have said that, the problem of dissidence would disappear and peace would reign. I don't visualize that because the analyst or any human being does not approach a patient with a totally open mind. To some extent we are open. To some extent we are not. But we can never be totally open. Otto Kernberg said, "I analyzed this patient and I couldn't touch him and the next analyst could not touch him either." Here I also see things differently. I know that an awful lot of energy was spent on the question of analyzability. Who is analyzable and who is not? I would tend to consider this effort misguided because, as André Green once said, "Analyzable by whom? Under what conditions?" So that the analyzability is as much a function of the analyst as a function of the patient. Otto, I would suggest to you, and I think that this is closer to something that André Green said, that it's actually not possible for any two people to meet for a long period of time and the patient not being touched by it. What I think is really meant by your statement is that the patient was not touched along the direction that you wished him to be touched. I didn't ever see a patient who was not touched by the previous analyst because some change took place—even the fact that he succeeded to win victory over the therapy did change something in his superego, his ego, or his id. In other words, the stream is never the same and even the most difficult patients are actually in some way or another influenced by us.

Kernberg: Martin, in response to that, if I may interrupt for a moment. I think I expressed myself wrongly or you misunderstood me. I fully agree with everything you are saying but I was trying to say that the theory of technique— or the technique that I was applying—didn't work analytically with him. I surely touched him in other ways. The same approach by the next person within that institution didn't work either. I used it to illustrate that there was a need for a change in technique and to illustrate that a different way of treating different types of pathology is important to integrate in our psychoanalytic knowledge.

On the positive side, what seems to be the important issue is the level of technique. We develop different techniques with different patients and it's easy to say then, "This is not analysis." It is possible that these different technical approaches again are related to a higher level of theory of technique that brings them together, and progress can thus be achieved. André Green has described how borderline patients disrupt the flow of free association in order to avoid a potential trauma in the central phobic position. That means that the attitude of the analyst who sits back and waits for free association to clarify things will fail. André could have said—if he were a dissident—free association is out. Forget free association. However, what he says instead is that some people in analytic treatment cannot free associate, but free association is nevertheless an integral part of psychoanalysis. The analyst has to look at each segment of communication and attempt to understand it before he decides that Freud was mistaken. What André said was, "Yes, the patients have this problem. Therefore, our standard analytic technique has to be modified. The concept of free association still stands, but at a higher level of abstraction it may take different forms." I think the same could be applied to the concept of resistance.

Bergmann: When André presented one of those difficult patients, what he said was that he did not even try to cure him. What he tried to do is to understand him, and if you are thinking about an analytic core, it is, at least to me, one of the most precious parts of the psychoanalytic core that we try to understand our patients. Understanding may or may not cure, but it is at the very core of analysis.

Green: It saves his life at least.

Bergmann: When we feel that we did not touch our patients we really mean that we did not achieve what we intended to achieve, we tend to say that this person was unanalyzable, not that he changed in an unexpected way. But if you look at the untouched patient microscopically, you will notice that with all of the resistance, the fact that he spent all of these years coming and that there was a genuine effort on the part of the analyst to understand the patient— that created a bond to have a certain effect. We are all here basically opposed to eclecticism because eclecticism is a form of not really taking seriously any particular point of view. But we are all, I think, in favor of pluralism. Whether time will eventually bring theories together, create a new synthesis, or whether time will be more destructive and divisive, it seems to me that on the basis of psychoanalysis we can never be sure whether libido, the builder of cities, or destrudo, the destroyer of society, will win. But at least we are trying by this meeting to put our energy in the direction of trying to understand not only the patient but also trying to understand ourselves and our dissidents and arrive at a greater understanding.

Ostow: Martin, can I ask you to clarify the difference between eclecticism and pluralism?

Bergmann: Pluralism means that we don't agree with each other. We have different views but with the effect of last night's discussion, we are better able to tolerate each other, to work together, to be interested in each other's ideas, and to hope for some kind of a deepening understanding that eventually will be enriching and will help us to tolerate disagreements.

Eclecticism is something very different and it has its base because even Otto and André are to a certain extent eclectic. But the danger is that you take a little bit from here, a little bit from there, and you don't really pay too much attention to what the theory is all about. Sometimes when you are trying to win a patient, you use this kind of a hypothesis or this kind of an idea. And other times, you use another. Your main aim is to make a living. You are trying to keep your patients and you are trying to continue your development and you kind of draw upon theory—but not really with any deeper attempt to arrive at what amounts to your own therapeutic philosophy, your own point of view. I am not quite so convinced that time is necessarily on our side because I think there is always the destructive drive to be taken into account. But we are soldiers in the field of the libido and we are trying to do what we can to bring more libido, more understanding into the psychoanalytic discussions. Have I answered your question?

Ostow: You've answered it, but I don't know that you've clarified it.

Kris: I would like to make a plea for a measure of dissidence. Otto's beautiful formulation is very elegant, but it makes me a little nervous because I begin to see that anybody who has an idea is really required to integrate it and put it in perspective and that is a view that I don't share. I'd rather have dissidence, even those who want to destroy everything if they can at least get their idea out. We'll take care of it later.

Kernberg: Do you think I disagree with you? I see it as an institutional process. I think that Martin Bergmann clarified it. Eclecticism is an effort to bring different factions together to a common idea or concept or theory. True pluralism, in contrast to eclecticism, is often misunderstood. It means everyone continues what he is doing but you really have learned about alternative ways that may influence you, but particularly the next generation on doing what we are doing; creating new understanding so that a new generation that is not narcissistically involved in the new finding sometimes may use dissidents' ideas for a new development of thinking. In other words, I was thinking of a historical perspective in contrast to eclecticism. When I read an article saying, "Sometimes I behave like a Kohutian, sometimes like a Kleinian," the article is already a mediocrity for me, because it already precludes thinking about irresolvable differences that require a much more complex process than simply "Let's all be friends."

Kris: But all I'm saying is that I would not want to have us think that dissidence is bad.

Green: I'd like to say a few words about something, and it may sound pompous to you. It's about Freud's own dissidence. From the minute he introduced the death instinct, Freud was a dissident of himself. We all know that there were reactions in the psychoanalytic community. There was a lot of turmoil. Nobody understood why the old man had changed everything into a more speculative theory. After listening to Martin's clarification, which I think is helpful, there is an important shift in what I will call Freud's dissidence of 1920. It is my assumption that in 1920, Freud had a model on which he still lived: neurosis is the negative of perversion. This continued for him to be a theorem for psychoanalysis. I believe that after 1924—the two papers on neurosis and psychosis[32]—neurosis was not anymore compared to perversion but to psychosis. This brings a total change in the picture, because if you have to analyze the wish or the fantasy linked to the libido in relation to perversion, then with the help of repression and sublimation you can help the patient to change and to have a more, let's say, realistic aim. But when comparing neurosis to psychosis, repetition compulsion, which was not there before, comes into the picture, and with it masochism and splitting. So now we have this combination of splitting masochism and repetition compulsion in the ego, the ego being a kind of double agent.

   The ego being a double agent—splitting—and a reversal of the pleasure principle in masochism, this troubles our minds when we have to bend the theory because they are such negative aspects; it is difficult to have a clear picture of their actions. When we think of these patients—helping them or curing them or just listening to them—to listen to them is to be able to tolerate the splitting and the masochism and the repetition compulsion. The fact that you tolerate them means that, to some extent, they have not destroyed the mind of the analyst. If they have not destroyed the mind of the analyst, if the analyst can still think with these negative features, then he gets some sense, which can be brought back to the patient and maybe the patient has a glimpse of what he's doing—not an understanding but a glimpse. And if you have endurance, if you can endure the patient for years and years, you see sometimes changes that you did not expect or did not hope for anymore. Not that

---

32. Freud, S. (1924). The loss of reality in neurosis and psychosis. *Standard Edition* 19, pp. 183–187.

the patient is cured! But the patient is alive. The patient is not in a psychiatric hospital. The patient has a so-called normal, average life.

Kris: André, are you introducing now shifting goals of analysis as part of the reassessment of dissidence?

Green: Absolutely. I'm shifting goals in order to help the patient move from his position to the one that you have labeled as the libidinal elements. And it is here, surely, that the concept of object relationship is very helpful because when these patients get better, their relationship extends. They are less isolated and less sheltered, and they are less masochistic. I think that's what I would call Freud's dissidence, which we find in his late work and which explains why we have so much difficulty in building a coherent structure about these destructive features.

Neubauer: Let me ask you, when you use the term *endurance* or *tolerance*, there would be many today who would say, "Why don't you go further?" It is not just tolerance but empathic participation of our own unconscious rationality that must be available in order to tune in with the one of the patient, and it is more than the tolerance, of being able to withstand it, but even to go further. And you know there are also many today who feel the therapeutic intervention exactly depends on that dialogue of the internal reflection.

Green: Yes. I think they are boasting. I think there is a lot of illusion and I would feel satisfied with the word *endurance*. To endure it and survive—I have reservations about the magical powers of empathy. How can you empathize with someone who is so different from you? I am different from Otto but I know at least that he belongs to the same psychiatric category as I. We are not psychotic either of us—maybe you think differently but that's your problem. But how can empathy play with a deeply disorganized person. Bion, who probably was the most important author—Bion and Searles too didn't think of empathy. They thought of tolerating, yes. Tolerating the projected identification, the fragmentation, the split off parts of personalities—yes, to survive that is really enough. But empathy as all-loving relationship I don't believe. I think it's a religious statement.

Bergmann: We entered the discussion of Jill Scharff's paper.

Scharff: Well, the discussion is so fascinating, I can see that I'm at a disadvantage not having heard where you got to last evening. I've been trying to tune in. I'd like to start by responding to a few of the things I've heard. I hear the group returning to a preoccupation with dissidents, even though I believe this group carries an ideal of diversity, controversy, heated argument, and fine-tuning or throwing out lousy theories—trying to operate according to a principle of selective identification: that which is useful and makes sense leads one toward a higher level of understanding and abstraction. There must be a few definitions of what would qualify as dissident: Someone who disagreed with Freud? Someone who was disloyal to Freud? Someone who was hurt by Freud and had to avenge himself? Someone who wants to create a school rather than just offer ideas for use and for disruption if the ideas don't appeal to enough people to really validate them as useful organizing principles? And you may have come up with some others.

For my own part, I think of theories as existing all over—not an "I think" here and a "You think" there. Rather, they're all processing systems that are moving along in parallel lines and they bump into each other now and again. If we are fortunate enough to have people like André Green and Otto Kernberg, who can speak in various languages and then reach into depths of cultural experience that lead to the theory that wishes or does not wish to communicate with other theories and so on, then we can all move several steps ahead. These interdigitations are important to allow one theory to become a system of influence—not that it should take over but that it would come into contact with other systems of thought. All systems might reorganize somewhat, create multiple bifurcations, and ultimately come back into a chaotic form again out of which wonderful new ideas would emerge.

I know I've been identified with object relations theory. That was my first way of looking at things, my earliest training. And I'm not as far along in my development as an analyst as most of you here—in fact all of you here.

Young-Bruehl: Oh no. I'm the child.

Scharff: You're the child?

Kris: The *very* wise baby.

Scharff: So I'm seeing myself as coming from that base and I'm looking for ways to get beyond it, to see what's next, what is an orienting principle. I very much resonated with what André said about analysis being a masochistic profession. I feel aware of that. The converse of that is that it's also a sadistic profession. While Harold Searles did say a good analyst has to endure, to survive the attacks, he did also say it was important for the analyst to survive the wish to kill the patient, which I think we don't look at enough—Martin Bergmann might call it destrudo, and Harold Blum called it the wish to kill—that so pervades the analytic institutes and causes such havoc. It's not been analyzed individually or more particularly as a group in the analytic society.

I was very affected when you spoke about your situation, Otto, coming from Chile to New York. I should have known this would be the case but I was too caught in my own experience, coming up for certification, to think of how it might have affected senior people already certified. Certification was a very traumatic experience, which it shouldn't have been. It should have been a great pleasure to join a community of people so dedicated. It was traumatizing, but of course I experienced it within my own narcissism, instead of seeing that surely the examiners were traumatized too—that's why the trauma was being perpetuated. We live very much in a culture of transgenerational transmission of trauma; it goes right back to how much Freud suffered for thinking the way he did, for living in the times he did. Being the kind of person who, although he could allow himself to be a dissident of his theories, couldn't accept it in other people. Freud failed to bring about creative interchanges. That's what we're recovering from now in this culture of pluralism or—I prefer—diversity with points of conversion and divergence that lead to a more interesting and complex situation.

Bergmann: Does anybody want to start the discussion of Jill's paper?

Green: I just want to add one remark. I took to the habit of classifying my colleagues and the movements to which they belong. And I do it in a spirit of kinship. Often I would say, "Mr. So-and-so is my brother. Mr. So-and-so is my cousin. Mr. So-and-so is a far cousin. And Mr. So-and-so is really a foreigner for me." I had this discussion once with Daniel Stern at University College, and I told him I'm not a Kleinian. The Kleinians are my cousins. This way of reasoning introduces a dynamic perspective in dissidence. For instance, I do not find any common ground or agreement with the intersubjectivists. None. I can find one with Sutherland or Searles or Otto or Harold or many others. But there are people from whom I find myself really too distant to have a fruitful discussion. This is an approach for diversity or pluralism, but not for a general assembly of dissidents. I wouldn't have anything to say to a Jungian, for instance.

Scharff: In the discussion last evening, did you arrive at an agreement of what is the core from which people diverge or form dissidence?

Green: I gave my own idea of the core but I don't know how much my colleagues share my views.

Blum: Jill, may I ask you a question? If you could tell us—because we all want to learn something more about the so-called object relations school—in particular if you could tell us the core in a capsule about what you view as Fairbairn's contribution? What can we learn, in your view, from Fairbairn?

Scharff: The great thing about the object relations school is it really isn't a school. It's a bunch of analysts who have been grouped together—retrospectively almost—as all being interested in the same thing: namely, the process of analysis, the way that it moves between the analyst and the patient, and how it re-creates aspects of the mother–infant relationship. These analysts were more preoccupied with the mother–infant relationship rather than with the mother–father or father–infant relationship. It's a limitation but that is what connects them as you look back. Would you agree, Otto?

Kernberg: I'm probably closest to you in this group. I'm not totally sure of this. In many ways we work together but you already pointed to a significant difference and maybe that's of interest here. Object-relationist approaches are a broad spectrum to begin with, that cuts across from Klein to Sullivan. It probably includes also some of French analysts—certainly André Green. André, you have been stressing the importance of an object relations perspective that Freud relatively neglected. I see the core of psychoanalysis as somewhat different. I see that the expression of impulses from the beginning of life on as directly connected with objects, and there is an inseparable fusion between drive derivatives and the maternal object. There is an investment in the basic dyadic structures that can be simplified as stating that all internalizations are at the minimum dyadic. An internalization—whether it's introjection or identification—is one of the relationship between self and object under the impact of affect or drive derivatives—I'm leaving this open for the time being. The development of intrapsychic life is marked by the gradual separation or rupture of this dyadic stage under the impact of an implicit, at first excluded, object, the father. So I objected to your saying "mother–infant" because in "mother–infant,"—as I'm sure André will agree with me, there is already the shadow of father, at least in mother's mind, influencing the mother–infant relationship.

Scharff: But that's where you're influenced by Kleinian thinking.

Kernberg: Not necessarily. The Kleinians were very close to what you're saying until the last ten years, when they again focused on oedipal issues. I am talking about the contemporary Kleinians, not the earlier generation. This basic concept, the mother–infant dyadic, gradually becomes fortified; it is the building block of ego, superego, and id. The drives are organized in the context of these structures, so there's no such thing as pure drives or pure affects. They are indissolubly linked with objects, and a destructive drive is indissolubly linked to the attack on that dyad. That's what the destructive drive is all about. That is for me the essence—that basic dyadic structure, influenced from the start by an outside third party, is the indissoluble place in which drive and defenses against the drives get organized. The Kleinians say they're not object-relationist because they're pure Kleinians. This is a political statement. In the same way, Jacobson and Mahler would not say that they are object-relation theorists. They would only confess that they are interested in Melanie Klein privately. But Mahler and Jacobson told me how much they were interested and influenced by Klein but would never say that publicly at the New York Psychoanalytic Society in their time.

The real big difference is whether you believe that to establish that relation is a core motivation of human behavior, or whether that relationship is dominated by the control of unconscious drives, libido, and aggression. I think that this is what divided the object relations school into two big groups. On the one hand, you have Klein, Jacobson, and Mahler. Winnicott straddles the middle although he's closer to them. On the other hand, you have Fairbairn, although he's the closest one to the others because clinically he sees the duality. Fairbairn theoretically rejects drives and practically always affirms them. There is a deep contradiction inside of Fairbairn in this regard, not necessarily a contradiction but a separation. But then you have Guntrip and Kohut and the intersubjectivists like Mitchell and Greenberg—although Greenberg is coming back—who reject drive theory. I don't know exactly where Greenberg stands now. All those accept an object-relationist approach in contrast to drives. As I put it in my paper, this is a crucial issue: to what extent this involves the core of psychoanalysis or not. It seems to me that the drive theory is a core concept that permits object relations and non–object relations schools to evolve, and that the object relations school is divided between those who reject drives and those who accept them. History will show. For me, object relations theory has been a fundamental contribution to psychoanalysis, a major bridge bringing together ego psychologists, independents, Kleinians, and potentially also the contemporary French psychoanalytic school. Lacan was not an object relations theorist. He was almost the opposite. Lacan, as I put it in my paper, ironically was a two-person psychologist, meaning that two persons independently have their unconscious being stirred up in the analytic session. He denied the analysis of transference. Therefore, he totally ignored character analysis, and that was a weakness of French psychoanalysis. André Green pointed that out in his most recent book.[33] I was very pleased to see that.

---

33. Green, A. (2003). *Diachrony in Psychoanalysis*. New York: Free Association Books.

Object relations theory is an integrative frame that has wonderful technical implications that cut across the healthiest patients and the sickest patients. It permits us to put different techniques together, and there lies it's great value. When I study people who adhere to object relations theory while rejecting drive theory, there is in their approach a tendency to deny the negative transference, to deny the importance of sexuality—not necessarily, but there's a certain tendency that you don't find in those who maintain drive theory. While there is disagreement about the role of drives, there is a common emphasis on the original dyad—the indissoluble, basic nature of dyadic internalizations, on the assumption that subjectivity arises out of this intersubjectivity. That seems to me important. Stern and all those who have rejected, rightly so in my opinion, the autistic state of development and the symbiotic stage of development of Margaret Mahler—I very much agree with them. I don't think there's a symbiotic stage of development. There's a sharp differentiation between self and nonself under conditions of relative low affect. Under conditions of intense affect activation by the mechanisms of projection and introjection, I think that such intersubjectivity becomes the very core of what is the psychic apparatus. Symbiotic experience and the basic matrix of undifferentiated self-object representations are not a stage of development, and do not deny the capacity of sharp differentiation between self and object under other circumstances from birth on.

Neubauer: I'd like to ask you a question. You spoke about Jacobson and Mahler. For me one of the significant contributions of Mahler is that she doesn't just speak of attachment and interrelationship of the object. She speaks of the equally significant need for autonomy, for the reaching independence and individuation. This is left out of the usual discussion when one speaks about object interaction—that in it, on top of the object interaction and the duality, there is also the internal quest for the differentiation and individuation. This cannot be reduced to the matrix of mother–child interaction. But there are additional factors involved, psychic factors that demand that the individual emerge within its own possibilities and frame of reference that counteract somewhat an attachment to the object, which seems not to permit the right to autonomous development. Mahler spoke about separation and individuation steps. She did not speak about attachment steps, because she recognized that there is an additional step that has to be taken side by side with the object interaction. There's also a question about the primacy of the duality. You think of infant development—it is amazing how early infants have differentiated relationships to different objects. In our studies and our research there is always the mother and the baby. It is never the father and the baby, or the uncle of the baby, or the brother of the baby. It is always reduced to one interactive system, which I don't think does justice to the complexity of demands of the infant. Look at the diversity of differentiation—continue a search for it. We have to include the urge for differentiation and autonomy in our deliberations.

Kernberg: You're absolutely right. This is really important.

Ostow: Autonomy is an important root of dissidence. I think Peter's point is very important in this conference.

Scharff: Fairbairn could not agree that the infant was born with undifferentiated drives toward sexuality or aggression. He felt that the infant was born with a pristine ego, and then in the course of development—meeting frustrating experiences that challenge the ego—the infant would have to develop psychic structures to cope with these frustrations and delays that were necessary. He assumes a driving force for internalization and the creation of psychic structure. Once the object was internalized, the ego then acted upon it, dividing it into a couple of categories that basically might be good or bad. What has been useful to me from Fairbairn was that he saw that a part of the ego had to be split off and repressed along with the affect pertaining to the exciting or rejecting element of the object. So that in unconscious areas of the mind these are objects, parts of the ego, and the affects that connect the ego to the repressed split-off part/object. Now all of these parts of the self are in dynamic relationship. The healthier person has less need of repressing parts of the object or parts of the self. So there is more of the central self available for interaction and for learning from new experience and therefore for having the more repressed areas benefit from, and be modified in the light of, experience.

I have found Fairbairn's way of thinking helpful because since he offers this view of the self as a dynamic system, it's a simple step then to see one person communicating through introjection and projection with another, particularly in marriage and family. It helps you to see how a family group will identify with a repressed, internal object relationship and project it into one of its members and scapegoat him or her. Often, the adolescent will become the exciting object the family members are longing for by rejecting them or teasing them with burgeoning sexuality, playing with the risks of drug taking or whatever. Here is where I feel I'm often viewed as a dissident from the analytic mainstream: Not all my colleagues think analysts should be working with families and couples. But if you work with a couple that has a sexual problem, for instance, it's very helpful to think in terms of how the partners view each other as an ideal object, an exciting object, a rejecting object. Those very objects, I have found, are projected not just into the self or into the partner but into genital parts of the body. Breasts can become a rejecting object. The genitals can become a rejecting object, rejecting not only to the partner but to the self and the self's wish for a sexual pleasure fulfillment and an enduring bond.

I'm sure I could go on about why Fairbairn appeals to me, but there are also reasons that he does not: One is the need to internalize bad object experience as the way to cope with it. Fairbairn is weak on how we deal with good experiences. Yes, there's the satisfactory object inside the self but how does it get there if it isn't introjected? The drive to be autonomous and the drive to be in a relationship are in balance all the time, supported, it is hoped, by the parents, family group, extended family.

Green: I want to classify two categories of theory. On one side we have the theories that focus on drives and ego—ego psychology, self psychology, and Lacan's theory, which I would call the theory of the signifier. This is one group. The other group is opposite and implies a relationship to something else, object relationships, with all the varieties Otto described; included also is attachment theory, which implies the object to which babies attach, and the intersubjective. The first group implies two subjects; Lacanian theory is one of them—it contains the theory of "the other," the relationship to the other. With these two groups of theory, we can see that one group is ego- or self-centered, and the other is centered on the non-ego—nonself, whether it's the object, whether it's attachment to an object, the relational, intersubjective. This is a great split in psychoanalysis—the theories that bring to the fore relations to something else, an object, a person, or those that are, I would say, ego- or drive- or self-centered, implying that the not-me will come in the relationship after a certain while. We have to discuss the difference between the object relationship theory and the subjective theory. What is the difference between an object and a subject? Whether you think of Fairbairn or Melanie Klein, it is misleading how these people can talk about intersubjectivity without taking pains to define what the subject is.

Kernberg: André, you mentioned this already last night. Would you expand a little on what you see as the issue of the theory of *"le sujet"*—the subject in psychoanalysis?

Green: Very difficult question because if you take the dictionary of the Academie Française, when you look up "object" and when you look up "subject," they're exactly the same formulation—in French at least. I don't know if this holds in English. The object is something that is taken as a not-me. As for the subject, one can say there can only be a subject for another subject. If I consider

Otto Kernberg—Otto Kernberg for me is a subject and only a subject can think of another subject. We have all kinds of objects. We have the object of the fantasy, object in reality. I've written a paper in which you see that the conception of the object includes seven or eight meanings, and there is no conception unifying the object.

When you deal with the term *subject*, the subject will always have to do with the most sophisticated levels of actions of the person—his intentions. If you speak of the intentionality, you must imply a subject. So the subject is really more than an ego and more than a self. It has to be endowed with intelligence, and in my conception the subject is the combination of all types of representations, which are within the self. Lacan, using Freud's idea, the splitting of the ego, said, "No, it's not the splitting of the ego. It's the splitting of the subject." What he meant, of course, is that you cannot rely on something, which is a totality. Even the ego is split. I think the idea is that the subject is split—split in contradictions within himself because of inner conflict. It's split because of the mechanism of splitting. When I try to listen to a patient, I don't try to ask, What is his ego saying? What is the subject saying? What does he want? What does he want from me? Ego/object, subject/other—not self/other because self is always the person. For instance, Lacan would say there is a subject of the unconscious. This is a point of disagreement with Otto. But the subject of the unconscious is to try to find out who is doing what to whom, unconsciously. Apart from Lacan, nobody gave us a theory of the subject. The subject lacks a theory.

Blum: Okay, like everyone else we're digesting a great deal. I wonder, André, if you also consider Lacan a theoretician who was antitheory? Sometimes when I read Lacan, I get the impression—not good or bad necessarily; you can react to it either way—of someone who really is antitheory and destroys theories as well as builds theories. He plays games with ideas.

Green: He plays games for sure. Lacan being anti anything is also something to consider, but the true question is Lacan being anti-total. Anything that aims at bringing the total picture of anything he is radically opposed to by definition.

Blum: In addition to the different forms of theory we might consider different levels of theory: theories that are more or less experienced near or experienced distant, theories that are more clinical theories, theories that are more or less abstract, theories that are the highest level of metapsychology but very distanced from the clinical experience, and theories that are public versus theories that are private. The analyst may espouse one theory publicly, but the way the analyst works entails incorporating several different aspects of theory without being necessarily fully aware of it. And then theories have to be looked at in terms of whether they're internally consistent and whether they're used consistently. To add a little more spice to the discussion with Jill, Guntrip took elaborate notes, apparently after each session with Fairbairn, and he wrote them up.

Green: They had discussions after their session.

Blum: They had discussions, apparently less than appeared as Guntrip later wrote in his psychoanalytic autobiography. But he took extensive notes of his treatment with Fairbairn, apparently after each session. He took notes of his treatment with Winnicott after the sessions with Winnicott. With respect to diversity, consistency, contradiction, separation, and a variety of other issues, let me read this from Guntrip. I think it will add a little spice to the discussion.

Guntrip[34] is referring here to the interpretations that he received from Fairbairn. "His conservatism slowly pushed through into his work." Guntrip meant above all interpretations framed in terms of castration anxiety and incestuous wishes—more specifically, the penis. During the three hundred sessions—Guntrip numbered each session—Guntrip is saying, "Maybe as a small boy, I could never grow as big as father. Father is a being of a different order." Fairbairn quickly interpreted: "You felt forbidden to have a penis of your own. It's not for little boys to have a penis and be sexual." This is one of the points where Guntrip feels that Fairbairn's consistent reiteration of interpretation in terms of penises was a survival of classical Freudian sexology and that his theory had moved beyond his own interpretation. Guntrip continues: "I felt that kept me stationary whereas interpretations in terms of the penis ultimately standing for the whole personality which my mother [Guntrip's mother] did her best to restrict and dominate, would have been much more realistic." In effect, his analysis, that is, Fairbairn's analysis of Guntrip, was a penis analysis not an ego analysis. Then in session 512, a couple of years later, Fainbairn behaved as if he were heeding the analysand's retrospective advice. "Castration, Fairbairn remarked, was really symbolic of a total personality situation and related to fears of loss of individuality and personality."

I hope we can have time to discuss the difference among the schools—the different theoreticians within this so-called object relations school because it's not appropriate to call this a school as if it's homogeneous. In fact they're very

---

34. Guntrip, H. (1975). My experience of analysis with Fairbairn and Winnicott. *International Review of Psychoanalysis* 2:145–156.

heterogeneous, and Winnicott is very different, as one would hear from Guntrip's analysis with Winnicott. Very different from Fairbairn.

Kernberg: In all fairness, I wonder whether Guntrip is presenting Fairbairn accurately. When you read Fairbairn, there is a subtlety that is denied in Guntrip's writing.

Scharff: What Harold read from Guntrip is a perfect example of splitting: Guntrip focused everything on the penis. Fairbairn himself had a urinary phobia so he may have been connected to his own penis and whatever destruction it could do. In that piece of writing, Guntrip, while complaining about the overemphasis on the penis, is actually saying that Fairbairn dominated his analysis with his regressive conservatism, just like his mother dominated his own life.

Blum: There's certainly a question of distortion. But I also wanted to bring up the effect of these theoreticians on each other. In other words, to what degree did Guntrip influence Fairbairn?

Scharff: He did. Fairbairn enjoyed working with Guntrip. He thought he learned a lot from him. I'm sure they had kind of an intellectual dance at the end of every session, which must have wreaked havoc with the transference. He did accept Guntrip's modification of including the even more split-off and repressed part of the ego in schizoid personalities, and he was certainly influenced theoretically. You mentioned Guntrip's analysis with Winnicott, which he presented as much more satisfactory than the one with Fairbairn. Guntrip's account can be seen as more evidence of his splitting. But the whole point of the story was that he really didn't get better until after both analysts were dead and he tried to cure himself, based on the work he'd done formerly, certainly, but the great realization came once he was on his own.

Blum: He wanted to claim and promote that it was only after Winnicott's death that the great revelation came. All such memoirs probably have a self-serving component in some degree. The subtleties, anxieties, and satisfactions of mutual influence and autonomous innovation are congealed, requiring analytic and historical reconstruction.

Scharff: But he isn't quite fair. Guntrip did say that Fairbairn was radical in his theory and highly intellectual and conservative. Whereas Winnicott, he thought, was conservative in his theory, because he wouldn't admit how different he was from Freud, but radical in his proceeding.

Green: Fairbairn used to analyze his patients from above the couch.

Scharff: Actually, he had the patients, I think, at a right angle to his chair.

Blum: The location, the setting is meticulously described by Guntrip.

Grossman: Guntrip's analysis brings up an important point. He is one of those people who is reporting his own case. The interesting thing about it, to my way of thinking, at least, is that none of the people who do this ever take another step and say, "Now everything I've been saying is about my transference and now I have to think about what is the meaning of this as my transference." They don't do that. They essentially say, "I have the last word. The analysts are dead. They're not responding. After them, it's me." I don't know the dynamics exactly—an intrinsic problem in the processing of our understanding of how people evolve their opinions and how they evaluate their analysis. It seems to me that it can be discussed because we see features of it not only in individual accounts of personal history but also in terms of the way history is presented in terms of personal accounts. It is the nature of the thinking in our field as analysts, as patients, as historians of the field—and we can't escape it. Material like this needs to be examined but not as evidence of what it purports to be evidence of.

Scharff: If you put together a person's theories alongside their biography, you get some insight into the transferences that have driven the innovations.

Young-Bruehl: Let me note one of the things that has interestingly disappeared, or is interestingly missing from André Green's discussion of the subject. When I was a philosophy student and listened to endless discussions about the subject—a long list of what the subject is, motivation, intentionality, etc.— the thing that was usually missing from the list was self-consciousness. The way Peter Neubauer develops it is interesting, but I think so far we've had a not very elaborate or particularly rich understanding of the self-consciousness with which people generate theories. Psychobiography has been within the field the way to understand the relationship between the person and the theory. But that's of course the psychobiographer making the connection. In many instances, it's a very rich literature. But the autobiographical literature or the self-reflexive literature about the relationship between the self or the subject, and no theory he or she creates is very scant and interestingly enough, is a literature that began right in the object relations traditions—the "report on my analysis" as though that were the place to study the cultivation of self-consciousness.

Bergmann: Just for the record, Elisabeth is referring to Bill Grossman.

Young-Bruehl: Yes, Bill Grossman. We have some indications of how some people can think about the context of how their theory emerged—"I distinguished myself from Fairbairn in this way and I distinguished myself from Freud in that way"—a relational context. But what's not in the literature is much self-consciousness that goes along on this level: "I understand that I am a narcissist and so, of course, my theory is going to reflect that characterological foundations in my self. It's going to be a narcissistic sounding theory and it's also going to be a theory that will be most applicable to narcissistic personality disorders. I may not be one; I may be a more sedate version of narcissism and there may be a more florid one, but we will be, so to speak, on the same page. My theory is narcissistically grounded, as their theories are narcissistically constructed." That level of self-consciousness would be the precondition for theoretical plurality as opposed to aggression. People who are involved in a pluralistic discussion would need to say not only, "There is this theory and this one is mine and this one is yours," but also, "This one is mine and it makes it more difficult for me to understand your theory because it's grounded in this way and it restricts me in this way or it reflects me in this other way." That level of discussion, which would also have been a discussion leading to self-consciousness, is almost missing. The field is at a moment where it can sustain that kind of self-consciousness because it has stopped being so constrained by the dissidence per se. But the object relations tradition may very well be the tradition out of which such a move forward comes because of what it is preoccupied with—awareness of our own subjectivity.

Grossman: Actually Freud made a comment. I think it was in 1912 in one of the technique papers.[35] He calls it internal resistances to the recognition of parts of one's own unconscious, but he talks about it unfortunately in terms of resistance, which always seems to me contaminates it. But he says at that point that if this is the case, if the analyst has some resistance to accepting or recognizing products of his own unconscious, he's likely to project these out as a general theory. I forget exactly the words he used but that was essentially the idea: that it's out of this kind of experience, the failure to recognize the source and the significance, that then gets projected as a general theory about the external world. [Editor's note: Freud (1912b) said, "Any one who has scorned to take the precaution of being analyzed himself will not merely be punished by being incapable of learning more than a certain amount from his patients,

---

35. Freud, S. (1912a). The dynamics of transference. *Standard Edition* 12, p. 103.

he will risk a more serious danger and one that may become a danger to others. He will easily fall into the temptation of projecting outwards some of the peculiarities of his own personality, which he has dimly perceived, into the field of science, as a theory having universal validity" (p. 117).][36]

Young-Bruehl: Freud was interested in just this question at the end of his life. A place where it's most impressive to me is in the little essay on libidinal types, where he's delineating the erotic, the narcissistic, and the obsessional types. He makes a side comment that "on the strength of this type one would scarcely have arrived at the hypothesis of the superego (p. 218).[37] This is an autobiographical remark. He is saying, "It took me a long time to come up with a notion of the superego because I couldn't really feature another self in myself, or I couldn't really feature another voice inside myself." But it's at that level of self-reflection about the characterological inhibitions of one theorizing or the characterological strengths of theorizing that the superego can be discovered.

Neubauer: You speak of self-consciousness, you just said self-reflection. There are perceptions of oneself, or the knowing about myself and reflection about it.

Young-Bruehl: You're coming to a very knotty philosophical question, which is the whole last part of the *Critique of Pure Reason*.[38] I'm not sure that we can ever expect to have just knowledge in a static way. What we do have is a self-perception about ourselves, usually in relationship to other people; you say, "I'm not like that." You distinguish yourself characterologically or in terms of your psychic formation from another person. You have the experience here all the time. "Well, I don't think like that. That's interesting. I would never have formulated it that way. I would never have come up with that particular idea," and then the next question is, "Why not?" Why wouldn't I have thought that way or why would that person have thought that. On that level, you have room to grow because there is not so much narcissistic investment in your own theory, your own vision.

Kernberg: I wanted to point to something that Jill said before we change the subject. I think that Jill very beautifully described Fairbairn's theory about

---

36. Freud, S. (1912b). Recommendations to physicians practicing psychoanalysis. *Standard Edition* 12, p. 117.

37. ———— (1931). Libidinal types. *Standard Edition* 21, pp. 215–220.

38. Kant, E. (1781). *The Critique of Pure Reason*.

the origin of the dyadic relationship and the internalization of the parental object that is split. It brings me back to something we discussed last night in the sense that very often a theoretician describes something crucial, but then tries to trace it back to the beginning of life, before we have any evidence, and this then creates dissidence because it creates the illusion—which is a cultural illusion of psychoanalysts—that that which comes first is the most important. This is a funny theoretical bias. If we leave aside Fairbairn's idea about sequence of development, his description of mental structure is the most clear and convincing analysis of the relationship between internalization of object relations and the structural theory, and it has practical implications for technique. Unconscious fantasy can be translated structurally in the affective or impulsive relation between self and other. When he says a piece of ego goes along with the object representation, that piece of ego is really a self representation. Fairbairn didn't use the term *self*; he used the term *ego* all the time. So if we leave aside origin, Fairbairn's structure and Jacobson's are compatible, but not when we talk about the origin of the structures.

We have a problem of semantics, a problem in psychoanalysis in general. André Green defined beautifully ego, self, and subject. Perhaps there should be more of an effort to spell out what's the difference between self and self representation. André said self is the personality. Well, that's a different definition of self as integration of the self-concept, which speaks to subjectivity. And certainly there is a difference between self and ego. But what he calls *"le sujet,"* the subject, is really involved in the concept of self with the object relations theory.

Green: In French there is the verb *assujetir*, for example, the subjects are *assujetis* to the law. *Assujetir* means subjected, which makes a difference between self and subject. *Les sujets* are the people of His Majesty.

Kernberg: When you use the term *object*, you refer to two things. Object is another person and object is the object of libidinal interest—of libidinal investment. But in French, there's one word for it. In Spanish, there are two words. There is *el objeto y el objetivo*. In English, there is again only one word. Language is important.

Green: In French we have two words: *objectal* and *objectif*.

Kernberg: Those are not nouns. In Spanish you have two nouns that separate that, so that the kind of misunderstanding that happens in French and English doesn't happen in Spanish. On the other hand, in English, because of the terrible translation of the *Standard Edition*, we use *instinct*. And even you,

André, when you talk English, you talk about death instinct, where theoretically you should always talk about death drive.

Green: Yes, you are right.

Kernberg: We all do it. But it's a problem because psychoanalysis has no instinct theory—it has a drive theory. And that has created misunderstandings. So we need some translation that respects the constraints of our concepts given by one or another language.

Bergmann: It's a pleasure to listen to all of that but I would like to change the direction of our discussion and raise a different question. First about Guntrip, I can testify that his two analyses are an extremely good subject in teaching. I have taught it a number of times and it always generates a lively discussion because it has in it the deeply personal and at the same time the general, and the question always is left over: How much of the superiority that he attributes to Winnicott over Fairbairn is the superiority of theory or the difference in the accessibility of two human beings?

When I read your paper, Jill, the following statement struck me: "Pleasure seeking is entirely secondary to the main role of securing attachment and survival. Aggression does not result from the death instinct but from fear when the child is unprotected" (p. 11). When I read that, I suddenly realized what Nietzsche meant by "the eternal return," because these questions come and go and appear again, and the question that interests me is whether a sentence like that can ever be subjected to any kind of empirical study or whether those are ultimately some basic ideas over which we ourselves have relatively little control. I was struck also by the fact that you found Fairbairn helpful. We all have in our biography certain articles that were particularly helpful to us at certain times. In my case, it was Ernst Kris's (1956) paper on the good hour,[39] because when I read it, I said to myself; as an analyst, you cannot bring about the good session, but by God you can do an awful lot to spoil it. So I built up a whole educational theory in terms of what can the analyst do to maximize the possibility of the good session. In 1956 that was a very important paper for me, just as for you Fairbairn was important. Any reading is in some way connected with where we are and what we are searching for. And of course, anybody who comes to our assistance at a certain point in our development and helps us out of a dilemma, we will remain

---

39. Kris, E. (1956). On the vicissitudes of insight in the course of psychoanalysis. In *The Selected Papers of Ernst Kris*, pp. 252–271. New Haven, CT: Yale University Press, 1975.

particularly grateful to him or her. Each one of us has his or her list of papers or books that were particularly important at a given time.

As to your statement, Jill, I ask myself whether there ever will be a time when there will be an objective answer to the question of whether we are plea-sure seekers or safety seekers, whether this question will ever be answered with a yes or no, or whether we have to say to ourselves certain questions are and will be unanswerable. And the same question comes up whether the death instinct is inborn or whether it is a result of frustration or fear? I would like some discussion on the subject whether we do believe that eventually empiri-cal data will answer the questions we raised or are we dealing with a subject where even in the long stretch, empirical data are going to leave us in doubt or forever dependent on irrational aspects of ourselves. This is a personal pre-occupation of mine but it was an important reason why I asked for this sym-posium. I would like some discussion on that.

Scharff: That's not my belief. That is a description of Bowlby.

Bergmann: But you brought it up with approval.

Scharff: Well I was asked to present Fairbairn and the object relations theo-rists, so I did that. Bowlby's position about the child's primary need for at-tachment is, to me, obvious. Without that, the child dies. It's a necessary condition within which other necessary interactions occur for the creation of psychic structure.

Green: Primal attachment could not be automatic.

Scharff: I think it is—absolutely fundamental, supported by instincts of cry-ing and smiling and so on.

Kernberg: We are touching here a fundamental question. For me, the dual drive theory is Freud's final theory. The basic motivational forces that determine the organization of the psychic apparatus for me are libido and aggression. Under certain conditions, aggression can be become so dominant and develop in such a pathological way that it justifies the concept of the death drive as a dominant motivation in certain individuals and that is of enormous importance, clinically. The most fundamental drives of Freud may not be inborn, as I have suggested, and I'm not alone anymore. I used to be. We have solid evidence of genetically determined, inborn, complex structures that we call affects that have cognitive elements, subjective elements, behavioral elements, neurovegetative elements, and expressive-communicative elements; they come in two packages. One is going to be integrated eventually as libido, and the aversive one is going to be integrated eventually as aggression. Affect theory is a potential that comes from other areas of discourse—not from psychoanalysis—but is potentially a bridge between neurobiology and psychoanalysis. There are other bridges. Cognitive developments lead to representation and consciousness. Basic feedback mechanisms may lead to reflectiveness. There are three bridges from which I believe we can get answers to the problem of origins. But those don't tell about psychic structures. There psychoanalysis comes in. It's equally problematic, for me, to look for purely psychic origins as it is to derive psychic structure from what we know about neurobiology. Freud wisely separated these areas, but at the same time, the way he did it and the way he hooked up drives to the body no longer needs to be accepted.

Green: I'd like to come back to the idea of attachment and the drives. I'm very happy to hear that you consider attachment as a manifestation of drives. I have said many times during this meeting that if I refer to drives, it doesn't mean that I refer to the classical, orthodox definition. What I consider as drives are primitive structure, and, as Otto reminded us, in which the characteristic element is force. These forces, as Freud said, are not influenced by reason. They escape the influence of reason. The question of discharge, to which you, Otto, refer many times in your paper, is not so important for me. What is important for me is that they call for satisfaction. Here is also a discrepancy and maybe a way of finding a bridge. What is object seeking? The object that is sought because it is the object that can bring satisfaction.

Scharff: What is satisfaction?

Green: What is satisfaction? Are you hungry?

Scharff: Well, that would be only one.

Green: I'm starting from the most basic. Satisfaction is what brings relief from unpleasure and provides pleasure. When you say pleasure, you have to extend the meaning of pleasure not only to the basic needs but also to the pleasure of seeing my friends, the pleasure of looking at you, the pleasure of being in New York. Pleasure is what makes life enjoyable. If you have no pleasure, then you have no reason to live.

Scharff: That brings it very close to the object relations point of view, where there is drive not just for physical satisfaction, pleasure, and enjoyment, but a drive to find a meaning in existence, an awareness of one's own identity.

Green: I agree! The pleasure of being connected to an object is not denied by me. Of course! But I am not sure, to come back to what Otto said, that objects and the ego exist from the beginning. Winnicott never said that. Winnicott supposed some primitive fusion and the progressive differentiation of the object from the ego. In the posthumously published outline, Freud observes that it is interesting that in the beginning we see the effects of the drives and also the reaction contrary to them; only later do the two become distinct. It is not possible to disassociate the primitive drive from the defense raised against it. You have it as one block. And if you take, for instance, the model of charac-ter—the character as the result of the fixations, of the reaction formations, and of sublimations—you have here a new model of the drive that can include the drive manifestation itself, the defense against it, reaction formation, and some kind of very elementary sublimation. I prefer to see drives today this way because it has not this biological background, which gives rise to many com-plaints. I prefer the word *force*; I never use the word *motivation*.

Kernberg: Would you like to explain why you think motivation is for rats and not for humans?

Green: Because if I fall in love with Otto, which can happen, it is not a moti-vation. Love is not a motivation. Love is like an inner urge. It is a complex intention. *Motivation* is the word that is used in the laboratory to understand what animals do—how you motivate animals to do this or that. They go into the labyrinth in order to find the bit of cheese. But motivation is not an ap-propriate word for studying what is meaning for humans. I say that attach-ment theory is wrong. Why? Because I don't think that the baby is attached to the mother. I don't think that the mother is attached to the baby. I think they are in love with each other. And being in love is not to be attached.

Ostow: Why not?

Green: Because the most elementary experience in your life, if you remem-ber when you fell in love at 18, is not the same as saying that you have been attached to this girl. *Attached* is a weak word. Would you say that Romeo is attached to Juliet?

Ostow: Yes.

Green: I wouldn't. I say Romeo is attached to Tybalt. He is attached to many people, but he is in love with one person—Juliet. To be in love—and this is very essential because motivation means that it can be reasonably explained. Love cannot.

Kernberg: No, in English, the word *motivation*, in the literature, is used as a force that moves toward doing, wishing, willing, whatever one wishes, whatever one wants to change. Perhaps in French it is linked with rats but there exists an entire literature on what moves human beings outside of psychoanalysis. I don't know any other term.

Grossman: It's the most general wastebasket.

Green: I don't think we should waste time on that. About love, there is an element of madness, which is not in attachment.

Bergmann: We should stop now. There are some urgent issues to discuss around André's paper (Chapter 2, this volume). I would also like to raise some issues connected with your paper, Elisabeth. So I think if you all agree, we will have now a working lunch, a short break, and then we will resume around 3 or 3:30.

(Break for lunch)

Kris: There's one more point I would like to respond to. Otto Kernberg tried to show in his paper that cultural shifts affect what goes on in the analytic world. He speaks of the recent interest of psychoanalysts in the neurosciences. I confess that I am not as optimistic about that new interest being the great reward ahead of us. The rejoicing is premature. It is a flight from psychoanalysis because so many analysts are disappointed in psychoanalysis, and therefore they reach for another God. I was struck by the emphasis on recasting a wide net—"We include this; we include that." Then I read the end of Jill's paper and it's exactly the same, that is, she's speaking about "We now include this and this and this" and all these child observations—wonderful self-regulating, self-renewing, and self-transforming self ideas. We are in a phase where the right thing to be is ecumenical, and cast one's net even broader and wider than Freud did. I'm a curmudgeon and I perhaps am emboldened to take my position because André Green is nearby, and even though he casts a pretty wide net, he also has a view that ultimately psychoanalysis is more limited. He starts with the drives and I start with free association.

Green: I also start with free association.

Kris: There you have it. I don't think we're very far apart on that, but for me the center of analysis is what you can learn in the analytic situation; I need—and you will forgive the English word—a motivation as part of my theory. But I don't care whether it's the drive concept. We have the somewhat paradoxical situation of including everything in psychoanalysis today and being unable to really stay with the center. Now all this was motivated for me and stimulated for me by Martin's question: "What will the future do? Will there be a confirmation of some of these ideas? Will it be possible on the basis of some evidence to discriminate?" I want to offer this provisional answer: yes. We have evidence already that many theories have been modified or eliminated on the basis of new evidence. The empirical evidence about the development of the child, the baby, simply doesn't permit the tabula rasa notion that we started with, that Freud started with.

The same thing can be said of psychoanalysis and psychotherapy. In the 1950s there was the great absolute division between psychoanalysis and psychotherapy. It was a fundamental error. I'm very pleased that Bob Wallerstein agreed with me when I pointed this out in a book in his honor—that the false distinction was between psychoanalysis that was an exploration and psychotherapy that was supportive. Whereas psychoanalysis is the most supportive of all treatments but the ultimate questions is, Is it exploratory or is it suppressive? We don't think today about psychoanalysis and psychotherapy the way we did half a century ago. Jill Scharff points out that she actually works with couples. Yes, but the fact is that many analysts not only work with couples but take it for granted that couples therapy is compatible with analysis, to have the analysand in couple's therapy at the same time. Morty Ostow's use of medication is another example. I know how hard it was for me even to get to use medication. I had a number of steps to get over, but what I'm getting at is that I do believe empirical observation, accumulated evidence will be able to differentiate between some theoretical formulations and others. To the extent that there is anything like psychoanalysis half a century from now, uncertainty must be part of it or it will be dissidence.

Neubauer: Tony, can I ask you, maybe I'm very old fashioned when I think this way, when we speak about psychoanalysis, where it fails and doesn't fail, the drive concept in psychoanalysis is a tool of investigation. Is the drive concept really our favorite way of proceeding? Analysis is a theory of the mind and analysis is a technique of intervention. Most of us emphasize understanding the patients. Understanding the patients and the means to intervene are two different issues. We cannot just say, "The analyst's role in connection with the patient is to understand what goes on, listen to it without any intention of translating this understanding into a component of change." And there may be our problem. When we speak about the history of analysis and the dissenters, in which area was there dissent? Was the dissent in the area of understanding the mind? André Green says, "I want to start with the core component—what I consider to be there—as a basis for my discussion." Did others interfere with the capacity to listen in order to find modes of intervention? For instance, the theory—and you mentioned it, Tony—the psychoanalytic theory of development is a very special, basic component to understand psychoanalysis. Why? Because Freud in certain aspects very early linked the normal stages of development to the pathology. He made an incredible statement from a viewpoint of medicine or psychology by making that link. That link is how we see the psychoanalytic theory of development, not only as Otto said, very much the beginning as if this were the baseline, but also as the components of transformation from period to period, and not just up to the oedipal one but continuing in all subsequent developments.

When we discuss where we are in connection with different dissensions, I wish we would pin it down in more detail, into various components of it, in which we may be in agreement and those places where we may really fall apart in disagreement. Narcissism was a theory of the mind and an intervention at the same time. When we go to other issues, there may be much more a question of how to understand the origins of psychic life and therefore interpretations.

Blum: The way history is written is always a matter of interpretation. It would have been a different conference had we had as topics the evolution of psychoanalytic thought, or transformations in psychoanalytic theory, or differences in technique among psychoanalysts. The term *dissidence* is hardly neutral. The language here has its own special connotation. Even the word *divergence* has a different connotation than *dissidence*. Perhaps this issue is also related, Martin, to your concerns about how exercised everyone has become about the term *dissident*. We have to understand more about why we tended to view theoretical divergence as dissidence. Bowlby may be a particular point of entry into this overall discussion because he was treated as such in the 1960 *Psychoanalytic Study of the Child*,[40] where he introduced his ideas. There are responses from Anna Freud and Max Schur. Various responses continued over the next several years and some of the responses were particularly vehement, Max's was much more so than Anna Freud's. The limitations and constructive innovations in Bowlby's thought are carefully considered in current psychoanalysis. Attachment perspectives are being integrated into our developmental

---

40. Bowlby, J. (1960). Grief and mourning in infancy and early childhood. *Psychoanalytic Study of the Child* 15:9–52. New York: International Universities Press.

theory, an example of a dissident's ideas retrospectively reintegrated as a contribution.

Kris: Anna Freud was very measured. Max Schur was over the top, irate.

Blum: Anna Freud, as you know, could be also a guardian of the gate.

Kris: But she did not publicly talk that way.

Blum: No, she didn't publicly talk that way but there was this dismissive reaction, rather than a more dispassionate consideration of the points of view, agreement and disagreement. There were cogent reasons for not uncritically accepting attachment theory on the part of those who dissented from Bowlby. However, what Bowlby might be contributing, what his ideas were, what his reasons for bringing up his different point of view, his attempts to devalue and really eliminate drive theory and introduce his own theory—I think all of that could have been debated in a much more dispassionate, calm, tranquil fashion. Open and respectful debate would have allowed a real dialogue to emerge in a way that was not possible at the time. Here today we have that calm, but unfortunately in the analytic community we have what Peter Neubauer and Tony Kris were bringing up—we have not only ecumenicism, we have eclecticism. Instead of theoretical pluralism with awareness and investigation of differences, we have theoretical splitting, fusion, and confusion. We have a kind of fragmentation or dissolution of psychoanalysis with all kinds of burgeoning theories and "every flower should blossom." Every theory can be viewed as potentially valid or equally valid. And that's a danger on the other side of monolithic orthodoxy.

Bowlby is a very interesting question—the whole question of the prevalence, the popularity of attachment theory at this time is very important. Our reaction now to the potential fragmentation of psychoanalysis includes what Tony brought up about neuroscience. Though neuroscience can enrich psychoanalysis, it can be not only a flight from analysis, but also the enactment of a rescue fantasy. There is a fantasy and hope that neuroscience is going to rescue psychoanalysis. And I think that the issue of rescue when there's insecurity, when there's uncertainty, when there's a great deal of underlying anxiety, is an important issue in the whole history of dissidence. But still, I would particularly like to have your points of view, since you brought up Bowlby, about what we can learn from him and also the treatment of Bowlby, then and now.

Scharff: To me, he was interesting in that he took an ethological point of view and he compared the human young with the young of other species and found that what was common to all young was that they required an object of attachment for security. And that they were all driven by instinctual behaviors such as crying, rooting, clinging, following, and smiling to connect with that person, to keep that person in a state of proximity for their own safety. He could prove that with his various research procedures. The problem with Bowlby was partly personality. He was extremely self-righteous. He felt what he thought was right and he had no hesitation telling people that their work was flawed or false.

Ostow: He was an analyst.

Scharff: Yes, he was an analyst. In his seminar he was quite abrasive. I think you could say the two are not mutually exclusive. Also he was quite contemptuous of the unconscious because it couldn't be proven.

Green: That was his great success.

Scharff: That really upset the analysts who had devoted their lives to working with that which can't be proved but which was so rich in the understanding that it brought to people. His work was really ignored except by people in the middle group, the object relations people I have mentioned. They were interested in Bowlby. Bowlby felt that he had taken his work from Fairbairn in particular, and he was trying to develop research methods to investigate Fairbairn's revision of Freud. They appreciated attachment research but they didn't develop it themselves and it didn't help them clinically.

It did not make a big impact clinically until it was picked up by women: Mary Main, Mary Ainsworth. I think the turning point came when they were able to show that adult attachment behaviors reflected earlier infant attachment style, particularly pointing out that the way an adult recollects childhood is characteristic for the type of attachment he or she had for the parent being discussed, revealed in lapses in communication, hesitations, and affective outpouring. These are things that an analyst is looking for and responding to as the harmonics to the music of the verbal output of the analytic patient. Fonagy has taken it a step further, being able to show how the mother's capacity to mentalize the child's experience has an effect on the security of attachment a child becomes capable of with her. (It's always specific to the one parent.) His research methodologies reduce extremely complex behaviors to a manageable amount to measure and comment on. What captured the imagination not just of analysts now but of psychotherapists, teachers, and child-developmentalists is that attachment research has the potential to carry forward analytic ideas, is not contemptuous of unconscious processes, and is relevant to clinical work.

Ostow: I want to state that attachment is an instinct. It behaves like an instinct. It's different from other instincts in one respect. Most instincts are phasic—the sexual instinct rises to a climax and then declines. The nutritional instinct rises to a climax and declines. The attachment instinct can be maintained over a long period of time. It does have to be refreshed but it's maintained—it's tonic, it's not phasic.

There are different kinds of pleasure, affective pleasure. Turndike talks here about pleasure as though it's a unitary thing. Pleasure is not unitary. There are many kinds of pleasure. If again we turn to neurobiology, we turn to the pleasures associated with instinctual gratification. There are several, to take the sexual pleasure as the paradigm: There's the pleasure of catching the eye of someone you're attracted to, the pleasure of temptation. There's the pleasure of the pursuit, which is a different pleasure. There's the pleasure of the gratification, which is a different pleasure. There's the pleasure of the detumescence relaxation after climax, which is a different pleasure. These are different sources of pleasure. Each instinct has that same distribution of different pleasures.

But there's a different kind of pleasure—completely different aside from those things. And that is the issue of mood regulation. Everybody spends most of his time trying to maintain a certain degree of equanimity, if not happiness, and trying to avoid distress. But there's a sense of pleasure associated with a good mood—it's not attached to any specific instinct that can be formulated. It can be reinforced by instinctual gratification. It can be destroyed by instinctual frustration, by threat. But the pleasure of the mood regulation, the overall mood, is uppermost in everybody's mind at every time. It's a different kind of pleasure. The death instinct is associated with the loss of composure, with the loss of self-control, with the fear of losing the feeling of composure and happiness.

Bergmann: I would like to enter this discussion along my own lines and to say sure, I know that attachment is important—the fact that you are all here to celebrate my birthday, I feel very thankful and very attached. But I think that psychoanalysis needs something else. What I think André Green is questioning, and I am inclined to agree with him, is the productivity of the concept. What can you do with it? Attachment is opposed to nonattachment—we need the kind of concepts that are helping us in terms of the struggle that we are engaged in. With all due respect to the attachment theory, I don't see how useful it is in our understanding and in our struggle with our patients and also with our basic philosophy. I don't question it, but I don't see its productivity and how to utilize it and I think that is really the issue: how useful is the concept.

Ostow: You relate attachment theory to separation anxiety?

Bergmann: Yes, sure. All of that is there, but it lacks something useful for me to attach to.

Ostow: Isn't separation anxiety useful in analysis?

Grossman: Peter Neubauer enunciated a very important principle that if we want to understand these things more, we have to break them down into their components and talk about the vicissitudes of the components. But he has a general principle of investigation—this is really what it's about. In a way, I disagree with Tony Kris because I think the idea that we should separate psychotherapy from analysis leads us to consider a certain number of components, and then we can begin to talk about what's relevant to what. I disagree with Harold Blum that neuroscience has the function of finding a rescuer because I think that the relationship is much more along the lines of what Peter is talking about. Why should we call attachment the motive? Why don't we talk about it as a desirable process that has components and that these components could be studied? If you know the work of Myron Hofer, for instance, who is a neurobiologist—Myron is well informed analytically but that's not his work. He works with rats and motivation and he has gradually broken down the attachment processes in baby rats, showing that what looks like an organized drive for attachment to the mother can be broken down into specific components that influence different features of the separation response. Those individual features are not motivated. They're part of an overall adaptive process. And yes, at some point, these things become operative along the same model in the mental life and that's where we come into it. And so your question about how useful is answerable to some extent. It may not be tremendously useful to know all of this to work in with your patient the next day but if you want a framework for thinking about these things, it's extremely useful because it gives you a way to organize the conception of what it is we're trying to do. And if we ask where is change going to come in analysis, it's partly from the fact that people will, out of their experience, generate different ways of dealing with patients as André described this morning—the whole idea that for certain types of people who react in a certain way to free association, you have to modify your stance on free association. This is part of the fractionating process that you have to go through. But you have to go through it at every level and that's what the organizing framework tells us—that at every level, this process of fractionating and the pursuit of the individual factors is what we have to do. And we have to know what level we're working at so that we don't pull concepts from one place into concepts of another place where they really don't fit. Neuroscience is important from that point of view because it also breaks down many functions that we know are synthesized in behavioral responses, in mental function, and it's in that way that we sharpen our perception of those mental functions that play a role in the analytic process. I don't think it's a rescue fantasy. I think it's a question of providing a new framework and conceptual methodology for thinking about problems that are very important to analysis and analytic theory.

Neubauer: One point about the attachment theory—not only about Bowlby but also Peter Fonagy. It violates my understanding of development because he reduces the proposition of relationship to the first years of life, and it's pattern is then echoing and reverberating all through life without the influence of the oedipal period, without latency, without the adolescence, without the capacity of the transformation of the attachment into various different objects and experiences, and then Fonagy says, "When I know what the mother does with the infant, I can tell you then whether the mother mentalizes. . . . I can predict then the outcome." It is so against everything we know; it violates our theory of development. And for me it does something else. When one studies the literature of identical twins separated at birth into different homes and sees after ten years, or fifteen years, or twenty years the outcome and sees in each area these identical twins—the reaction to the external world and in which areas they are influenced by the environment, then you will see disposition is a component which is a part of the interplay, not just the reaction to the mother. The attachment theory is a reductionistic theory, which cannot do justice to the complexity we are dealing with.

Blum: I want to respond to Bill. What Bill brought up was significant and he misunderstood me. I was not in any way saying, especially in the inclusive, thoughtful atmosphere of today's discussion, that we should exclude neuroscience or considerations of neuroscience. Neuroscience is very important and very valuable for psychoanalysis. I was referring to tendencies to go overboard and to make premature assumptions during our current attempts at building bridges between neuroscience and psychoanalysis. This kind of exuberance was related to rescue fantasies. The rational side of our interest in neuroscience is important. Neuroscience does hold out great promise for advancing psychoanalysis, and I also think the other way around. I think psychoanalysis has something to say to neuroscience and can be very helpful to neuroscientists. Tony wasn't objecting to neuroscientific research or to attempts at integration and for mutual interdisciplinary enrichment, but he was concerned about "going overboard" and viewing neuroscience as the answer that will solve our problems. No other discipline can solve our problems, internally within psychoanalysis and externally in terms of the loss of prestige of psychoanalysis in the general public. This is irrational and an exercise in futility.

Grossman: So it's a clinical judgment?

Blum: Not at all, a purely clinical judgment since it incorporates theoretical perspectives.

Kris: Peter Fonagy is a very good example. It's wonderful that he's doing what he's doing but I don't have to be entirely in agreement, and I wanted to respond to Peter Neubauer. You know, I've heard exactly the same mistake made with Margaret Mahler's ideas, that is, somebody discusses an adult case and talks about separation and individuation as though there were never an adolescence.

Kernberg: The basic misuse of the relationship to boundary fields such as neuroscience is a symptom of the current insecurity of psychoanalysis, picking up one thing to explain everything. That is a problem that is stemming from the insecurity of our field. Attachment theory is helpful because it indicates one way in which the capacity for integrating affects as representational experience is made possible. Attachment has something to do with bringing together affect and representation of the same thing—the cognitive is the skin, so to speak, of affective experience. When Peter Fonagy says that if the mother overidentifies with the infant, then the infant can't integrate his affect, that's a good observation. Or when the mother denies the affect, the infant then doesn't have the kind of reflection that permits him to integrate his own affect, which by the way is quite similar to Bion's idea of mother's function to transform beta into alpha elements.

That's useful. On the other hand, from there to go directly to what's happening later about affective pathology is unfortunate. Peter may have been seduced by all that interest in talking about mentalization as if the mother–infant relationship by itself determines how affects are going to be integrated, and that's problematic. And you know there's attachment therapy, trauma therapy, attachment-trauma therapy. These are fashions that unfortunately infiltrate rescue mentality. It happens also in the area of neurobiology. Some people pick up some elements from neurobiology to show how Freud "was right." It makes me cringe. We are going to create a very problematic impression in the fields that we want to relate to. I think that as knowledge accumulates in neurobiology, we have elements that may help us understand how some components relate from biology to psycho dynamics, but the internal dynamics or psychodynamics cannot be washed away by that. Very concretely—as you know, I'm involved in studying affect development in borderline patients. Using Posner's work on neurocognitive development there is good evidence that there is an inborn disposition to intensity of affective reaction—reflected in amygdala activation—which has something to do with the function of temperament in affective relationships. On the other hand, there's an inborn disposition to focus on the cognitive implications of affect activation to sort out contradictory cognitive information and to establish the priority of what needs to be focused upon—that's located in the prefrontal and preorbital cortex. These two areas are part of a neurobiological system that has something to do with the way in which affects are tolerated and integrated. From there you can't go directly into psychoanalytic theory. That's just a component of how representations develop, how affects develop—the relation between representation and affects. That is of real interest, but doesn't replace or explain psychoanalytic theories of development.

Another dramatic example—the concept of the self. There is now beginning evidence of the neurobiology of the concept of the self. The concept of self is a subjective experience. There are about six or seven areas of the brain that jointly determine whatever we think of ourselves at a given moment, how we quickly put together, memory about our past, our location in space, affective memory, demands regarding our relations to the environment—and you can localize these components in different brain areas. To us, it feels of course as if our self sits there all the time and we are just calling on it. From a neurobiological viewpoint, these are momentary integrations—flickering momentary integrations of completely separate neurobiological structures. Neurobiological structures determine a function, which becomes psychic. But that momentary function then gets into the complication of the development of normal or abnormal identity or a split self, about which neurobiology has nothing to say anymore. And it seems to me that that's both interesting and on the other hand tempting for oversimplification and the reductionism that every time something new is discovered, is brought into psychoanalytic theory. So now we have a solid basis in neurobiology and we are good friends with neuroscientists. It is an irrational integration of other fields that may take the form of dissidence because of this artificiality at some times. As Harold Blum pointed out, we oscillate between an artificial taking *pars pro toto* [the part for the whole], or as a defense against that, a premature integration that blurs our own science and prevents us from developing psychoanalysis or studying purely psychic structures.

Overestimation of our field and underestimation tend to go hand in hand.

Scharff: Actually, I don't agree with you that the conditions of attachment have nothing to do with the regulation of mood.

Kernberg: Once you have problematic attachments this could develop into many different directions. If attachment is in a mess, there will be a terrible chaos of mood. If the patient becomes a narcissistic personality, then there may be high stability of mood and narcissistic invulnerability except at certain moments when severe inferiority feelings come about, but that already contains a pathologically grandiose self. There are many things that go way beyond the attachment experience.

Scharff: Bion is talking about how the mother contains the infant's experience—absorbing the "unthinkable anxiety" of the infant and giving back to the infant "thinkable anxiety"—this being the beginning of thought and the shaping of affect. The child identifies with the mother's capacity for this alpha function. This relationship is crucial in the management of affect.

Kernberg: That is one aspect of the development of thinking. There are many others. As I just mentioned, there's an inborn capacity for what Posner calls effortful control. There's an inborn capacity for cognitive functioning. This is equally important.

Scharff: Indeed, but neurobiological research also shows that there's interaction between the brains of mother and infant. This mother–infant mutual interaction proceeds along the developmental path. For instance, the light in the mother's eyes lights up the light in the infant's eye, through reciprocal responses in their serotonin systems.

Kernberg: We cannot assume that all is decided in the first six months of life, and therefore to talk about attachment without considering the complexity of unconscious, intrafamilial development is an oversimplification. I've seen cases presented using attachment theory for analyzing negative transference. It is a gross oversimplification that usually misses aggressive and erotic impulses. Kohut was a kind of preattachment attachment theorist.

Green: I want to tell you about an experience I had last month. Peter Fonagy invited me for a dialogue during a holiday at University College, London. The title was, "Can Infancy Research Contribute to Clinical Psychoanalysis?" What he did was present a clinical case. Infancy was completely out. I told him, "Well, Peter, here is the title. Why didn't you speak about research on infancy because that's your field? It's not mine." He said, "Because when I talk about infancy research, people get bored." What does that mean? He was speaking to an audience of psychoanalysts. It means that psychoanalysts do not see the bridge between what he says and what he does in his clinical work.

About attachment theory, I have many criticisms, and all criticism flows in the same direction: it's an oversimplification. But I would just ask why should we spend such a lot of time to study an author who said that he was not interested in the unconscious because it was unproven. He is not interested in what we are interested in. At the present moment in this discussion attachment theory is a matter of dissidence, but as Harold said it is also an evolution and transformation. Why shouldn't we say that Bowlby is an evolution of psychoanalysis toward a dynamic psychology? Which is different from what we are doing—research about the unconscious. Even when we decide on giving drugs, we can read it in giving drugs to the patient—the unconscious is still there. We deal with the unconscious differently. It is modified but it is still there. Seeing it in groups when studying in psychodrama and group analysis, the unconscious is omnipresent. We are coming to the paper I wrote and you said you wished to discuss. The problem is first to determine what is the core of psychoanalysis. There are two steps in the core. If we have an identity here, it is an identity because we share the same core. We may differ in our theories. We may differ in what we consider developments within psychoanalysis, but we share the same core. There will always be a shorter distance between an analyst and another analyst—whatever he is—than between an analyst and a nonanalyst.

Kernberg: Not necessarily. The codirector of my institute is a behavior therapist—John Clarkin. Some of you know him. He is very active in international psychoanalysis, providing research methodology. He is not a psychoanalyst. I am extremely close to him in our way of thinking. He is interested in knowing what do we observe and why we think that this is so and what is our basis, and he helps me to sharpen my thinking.

Green: He is under your orders.

Kernberg: He is not under my orders.

Blum: André, you know that in our country—I don't know if this is true at all in France—Freud is being ever more reduced in the psychoanalytic curriculum across the country. Institutes are spending less and less time teaching Freud—reading Freud's papers, discussing those papers, speaking of the core of psychoanalysis. Freud is being treated more and more as if he is, in the English idiomatic expression, "old hat," antiquated.

Green: We know that.

Blum: There is a question about how do we define the core and Freud's essential connection with the core of psychoanalysis. Having said that, I think it's important that we don't prematurely exclude attachment theory. It appears to contribute further to our understanding of the development of the child. Attachment theory has significant connection with object relations, with ego development, and so forth. One reason that attachment theory is so popular—it's something Jill Scharff alluded to, she said 75 percent—is our unspoken search for certainty and predictability. The strange situation, which Mary Ainsworth introduced, really became so popular because it was predictable and reliable and it could be replicated by many other investigators. As attachment theory evolved, it wasn't the work of one particular person, and other people could observe the findings. So for this reason, partly because of the clinical difficulty in dealing with ambiguity and uncertainty, interest in attachment theory burgeoned. Here was something that promised reliability, replicability, making certain predictions, 75 percent accuracy, and so forth. Attachment gave the appearance of hard science.

Green: But there are many human sciences in which predictability is not possible but they are not denied as sciences.

Blum: Attachment theory emphasizes, even in the context of mentalization, the mother's effect on the infant. The adult attachment interview of the mother predicts the quality of her infant's attachment. The theory does not emphasize the infant's effect on the mother. Each infant has a different effect on the mother. A mother may be better adapted to a particular child, may even have a postpartum depression with the second child and may function much better with the first or the third. The complexity of development is such that it involves a continuous interaction between the innate endowment and a thousand other factors. A complex set of interactions go on between mother and infant. The infants elicit from the mother different kinds of mothering experiences, and the infant has other experiences besides the mother—sibling experiences, a twin experience, etc.

The claim of attachment theory that it's possible to predict the psychopathology of the child, even before the child's birth, from the adult attachment interviews strikes me as fascinating. We can learn from these findings but it certainly seems to challenge what we know about the complexities of development and of developmental transformations. But so many processes go on that would have to influence the infant. We are dealing with what Winnicott would call "impingement"—that is a mother whose impingement is so powerful that it really has a determining influence on that particular child. Attachment is complementary to the process of separation and individuation, but regrettably disregards unconscious fantasy.

Young-Bruehl: I agree about the limitations of the attachment theory but then comes the question: What follows if we agree that this theory is limited in terms of what it can yield to psychoanalysis or in terms of what elements of human development it studies—two very different attitudes? One is a kind of laissez-faire—let them do attachment theory and we'll see what turns out to be interesting about it. The other is a more active kind of approach that says, "Look, it's quite possible that attachment theory is a very good way to study certain features of development." If we think in terms of a large orchestration of factors that are involved in development, if you were, say, an Anna Freudian thinking in terms of many developmental models, which of our interests can attachment theory address? And which can it not? The focus then would be on where attachment theory can fit into the much broader, much more interesting panoply of psychoanalytic context. For example, it's possible that there are features of attachment that can deal with the concept of intergenerational transmission in ways that are different from the ways we do it.

Neubauer: Peter Fonagy's mentalization of the mother, namely her capacity to observe, to be aware of herself and look at the child, and if she has that capacity, she does not just transmit unconsciously—that the path of knowing what it is, is very useful because that would separate the symbiotic sort of transmission idea from the intervening idea of a mother who may be able to see the child, as you say, Harold, in his own right. The child selects from the environment what he needs. He's not just absorbing the environment; with the idea of mentalization there is a quality that I like to detect in the mother that is useful for me as a possible additional factor, but what the analyst made out of it—the predictive component of it, the abolition of transformation—this is the danger.

Young-Bruehl: It's a sign of the un-confidence within psychoanalysis itself to be able to focus actively and delineate and say what the limitations are. There's a lack of confidence over the "psychoanalytic core."

Bergmann: I would like to move the discussion now from attachment theory to the question that is central to your paper, André, about the core of psychoanalysis. If we have time, I would like also to have a discussion about Ian Suttie—your paper, Elisabeth. So I would like to ask if anybody wants to begin this discussion of André Green's paper. No one is volunteering? Then I will read to you the notes that I wrote because I thought that I ought to be prepared to start a discussion.

I wish to thank André for his contribution, which in scope and in depth goes in many ways beyond the confines of our symposium. I can see his paper, perhaps with the first laudatory paragraph about me omitted, as another significant contribution to a future collection of psychoanalytic essays. But I am happy that its first appearance will be in this symposium. Following my lines of reasoning, André assumes that in some respects, all of us are dissidents in one way or another. Our task is to state as clearly as possible what constitutes the Freudian core. To our great surprise, this psychoanalytic core does not turn out to be rather tedious repetition of what we all know, but a highly original group of ideas. We have long known that one of Freud's great achievements was building a royal bridge between neurosis and normalcy. André extends this structure to include psychosis. In the outline, the dream is seen as a psychosis in a state of sleep. Ignoring the studies on hysteria, André postulates that Freud started with the normal mind by studying the dream, while Melanie Klein reversed the process, starting with what the analyst considers the most primitive. To my understanding, this is a normal way of approaching Melanie Klein. From here André Green takes the more familiar road traveled by Freud to discover censorship, resistance, transference, psychic reality, repression, primary impulses, wish fulfillment, and free association.

I noticed with some astonishment that if I understood your psychoanalytic core correctly, it goes back to Freud before 1920. After establishing the Freudian core, André concludes that every dissident has a quarrel with this core. The core is a guide to treatment of psychic illness but it is just as relevant to the understanding of art via sublimation and culture. Many of the dissidents, including Wilhelm Reich and the culturalists, return to the emphasis of external reality at the expense of inner reality. André divides the history of psychoanalysis into four stages. I was surprised that he did not give a special section to the Wolf Man since he did so much to heighten our attention to this particular patient, whose treatment haunted psychoanalysis because the Wolf Man remained bisexual with two types of orgasms—feminine and masculine. He was interviewed and cared for by a series of psychoanalysts; instead of becoming cured he became, at least until close to his death, an apostle of psychoanalysis, raising the question that sometimes when we don't cure our patients, we convert them into missionaries for psychoanalysis. André stands on the other side of Bob Wallerstein in his opposition to tolerance of fragmentation, which he considers a step toward the death of psychoanalysis. Much that passes for reconciliation is to André only—or at best—a cease-fire.

Blum: It's a shame we don't have Bob Wallerstein to engage in a dialogue.

Bergmann: Bob expressed the idea that you would act as his substitute, Otto.

Kernberg: Yes, I know his thinking and I talked with him by phone and I can summarize what we were discussing very briefly. Bob Wallerstein saw my paper "Convergences and Divergences" as illustrating that at the level of technique, analysis is coming together. He was questioning my latest paper about the history of psychoanalytic technique in the English-language contributions where I point out there are three major technical approaches in our day. What I called the mainstream of Kleinian independent ego psychology, as opposed to French psychoanalytic technique, as opposed to the New York Kohutian intersubjectivists. I told Bob that I disagreed with his assumption that theories are only metaphors and that we are in agreement on clinical reality. We must be capable of establishing valid hypotheses and testing them out—there's a certain kind of nihilistic quality about doing this. So I disagree with Bob Wallerstein, but on the other hand, I agree with him that there is a tendency to coming together in the technical field, but that is relative, because there are certain divergences that emerge again and again under the influence of certain cultural currents that tend to deny it some basic tenets of psychoanalysis, particularly regarding the theory of drives, the negation of the importance of aggression, and the importance of infantile sexuality. This may be a constant struggle that psychoanalysis has to maintain itself against the constant cultural threat to erase this because it runs counter to mass psychology—against conventional wisdom. Bob Wallerstein said that he was in agreement with me on that. So in a nutshell, we agree that there has been a tendency toward overcoming differences, a more dramatic one between ego psychology and Kleinians—neither of the two in many ways accepted that. I mean particularly Kleinians never accepted anything from anybody else as part of the psychology of the school. It is an indication of the nature of Kleinian training. The Kleinians are more at risk than anybody else of becoming sterile because of this dogmatic nature of their education.

Green: They are changing.

Kernberg: I am agreeing with Bob that there is a basic core and I think that Bob would agree with André Green that the basic core is the nature of the drives—the determination of the unconscious, with your permission, motivation—and a fundamental aspect of personality and psychopathology. The disagreement with Bob is more about his basic stand about the common ground because I don't think that the common ground lies only in a technical approach—it lies in theory. And if we deny the theory, we are in trouble.

Neubauer: Otto, could you explain this to me—if Bob were indeed in agreement with André about the basic core, how can he then assume that the various people who diverge in their interpretation accept that basic core when he says there may be a commonality? I don't think they do.

Kernberg: Bob's position, personally, is in agreement with this basic core. I don't think he would say that the different theoreticians all agreed with it.

Neubauer: But does he exclude them from his ecumenical spirit of integration?

Kernberg: There is an ecumenical theory. He just said these are metaphors and we are coming together in the clinical theory—that's his ecumenical thinking. It's in the clinical approach to patients—this is an illusion of psychoanalysis by which we patch our techniques together and develop a mainstream. There is such a psychoanalytic mainstream in the technical approach, although it has limitations and problems. I would not say that there is an ecumenical attitude about theory. I'm talking about where he stands in his theory. He stands close to André and myself and most of us here. But he would say that he tends to ignore where people stand in different ways to that one because these are only metaphors. And I had not asked him whether he thinks that his own theories are only metaphors. If he said it's only a metaphor, he would disqualify himself.

Bergmann: If we could decide what is the core and what is not the core of psychoanalysis we could say as long as we have this in common, we have the core. If we disagree on the other things, then it is not dissidence but just a disagreement. However, the controversial discussions have taught me that that's not so easy because they obviously thought that whatever they talked about was the core. And when Melanie Klein said, "I am a Freudian but not an Anna Freudian," she meant that she is staying within the core. The difficulty I have with the concept is how and who decides what the core is. Let us take the death instinct. Is the belief in it core or not core, mere disagreement?

Green: I will tell you first how I wrote the paper. I wrote the paper after reading all the papers I received at the time and mainly Bob's paper. And I must say— I'm happy to say that while he is not here—I disagree very much with Bob's paper because in fact, he took sides and the paper was published in the *International Journal of Psycho-Analysis*. He patronized the relational point of view and extended it. I wanted to present a position showing why I think the intersubjective could not replace the intrapsychic. I thought that we have to find something acting as a core in the intrapsychic. What I have described is what appears from *The Interpretation of Dreams*—the description of the "dream processes" of the "dream work," and I cannot see how a relational point of view or even an object relations point of view can explain the dream process. The dream process is really something that I consider as intrapsychic, and whatever we think of how it comes to happen, in the end when we are with a patient who tells us a dream and we try to analyze the dream and we get the interpretation and I think we all agree around this table that the core is the unconscious—whatever you think of the unconscious, whatever you think of how it is built, whatever you think of what it is made of—it is really our business, the unconscious.

As Martin has noticed, I had to make a distinction between this model, which I called the dream pattern, with what happened after 1920 in which instead of the dream, the narrative of the dream, the interpretation—all based on the monologue representations—was replaced by what happens in the second aspect of the core: the reference to acting out. This, for me, is the second aspect—the acting out, replacing, remembering. How can we connect the two? We can connect the two by saying that the acting out is the result of the unsuccessful attempt to create the representation. It is because there is a failure in the making of representation that acting out comes to the front.

Neubauer: Can you differentiate enactment from acting out?

Green: *Enactment* is a modern term because *acting out* was considered old-fashioned, and so enactment was brought in. Gabbard was really doing an extraordinary acrobatic number to show that enactment and projective identification have a common ground. I don't think that's true. Projective identification is a purely Kleinian concept. The degree of dissidence between us can be measured by the distance that we take from that core principle. Those people who take the greatest distance I don't want to hear about; they are too far away from my thinking. The unconscious leads us to the drives. The unconscious is a product of the drives; we see that we are dissidents in the things that we refuse. And we can refuse it massively like Adler and Jung—more subtly with object relationships, even more with attachment theory, and even more with intersubjective theory. If you read Owen Renik's last paper on technique, where he recommends seeing the families of our patients—I will only say to Renik, Why do you claim to be a psychoanalyst? This is dynamic psychology and I think that we have to make a difference between dynamic psychology and psychoanalysis. I do not consider that Melanie Klein's theory is dynamic psychology. I think it is psychoanalysis. She is my "cousin," as I said. But these are the explanations I wanted to give on how I wrote that paper, a way to find a core, to define a center from which we are all at different distances.

Young-Bruehl: Could I just ask you to go back and clarify one step, just to make sure that I understand what you say about the core and the unconscious. The step of turning to Renik's paper.

Green: To say in two words that the answer to our problem is to bring together the intrapsychic and the intrasubjective in the body that you are studying. It may be individual therapy. It may be a couples therapy, but that's something else. It may be in group therapy, but the idea remains that it is to bring together what happens between me and me and what happens between me and Otto. And for Otto it's about Otto and myself and between Otto and himself. So I would say that the intrasubjective point of view, in the end, connects two intrapsychic worlds—the unconscious of Green and the unconscious of Kernberg.

Young-Bruehl: I agree, but why not see the other person? Why is Renik a departure—to see the friend of your analysand—why is that a departure?

Green: Ah! Because you are introducing something alien to your body of study. If you had decided to do couples therapy, okay! It is your purpose. It is what you have decided to do—to study the interaction between two people who are engaged or attached to each other or whatever. But if you had decided that you want to study the internal and external mechanisms of a person, then you have to answer it yourself. You cannot call in a friend or family member. You're missing two things. For instance, if you have a young woman in treatment, you know her from the transference. You know her past history, her mechanism of defense. If you now say, "Well, ask your boyfriend to come and see me," you don't know anything about the boyfriend. What you know about the boyfriend is what the young woman tells you about the boyfriend, so how can you in one consultation . . . We know from the experience with patients that when a patient agrees that you see somebody else, she will become very resentful that you did.

Young-Bruehl: It happens in child and adolescent treatments all the time.

Green: Children are not adults. There is a dependency, which is normal to children. Of course, if you have a baby—the study of the baby, you have to go to the mother too. But for an adult, it is a breach of confidentiality to see another person. Or else you are doing family therapy, which is something else.

Bergmann: Among my many sins, there is a paper in 1966 called "The Intrapsychic and Communicative Aspect of the Dream."[41] I was not the only one,

41. Bergmann, M. S. (1966). The intrapsychic and communicative aspect of the dream. *International Journal of Psycho-Analysis* 47(2/3):356–363.

before object relations theory came into being, but I kind of stumbled into it. But I was not the only one. Mark Kanzer wrote a paper about it and so did John Klauber. You, André, are making the dream the center of the psychoanalytic core and yet it's not so sure because at least in the theory that I developed then, the dream serves as a communication, that is, what the patient cannot tell you directly, he tells you in a dream. So what does that mean? That the dream that is from one point of view, the center of the intrapsychic, has also a communicative aspect to it. I come back to the question that the core is not so easy to define.

Green: The core is not as easy to define—I agree. And about the communicative aspect of the dream, I do not mind at all. But what remains in the dream is made up out of nothing conscious. It is because consciousness takes no part in the dream that the dream is important. The only answer I could find is to say, "Well, I am going to close myself in my dreams and see what happens." It is because consciousness takes no part in the dream that the dream is precious. Even Winnicott said that you direct your fantasies but you cannot direct your dreams.

Kris: We're talking about Bob Wallerstein's ideas; it comes down to a matter of praxis. He is saying, "The core is praxis and can we compare praxes?" And André is saying the core is ultimately a set of ideas. I don't believe we can distinguish the dancer from the dance. We are left with uncertainty. I don't think it is possible for any two analysts absolutely to say this is the core we agree on. I think there's always going to be overlapping, and furthermore I don't think you will agree with yourself the day after tomorrow. You will have another perspective and you will say, "No, this has to be included." That's how it should be. There are some things that are fundamental, but what may be very fundamental to you is perhaps a little less fundamental to me. There's a lot of overlap. I do have a feeling that we are cousins, but I think it is not conceivable that there be identity congruence. So that even though we have a concept of the core, it can't really be *the* core.

Kernberg: As I tried to put in my paper also, I am very close to André. I believe the core consists in the influence of the unconscious—with your permission, the word *motivation*—the dynamic unconscious in the sense of the unconscious that has a motivational force. I am not saying that the drives are something with which we are born. I believe they are constituted by primitive effects. But for me they are psychic organizations that come into being in the context of unconscious developments. I think that the unconscious determination of behavior, particularly expressed in intrapsychic structures that are manifest throughout life, determines the life of fantasy and unconscious fantasy represented by the dream, and acting out in terms of expression in habitual behavior. Behavior is determined to quite an extent by the structural transformation of the drive-invested internalized object relations into templates, that may again be dissolved into their constituent object relations as part of character analysis. The drives are packed into an internal world of object relations; they are indissolubly linked with them. A theory of drives without a theory of structured object relations gets nowhere. For me the core is drives, determining unconscious motivations packed into internalized object relations that determines the tripartite structure of ego, id, and superego, which manifest themselves in habitual behavior patterns that we call character, and they determine the transference and subjective experience that is the world of object relations—quoting Sandler—constituted by the concept of self and the concept of significant others. These are fundamental in our subjectivity, so that simultaneously the unconscious shows up in subjective structures and is expressed in behavior, or let's say in behavior corresponding to subjective structures. For me, that's the essence of psychoanalytic theory. It means that identity and character are determined mostly by unconscious factors and by the derived system of ethical structure—the superego. I consider the superego as a fundamental structure, the conscious and unconscious internal structure of ethical commitments. These commitments are also determined, to quite an extent, unconsciously, which is extremely important because superego pathology is crucial in determining the severity of all other pathology. Again, that comes from Freud. So for me all this constitutes the core. But psychoanalytic technique as treatment is not the core. Psychoanalytic treatment is a specific instrument for the investigation of the unconscious, yes. Psychoanalysis has developed its own methodology, which is the psychoanalytic situation, which is an essential research situation. Perhaps as a specific instrument of investigation it may be considered as part of the core, insofar as it is an important source of new knowledge. But I don't think that the psychoanalytic situation is the unique, privileged instrument for learning about the unconscious. There may be other instruments. It is a rigidity and narrowness to consider the psychoanalytic instrument as the only instrument of investigation. But in terms of treatment, I think that psychoanalysis contains a potential for multiple modalities of treatment, which are all psychoanalytic as long as they accept the basic core and as long as these techniques have a clear relationship with that core. From this viewpoint, what we call standard psychoanalysis for neurotic patients is essential, while psychoanalytic psychotherapy is also a legitimate psychoanalytic technique. I think that the psychoanalytic couple therapy developed by Henry Dicks on the basis of Fairbairn's concepts is a legitimate psychoanalytic contribution, which has influenced all other couple therapies, and I think that supportive psychotherapy based on psychoanalytic concepts as it has been spelled out in the work of Wallerstein also needs to be included. Ann Applebaum is about to publish a book on supportive therapy for borderline patients, stressing that this is also a legitimate psychoanalytically derived therapy.

Psychoanalysis has done itself a disservice in not realizing that broad potential. We cannot abandon a search for a basic, global theory that has to be elaborated, researched, made fresh as we learn more, and critically reexamined all the time.

Bergmann: I hope that nobody is left too frustrated if we end now. You are all invited with your significant others at 7:30 to my house and I promise there will be no more debate. We will devote the evening to the pleasure principle, although this conference had a great deal of pleasure in it. I want to thank you once more and I want to thank the Psychoanalytic Research and Development Fund for sponsoring and I do hope that when these deliberations are edited, that we have contributed something important to contemporary psychoanalysis.

IV

A RESPONSE TO THE SYMPOSIUM "UNDERSTANDING DISSIDENCE" —AFTER THE FACT

ROBERT S. WALLERSTEIN

Martin Bergmann sent me the edited transcript of the weekend symposium on "Understanding Dissidence," for which I had written an invited preparatory paper, but which I could not attend because of a sudden illness in my family. Martin requested that I read this discussion, and as much as I felt able and willing, respond to it with my own commentary, approximating as closely as possible what my own participation could have been had I been present. I indeed found the symposium discussion over the two days far-ranging in the scope of issues covered, provocatively informative, often fascinating and dialectically argumentative in the best sense, making me regret all the more that I had not been present to participate personally. Therefore, I am happy to accept Martin's offer and at least to join the discussion this way, after the fact.

I do applaud very much Martin's spirit through the symposium, his constant push (and exhortation) for increased understanding of disparate viewpoints, not necessarily overall agreements. I liked very much also the elaboration of the history of dissidence begun in Martin's paper and contributed to by others of the papers, and the delineation of the dynamics of dissidence initiated by Otto Kernberg's paper with his outlining then of the interplay of personal character structure (or psychopathology), of the institutional dynamics of our societies and institutes, and of the sociocultural currents in our various centers of activity worldwide in bringing about our recurring dissident formulations. In this connection, I found Elisabeth Young-Bruehl's distinction between dissidence in the realm of general theory (our various metapsychologies) and dissidence in the realm of theory of technique (of which, as was stated, Ferenczi is such a compelling example, though from another perspective, Ferenczi can also be looked at as the original great dissident in theory, the progenitor of all relational-based psychoanalysis) very useful and clarifying.

What I am not so much in accord with was the constant linking, certainly on the first discussion day, of the issue of dissidence with concern for the vehemence with which it has historically so often been expressed, and with the repeated injunction that any tendency to vehemence in the symposium discussion be curbed in the interest of dispassionate discussion and clarification. The word *vehemence* always carries a most pejorative connotation and often enough can be a proper characterization, but there can always be a positive valence given to strongly held beliefs, using words such as *passion* and *conviction*. Certainly we, of all people, are aware of the ambivalence that characteristically endows and shapes human behaviors and interrelations, and I think that the multifaceted nature of human thoughts and feelings was not given its due in the emphases that first evening upon the vehemence that was depicted in the stories of dissidence and dissidents.

But now let me go on to disagreements, and to what I feel were misunderstandings in relation to which I would have entered contrary views had I been present. A small one occurs with Martin's placing Leo Rangell into the same position that Otto Kernberg and I entertain in seeing the pendulum beginning to swing back, away from the era of increasing divergences, leading to our current theoretical diversity, or pluralism as we have come to call it, back now to telltale signs of growing convergences, at least at the technical and clinical levels, from what have been highly divergent theoretical positions. I have read Rangell closely, and discussed with him publicly, and I do not feel that he agrees at all with any sense of growing convergences from once highly different and divergent clinical or theoretical perspectives.

Rather, I see him holding in a steadfast way to a lifetime conviction of the centrality of the ego psychological structural theory, handed down in a direct line from Sigmund Freud, through Anna Freud, Hartmann, and Fenichel, that Rangell calls "total composite psychoanalytic theory," with all other metapsychologies being viewed as partial theory offshoots, taking part of the Freudian corpus and elevating it to a rival effort at a full explanatory system (which, of course, proponents of other theoretical viewpoints see as expressions of American imperialism). But so much for that as a minor enough point.

Also, I disagree on another minor enough point made by Mort Ostow that our theories don't allow us to predict anything. Actually, I and others have written at length about the possibility of (and the place of) formal prediction—

based on theory—in psychoanalytic therapy and in psychoanalytically understood development. Suffice it to say, for simple example, that when we diagnose someone as a paranoid personality (or as any other character configuration) we are involved in all kinds of predictions about characteristic defenses, dynamics, conflicts, etc., that we expect will emerge over the course of a therapeutic undertaking. To be sure, I feel that Mort retreated somewhat from this flat assertion, and he and I do agree that a major value of valid theory is that it does enable us to make predictions about empirically expectable phenomena, and that properly made observations (experiments, natural or contrived) can therefore test theory by determining whether its predictions are sustained or refuted.

But all this is of far less import than the much more major issues to which I now turn, the proper delineation of my views on what we can call our common ground as analysts, and where we currently diverge widely, our pluralism, which has of course been brought into being by those who have been described in this symposium (and throughout our literature) as psychoanalytic dissidents. I have always felt that my views on these issues have been described simply and clearly enough in my two plenary addresses to the International Psychoanalytic Association congresses in Montreal in 1987 and in Rome in 1989. But this may well not have been so, because I have been surprised any number of times—and again in this symposium—at how differently my views seem to be understood by others, and so I do welcome another very appropriate opportunity to try to restate and clarify my own position on these issues.

But first on the issue of our psychoanalytic core around which André Green formulated his presentation and which came under such intense discussion during the symposium days. I do of course agree, and I think that all those who consider themselves analysts agree, on the fundamentals of the core: (1) the unconscious and therefore hidden workings of the mind, which so powerfully mold our thoughts, feelings, and behaviors; and (2) the conception of psychic determinism, of what comes before helping determine what comes after (i.e., the enduring impact of experience or nurture in the nature/nurture dialectic), or put differently, of the past influencing and imprinting the present and future. More than one psychoanalytic theoretician (and certainly David Rapaport) has asserted that all else that is psychoanalytic can be derived from these two basic propositions of unconscious mental activity and psychic determinism.

I think that all those who have been labeled psychoanalytic dissidents would agree with these central propositions. Where they disagree and diverge, and perhaps ultimately come to differing metapsychologies, is in what shape and form this all takes, what factors or emphases are more central or meaningful or salient, and here is where all the issues of drives and affects and internalized object relationships, of developmental stages or developmental positions, of gratification seeking or object seeking, and all the other things in our various metapsychologies, divide us.

Even further along the same line, a number of psychoanalytic authors, myself included, have speculated that had the great defections involving the earliest schismatics, like Adler and Jung, occurred not during Freud's earliest active years when those individuals were so embroiled in tangled personal ambivalences and competitive rivalries and envies vis-à-vis the persona of Freud, on top of their different preferred theoretical formulations, but more currently, and therefore without complicated personal involvements with Freud, they might very well have persisted as alternative metapsychologies within the house of organized psychoanalysis. After all, several of Adler's central conceptions, like those of the ego and adaptation, or of the motive power of aggression (masculine protest, overcompensation for organ inferiority, etc.) have been actively reincorporated into the main body of psychoanalysis, first by Freud, and then by others who came after, like Hartmann, and perhaps this is related to the near collapse of Adlerian psychology as a separate therapeutic enterprise.

There have been lesser, but nonetheless still substantial, reincorporations also from Jungian psychology, or at least cognate developments within the psychoanalytic framework, like Erikson's life span focus with its shift in emphasis to the co-equal concern with the second half of the life cycle, or like our enhanced focus on unconscious fantasy systems as guides to understanding motivation and behavior—albeit in a different way than the Jungians—and this somewhat lesser reappropriation of concepts from Jung's theoretical system may relate to its continuing greater vigor as a separate psychology and therapy than its Adlerian counterpart.

My overall point here—and of course some of the colleagues at the symposium might disagree—is that all the different metapsychologies that comprise our pluralism, including possibly even the Adlerian and the Jungian, could fit comfortably enough within our (common) core, at least as I have indicated my understanding of what comprises the fundamental psychoanalytic core.

But now to where I feel that my own stated positions have been misunderstood or misconstrued. Most importantly, I do not regard our various metapsychologies (or general theories) as all the same, in the sense of being in some way equally valid depictions of the workings of the mind, as was stated about me a number of times by a number of symposium participants (for example, by Otto Kernberg). Clearly, the adherents of each theoretical framework do proclaim the unique value of their own preferred perspective as giving them the best handle on understanding the workings of the normal and abnormal mind, and on being best able to guide the amelioration of the disordered malfunctionings of the mind (and correspondingly, they diminish the value of the alternative metapsychologies). This near-universal stance among us is, to me, a function of, and the outcome of, our chosen training immersions and practice communities in variable combination with our individual character proclivities, and this is obviously true in my own case, as well as in everyone else's.

In the spirit of personal statements that pervaded the symposium proceedings, I should state that I was trained psychoanalytically in the United States during the decade of the 1950s, during the era of the almost monolithic hegemony within the American Psychoanalytic Association of the ego psychology metapsychological paradigm, architected by Heinz Hartmann and his collaborators, and systematized to the extent feasible by David Rapaport, and declared to be the true descendant of Freud's structural theory as further elaborated through the landmark contributions of Anna Freud (on the defensive functions of the ego) and Hartmann (on its adaptive functions). That was the training context that molded my own psychoanalytic perspectives, as subsequently modified and enlarged, however, by my contacts over the decades since with the various object relations perspectives, brought together currently under the rubric of the "relational turn"—with then all of the interplay within me of what are called the two-person psychology and one-person psychology conceptualizations.

But to me, all these theoretical perspectives that we variously espouse, my own no less than the others, have still today the status of scientific metaphors—not yet coherent and full-fledged theories—and this is not to denigrate metaphors as un- or antiscientific, but rather to place them as proper and necessary precursor steps in theory construction, as proto-theoretical structures. (For a spirited and persuasive statement of the facilitating role of scientific metaphor formation in the early stages of theory building, see Wurmser 1977.) As still metaphoric in nature, our various general theories do not have established canons of inference linking them securely to observable and demonstrable phenomena in our consulting rooms, and are thus, at this time, not amenable to the scientific testing that could establish differentially the greater explanatory power or validity of any one of them over any of the others.

That is the reason that I have contended that we have no warrant at this time in the evolving construction of our discipline to declare any of our metapsychologies as indubitably superior as theory (or as derived therapy) to any of the others (including my own preferred framework). Some theoretical frameworks may indeed have greater explanatory power than others in particular contexts, or with particular portions of the psychopathological spectrum, but in my mind, we simply have no valid basis at this point for declaring that to be so, and certainly no basis for persuading the holders of other theoretical perspectives to that effect.

It is on the basis of these currently irreconcilable theoretical divergences that I have sought our common ground in our clinical theory (as distinct from our general theories), which is linked directly to the phenomena discernible and demonstrable in our consulting rooms, and in this sense I agree wholeheartedly with Tony Kris's statement, that I find our core manifest in our praxis, and by implication then in the growing convergences that I am discerning in our practices, and I would think that Otto would certainly agree with this last statement. Tony at that point contrasted this position with André Green's, that our core is ultimately a set of ideas. I would agree with André on that also, but in a more restricted sense; I would certainly agree that we have a psychoanalytic core in the conceptions of unconscious mental life and psychic determinism, but I would exclude from the agreed core the variously divergent metapsychologies to which we differentially adhere and within which we seek to explain the phenomena that we deal with in our consulting rooms.

But all of this is very far indeed from what is so widely (and wrongly) imputed to me, that all our differing theoretical frameworks are equal, and it is very far indeed from mixing them together into an (intellectually lazy) eclecticism, usually stated even more pejoratively, as a mindless eclecticism. I thus disagree heartily with Harold Blum's statement that my position is that "you can accept, integrate, reconcile radically theoretically different frameworks and systems." That would indeed be a mindless eclecticism or a Hungarian goulash as is stated there; it just is not my position.

My position here is, rather, twofold. The first part is rather to look for growing convergences as they develop out of our clinical activities over time, starting, as I have written elsewhere at length, in the realm of technique and clinical conceptualization, and, it is hoped, as our consensually accepted clinical theory grows, perhaps building upward into converging elements of the more general theory (or metapsychology). In my paper prepared for this symposium I give examples of just these evolving convergences that I see in the current beginning swing of the pendulum back from the era of growing divergences established by all the charismatic dissidents that have been the subject of this symposium (and many of these telltale markers of these growing convergences at this time are quoted from two papers of Otto's in 1993 and 2001).

The second part of this twofold position is to concomitantly work out ways to more definitively evaluate, and to more systematically compare and contrast, the extent to which our different metapsychologies actually do or do not enhance our understandings of our efforts to ameliorate the malfunctionings of the minds of our patients as they come to light in our consulting rooms. This is the realm of systematic and formal research, and I discuss the potential role of such research in the next part of these discussion comments. Meanwhile, we all live—and practice—by the theoretical allegiances we have individually evolved within our own training and practice communities, and mine, as I have indicated, can be stated as a transformed ego psychology core as modified by the theoretical amalgamating efforts of people like Otto and Joe Sandler, and as strongly influenced by the many proponents of the current "relational turn" (an overall position that has been articulated in quite comparable terms by people as different as Merton Gill in his final book [1994] and Nancy Chodorow in her most recent book [1999]).

All this brings me to the question of where I feel we can best go from here, and here I do want to enter into the discussion material that I felt was not advanced by any of the participants (except by allusion, and in a very limited way, by Otto), and yet that I feel is shared—I hope I am not wrong—by at least some of those who were present, but I know not by all. This has to do with the potential role of systematic and formal empirical research in making possible the more adequate comparative evaluation of our welter of competing metapsychologies—Freudian, Kleinian, Bionian, object relational, Lacanian, Kohutian, intersubjective, etc.—by way of empirically guided comparisons and contrasts. This would need to be done by methods at once meaningful and responsive to the subtlety and the complexity of our psychoanalytic phenomena and at the same time scientific in the best sense of that term, of loyalty to the reality principle as embodied in appropriate canons of scientific inference.

Over the half-century since my own career as a psychoanalytic therapy researcher started, with the creation (in the early 1950s) by myself and colleagues of the thirty-year-long Psychotherapy Research Project of the Menninger Foundation, there has been a gradually accelerating increase of varieties of both outcome and process measures of the course of psychoanalytic therapies that more and more adequately meet the combined criteria that I have indicated, and this is now the subject of a very substantial literature contributed to by a rapidly increasing cadre worldwide of trained psychoanalyst empirical researchers.

This research is in opposition to the stance taken by Roy Schafer in his discussion of my 1989 Rome Congress plenary presentation, decrying my goal of overcoming our then regnant theoretical diversity as the holding to a stodgy and conservative sociopolitical posture, and, rather, espousing the celebration of our differences as the fount of a progressive and creative disciplinary future. As I have written elsewhere, no discipline with claims to stature as a science lives by celebrating theoretical diversity, and I have used as a prominent example the current struggle within theoretical physics to overcome problems in reconciling modern relativity theory, essential to explaining the world of the very large (cosmology, the operations of the universe), with modern quantum theory, essential to explaining the world of the very small (subatomic particles and forces). The problem as it stands now is that these two vital theories, both necessary to our understanding of the natural universe, stand in stark contradicion to each other, so that if the one is valid, the other cannot be. An entire generation of theoretical physicists is currently at work in an effort to comprehend both of these theories within an encompassing umbrella of super-string theory, or as wryly put, TOE, a theory of everything. (For a fascinating account of this quest, see the 1999 book, *The Elegant Universe*, by Brian Greene, a theoretical physicist who is himself a major player in this effort.) Physics is far indeed from celebrating this kind of diversity and contradiction.

Which brings me to my response to the question raised by Martin in the discussion: "Will there ever be a time when there will be an objective answer to the question of whether we are pleasure seekers or safety seekers? Will this question ever be answered with a yes or no, or will we have to say to our-selves that certain questions are and will be unanswerable? And another ques-tion comes up: Is the death instinct inborn, or is it a result of frustration or fear? I would like some discussion on the subject of whether we do believe that eventually empirical data will answer the questions we raised, or are we dealing with a subject where even in the long stretch, empirical data are going to leave us in doubt or forever dependent on irrational [Editorial comment: I would have used the word *subjective*] aspects of ourselves."

Here I am sure that my answer may not be widely shared in the group. I don't think that our clinical psychoanalytic work, and the theorizing inspired by it, will ever lead us to the definitive answers Martin is speculating about. We have seen too many examples among our analytic forebears, as well as in our own generation, of extraordinarily gifted and insightful analytic clinicians and theoreticians come to starkly different perspectives on these issues that divide us, each with a quite plausible, and at times seemingly compelling, overall for-mulation. There is no reason to think that that state of affairs will ever be over-come in the course of our ongoing clinical and theoretical thinking and working.

Empirical research never carries guarantees and can always lead into its own blind alleys. But it can give us hope—though we can never be sure that it will succeed or not—of yielding persuasive enough agreed-upon answers to Martin's questions, whether in our current generation or with those who come after us. At least that is my belief, and I know for one that at least André thoroughly disagrees with me over the place of, and the promise of, the em-pirical research process in carrying the total psychoanalytic enterprise forward. (Part of our disagreements have been articulated in written exchange in the pages of *International Psychoanalysis* (1996), the news magazine of the Inter-national Psychoanalytic Association.)

I should end this commentary with some discussion about the nature of my convictions concerning the role of empirical research in the advance of psychoanalysis as a science, whether as part of the family of natural or biological sciences, as Freud believed, or as a social or behavioral science, with whatever its different methods, or as a quite separate and unique science, in Merton Gill's terms a "hermeneutic science." I grew up with many expectations, for complicated reasons, that I would follow in my father's footsteps in the practice of medicine. These feelings were nourished in my growing-up years by two books, very influential in America at that time, Sinclair Lewis's *Arrowsmith*, and Paul de Kruif's *Microbe Hunters*. During the course of my medical training, I was drawn, again for complicated reasons, to psychiatry as the avenue to psychoanalysis.

Hence I fell in congenially with Freud's vision (carried on later by Hartmann) of psychoanalysis as a (natural biologically based?) science, though I was puzzled by Freud's paradoxically dismissive attitude toward empirical research. Clearly, science advances incrementally by research, and yet the only empirical study that Freud spoke favorably of (1900, pp. 181–182) was Otto Pötzl's investigations of subliminal perceptual phenomena, and, in 1934, he responded dismissively to the American psychologist, Saul Rosenzweig, who had written Freud of his experimental confirmation of basic psychoanalytic propositions, saying that such confirmations were not necessary since the psychoanalytic propositions rested on repeated clinical demonstrations, but in any case the experimental work could do no harm. It was despite this chilling assessment by Freud that I and many others by now have embraced empirical psychoanalytic research as a necessary road to our advancement as a science— and as then a more secure way to answer Martin's questions. This is the position that I felt should have been entered explicitly into the symposium discussion.

All of this makes me all the more regretful that I was not able to be present and participate in the symposium discussions. I would have welcomed the responses of my colleagues to my (hopefully clearly) restated views, and who knows what additional productive avenues might then have been opened up in the symposium proceedings.

References

Chodorow, N. (1999). *The Power of Feelings: Personal Meaning in Psychoanalysis, Gender, and Culture*. New Haven, CT: Yale University Press.

Freud, S. (1900). The interpretation of dreams. *Standard Edition* 4:xi–338.

Gill, M. (1994). *Psychoanalysis in Transition: A Personal View*. Hillsdale, NJ: Analytic Press.

Green, A. and Wallerstein, R. S. (1996). What kind of research for psychoanalysis?; Psychoanalytic research: where do we disagree?; Response to Robert Wallerstein. Newsletter of the International Psychoanalytical Association v(1):10–21.

Greene, B. (1999). *The Elegant Universe*. New York/London: Norton.

Wurmser, L. (1977). A defense of the use of metaphor in analytic theory formation. *Psychoanalytic Quarterly* 46:466–498.

Index

abandonment, 42, 59
Abraham, K., 47
   contributions of, 14, 28, 261
   on female psychology, 39–40
   Ferenczi's analysis of, 177
   Horney's analysis with, 39–40, 89
   Klein's analysis with, 287
   on Rank, 26–27
"accommodationist theorists," 213
acting out. *See* enactments
actual neurosis, psychoneurosis *vs.*, 33,
   35–36, 47–48
adaptation, U.S. emphasis on, 135
Adler, A., 20, 42, 94, 134
   adherents of, 11, 176
   aggression theories of, 5, 12
   compared to Freud, 7–8, 11
   dissidence of, 14, 23, 26, 120, 124,
      149, 364
   as first-generation dissident, 4, 234, 364
   Freud's response to dissidence of, 10,
      202
   rejection of Freud's theories, 7–11,
      237–238
   relationship with Freud, 6–7, 10, 13,
      131
   response to ideas of, 12, 132, 205
adolescence, masturbation in, 34–35
adults, continuing development of, 205
affect, 137, 215, 301
   influence of mother on child's, 345,
      347
   intensity of, 323, 346

aggression, 9–10, 12, 74, 80, 164, 193,
   278, 301
   Adler on, 5, 8, 132, 205
   compared to other drives, 138, 240–
      241
   defensive v. malignant, 64
   in dual drive theory, 5, 137–138,
      334–335
   fear as cause of, 182, 333
   importance of, 135, 352
   in institutional structures of
      psychoanalysis, 140–141
   Klein on, 54, 240
   repression of, 12, 42, 90–91
Ainsworth, M., 341, 349
Alexander, F., 42–44
"alternative theorists," 213
Althusser, 134
ambivalence, of dissidents toward
   Freud, 88–89, 170
American Psychoanalytic Association,
   203, 218, 234–235
   hegemony in, 178, 206
   Kernberg and, 303–304
Analysis of the Self, The (Kohut), 74, 77
"Analysis Terminable and
   Interminable" (Freud), 27–28, 29,
   310
analysts, 95, 141. *See also* training
   analysts
   choice of, 80, 252
   disruption of community of, 156–157
   dissatisfaction with, 78, 274